M Y T H S   A N D   L E G E N D S
S E R I E S

MIDDLE AGES

H. A. GUERBER

The Castle of the Holy Grail

MYTHS AND LEGENDS SERIES

MIDDLE AGES

H. A. GUERBER

WITH ILLUSTRATIONS FROM DRAWINGS AND FAMOUS PAINTINGS

AVENEL BOOKS
NEW YORK

Previously published by Gresham Publishing Co

This edition published 1986 by Avenel Books
distributed by Crown Publishers Inc.,
225 Park Avenue South
New York, New York 10003

ISBN 0-517-60442-6

Printed and bound by
Grafoimpex, Yugoslavia

h g f e d c b

" Men lykyn jestis for to here,
    And romans rede in diuers manere

" Of Brute that baron bold of hond,
    The first conqueroure of Englond ;
    Of kyng Artour that was so riche,
    Was non in his tyme him liche.

" How kyng Charlis and Rowlond fawght
    With sarzyns nold they be cawght ;
    Of Tristrem and of Ysoude the swete,
    How they with love first gan mete ;

" Stories of diuerce thynggis,
    Of pryncis, prelatis, and of kynggis ;
    Many songgis of diuers ryme,
    As english, frensh, and latyne."

Cursor Mundi.

CONTENTS

CHAP.   PAGE
      INTRODUCTION xi

    I. BEOWULF 1

   II. GUDRUN 18

  III. REYNARD THE FOX 35

  IV. THE NIBELUNGENLIED 59

   V. THE LANGOBARDIAN CYCLE 102

  VI. THE AMELINGS 122

 VII. DIETRICH VON BERN 135

VIII. CHARLEMAGNE AND HIS PALADINS 162

  IX. THE SONS OF AYMON 199

   X. HUON OF BORDEAUX 215

  XI. TITUREL AND THE HOLY GRAIL 241

 XII. MERLIN 273

XIII. THE ROUND TABLE 285

XIV. TRISTAN AND ISEULT 312

 XV. RAGNAR LODBROK 327

XVI. THE CID 344

XVII. GENERAL SURVEY OF ROMANCE LITERATURE . . 369

INDEX TO POETICAL QUOTATIONS 381

GLOSSARY AND INDEX 383

LIST OF ILLUSTRATIONS

To face page

Queen Guinevere   287

The Dream of Sir Launcelot   300

Elaine   301

The Passing of Arthur   308

Tristan and Iseult   309

Tristan and Iseult   320

" Brangwaine sorrowed with many
Tears "   321

Iseult compelled to undergo the
Ordeal of Fire   324

Sigurd Ring   325

Krake   332

The Valkyrs   333

" Doña Ximena demanded
Justice "   346

Envoys of Henry III. and the
Pope   347

The Cid and the Lion   360

The Cid's Last Battle   361

Tomb of the Cid and Ximena at
San Pedro de Cardeña   368

LIST OF ILLUSTRATIONS

The Castle of the Holy Grail	*Frontispiece*
	To face page
A Sea-King's Grave	2
Beowulf vows to slay Grendel	3
Beowulf Challenged by the Coast-guard	6
Funeral of a Northern Chief	7
Horant	22
The Conflict at Wülpensand	23
Gudrun and the Swan	30
The Triumph of the Hegelings	31
Reynard's Trial	36
Reynard in the Fowl-yard	37
Bruin as Messenger	40
Reynard at the Place of Execution	41
Reynard and Bellyn	50
The Combat	51
Siegfried and the Dragon	60
Siegfried Captures Ludegast	61
The Death of Siegfried	76
The Funeral of Siegfried	77
Hagen slays Ortlieb	94
The Burgundians and the Huns	95
Alboin and Rosamund	104
Ortnit and Alberich	105
Wolfdietrich and the Cubs	124
Rauch-Else and Wolfdietrich	125

LIST OF ILLUSTRATIONS

To face page

The Dwarf Laurin   148

The Huns   149

The Tomb of Theodoric   160

The Emperor Charlemagne   161

The Coronation of Charlemagne   170

Ogier in Avalon   171

Charlemagne at the Healing   188
    Spring at Aachen   189

Rogero delivering Angelica   198

The Burial of Charlemagne   199

Satan pursues Malagigi

Charlemagne and the Wife of   210
    Aymon   211

Huon before the Pope

" Oberon appeared like a brilliant   220
    Meteor"   221

Huon and Angoulaffre   232

Neptune   233

The Holy Grail

Parzival at the Court of King   254
    Arthur   255

Parzival prays for guidance   270

Lohengrin and Else   271

The Wizard   278

Stonehenge   279

Tintagel .   286

King Arthur

viii

INTRODUCTION

IF there is a phrase in our tongue which connotes the atmosphere of romance it is that of " the Middle Ages." Do but mention the words, and it is as another opening of Pandora's box. Out there streams a retinue of goodly knights, each armed *cap-à-pie*, each bearing in his helmet some gaily coloured thread or ribbon, the favour of the lady of his allegiance. Yonder before them tower the battlements of an ancient city, its walls grim and grey even beneath the dazzling shafts of sunlight, which make armour and weapons shine like very silver. As the knights ride two by two over the sharp cobble-stones and under the low, overhanging turret archway, the clatter of their steeds and the shrill notes of the bugle mingle in the air. Thus they disappear, a gallant company, followed as they go by the timid glance of many a gentle-eyed maiden, peeping shyly through her casement after the knight of her heart, bound, perchance, on some perilous adventure. The noise of the bugles grows louder, sounding more and more defiant as it cuts through the air. Then as it dies away is heard the flutter of little sighs. For who can tell which of these brave knights will ever return, bringing the tattered remnants of the ribbon now floating so bravely in the breeze ?

Something of the fascination which emanates from the Middle Ages with a spell strong as that of the strains of the Pied Piper is due to matters of chronology. However elastic the boundaries of that period may be, they circumscribe a time not too remote to have passed beyond the grasp of imagination, yet not too near for things of magic and faery chance to appear incongruous. Thus in greater degree than is true in the case of the legends of either a more ancient or a more modern day these tales of the Middle Ages have a dual charm as being familiar yet unfamiliar. They are real, yet unreal ; reflections of what was, yet not wholly unlike that which still is.

The outside influence which has impressed its stamp most clearly upon the legends of mediæval Europe is undoubtedly that of the crusades. These form the dividing line cutting off the mythology that is purely pagan. It is true, nevertheless, that many of the mediæval romances are distinguished by an extraordinary mixture of heathen and Christian lore ; yet in the main the crusades constitute the most satisfactory division that can be found, since they are indications, not of a change confined to a single area, but of one which concerned the general temper of the atmosphere of all Europe. The warmth that marked the Norse legends of Odin and Thor gives place in mediæval romance to tales of a colder conception. Spontaneity becomes more or less lost in creed, and doctrine begins to assume an important position in daily life. All who are not of the Christian faith are alike Saracens or Paynims, followers of the head of the faith of Mohammed, as opposed to the followers of the Pope as the head of the Christian Church. Hence it is no uncommon thing to come upon scenes in which a Christian knight, fighting against a Paynim, makes use of the pauses between the rounds to expound the most intricate theological doctrines ; while not seldom his opponent is won over by the other's eloquence, and so they part friends. The romances of mediæval days, therefore, are romances of a transition stage. They are not purely legendary, nor can they be considered historical ; they represent the new faith, yet they have not shaken themselves altogether free from the old ; they exhibit scenes of knighthood and Christian orders, but the heroes are

xii

commonly heroes of a much earlier period, decked out in local colour ; the Holy Grail is an object for diligent search, but magic and witchcraft are still in common acceptance.

Like everything else belonging to an epoch which links together two more clearly defined periods, the legends have some of the drawbacks that are peculiar to transition. They lack something in the way both of crystallisation and unity. The directness and simplicity that characterise the stories of Odin or Pallas are necessarily somewhat encumbered in recitals of a time when creeds were first being evolved, when old ideals were being overturned and new ideals were coming thick and fast to take their place. Knighthood emerged, and then gradually began to mean something more than allegiance to a chief or devotion to those in distress ; it acquired a mystical significance, with a root firmly fixed in an earnest endeavour after everything noble. Jousts became more than mere plays ; quests turned less upon personal glory and more upon self-purification ; the conversion of the enemy was even more eagerly welcomed than his overthrow. Moreover, everywhere the presence of knowledge was being made manifest by signs as yet only portents in the air, but by-and-by to spring into being. A great stirring was abroad ; involuntarily men were struggling through a cloud to the top of the mountain. One age was drawing to a close ; the next was already in sight.

This tendency of the time has been well expressed by Emerson in one of his essays, where he declares : " All the fictions of the Middle Age explain themselves as a masked or frolic expression of that which in grave earnest the mind of that period toiled to achieve. Magic, and all that is ascribed to it, is manifestly a deep presentment of the powers of science. The shoes of swiftness, the sword of sharpness, the power of subduing the elements, of using the secret virtues of minerals, of understanding the voices of birds, are the obscure efforts of the mind in a right direction. The preternatural prowess of the hero, the gift of perpetual youth, and the like, are alike the endeavour of the human spirit 'to bend the shows of things to the desires of the mind.'"

The extreme popularity of these stories, which with delightful *naïveté* exhibit the attitude of mind which sees in events those characteristics which it most desires to see, is readily evidenced by the many different versions of each which still exist. They were everywhere familiarised to rich and poor alike by the scalds, bards, *trouvères*, troubadours, minstrels, and *minnesingers*, who passed from castle to cottage, or inn to palace, in each a welcome guest. As a historical record of the customs, habits, dress, manners, and characteristics of the people, the stories are inestimable, though it should be remembered that the setting is not necessarily true to the time which the events describe. More often than not it is false, and the setting is later than the germ of the story itself. Nevertheless, with this reservation these old romances afford a valuable picture of the colour of bygone days. For nothing gave greater delight to the heart of the bard than any opportunity for indulging his passion for minute embroidery in a long and detailed account of a tournament, a banquet, or a wedding feast. In this connection, too, Carlyle's observation that history is only "the biography of great men" is not without a measure of application. Obscure occurrences are often of greater importance than is generally suspected, and what is seen must always be the outcome of much that is unseen. These mediæval heroes, with a personality half legendary, half historical, have a very real significance. They are the landmarks of an age, and stand for the crises which signalised the struggle of the nations. By sifting out the impossible, and separating that which is minor from that which is of greater importance, a fairly complete sequence of events can be perceived, in which are reflected those changes through which the people had to pass before the era of history and reason could be fully established upon those magnificent relics of ancient time which are still its glory and its delight.

> "Saddle the Hippogriffs, ye Muses nine,
> And straight we'll ride to the land of old Romance."
> *Wieland.*

CHAPTER I : BEOWULF

The Importance of "Beowulf"

THE most ancient relic of literature of the spoken languages of modern Europe is undoubtedly the epic poem "Beowulf," which is supposed to have been composed by the Anglo-Saxons previous to their invasion of England. Although the poem probably belongs to the fifth century, the only existing manuscript is said to date from the ninth or tenth century.

> "List! we have learnt a tale of other years,
> Of kings and warrior Danes, a wondrous tale,
> How æthelings bore them in the brunt of war."
> *Beowulf (Conybeare's tr.).*

This curious work is the most valuable old English manuscript in the British Museum. It is written in rude alliterative verse, rhyme not being known in England before the date of the Norman Conquest. Although much damaged by fire, the manuscript has been carefully studied by authorities who have patiently restored the poem, the story of which is as follows :

The Coming of Skeaf

Hrothgar (the modern Roger), King of Denmark, was a descendant of Odin, being the third monarch of the celebrated dynasty of the Skioldungs, whose chief boast was their descent from Skeaf, or Skiold, Odin's son, who had one day drifted mysteriously to their shores. Full of excitement the people crowded round to look at this wonderful infant, who lay smiling sweetly in the middle of a boat, on a sheaf of ripe wheat, surrounded by priceless weapons and jewels. Now it happened that at that very time the Danes were seeking

1

for a ruler. They therefore immediately recognised the hand of Odin in this mysterious advent, proclaimed the child king, and obeyed him loyally as long as he lived. Years went by, and at last Skeaf felt the sure hand of death closing upon him. Anxiously he called his nobles about him and explained to them the manner in which he must needs leave them. Obeying his orders, therefore, they prepared a boat, and decked it lavishly with gold and jewels. Then, seeing that all was ready, the dying monarch dragged himself on board and stretched his limbs on a funeral pyre, in the midst of which rose a sheaf of corn. So he drifted out into the wide ocean, disappearing as mysteriously as he had come.

The Building of Heorot

Such being his lineage, it is no wonder that Hrothgar grew into a mighty chief, nor that during a long life of warfare he became possessed of much treasure. Part of this he resolved to devote to the construction of a magnificent hall, to be called Heorot, where he might feast his retainers and listen to the heroic lays of the scalds during the long winter evenings.

> " A hall of mead, such as for space and state
> The elder time ne'er boasted; there with free
> And princely hand he might dispense to all
> (Save the rude crowd and men of evil minds)
> The good he held from Heaven. That gallant work,
> Full well I wot, through many a land was known
> Of festal halls the brightest and the best."
>
> *Beowulf (Conybeare's tr.).*

For months the sound of hammer and chisel could be heard as the masons toiled over their laborious task and stone after stone was put in its place. But at last all was ready, and the great building was thrown open

2

A Sea-King's Grave

Beowulf vows to slay Grendel

amidst the acclamations of all the court. The occasion was fittingly celebrated by a sumptuous banquet, to which came all the most noble knights in the land. Then, when the guests had all retired, the king's bodyguard lay down in the hall to take their rest. When morning dawned the servants appeared to remove the couches. With horror they beheld the floor and walls all stained with blood, and not a trace of the knights who in full armour had gone to rest there! This was the more terrifying since the bodyguard had been composed of thirty-two of the bravest of the king's warriors, known everywhere for their valour in fighting. Yet now nothing remained to give a clue to their disappearance save some gigantic blood-stained footsteps, leading directly from the festive hall to the sluggish waters of a deep mountain lake, or fiord.

Grendel

No sooner did Hrothgar, the king, see these than he declared that they had been made by Grendel, a fearsome monster, long ago driven out of the country by a magician, but now evidently returned to carry on his savage outrages.

> " A haunter of marshes, a holder of moors.
> .   .   .   .   . Secret
> The land he inhabits ; dark, wolf-haunted ways
> Of the windy hillside, by the treacherous tarn ;
> Or where, covered up in its mist, the hill stream
> Downward flows."
>
> *Beowulf* (*Keary's tr.*).

As Hrothgar was now too old to wield a sword with his former skill, he lost no time in offering a princely reward to any man brave enough to free the country from this terrible scourge. Scarcely had the proclamation been made when ten of the doughtiest of his followers volunteered to camp in the hall on the following night, and attack the monster Grendel should he venture to reappear.

The Court of Hygelac the Geate

But in spite of the valour of these experienced warriors, and of the efficacy of their oft-tried weapons, they too succumbed. A minstrel, hiding in a dark corner of the hall, was the only one who escaped Grendel's fury, and after shudderingly describing the massacre he had witnessed he fled in terror to the kingdom of the Geates, a race later known by the name of Jutes or Goths. There he sang his lays in the presence of Hygelac, the king, and of his nephew Beowulf (the Bee-hunter), and roused their deepest attention by describing the visit of Grendel, and the vain but heroic defence of the brave knights. To all this Beowulf listened with intense interest. Then afterwards he eagerly questioned the scald, and, having learnt from him that the monster still haunted those regions, he impetuously declared that it was his intention to visit Hrothgar's kingdom, and at least fight, if not slay, the dragon.

> " He was of mankind
> In might the strongest,
> At that day
> Of this life,
> Noble and stalwart.
> He bade him a sea ship,
> A goodly one, prepare.
> Quoth he, the war king,
> Over the swan's road,
> Seek he would
> The mighty monarch,
> Since he wanted men."
>
> *Beowulf* (*Longfellow's tr.*).

BEOWULF SETS SAIL

Beowulf and Breka

At this time Beowulf was still very young, yet he had already won great honour in a battle against the Swedes. He had also proved his endurance by entering into a swimming match with Breka, one of the lords at the court of Hygelac, his uncle. Together the two champions had started out, sword in hand and fully armed ; together they had flung themselves into the waters, where, after swimming in company for five whole days, they were at last parted by a great tempest. After a terrible struggle Breka was driven ashore, but Beowulf was carried by the current toward some jagged cliffs. Here he clung on desperately, trying to resist the fury of the waves, and using his sword to ward off the attacks of hostile mermaids, nicors (nixies), and other sea monsters. By-and-by the gashed bodies of these slain foes drifted ashore, to the amazement of all who saw them. Swiftly they ran and told Hygelac the tidings ; ·yet he too could find no explanation for the matter. His delight may therefore be imagined when Beowulf himself suddenly reappeared and explained that by his hand the creatures had been slain. As Breka had been the first to return, he received the prize for swimming ; but the king gave Beowulf his treasured sword, Nägeling, and praised him publicly for his valour.

Beowulf Sets Sail

Now since Beowulf had successfully encountered these monsters of the deep in the roaring tide, he expressed a hope that he might prevail against Grendel also. He therefore embarked with fourteen chosen men and sailed to Denmark. Here he was challenged by the coastguard, who took him to be an enemy.

But no sooner had Beowulf made clear his errand than he received the warmest of welcomes for himself and his men.

Beowulf in Heorot

Blithely the warriors strode from the strand to Heorot, where Hrothgar received them most hospitably.

> " ' Lord of the Scyldings,
> Friend-lord of folks, so far have I sought thee,
> That *I* may unaided, my earlmen assisting me,
> This brave-mooded war-band, purify Heorot.' "
>
> *Beowulf* (*J. L. Hall's tr.*)

In vain the king tried to dissuade Beowulf from his perilous undertaking: the hero had made up his mind. Then, after a sumptuous banquet, where the mead flowed with true Northern lavishness, Hrothgar and his suite sadly departed, leaving the hall Heorot in charge of the brave band of strangers, whom they never expected to see again. As soon as the king had gone Beowulf bade his companions lie down and sleep in peace, promising that he would himself watch over them. Yet at the same time he laid aside both armour and sword ; for he knew that weapons were of no avail against the monster, with which he intended to grapple hand to hand should it really appear.

> " ' I have heard
> That that foul miscreant's dark and stubborn flesh
> Recks not the force of arms :—such I forswear,
> Nor sword nor burnish'd shield of ample round
> Ask for the war ; all weaponless, hand to hand
> (So may great Higelac's smile repay my toil)
> Beowulf will grapple with the mighty foe.' "
>
> *Beowulf* (*Conybeare's tr.*).

The Night Vigil

No sooner had the warriors stretched themselves out upon the benches in the hall than, overcome by the op-

Beowulf challenged by the Coastguard

Funeral of a Northern Chief

pressive air as well as by the mead, they sank into a profound sleep. Beowulf alone remained awake, watching for Grendel's coming. The night wore on ; still Beowulf kept his vigil ; still no beast was to be seen. But at last as darkness was turning into dawn there came a stealthy tread. Nearer and nearer it drew, till it reached the very hall. It was Grendel. With one powerful wrench the monster tore asunder the iron bolts and bars which secured the door. Then, striding swiftly within, he pounced upon one of the sleepers. Quivering with eagerness, he tore his victim limb from limb, greedily drank his blood, and devoured his flesh, leaving naught but the head, hands, and feet of the unhappy warrior. Yet this ghastly repast only whetted the fiend's ravenous appetite. Again he stretched out his hands in the darkness to seize and devour another warrior ; again he felt his grasp closing on another man. But this was no ordinary knight that he now touched. It was Beowulf. Burning with anger, the hero turned on the monster, and seized him in a grip that even Grendel could by no means shake off.

Grendel and Beowulf

Then began a fearful struggle in the darkness, till the great hall itself rocked to its very foundations, while the walls creaked and groaned under the violence of the furious blows. But in spite of the monster's gigantic stature Beowulf clung so fast to the hand and arm he had grasped that at last Grendel, making a desperate effort to free himself by a jerk, tore the whole limb out of its socket ! Bleeding and mortally wounded, he then beat a hasty retreat to his marshy den, leaving a long bloody trail behind him. And as he went he knew in his heart that his doom was writ and his death nigh at hand.

7

Beowulf's Triumph

As for Beowulf, exhaused but triumphant, he stood in the middle of the hall, where his companions crowded around him, gazing in speechless awe at the mighty hand and limb, and the clawlike fingers, far harder than steel, which no power had hitherto been able to resist.

At dawn Hrothgar and his subjects approached again. For a moment they lingered, dreading to enter Heorot for fear of finding the dead bodies of the knights within. When they heard what had really happened, and how Beowulf had fought with and conquered Grendel, their wonder knew no bounds. Open-mouthed they gazed upon the monster's limb, which hung like a trophy from the ceiling of Heorot. As for the king, he was carried away with delight. Warmly he congratulated the hero, and bestowed upon him many rich gifts. Then he gave orders to cleanse the hall, hang it with tapestry, and prepare a banquet in honour of the mighty champion from over the sea.

The Banquet of Gladness

While the men were feasting, listening to the lays of the scalds, and drinking many a toast, Wealtheow, Hrothgar's beautiful wife, the Queen of Denmark, appeared. She pledged Beowulf in a cup of wine, which he gallantly drained after she had touched it with her lips. Then she bestowed upon him a ring of the purest gold and a costly necklace, even the famous Brisingamen, or at least so say some authorities.[1]

> " 'Wear these,' she cried, 'since thou hast in the fight
> So borne thyself, that wide as ocean rolls
> Round our wind-beaten cliffs his brimming waves,
> All gallant souls shall speak thy eulogy.' "
>
> *Beowulf* (*Conybeare's tr.*).

[1] *See* " Myths of the Norsemen," Guerber, p. 134.

8

BEOWULF'S SECOND EXPLOIT

The Second Vigil

When the banquet was ended Hrothgar escorted his guests to more pleasant sleeping apartments than they had occupied the night before, leaving his own men to guard the hall, where Grendel would never again appear. The warriors, fearing no danger, slept in peace. But in the dead of night there came yet another foe ; for the mother of the giant, as loathsome and uncanny a monster as he, glided softly into the hall. Swiftly she secured the bloody trophy still hanging from the ceiling, then away she bore it into the darkness, together with Æschere (Askher), the king's bosom friend.

When Hrothgar learned this new loss at early dawn he was overcome with grief, and spent the hours in bitter weeping. "Alas !" he cried when he saw Beowulf, " Æschere, my best-beloved, is dead, snatched from me during the night by a loathly foe, even the mother of Grendel !"

> " ' Æschere is dead,
> Yrmenlaf's
> Elder brother,
> The partaker of my secrets
> And my counsellor,
> Who stood at my elbow
> When we in battle
> Our mail hoods defended,
> When troops rushed together
> And boar crests crashed.' "
>
> *Beowulf (Metcalfe's tr.).*

Beowulf's Second Exploit

No sooner had the king finished speaking than Beowulf volunteered to finish his work and avenge Æschere by seeking and attacking Grendel's mother in her own retreat. In doing so he knew full well the perils of the expedition, and so he first gave careful directions for the disposal of his personal property, in case he

9

should never return. Then, escorted by the Danes and Geates, he followed the bloody track until he came to a cliff overhanging the waters of the mountain pool. There the bloody traces ceased, but Æschere's gory head was placed aloft as a trophy, a warning to all that vengeance awaited the man who should dare venture further.

> " For they saw
> On that rude cliff young Æschere's mangled head."
>   *Beowulf* (*Conybeare's tr.*).

Then as Beowulf gazed down into the deep waters he saw that they also were darkly dyed with the monster's blood, and by this he knew that he must seek his foe beneath the waves. After taking leave of Hrothgar he bade his men await his return for two whole days and nights before giving him up for lost. Sadly they gave the promise, for each man believed in his heart that never again would he see the face of his brave leader. But as for Beowulf, he laughed and bade them be of good cheer, after which he flung himself courageously into the depths of the horrible pool. Further and further into the recesses of the waters he dived, till it seemed as if he would never reach the bottom. But at last a gleam of phosphorescent light told him that now he was nearing the dread hiding-place of his cruel foe. Quickly he made his way thither, yet even as he went he was repeatedly obliged to have recourse to his sword to defend himself against the clutches of countless hideous sea-monsters, which came rushing toward him from all sides.

> " While thro' crystal gulfs were gleaming
> Ocean depths, with wonders teeming ;
> Shapes of terror, huge, unsightly,
> Loom'd thro' vaulted roof translucent."
>   *Valhalla* (*J. C. Jones*)

BEOWULF'S RETURN

The Encounter

In the midst of this fearful struggle a strong current suddenly seized Beowulf, and swept him irresistibly along into the slimy retreat of Grendel's mother. The loathly beast was ready for her prey. Fast in her grip she clasped him, and strove to crush out his life. Then, snatching the hero's sword from his hand, she attempted to plunge her own knife into her foe. Fortunately, however, the hero's armour was weapon-proof, and his muscles were so strong that before she could do him any harm he had freed himself from her grasp. Instantly he seized a large sword hanging upon a projection of rock near by, and dealt her a mighty blow, which severed her head from the trunk at a single stroke. The blood poured from the cave and mingled with the waters without, turning them to such a lurid hue that Hrothgar and his men sorrowfully departed, leaving the Geates alone to watch for the return of the hero, whom they felt sure they would never see again.

In the meantime Beowulf had rushed to the rear of the cave, where, finding Grendel in the last throes, he cut off his head also. Then, seizing this ghastly trophy, he rapidly made his way up through the tainted waters, which the fiery blood of the two monsters had so overheated that as he went his sword melted in its scabbard till naught but the hilt remained.

> "That stout sword of proof,
> Its warrior task fulfill'd, dropp'd to the ground
> (So work'd the venom of the felons' blood)
> A molten mass."
> *Beowulf (Conybeare's tr.).*

Beowulf's Return

By this time the aspect of the boiling waters had become so terrible that even the Geates were about to depart in sorrow, nothwithstanding the orders they had received, when they suddenly beheld their beloved chiet safe and sound, bearing in his hand the evidences of his success. Their ecstasy was now extreme. Again and again they shouted, till the neighbouring hills echoed and re-echoed with their cries of joy. Then began the march back to Heorot, where Beowulf was almost over-whelmed with gifts by the grateful Danes.

A few days later the hero and his companions returned home to Jutland to recount their adventures and exhibit the treasures they had won. Pride rose in the heart ot Hygelac as he heard of the prowess of his nephew, and he ordered the most splendid of feasts to be prepared in his honour. Then as the cups of mead passed round and the songs of the scalds resounded, the name that rang through the hall was "Beowulf," "Beowulf." And as Beowulf heard it his eyes shone ; yet in his heart he resolved that ere he died even greater deeds than this should be placed against his name.

The Death of Hygelac

Several years of comparative peace ensued, till the land was invaded by the Friesians, who raided the coast, burning and plundering all in their way, yet always retreating into their ships before Hygelac or Beowulf could overtake and punish them. The immediate result of this invasion was a counter-movement on Hygelac's part. But although he successfully harried Friesland, he fell into an ambush just as he was about to leave the country, and was cruelly slain, his nephew Beowulf barely escaping a similar untoward fate.

When the little army of the Geates reached home once more, their first task was to consume the remains of Hygelac on a funeral pyre, together with his weapons and battle-steed, as was customary in the North. Meanwhile Queen Hygd, overwhelmed with grief at the loss of her brave husband, was also harassed by the fear of the dissensions that would be certain to arise during the minority of an infant king. She therefore convened the popular assembly known as the Thing, and bade the people set her own child's claims aside in favour of Beowulf. This proposal was hailed with enthusiasm ; for the people felt that in him they would find an ideal ruler. But Beowulf honourably refused to usurp his kinsman's throne, and, raising Hardred, Hygelac's infant son, upon his shield, he declared that he would protect and uphold him as long as he lived. The people, following his example, swore fealty to the new king, and faithfully kept this oath until he died.

Hardred's Reign

Hardred, having attained his majority, ruled wisely and well ; but his career was cut short by the sons of Othere, the discoverer of the North Cape. These youths had rebelled against their father's authority and had taken refuge at Hardred's court. But when the latter advised a reconciliation the eldest youth angrily drew his sword and slew him, a crime which was avenged with true Northern promptitude by Wiglaf, one of the king's followers. After this, fearing lest he should meet the same fate as his brother, the second son contrived to effect an escape. Meanwhile Beowulf was summoned by the Thing to accept the now vacant throne, and as there was none to dispute his claims the hero no longer refused to rule. His first action was to defend his kingdom against Eadgils, Othere's second son, who had sought refuge in flight. Eadgils was now king of Sweden, and thus came with an armed host to avenge his brother's death. But his expedition was of no avail, for he only succeeded in losing his own life.

13

Beowulf's Last Fight

A reign of forty years of comparative peace brought Beowulf to extreme old age. His early vigour had gone from him, and though he was still full of courage, yet he had not the strength that once had been his. His peace of mind was thus greatly disturbed by the news one day of the sudden advent of a fire-breathing dragon, which had taken up its abode in the mountains near by, where it gloated over a hoard of glittering gold.

> "The ranger of the darksome night,
> The Firedrake, came."
>
> *Beowulf (Conybeare's tr.).*

The presence of this fearsome monster had been discovered by a fugitive slave, who had made his way unseen into the monster's den during one of its temporary absences, and brought away a small portion of this gold. On its return the Firedrake discovered the theft, and became so furious that its howling and writhing shook the mountain like an earthquake. When night came on its rage was still unappeased, and it flew all over the land, vomiting venom and flames, setting houses and crops afire, and causing so much damage that the people were almost beside themselves with terror. Seeing that all their attempts to appease the dragon were utterly fruitless, and being afraid to attack it in its lair, they finally implored Beowulf to deliver them as he had delivered the Danes, and to slay this oppressor, which was even worse than the terrible Grendel.

Such an appeal could not be disregarded, and, in spite of his advanced years, Beowulf donned his armour once more. Accompanied by Wiglaf and eleven of his bravest men, he then went out to seek the monster in its lair. At the entrance of the mountain gorge the dauntless

14

BEOWULF AND THE FIREDRAKE

Beowulf bade his followers pause, and, advancing alone to the monster's den, he boldly challenged it to come forth and begin the fray. A moment later the mountain shook as the dragon rushed out, breathing fire and flame, and Beowulf felt the first gust of its hot breath even through his massive shield.

Beowulf and the Firedrake

A desperate struggle followed, in the course of which Beowulf's sword and strength both failed him. Then the Firedrake coiled its long, scaly folds about the aged hero, and was about to crush him to death, when the faithful Wiglaf, perceiving his master's imminent danger, sprang forward. This second attack diverted the attention of the monster, and it dropped Beowulf from its grasp to concentrate upon its new assailant.

Thus Beowulf, recovering himself, drew his dagger, and soon put an end to the dragon's life. But alas! even as his enemy breathed its last the hero himself sank fainting to the ground. Feeling that his end was near he warmly thanked Wiglaf for his timely aid, and rejoiced in the death of the monster.

Sadly Wiglaf pressed his hand and listened while the hero commanded that his faithful follower should bring out the concealed treasure and lay it at his feet, that he might feast his eyes upon the glittering gold he had won for his people's use.

At last the whole of the magnificent treasure was dragged from its darksome hold and spread by the side of the old warrior. The great pile of gold and jewels glittered in the rays of the sun like a thousand stars and dazzled the eyes of all who looked on. A smile of satisfaction quivered on the lips of the dying man as he saw the splendid pile. If he had lost his life he had at least lost it in doing a brave deed, and a deed that

15

would bring his people not only renown, but material riches. A fluttering sigh came from his lips, which told that he was well satisfied; that death had come to him in the way he had always hoped to meet it.

> " Saw then the bold thane
> Treasure jewels many,
> Glittering gold
> Heavy on the ground,
> Wonders in the mound
> And the worm's den,
> The old twilight flier's,
> Bowls standing ;
> Vessels of men of yore,
> With the mountings fall'n off.
> There was many a helm
> Old and rusty,
> Armlets many
> Cunningly fastened.
> He also saw hang heavily
> An ensign all golden
> High o'er the hoard,
> Of hand wonders greatest,
> Wrought by spells of song,
> From which shot a light
> So that he the ground surface
> Might perceive,
> The wonders overscan."
>
> *Beowulf* (*Metcalfe's tr.*).

The Death and Burial of Beowulf

Meanwhile the warriors were standing helplessly by, trying to conceal their grief over the death of their dear chief. Beowulf, seeing their sorrow, made one last effort to address them. In a faint but eager voice he spoke to them all of the love that he felt for them, and reminded them of the great deeds that had marked his reign. With some of his old fire he urged them to maintain the honour of their race, so that the name of Geate should still be known far and wide among all men

16

THE BURIAL OF BEOWULF

as the symbol of courage and loyalty. Finally he expressed a desire to be buried in a mighty mound on a projecting headland, which could be seen far out at sea, and would be called by his name.

> " 'And now,
> Short while I tarry here—when I am gone,
> Bid them upon yon headland's summit rear
> A lofty mound, by Rona's seagirt cliff;
> So shall my people hold to after times
> Their chieftain's memory, and the mariners
> That drive afar to sea, oft as they pass,
> Shall point to Beowulf's tomb.' "
> *Beowulf (Conybeare's tr.).*

These directions were all piously carried out by a mourning people, who decked his mound with the gold he had won, and erected above it a Bauta, or memorial stone, to show how dearly they had loved their brave king Beowulf, who had died to save them from the fury of the dragon.

CHAPTER II : GUDRUN

The Origin of the Poem

MAXIMILIAN I., Emperor of Germany, rendered a great service to posterity by ordering that copies of many of the ancient national manuscripts should be made. These copies were placed in the imperial library at Vienna, where, after several centuries of almost complete neglect, they were discovered by lovers of early literature. In spite of the years which had gone by, the manuscripts were happily in a very satisfactory state of preservation, and they excited the interest of learned men, for their historical importance and their literary value. Nevertheless only now are they beginning to receive the appreciation which they deserve.

Among these manuscripts is the poem "Gudrun," belonging to the twelfth or thirteenth century. It is evidently compiled from two or more much older lays, which are now lost, but which are alluded to in the "Nibelungenlied." The original poem was probably Norse, and not German, like the only existing manuscript, for there is an undoubted parallel to the story of the kidnapping of Hilde in the "Edda." In the "Edda," Hilde, the daughter of Högni, escapes from home with her lover, Hedin, and is pursued by her irate father. He overtakes the fugitives on an island, where a bloody conflict takes place, in which many of the bravest warriors die. Every night, however, a sorceress recalls the dead to life to renew the strife and to exterminate one another afresh.

The poem "Gudrun," which is probably as old as the "Nibelungenlied," and almost rivals it in interest, is one of the most valuable remains of ancient German literature. It consists of thirty-two songs, in which are

18

related the adventures of three generations of the heroic family of the Hegelings. Hence it is often termed the "Hegeling Legend."

The Boyhood of Hagen

The poem opens by telling us that Hagen was the son of Sigeband, King of Ireland, which was evidently a place in Holland, and not the well-known Emerald Isle. During a great feast, when countless guests were assembled around his father's hospitable board, this prince, who was then but seven years of age, was seized by a griffin and rapidly borne away.

In vain Sigeband's men sprang to their feet and sent arrow after arrow in the direction of the bird. It merely went on its way, heedless alike of the cries of the child and the arrows of the knights. Over land and sea it flew, till it finally deposited its prey in its nest, on the top of a great cliff on a desert island. Here one of the griffin's brood, wishing to reserve this delicate morsel for its own delectation, caught the boy up in its talons and flew away to a neighbouring tree. But it happened that the branch upon which it perched was too weak to support a double load, and as it broke the frightened griffin dropped Hagen into a thicket. Undismayed by the sharp thorns, and only too thankful to have escaped from his enemy, Hagen crept quickly out of the griffin's reach and took refuge in a cave. A great surprise awaited him here, for he found within three little girls who had escaped from the griffins in the same way.

The Three Maidens

One of these children was Hilde, an Indian princess; the second Hildburg, daughter of the King of Portugal; and the third belonged to the royal family of Isenland.

19

At once Hagen became the protector of these maidens, and together they spent several happy years in the cave. The only thing there was to trouble them was the thought of the griffins near by, for fear of whom they never dared to leave the cave. Only when they knew from the whirring of wings that their cruel enemies had left their nest for a while did Hagen venture to go out in search of food. On these occasions he was in the habit of using a small bow, which he had made for himself in imitation of those he had seen long ago in his father's hall. Years went by, and still Hagen and the three maidens lived together in their cave. Gradually the hope of being rescued had died from their hearts. Not one of them would have confessed as much to the others, yet each had long ere this given up all expectation of seeing any other human being again. Sadly they used to sit together and talk of the days of old, now so long gone by that their very recollections of them were dim and faded.

Hagen Slays the Griffins

Then a strange thing happened one day which made the hearts of them all beat with sudden eager longings. The reason for this excitement was a discovery made by Hagen, a discovery of nothing less than the body of a dead knight, clad in armour, which had been washed up on the shore by the storm! Trembling with wild joy, Hagen pulled off the armour for which he had so long and vainly sighed. Then, hardly waiting to snatch up the weapons, he strode off to slay the griffins which had kept the four children in terror for so many years. After a sharp struggle the youth succeeded in killing all of the hideous birds, after which he hurried back to the cave to tell the three maidens what had happened. Scarcely able to believe in their good fortune, the four strolled up and down the island where they had been so long prisoners. Their eyes shone and their cheeks flushed as they said to one another that perhaps now they might be seen by a passing ship and taken again to their homes. Yet so used had they become to disappointment that they did not venture to hope their rescue would soon come about.

Nevertheless before very long a white sail appeared on the dim horizon. One and all they lifted up their voices and cried out, while as for Hagen, he climbed on to the top of a high rock, from which he waved and shouted with frantic energy.

The Rescue

At last their desperate appeals floated on the wind to the ears of the sailors, who reluctantly drew near. As they came they gazed fearfully upon the three maidens, who, clad in furs and moss, resembled mermaids or woodnymphs. When they heard their story, however, they gladly took them on board. Joyfully the four stepped into the vessel, never stopping to consider if the men were friend or foe. Thus it was only when the island was out of sight and they were in mid-ocean that Hagen discovered that he had fallen into the hands of Count Garadie, his father's inveterate enemy, who now proposed to use his power to treat the young prince as a slave. But Hagen's rude fare, and the constant exposure of the past few years, had so developed his strength and courage that he now flew into a Berserker rage,[1] flung thirty men one after another into the sea, and so terrified his would-be master that he promised to bear him and the three maidens in safety to his father's court at Balian.

[1] *See* " Myths of the Norsemen," Guerber, p. 23.

Hagen the King

When Hagen at last arrived home he found that his
father, Sigeband, had died without leaving any other heir.
The people, however, welcomed the son warmly, and
hailed him as king, after which Hagen ascended the throne,
and took to wife Hilde, one of the fair maidens with
whom he had lived in the cave for so many years.
The royal couple were very happy, and Hagen ruled so
wisely that he became a terror to his enemies and a
blessing to his own subjects. Even when engaged in
warfare he proved himself an upright and generous
man, never attacking the poor or weak.

Hagen's Daughter, Hilde

In course of time Hagen and Hilde became the
parents of an only daughter, who was called by her
mother's name. As she grew up she was so beautiful
that many suitors soon came to Ireland to ask for her
hand. Hagen, who loved his daughter dearly, was in
no haste to part from her. Therefore to put off the
time for a while, he replied that she was far too young
to think of marriage ; then when this plea was disputed
he declared that Hilde should only marry the man who
had defeated her father in single fight.

Now as Hagen was unusually tall and strong, as well
as famous for his courage, he was considered well-nigh
invincible. Dismayed by these difficult terms, the
suitors reluctantly withdrew. Yet they too, one and all,
were men of great bravery and daring.

For some time no other knights ventured to ask for
the right to woo the fair Hilde, and the heart of Hagen
was exceedingly glad. But by-and-by news of her great
beauty drifted to the land of the Hegelings, in North
Germany, where Hettel was king. As Hettel listened

Horant

The Conflict at Wulpensand

to the stories of the marvellous beauty of the maiden across the seas his heart burned with desire to have her for his wife, and he set about thinking how he might best secure her. He dared not send an ambassador with a direct proposal lest Hagen in his wrath should slay the messenger, and rather than lose any of his brave knights Hettel decided he would give up all thought of the marriage. Yet the desire of his heart grew daily stronger, till at last three of his most loyal followers, seeing how great was the longing of their chief to possess the lovely Hilde, rose and said they would carry her off, even if they should be forced to do so by strategy. Thus they set off, these three, Wat, Horant, and Frute, upon the quest they had of their own free will undertaken, resolved not to return unless the fair Hilde herself were with them.

The Quest of the Three Knights

Afraid, however, of venturing into Hagen's kingdom except in disguise, they loaded their vessel with merchandise and hid their weapons, so that they should be taken for traders. Thus they sailed boldly into Hagen's port, where, spreading out their wares, they invited all the people to buy.

Attracted by the extraordinary bargains they offered, the people soon came in crowds, and before long all the inhabitants of Balian were busy talking about the strange peddlers and praising their wares. By-and-by these stories came to the ears of both queen and princess, who, summoning the merchants into their presence, asked them who they were and whence they came.

In reply all three asserted that they were warriors who had been banished from Hettel's court, so that they had been forced to take up their present occupation to make a living. To prove the truth of their assertions Wat thereupon exhibited his skill in athletic sports.

When these games were at last over Horant said he would sing them a song. The queen gladly assented, and soon all were listening breathlessly as Horant's fine voice rang out in song after song.

" When now the night was ended and there drew near the dawn,
Horant began his singing, so that in grove and lawn
The birds became all silent, because he sang so sweetly ;
The people who were sleeping sprang from their couches fleetly.

" The cattle in the forests forsook their pasture ground ;
The creeping creatures playing among the grass around,
The fishes in the water,—all in their sports were ceasing.
The minstrel might most truly rejoice in art so pleasing.

" Whate'er he might be singing, to no one seemed it long ;
Forgotten in the minster were priest and choral song,
Church bells no longer sounded so sweetly as before,
And every one who heard him longed for the minstrel sore."

Gudrun (*Dippold's tr.*).

Hilde's Wooing

These soft strains pleased the younger Hilde so much that she soon sent for the minstrel again, and Horant, finding her alone, made use of this opportunity to tell her of Hettel's love and longing. Modestly Hilde listened till the knight had finished his story. But long ere it had come to an end her heart had been won ; and when Horant begged her to flee with himself and his comrades she willingly assented.

The pretended merchants, having now achieved the real object of their journey, made haste to dispose of their remaining wares. They then invited the king and the royal family to visit their ship, during which they cleverly managed to secrete the willing princess. The royal party returned without the absence of the princess being noticed, and the vessel was well under way before the angry king discovered his loss. His wrath on realising the deception was terrible to behold. But spears, threats, and curses were all of no avail : the strangers were far beyond reach.

Marriage of Hettel and Hilde

The Hegelings sailed with their prize direct to Waleis, in Holland, near to the river Waal, where the impatient Hettel came to meet them. With eager tenderness he embraced his beautiful young bride, whose loveliness was even greater than he had pictured. Their hasty nuptials were at once celebrated, after which they prepared to sail away on the morrow. But ere the ships had sailed off Hettel became aware of the rapid approach of a large fleet. It was Hagen in pursuit of his kidnapped daughter. Full of confusion and consternation, the Hegelings hastily prepared themselves for battle. Nor were they ready a moment too soon, for

> " King Hagen, full of anger, leaped forward in the sea.
> Unto the shore he waded ; no braver knight than he !
> Full many pointed arrows against him were seen flying,
> Like flakes of snow, from warriors of Hetel's host defying."
> *Gudrun* (*Dippold's tr.*).

For a time the battle raged fiercely, till at last it happened that Hettel was wounded by Hagen, who, in his turn, was injured by Wat. Upon seeing this the distracted Hilde suddenly flung herself between the contending parties, and by her tears and prayers soon brought about a reconciliation. Hagen, who had tested the courage of his new son-in-law and had not found it wanting, now permitted his daughter to accompany her husband home to Matelan, where she became the mother of a son, Ortwine, and of a daughter, Gudrun, who was even fairer than herself.

25

Ortwine was chiefly brought up by Wat, the daunt-less hero, who taught him to fight with consummate skill ; while Hilde herself presided over the education of Gudrun.

Gudrun the Beautiful

Years went by, and Gudrun had grown from a little girl into a lovely woman whose hand was sought by many suitors.

Among the number were Siegfried, King of Moor-land, a pagan of dark complexion ; Hartmut, son of Ludwig, King of Normandy ; and, thirdly, Herwig of Zealand. Although the last of these fancied that he had won some favour in the fair Gudrun's sight, Hettel dismissed him as well as the others with the answer that his daughter was yet too young to leave the parental roof.

But Herwig was not ready to give up the maiden so easily, and he set about planning how he could win his bride. He remembered that Hettel had gained his own bride only after he had measured his strength against her father. So he collected an army, invaded Matelan, and proved his courage by encountering Hettel himself in the fray. Gudrun, who stood watching the battle from the palace window, seeing them face to face, loudly implored them to spare each other, an entreaty to which they both lent a willing ear, for Hettel had satisfied himself that Herwig was a man of courage, and as for Herwig himself he was by no means eager to kill the father of the one he desired as his bride.

In answer to Gudrun's piteous cries, therefore, the two men threw down their weapons and parted in peace. Before separating Hettel gave Herwig a promise that he should have the hand of Gudrun and marry her, and that within a year. So full of joy was Herwig at the news that he tarried in Matelan with his betrothed until he heard that Siegfried, King of Moorland, jealous of his successful wooing of Gudrun, had invaded his kingdom and was raiding his unprotected lands.

Hartmut's Raid

These tidings caused the brave young warrior to bid Gudrun a hasty farewell and sail home as quickly as possible. Hettel, meanwhile, promised to follow him soon and help him in repelling the invaders, who were far superior in number to his small but oft-tried host. While Herwig and Hettel were thus occupied in warring against one of the disappointed suitors, Hartmut, the other, hearing that they were both away, invaded Matelan and carried off Gudrun and all her attendants to Normandy. He paused only once on his way thither to rest for a short time on an island called Wülpensand, at the mouth of the Scheldt.

The harassed Hilde, who had seen her beloved daughter thus carried away, promptly sent messengers to warn Hettel and Herwig of Gudrun's capture. These tidings put an immediate stop to their warfare with Siegfried, who instead joined forces with his former opponents. Thus they sailed off in pursuit of the Normans in the vessels of a party of pilgrims, for they had none of their own ready for instant departure.

By dint of hard sailing Hettel, Herwig, and Siegfried reached Wülpensand before the Normans had left it. A frightful conflict followed, in the course of which King Ludwig slew the aged Hettel. The struggle raged until nightfall, and although there were now but few Hegelings left, so fierce was their courage that they were all ready to renew the struggle on the morrow. Their chagrin was thus all the greater when

27

they rose and found that during the night the Normans had sailed away with their captives, and were already out of sight !

The Death of Hettel

It was useless to pursue them with so small an army ; so the Hegelings sorrowfully returned home, bearing Hettel's lifeless body back to the desolate Hilde. What to do next they did not know. So many able fighting men had perished during the last fight that they dared not go to war again. Very reluctantly, therefore, they agreed to wait till their children should be men before setting out to take vengeance on their foes.

Gudrun and Hartmut

In the meanwhile Gudrun had arrived in Normandy, where she persisted in refusing to marry Hartmut. On her way thither the haughty princess had even ventured to remind King Ludwig that he had once been her father's vassal. This remark so roused his anger that he threw her overboard. But Hartmut immediately plunged into the water after her, rescued her from drowning, and when he had again seen her safe in the boat angrily reproved his father for his hasty conduct.

" He said : ' Why would you drown her who is to be my wife,
The fair and charming Gudrun ?   I love her as my life.
Another than my father, if he had shown such daring,
Would lose his life and honour from wrath of mine unsparing.' "

Gudrun (Dippold's tr.).

After this declaration on the part of the young heir none dared at first treat Gudrun with any disrespect ; and as she landed Gerlinda and Ortrun, the mother and sister of Hartmut, came forward to welcome her. But Gerlinda's friendliness was a mere pretence, for she hated the proud maiden who scorned her son's proffered love. She therefore soon persuaded her son to give the gentle captive entirely into her charge, saying that she would make her consent to become his bride. Hartmut, who was about to depart for the war and little suspected his mother's cruel intentions, bade her do as she pleased, and handed Gudrun into her care. But no sooner was Hartmut out of sight than poor Gudrun was degraded to the rank of a servant, and treated with much harshness, and often with actual violence.

During three whole years Gudrun endured this cruelty in silence. Then Hartmut returned, and she was restored to her former state. Yet she still persisted in refusing his passionate suit. Discouraged by her obstinacy, the young man weakly consented to abandon her again to Gerlinda's tender mercies. The princess was now made to labour harder than ever, and she and Hildburg, her favourite companion and fellow captive, were daily sent down to the shore to wash the royal linen.

It was winter, the snow lay thick on the ground, and Gudrun and her companion, barefooted and miserably clad, suffered untold agonies from the cold. Besides this, their spirits were nearly exhausted, and the hope of rescue, which had sustained them during the past twelve years, had almost forsaken them. Yet their deliverance was near, had they but known it. For while Gudrun was washing on the shore, a mermaid, in the guise of a swan, came gently near her, and bade her be of good cheer, for her sufferings would soon be at an end.

" ' Rejoice in hope,' then answered the messenger divine ;
'Thou poor and homeless maiden, great joy shall yet be thine.
If thou wilt ask for tidings from thy dear native land,
To comfort thee, great Heaven has sent me to this strand.' "

Gudrun (Dippold's tr.).

Gudrun and the Swan

The swan maiden then informed her that her brother Ortwine had grown up, and that he would soon come with brave old Wat and the eager Herwig to deliver her.

The next day, in spite of the increased cold, Gerlinda again roughly bade the maidens go down to the shore and wash, refusing to allow them any covering except one coarse linen garment.

> "They then took up the garments and went upon their way.
> 'May God let me,' said Gudrun, 'remind you of this day.'
> With naked feet they waded there through the ice and snow :
> The noble maids, all homeless, were filled with pain and woe."
> *Gudrun (Dippold's tr.).*

Barely had Gudrun and Hildburg begun their usual task, however, when a small boat drew near, in which they recognised Herwig and Ortwine. All unconscious of their identity at first, the young men inquired about Gudrun. She herself, to test their affection, replied that the princess was dead Nor did she allow them to catch a glimpse of her face as she said this until she beheld Herwig's emotion at the tidings, and heard him protest that he would be faithful to her unto death.

> "There spoke the royal Herwig : 'As long as lasts my life,
> I'll mourn for her ; the maiden was to become my wife.'"
> *Gudrun (Dippold's tr.).*

A shiver of intense joy passed over Gudrun as she heard these words, and in a flash she turned round and discovered herself to her lover.

Gudrun's Wooing

Their meeting was one only to be imagined, but the hearts of both beat with wild happiness when Gudrun

Gudrun and the Swan

The Triumph of the Hegelings

found herself clasped in the strong arms of Herwig. Meanwhile Ortwine was equally happy. For not only was he overjoyed at finding his sister, but he had long loved her companion, though he had said nothing of his passion. Now, however, he poured out the story of his love, and soon won from Hildburg a promise that she would be his wife. The first moments of joyful reunion over, Herwig would fain have carried Gudrun and Hildburg back to camp with him ; but Ortwine proudly declared that he had come to claim them openly, and would bear them away from Normandy honourably, in the guise of princesses, rather than by stealth.

Then, after promising to return to rescue them on the morrow, the young men took leave of the maidens. Hildburg conscientiously finished her task, but Gudrun proudly flung the linen into the sea and returned to the palace empty-handed, saying that it did not become her to do any more menial labour. Gerlinda, hearing her confess that she had flung the linen into the sea, ordered her to be scourged. But at this Gudrun turned upon her and proudly announced that she would take her revenge on the morrow, when she would preside over the banquet-hall as queen. On hearing this Gerlinda concluded that she had decided to accept Hartmut, and she therefore flew to her son to impart to him the joyful tidings. In his delight he would fain have embraced Gudrun, who, however, haughtily bade him refrain from saluting a mere washer-woman. Aghast at the words, the prince inquired what she meant, and so for the first time learnt of all the hardships the princess had suffered. At once he ordered sternly that her maidens should again be restored to her, that her every command should be fulfilled as if she were already queen, and that all

31

should treat her with the utmost respect. These orders were executed without delay, and while Hartmut was preparing for his wedding on the morrow, Gudrun, again clad in royal attire, with her maidens around her, whispered to herself the tidings of coming deliverance. Morning had barely dawned when Hildburg, gazing out of the window, saw the castle entirely surrounded by the forces of the Hegelings. Even as she gazed the cock crew and old Wat's horn pealed forth a loud defiance, rousing the Normans from pleasant dreams, and calling them to battle instead of to the anticipated wedding.

The Rescue of Gudrun

As was to be expected, the encounter between such warriors was both long and fierce. The courtyard rang with the clamour of the men and the fierce noise of shield clashing on shield. Higher and higher rose the war-cries and fiercer and fiercer grew the blows. One after another brave men dropped to the ground, stiff and lifeless. Amongst these lay King Ludwig, slain by the hand of Herwig. Within the palace Gudrun sat with wide-open eyes, wondering what the result of the fearful struggle would be. Even as she wondered she felt herself grasped by the cruel hands of Gerlinda, who would have slain her and all her maidens, had not Hartmut rescued her at the moment. With his anger intensified by the thought of the fate that Gudrun had barely escaped, Herwig threw himself upon Hartmut. The prince made a brave resistance, but Herwig was too powerful for him, and he fell to the ground swooning. Then as Herwig swung back to fetch a blow that would make an end of his enemy for ever, Ortrun, the sister of Hartmut, darted forward to Gudrun and begged her to plead for her

32

brother's life. Her request touched Gudrun, for she liked Ortrun, who had ever been kind and gentle towards her. So she rose from her seat and leaned out of her casement and called to Herwig, who, at a word from her, sheathed his sword, and contented himself with taking Hartmut prisoner.

Death of Gerlinda

And now the enemy entered the castle and began to plunder. By-and-by the whole town was sacked, and Wat, bursting into the palace, proceeded to slay all he met. In terror the women then crowded round Gudrun, imploring her protection. Among these were Ortrun and Gerlinda. But while Gudrun would have protected the former at the cost of her life, she allowed Wat to kill the latter, for she felt that Gerlinda deserved such a death as a punishment for all her cruelty.

When the massacre was over the victors celebrated their triumph by a grand banquet, at which Gudrun, fulfilling her boast, actually presided as queen.

" Now from the bitter contest the warriors rested all.
There came the royal Herwig into King Ludwig's hall,
Together with his champions, their gear with blood yet streaming.
Dame Gudrun well received him ; her heart with love was teeming."
Gudrun (Dippola's tr.).

This great feast at last over, the Hegelings again set sail. Together with them they took the recovered maidens, all the spoil they had won, and their captives, Hartmut and Ortrun. Before long they were back again in Matelan, where they were warmly welcomed by Hilde, who was overcome with happiness at seeing her daughter once more. Silently the two kissed each other, and clung together as if they would never part again.

33

The Marriage of Gudrun

Scarcely had the people finished recounting the marvellous deeds of Herwig when a fourfold wedding took place. Gudrun married her faithful Herwig, Ortwine espoused Hildburg, Siegfried consoled himself for Gudrun's loss by taking the fair Ortrun to wife, and Hartmut received with the hand of Hergart, Herwig's sister, the restitution not only of his freedom, but also of his kingdom.

At the wedding banquet Horant, who, in spite of his advanced years, had lost none of his musical skill, played the wedding march with such success that the queens simultaneously flung their crowns at his feet. But the minstrel smilingly refused the offering, for he said that crowns were perishable, but a poet's song immortal. Then, taking up his harp, he sang :

> " ' Fair queens, I bid you wear them until your locks turn grey ;
> Those crowns, alas ! are fleeting, but song will live alway.' "
>
> *Niendorf* (*H. A. G.'s tr.*).

And the people, hearing him, applauded long ; for they knew that the words of the old minstrel were true.

CHAPTER III : REYNARD THE FOX

Origin of Animal Epics

AMONG primitive races, where the child instinct is still predominant, animal stories always find a leading place in the literature. The oldest of these tales current in the Middle Ages is the epic of "Reineke Fuchs," or "Reynard the Fox." This poem was carried by the ancient Franks across the Rhine into France, where it developed a new version with certain distinct characteristics of its own ; then it returned to Germany by way of Flanders, and here it was finally localised.

After circulating from mouth to mouth almost all over Europe, during many centuries, the story was first committed to writing in the Netherlands, where the earliest manuscript, dating from the eleventh or twelfth century, gives a Latin version of the tale.

"The root of this saga lies in the harmless natural simplicity of a primeval people. We see described the delight which the rude child of nature takes in all animals—in their slim forms, their gleaming eyes, their fierceness, their nimbleness and cunning. Such sagas would naturally have their origin in an age when the ideas of shepherd and hunter occupied a great portion of the intellectual horizon of the people ; when the herdman saw in the ravenous bear one who was his equal, and more than his equal, in force and adroitness, the champion of the woods and wilds ; when the hunter, in his lonely ramble through the depths of the forest, beheld in the hoary wolf and red fox, as they stole along—hunters like himself— mates, so to say, and companions, and whom he therefore addressed as such. . . . So that originally this kind of poetry was the exponent of a peculiar sort of

35

feeling prevailing among the people, and had nothing whatever to do with the didactic or satiric, although at a later period satiric allusions began to be interwoven with it."

The story has been rewritten by many poets and prose writers. It has been translated into almost every European language, and was remodelled from one of the old mediæval poems by Goethe, who has given it the form in which it will doubtless henceforth be known. His poem "Reineke Fuchs" has been commented upon by Carlyle and translated by Rogers, from whose version all the following quotations have been extracted.

The Assembly of the Animals

In those far-away days, when the Franks were under their old Merovingian rulers, it was the custom for all the animals to assemble at Whitsuntide around their king, Nobel the lion, who ruled over all the forest. This assembly, like its prototype, the Champ de Mars, was convened not only for the purpose of deciding upon the undertakings for the following year, but also as a special tribunal, where accusations were made, complaints heard, and justice meted out to all. On this occasion every animal was present except Reynard the fox. His absence was soon a matter for comment, for there was many a dark deed laid to his account. Every beast present testified to some crime committed by him, and all accused him loudly except his nephew, Grimbart the badger.

> " And yet there was one who was absent,
> Reineke Fox, the rascal ! who, deeply given to mischief,
> Held aloof from half the Court. As shuns a bad conscience
> Light and day, so the fox fought shy of the nobles assembled.
> One and all had complaints to make, he had all of them injured ;
> Grimbart the badger, his brother's son, alone was excepted."

36

Reynard's Trial

Reynard in the Fowl-yard

GRIMBART'S DEFENCE OF REYNARD

Reynard Accused

Of these complaints the chief was made by Isegrim the wolf, who told with much feeling how three of his beloved children had been cruelly blinded by the spiteful fox, who had also shamefully insulted his wife, the fair lady Gieremund. No sooner had Isegrim ended his accusation than Wackerlos the dog came forward. Pathetically he described how upon one occasion when he had found a little sausage in a thicket it had been ruthlessly purloined by Reynard, who seemed to have no regard whatever for the famished condition of the other.

The tom-cat Hintze, who at the mere mention of a sausage had listened more attentively, now cried out angrily that the sausage which Wackerlos had lost belonged by right to him, as he had concealed it in the thicket after stealing it from the miller's wife. He added that he too had had much to suffer from Reynard. In this he was supported by the panther, who described how he had once found the miscreant cruelly beating poor Lampe the hare.

> " Lampe he held by the collar,
> Yes, and had certainly taken his life, if I by good fortune
> Had not happened to pass by the road. There standing you
>   see him.
> Look and see the wounds of the gentle creature, who no one
> Ever would think of ill-treating."

Grimbart's Defence of Reynard

The king, Nobel, was beginning to look very stern as one after another rose to accuse the absent Reynard, when suddenly Grimbart the badger courageously began to defend him. So artfully did he plead that one by one the accusers found the tables were being turned upon themselves. Taking up their complaints in turn, he described how Reynard, his uncle, once entered into partnership with Isegrim. To obtain some fish which a carter was conveying to market, the fox had lain as if dead in the middle of the road. He had been picked up by the man for the sake of his fur, and tossed up on top of the load of fish. But no sooner had the carter's back been turned than the fox had sprung up and thrown all the fish into the road to the expectant wolf. As for himself, he had remained in the cart until the last bit of booty had been flung down. Meanwhile the wolf, ravenous as ever, devoured the fish as fast as they were thrown down, and when the fox claimed his share of the booty he had secured, Isegrim gave him only the bones.[1]

Moreover, not content with cheating his ally once, the wolf had induced the fox to steal a suckling pig from the larder of a sleeping peasant. With much exertion the cunning Reynard had thrown the prize out of the window to the waiting wolf. Then when he had asked for a portion of the meat as a reward he had been dismissed with nothing but the piece of wood upon which it had been hung.

The badger further proceeded to relate that Reynard had wooed Gieremund seven years before, when she was still unmated, and that if Isegrim chose to consider that an insult it was only on a par with the rest of his accusations, for the king could readily see that Reynard was sorely injured instead of being guilty.

Here Grimbart paused for a minute to take breath, and as he did so he cast a stealthy look round him and saw that all the animals were deeply impressed by his words. Flattered by the thought of his own eloquence, he proceeded to dispose airily of the cases of Wackerlos

---

[1] A translation into French of the Russian version of the story will be found in "Contes et Légendes," Guerber, vol. i. p. 84.

and Hintze by proving that they had both stolen the disputed sausage. After this he went on to say that Reynard had undertaken to instruct Lampe the hare in psalmody, and that the ill-treatment which the panther had described was only a little wholesome castigation inflicted by the teacher upon a lazy and refractory pupil.

> " Should not the master his pupil
> Sometimes chastise when he will not observe, and is stubborn in evil ?
> If boys were never punished, were thoughtlessness always passed over,
> Were bad behaviour allowed, how would our juveniles grow up ?"

These plausible explanations were not without their effect, and when Grimbart went on to declare that ever since Nobel had proclaimed a general truce and amnesty among all the animals of the forest Reynard had turned hermit and spent all his time in fasting, alms-giving, and prayer, it seemed as if the complaint would be dismissed.

Henning the Cock

And so it would probably have happened had not Henning the cock suddenly appeared, followed by his two sons, Kryant and Kantart, who bore upon a bier the mangled remains of a hen. In broken accents the bereaved father related how he had dwelt happily in a convent henyard, with the ten sons and fourteen daughters which his excellent consort had hatched and brought up in a single summer. His only anxiety had been caused by the constant prowling of Reynard, who, however, had been successfully kept at a distance by the watchdogs. But when the general truce had been proclaimed the dogs had been dismissed. Then came Reynard's opportunity. In the garb of a monk he had made his way into the hen-yard to show Henning the royal proclamation with the attached seal, and to assure him of his altered mode of living.

Thus reassured, Henning had led his family out into the forest in happiness of heart. But alas! scarcely had they got there when Reynard came out from his lurking-place and killed all but five of Henning's promising brood. They had not only been killed, but devoured, with the exception of Scratch-foot, whose mangled remains were laid at the monarch's feet in proof of the crime, as was customary in the mediæval courts of justice.

This circumstance at once altered the temper of the meeting. The king, angry that his truce should thus have been broken, and sorry for the evident grief of the father, ordered a sumptuous funeral for the deceased, and commanded that a stone should be placed upon her grave, bearing the epitaph :

" ' Scratch-foot, daughter of Henning, the cock, the best of the hen
      tribe.
   Many an egg did she lay in her nest, and was skilful in scratching.
   Here she lies, lost, alas! to her friends, by Reineke murdered.
   All the world should know of his false and cruel behaviour,
   As for the dead they lament.' Thus ran the words that were
      written."

Reynard Summoned to Court

Then, having given these directions, the king proceeded to take advice with his council, after which he solemnly bade Brown the bear proceed immediately to Malepartus, Reynard's home, and summon him to appear at court forthwith to answer to the grave charges which had been made against him. And he showed how greatly he suspected the loyalty of the fox by warning his messenger to behave circumspectly and to beware of the wiles of the crafty beast. However, the bear rather resented these well-meant recommendations, and, confidently asserting his ability to take care of himself, he set out for Reynard's abode.

Bruin as Messenger

REY-
NARD
AT THE
PLACE
OF
EXE-
CUTION

His way to the mountains led him through an arid, sandy waste, and thus by the time he reached Malepartus he was both weary and overheated. In no gentle voice, therefore, he stood before the entrance to Reynard's lair and called him to come out. For some time there was no reply, for Reynard was far too cautious to let himself be captured unawares. But at last he poked out his head, and, having satisfied himself that Brown was alone, he hastened out to welcome him.

With great volubility the fox commiserated the bear on his long journey, and excused the delay in admitting him under plea of an indisposition caused by eating too much honey, a diet which he abhorred. Indeed, his mention of this delicacy was only a ruse to distract the attention of the bear. It was more than successful, however, for at the mere mention of honey, Brown forgot all his fatigue, and when his host lamented the fact that he had nothing else to offer him he joyfully declared no food could suit him better, and that he could never get enough of it.

> " 'If that is so,' continued the Red one, ' I really can serve you,
> For the peasant Rüsteviel lives at the foot of the mountain.
> Honey he has, indeed, such that you and all of your kindred
> Never so much together have seen."

Reynard's Trick

Oblivious of everything else but the thought of such a treat, Brown the bear forgot all about the errand on which he had come, and set out willingly in Reynard's company. By-and-by they came to the peasant's yard, where a half-split tree-trunk lay in full view. Reynard bade his companion thrust his nose well down into the hollow and eat his fill of honey. Then as soon as he saw that the bear had thrust not only his nose but both forepaws into the crack, he cleverly removed the

41

wedges. Hereupon the tree clapped together and left the bear a prisoner, howling with pain.

These sounds soon attracted the peasant's attention, and he and his companions all fell upon the captive with every imaginable weapon, and proceeded to give him a sound beating. Frantic with pain and terror, the unfortunate animal finally succeeded in wrenching himself free, at the cost of the skin on his nose and forepaws. He made some attempt next to revenge himself on his foes, and succeeded in tumbling the fat cook into some water. After this he swam down the stream, and landed in a thicket, where he loudly bewailed his misfortunes. Here he was found by the fox, who added insult to injury by reproving him for his gluttony, and recalling the amusing picture he had made when he had been caught fast in the tree. All this was too much for Bruin, who felt as if he never again wished to see his spiteful companion, so he plunged headlong into the stream and swam away as fast as ever he could.

The Second Summons

Suddenly the remembrance of the errand on which he had come flashed into his mind, and he straightway resolved to return to Nobel and tell his miserable tale. Slowly he made his way back, for he was sore and stiff after the treatment he had received. But at last he stood before the assembly and pointed out his grievance. The king listened courteously to all that he had to say, but he was determined at all costs to be just to Reynard. So, after consulting with his principal courtiers, he declared it the right of any man to be thrice summoned. He also conceded that the bear's manners were not of a conciliatory nature, and therefore he selected Hintze the cat to bear his message to Malepartus. The cat, disheartened by unfavourable omens, was nevertheless compelled to go on this unwelcome journey.

On his arrival Reynard greeted him cordially, and promised to accompany him to court on the morrow. He then asked what kind of refreshment he could offer. When Hintze had confessed his preference for mice the fox replied that it was a very fortunate one, as there were plenty of them to be found in the parson's barn near by. At once Hintze asked to be led thither, that he might eat his fill.

> " ' Pray do me the kindness
> Hence to lead and show me the mice, for far above wild game
> Give me a mouse for delicate flavour.' "

With every mark of politeness Reynard conducted his guest to the parson's barn, and pointed out a little opening through which he had passed to steal chickens. For he happened to know that Martin, the parson's son, had recently laid a trap here to catch any intruder. Hintze at first demurred, but, urged by Reynard, he crept in, and straightway found himself caught in a noose. Reynard, pretending to take the cat's moans for cries of joy, banteringly inquired whether that was the way they sang at court. And as the screams of the unhappy animal grew louder and louder the unfeeling fox only laughed the more.

These sounds finally reached the ears of little Martin, who, accompanied by his father, came into the barn to catch the intruder. Poor Hintze, frightened at the sight of the bludgeon the parson was carrying, flew at his legs, and scratched and bit him so severely that his opponent fell to the ground in a swoon. Then, taking advantage of the confusion, Hintze managed to slip out of the noose, and so he effected his escape. As fast as he could he hobbled back to court, and there denounced

43

the hypocrisy of the fox, while as a proof of the cruel torture he had suffered he pointed to the socket from which his eye had been torn in the encounter.

Reynard and the Badger

The wrath of the king was now terrible to behold, and, assembling his council, he bade them decide how he should punish the miscreant who had twice ill-treated his messengers. Grimbart the badger, seeing that public opinion was decidedly against his relative, now begged that a third summons should be sent, and offered to carry the message himself. He furthermore declared that, even according to their own showing, the cat and bear had come to grief through their greediness. Leaving this thought to simmer in the minds of the assembly he then promptly departed.

The Third Summons

No sooner did Reynard hear Grimbart's voice than he ran out and bade him come in and tell him the news. Then he led the way into his lair, and told the badger to make himself at his ease. But Grimbart was in no mood for dallying. He hurriedly delivered his message, explained the grave case against Reynard, and urged the fox to obey the king's summons. By appearing at court, he added, there was still a chance that he might manage to save himself; but if he remained at home the king would certainly besiege his fortress and slay him and all his family. Reynard listened favourably to this advice, and, after bidding his wife a tender farewell, and committing his beloved children to her care, he set out with Grimbart to go to court.

The Journey to Court

On the way the recollection of his many transgressions began to lie very heavily upon his heart. The fear of death quickened his conscience, and, longing to make his peace with Heaven, he expressed a great wish to confess his sins and receive absolution. As no priest was near at hand, he begged Grimbart the badger to listen to him, and penitently confessed all the misdeeds that have been already recounted. He also added that once he had bound Isegrim to the rope of the convent bell at Elkinar, where his frantic tugging had made the bell ring repeatedly, and so brought the monks around him, who had cudgelled him severely. He related, too, how on another occasion he had induced Isegrim to enter the house of a priest through a window and then crawl along some beams in search of ham and bacon. As the wolf was carefully feeling his way, however, the mischievous fox had pushed him and made him fall on to the sleeping people below, who, awakening with a start, had fallen upon him and thrashed him severely. These and sundry other sins having duly been confessed, the badger ordered the fox to chastise himself with a switch which he plucked from the hedge. This being done, he next bade him lay it down in the road, jump over it thrice, and then meekly kiss it in token of obedience. Then he pronounced Reynard absolved from his former sins, and admonished him to lead an altered life in future.

> " 'My uncle, take care that your future amendment
> In good works be visible. Psalms you should read, and should visit
> Churches with diligence ; fast at the seasons duly appointed ;
> Him who asks you point out the way to ; give to the needy
> Willingly ; swear to forsake all evil habits of living,
> All kinds of theft and robbing, deceit and evil behaviour.
> Thus can you make quite sure that you will attain unto mercy ! ' "

The fox solemnly promised amendment, and with sanctimonious mien he continued his journey. But as he and the badger passed a convent some plump hens crossed their path. Immediately Reynard forgot all his promises and began to chase the chickens ; nor was it until he had been called sharply to a sense of duty by Grimbart that he gave up the chase, and even then only with reluctance. After this event the two proceeded without further drawback to the court, where Reynard's arrival created a great sensation.

> " When at the Court it was known that Reineke really was coming,
> Ev'ry one thronged out of doors to see him, the great and the little.
> Few with friendly intent ; for almost all were complaining.
> This, however, in Reineke's mind was of little importance ;
> Thus he pretended, at least, as he with Grimbart the badger,
> Boldly enough and with elegant mien now walked up the high street.
> Jauntily swung he along at his ease, as if he were truly
> Son of the king, and free and quit of ev'ry transgression.
> Thus he came before Nobel the king, and stood in the palace
> In the midst of the lords ; he knew how to pose as unruffled."

Reynard at Court

With consummate skill and unparalleled eloquence and impudence Reynard addressed the king, lauding himself as a faithful servant, and commiserating the fact that so many envious and backbiting people were ready to accuse him. But Nobel, in whose mind the recollection of the treatment inflicted upon Brown the bear and Hintze the cat was still very vivid, answered him sternly, and told him that it would be difficult for him to acquit himself of those two charges, to say nothing of the many others brought against him. Then Reynard, still undismayed, demanded with well-feigned indignation whether he was to be held responsible for the sins of those messengers, whose misfortunes were attributable to their gluttonous and thievish propensities only.

46

The Sentence

But in spite of this specious pleading all the other animals came crowding around with so many grievous charges that matters began to look very black indeed for the fox. In spite of all Reynard's eloquence, and of the fluent excuses ever on his tongue, the council pronounced him guilty, and condemned him to die an ignominious death. The announcement of this sentence was received with great joy by the enemies of the fox, who dragged him off with cheerful alacrity to the gallows, where all the animals assembled to witness his execution.

On his way to the place of punishment Reynard tried to think of some plan by means of which he could save himself even at the eleventh hour. But for the moment even his nimble wits failed him. Still, knowing that some scheme would occur to him if he could only gain a little time, he humbly implored permission to make a public confession of his manifold sins ere he paid the penalty of his crimes. Anxious to hear all that he might have to say, the king willingly granted him permission to speak. Cunningly the fox began to relate at length the story of his early and innocent childhood, his meeting and alliance with Isegrim the wolf, and his gradual induction by him into crooked paths and evil ways. He told, too, how the cruel wolf, presuming on his strength, had ever made use of it to deprive him, the fox, of his rightful share of plunder. Then he concluded by saying that he would often have suffered from hunger had it not been for the possession of a great treasure of gold, which had sufficed for all his wants.

" 'Thanks be to God, however, I never suffered from hunger ;
Secretly have I fed well by means of that excellent treasure,
All of silver and gold in a secret place that securely
Hidden I keep ; with this I've enough. And, I say it in earnest,
Not a waggon could carry it off, though sevenfold loaded.' "

47

Nothing that Reynard could have said could have helped him so much as the mention of this great hoard.

Reynard's Trick upon Nobel the King

At the word "treasure" Nobel pricked up his ears, and bade Reynard relate how this wealth was obtained and where it was concealed. The artful fox, seeing the king's evident interest, rapidly prepared more lies. Addressing himself more especially to the king and queen, he declared that he also felt that ere he died it would be better for him to reveal the carefully guarded secret of a conspiracy which would have resulted in the king's death had it not been for his devotion.

The mere thought of the danger to her royal consort made the queen shudder with terror, and she begged that Reynard might step down from the scaffold and speak privately to his Majesty and herself. In this interview Reynard, still pretending to prepare for immediate death, told how he discovered a conspiracy formed by his father, Isegrim the wolf, Brown the bear, and many others, to slay the king and seize the sceptre. He described the various secret conferences, the measures taken, and his father's promise to defray all the expenses of the enterprise and to subsidise mercenary troops by means of the hoard of King Ermenrich, which he had discovered and concealed for his own use.

As the tale went on Reynard invented more and more lies. He described his loyal fears for his beloved sovereign, his resolve to outwit the conspirators, and his efforts to deprive them of the sinews of war by discovering and abstracting the treasure. Thanks to his ceaseless vigilance, he saw his father steal forth one night, uncover his hoard, gloat over the gold, and then with the utmost skill efface the traces of his search.

THE PARDON OF REYNARD

> " ' Nor could one,
> Not having seen, have possibly known. And ere he went onwards
> Well he understood at the place where his feet had been planted,
> Cleverly backwards and forwards to draw his tail, and to smooth it,
> And to efface the trace with the aid of his mouth.' "

Next he told the king how with his wife, Ermelyn, he had laboured diligently to remove the gold and conceal it elsewhere ; how in consequence the conspiracy had come to naught when no gold could be found to pay the troops. He added sadly that his loyalty had further deprived him of a loving father, for the latter had hung himself in despair when he found his treasure gone and all his plans frustrated. With hypocritical tears Reynard then bewailed his own fate, saying that, although ready to risk all for another, there was no one near him to speak a good word for him in this his time of bitterest need.

The Pardon of Reynard

The queen's soft heart was so touched by this display of feeling that she immediately pleaded for his pardon from Nobel, who granted it only upon condition that the fox would give him his treasure. With elaborate care Reynard set himself to describe the exact spot where the treasure was to be found. To this the king listened carefully, resolved to inquire into the matter with all possible speed. Then, having given every possible direction, Reynard begged that he might be allowed to leave for Rome. He declared, in his wiliness, that he was under a ban from the Pope, so that his presence could only be an offence to their Majesties. "Certainly you may go," replied Nobel courteously. "But first I must ascertain whether the spot you have indicated really exists."

"By all means," assented Reynard willingly ; for he knew that the place was known.

49

So the king gave orders for the imprisonment of Isegrim, Brown, and Hintze—the three chief conspirators, according to Reynard's tale—and then made inquiries about the locality that the clever fox had mentioned. On being told that many knew of its whereabouts he was satisfied as to the truth of what he had heard. So with many good wishes he bade the fox set off on his pilgrimage.

Before his departure, however, Reynard spitefully asked for a fragment of Brown's hide to make a wallet, and a pair of socks from the skin of Isegrim and his wife. All these the king willingly granted, for he deemed the others vile traitors, and thus equipped the fox left the court. Anxious to show him every courtesy, the king, queen, and court then accompanied him a short way on the first stage of his journey, after which they turned back, leaving Bellyn the ram and Lampe the hare to escort him a little farther. These innocent companions accompanied Reynard to Malepartus, and while Bellyn waited patiently without Lampe entered the house with Reynard. Lady Ermelyn and her two young sons greeted Reynard with joy, listened breathlessly to the account of his adventures, and then helped him to slay and eat Lampe, through whom, he declared, all these evils had come upon him.

Thus Reynard and his family feasted upon the body of poor Lampe the hare, whose head was then securely fastened in the wallet made of Brown's skin. This the fox carefully carried out and placed upon Bellyn's back, assuring him volubly the while that it contained important despatches, and that in order to ensure him a suitable reward for his good offices he had told Nobel the king that the ram had given him valuable assistance in preparing the contents of the wallet.

Reynard and Bellyn

The Combat

GRIMBART TO THE RESCUE

The Death of Bellyn

Thus instructed, and reassured concerning the absence of Lampe, whom Reynard described as enjoying a chat with Ermelyn, Bellyn bounded off to court, where he did not fail to vaunt that he had helped Reynard to prepare the contents of the wallet. Nobel publicly opened it, and when he drew out Lampe's bleeding head his anger knew no bounds. Following the advice of his courtiers, Bellyn, in spite of all his protestations, was given in atonement to the bear, the wolf and the cat. For the king now was beginning to fear that these three subjects had been unjustly treated. They were therefore released from imprisonment and reinstated in royal favour, and twelve days of festivity ensued.

More Accusations against Reynard

Then in the midst of the dance and revelry a bloody rabbit appeared and accused Reynard of tearing off one of his ears. Scarcely had he finished when the garrulous crow, Merkinau, related how the same unscrupulous wretch had pretended death merely to befool Sharfenebbe, his wife, and induce her to come near enough for him to bite off her head. Upon hearing these complaints Nobel the king immediately swore that within six days he would besiege Reynard in his castle, and take him prisoner, and make him suffer the penalty of his crimes.

Grimbart to the Rescue

Isegrim the wolf and Brown the bear rejoiced at these tidings, while Grimbart the badger, seeing the peril his uncle had incurred, hastened off secretly to Malepartus to warn him of his danger and support him by his advice. He found Reynard sitting complacently

51

in front of his house, contemplating two young doves which he had just captured as they were making their first attempt to fly. Grimbart breathlessly related the arrival of Bellyn, the royal indignation at the sight of Lampe's head, and the plan for surrounding and capturing Reynard in his safe retreat.

In spite of this disquieting news Reynard's composure did not desert him. After vowing that he could easily acquit himself of these crimes if he could only win the king's ear for a moment, he invited his kinsman to share his meal and taste the delicate morsels he had secured. But Grimbart was too full of anxious thoughts to enjoy a meal just then. He feared the doom that might swiftly overtake his kinsman, and he begged the fox not to wait for the king's coming and expose his wife and children to the horrors of a siege, but to return boldly to court. "Only one thing remains to be done," he cried wildly :

"'Go with assurance before the lords, and put the best face on
    Your affairs. They will give you a hearing. Lupardus was also
    Willing you should not be punish'd before you had fully
    Made your defence, and the queen herself was not otherwise
        minded.
    Mark this fact, and try to make use of it.'"

Reynard again at Court

At last Grimbart's entreaties prevailed, and Reynard once more bade a tender farewell to his wife and sons, and set out with Grimbart to visit the court. On his way he again pretended repentance for his former sins, and, resuming his confession at the point where he had broken off, he told how maliciously he had secured a piece of the bear's hide for a wallet, and socks from Isegrim and his wife. He then went on to relate how he had murdered Lampe, charged the innocent Bellyn

with the ambiguous message which had cost him his
life, torn off one of the rabbit's ears, and eaten the
crow's wife. Lastly, he confessed how he had gone
out in company with the wolf, who, being hungry, and
seeing a mare with a little foal, had bidden Reynard
inquire at what price she would sell it. The mare
retorted that the price was written on her hoof. The
sly fox, understanding her meaning, yet longing to get
his companion into trouble, pretended not to know
how to read, and sent the wolf to ascertain the price.
The result was, of course, disastrous, for the mare
kicked so hard that the wolf lay almost dead for several
hours after.

Waxing more and more eloquent as they drew nearer to
court and his fears increased, Reynard began to moralise.
He excused himself for Lampe's murder on the plea of
the latter's aggravating behaviour ; said that the king
himself was nothing but a robber living by rapine ; and
proceeded to show how even the priests were guilty of
manifold sins, which he enumerated with much gusto.

Martin the Ape

All this he was declaiming lustily when they happened to come across Martin the ape, on his way to
Rome. At once Reynard hastened to implore him to
secure his release from the Pope's ban, and begged him
to intercede on his behalf with a cardinal who was uncle
to Martin. The ape not only promised his good offices
at the Papal court, but bade Reynard not hesitate to
consult his wife should he find himself in any predica-
ment at court.

Thus supported, Reynard again made his appearance
before the assembly, to the utter amazement and surprise
of all. Yet although he was well aware that his situation
was more dangerous than ever, his assurance did not seem

53

at all impaired. Kneeling with pretended humility before the king, he artfully opened his address by lamenting the fact that there were so many unscrupulous people ever ready to accuse the innocent ; and when the king angrily interrupted him to accuse him of maiming the rabbit and devouring the crow he began his defence.

Reynard's Second Defence

First, he explained that since Martin the ape had undertaken to free him from his ban his journey to Rome was of course unnecessary. Then he related how the rabbit, dining at his house, had insulted and quarrelled with his children, from whose clutches he had had much trouble to save him. The crow's death was caused by a fish-bone she had swallowed. Bellyn, the traitor, had slain Lampe himself, and evidently put his head in the wallet instead of some treasures which Reynard had entrusted to their care for the king and queen.

Reynard and Rückenau

The king, who had listened impatiently to all this discourse, angrily retired, refusing to believe a word, whereupon Reynard sought the ape's wife, Frau Rückenau, and bade her plead for him. She readily agreed, and at once entered the royal tent, where she reminded the king of her former services. Then, seeing his mood was somewhat softened, she ventured to recall how cleverly Reynard had once helped him to judge between the rival claims of a shepherd and a serpent. The latter, caught in a noose and about to die, had implored a passing shepherd to set it free. The peasant had done so, after exacting a solemn oath from the serpent that he would do him no harm. But the serpent, once released, and suffering from the pangs of hunger, threatened to devour the peasant. The latter called the raven, the wolf, and the bear, whom he met by the way, to his aid. But as they all hoped to get a share of him, they all decided in favour of the serpent's claim to eat him.

The case by this time had become so intricate that it was laid before the king, who, unable to judge wisely, had called Reynard to his aid. The fox declared that he could only settle so difficult a matter when plaintiff and defendant had assumed the relative positions which they occupied at the time of dispute. Then when the snake was safely in the noose once more Reynard decided that, knowing the serpent's treachery, the peasant might again set him free, but that he need not do so unless he chose.

> " ' Here now is each of the parties
> Once again in his former state, nor has either the contest
> Won or lost. The right, I think, of itself is apparent.
> For if it pleases the man, he again can deliver the serpent
> Out of the noose ; if not, he may let her remain and be hang'd there.
> Free he may go on his way with honour and see to his business,
> Since she has proved herself false, when she had accepted his kind-
> ness ;
> Fairly the man has the choice. This seems to me to be justice,
> True to the spirit. Let him who understands better declare it.' "

The king remembered this celebrated judgment well, so when Frau Rückenau went on to remind him of the well-known rapacity of both the bear and the wolf he consented at last to give Reynard a second hearing. Now that the fox had got yet another opportunity he did not fail to make use of it. He minutely described the treasures he had sent to court—a magic ring for the king, and a comb and mirror for the queen. Not only was the fable of the judgment of Paris engraved on the latter, but also that of the jealous donkey, who, imitating his master's lapdog by trying to climb into his lap, received nothing but blows. There was also the story of the cat and the fox, of the wolf and the crane ; and, lastly, the account of the miraculous way in which his father, a noted leech, had saved Nobel's sire by making him eat the flesh of a wolf just seven years old.

The pleader then reminded the king of a noted hunting party, where Isegrim, having secured a boar, gave the king one quarter, the queen another, reserved a half for himself, and gave the fox nothing but the head. This division was of course very disloyal, and the fox had shown that he thought so by dividing a calt more equitably. Thus he had given the queen one half, the king the other, the heart and liver to the princes, the head to the wolf, and reserved only the feet for himself.

Reynard's Great Fight

Reynard made a great show of parading these tokens of loyalty one by one, and so effective were his words that all the animals felt there was nothing to say in reply to him. Seeing that he had made a favourable impression, he volunteered, in spite of his small size, to meet the wolf in battle and leave the vindication of his claims to the judgment of God. This magnanimous behaviour filled the king with admiration, and the trial was appointed for the following day, the intervening hours being granted to both combatants for preparation. During the interval Reynard followed the advice of Frau Rückenau, by which he was shaved smooth, and rubbed with butter until he was as slippery as could be. He was then instructed to feign fear and run fleetly in front of the wolf, kicking up as much sand as possible, and using his brush to dash it into his opponent's eyes, and thus blind him.

REYNARD'S GREAT FIGHT

The night passed and day came. Every one crowded to watch the combat. Determined to win, Reynard carefully followed out the instructions Frau Rückenau had cunningly given him, till at last the eyes of his opponent were quite blinded with sand. Irritated by this circumstance, the wolf dashed furiously upon his enemy, and would have caught him had not the fox been too slippery to hold. At last, in spite of his size, Reynard succeeded in getting the victory. Then to win favour from the spectators he generously granted life to his foe, whom he had nearly torn and scratched to pieces. Thus Reynard, having proved his prowess, enjoyed the plaudits of the crowd, while the wolf, being vanquished, was publicly derided, and borne off by his few remaining friends to be nursed back to health, if possible.

" Such is ever the way of the world. They say to the lucky,
   'Long may you live in good health,' and friends he finds in abundance.
   When, however, ill fortune befalls him, alone he must bear it.
   Even so was it here ; each one of them wish'd to the victor
   Nearest to be, to show himself off."

After this famous encounter the king stood up and pronounced Reynard guiltless of all charges. Then he further showed his favour by making him one of his privy councillors. But the fox, after thanking the king for his kindness, humbly besought permission to return home, where his wife was awaiting him. Accordingly he departed, escorted by a deputation of his friends.

Authorities vary as to the exact end of this story. According to some versions of the tale, Reynard contented himself with blinding the wolf and maiming him for life ; according to others, he bided his time, and when the king was ill told him that nothing could save him short of the heart of a wolf just seven years old. Of course no wolf of the exact age could be found but

57

LEGENDS OF THE MIDDLE AGES

Isegrim, so he was sacrificed to save the king, who recovered. As for Reynard, he enjoyed great honour as long as he lived, and his adventures have long been the delight of the people, whom his tricks have never failed to amuse.

> " Highly honour'd is Reineke now ! To wisdom let all men
> Quickly apply them, and flee what is evil, and reverence virtue !
> This is the end and aim of the song, and in it the poet
> Fable and truth hath mixed, whereby the good from the evil
> Ye may discern, and wisdom esteem ; and thereby the buyers
> Of this book in the ways of the world may be daily instructed.
> For it was so created of old, and will ever remain so.
> Thus is our poem of Reineke's deeds and character ended.
> May God bring us all to eternal happiness. Amen ! "

CHAPTER IV : THE NIBELUNGENLIED

The Genesis of the Story

GERMANY'S greatest epic is, without doubt, the ancient poem entitled " Nibelungenlied," or the " Lay," " Fall," or " Calamity of the Nibelungs." Although nothing certain is known concerning the real authorship of this beautiful work, it is supposed to have been put into its present form either by the Austrian minstrel von Kürenberg or by the German poet von Ofterdingen, some time previous to the year 1210, the date inscribed on the oldest extant manuscript of that poem.

According to the best authorities on ancient German literature, the " Nibelungenlied " is compiled from pre-existing songs and rhapsodies, forming five distinct cycles of myths, but all referring in some way to the great treasure of the Nibelungs. One of these cycles is the Northern Volsunga Saga,[1] where Sigurd, Gudrun, Gunnar, Högni, and Atli, the principal characters, correspond to Siegfried, Kriemhild, Gunther, Hagen, and Etzel of the "Nibelungenlied." The story of the German poem, which can be given only in outline, is as follows :

Dankrat and Ute, King and Queen of Burgundy, were the fortunate parents of four children : three sons, Gunther, Gernot, and Giselher ; and one beautiful daughter, Kriemhild. When the king died his eldest son, Gunther, succeeded him. He reigned wisely and well, and resided at Worms, on the Rhine, his capital and favourite city.

The Girlhood of Kriemhild

Following the general custom of those days, Kriemhild lived a peaceful and secluded life, rarely leaving

[1] *See* " Myths of the Norsemen," Guerber, p. 251.

her mother's palace and protection. But one night her slumbers, which were usually very peaceful, were disturbed by a tormenting dream. Upon awaking she hastened to confide her fears to her mother, for she knew that Ute was skilled in magic and dreams, and she hoped she might give her a favourable interpretation, and thus rid her of her haunting uneasiness.

In her vision the princess had been possessed of a young falcon which she had trained with great care and love, until one day two fierce eagles had suddenly appeared, swooped down on the falcon, and carried it off even before her eyes. All these things Kriemhild falteringly told her mother. Then she stood anxiously waiting to hear what the explanation would be. But Ute shook her head as she declared that the falcon her daughter had seen in her dream must be some noble prince, whom she would love and marry, while the two eagles were base murderers, who would eventually slay her beloved. Instead of reassuring Kriemhild, this interpretation only saddened her the more, and made her loudly protest that she would rather forego all the joys of married estate than have to mourn for a beloved husband.

Kriemhild and Siegfried

Now in those days there flourished, farther down the Rhine, the kingdom of the Netherlands, governed by Siegmund and Siegelind. These two were proud about many things, but above all they were proud of their only son and heir, young Siegfried, who had already reached man's estate. To celebrate his knighthood, therefore, a great tournament was held at Xanten, on the Rhine, and thither flocked all the best-known knights in the land to try their fortunes at jousting. Yet in the contests the young prince won all the laurels, and in spite of

Siegfried and the Dragon

Siegfried captures Ludegast

the acknowledged skill of his several opponents he succeeded in carrying off all the glory.

For seven whole days the festivities continued, and when at last the guests departed they were all heavily laden with the costly gifts which the king and queen had lavished upon them. So splendid were these gifts and so generously were they given that it seemed as if the very palace itself must have been despoiled. For in their delight over their son's great achievement Siegmund and Siegelind found nothing too costly to give to their friends.

Then when the last of the guests had gone, and the decorations were being torn down from the lists, young Siegfried went to his parents and told them that he had heard such rumours of the beauty and attractions of Kriemhild of Burgundy that he would never be content till he had secured her as his wife.

In vain the fond parents tried to prevail upon him to remain quietly at home ; Siegfried would not be moved from his purpose. At last he won their reluctant consent, and so he set off on his errand. With eleven companions, all decked out in the richest garments that the queen's chests could furnish, the young prince rode down the Rhine, and reached Worms on the seventh day.

Siegfried's Wooing

The arrival of such a splendid company was soon noted by Gunther's subjects, who hastened out to meet the strangers and help them to dismount. Immediately Siegfried requested to be brought into the presence of their king, who in the meanwhile had inquired of his uncle, Hagen, the names and standing of the newcomers. Glancing down from the great hall window, Hagen said that the leader must be Siegfried, the knight who had slain

the owners of the Nibelungen hoard and appropriated
it for his own use, as well as the magic cloud cloak, or
Tarnkappe, which rendered its wearer invisible to mortal
eyes. He added that this same Siegfried was ruler of
the Nibelungen land, and the slayer of a terrible dragon,
whose blood had made him invulnerable. He therefore
advised Gunther to receive him most courteously.

> " Yet more I know of Siegfried, that well your ear may hold :
> A poison-spitting dragon he slew with courage bold,
> And in the blood then bath'd him ; thus turn'd to horn his skin,
> And now no weapons harm him, as often proved has been.

> " Receive then this young hero with all becoming state ;
> 'Twere ill advis'd to merit so fierce a champion's hate.
> So lovely is his presence, at once all hearts are won,
> And then his strength and courage such wondrous deeds have done."
>
> *Nibelungenlied* (*Lettsom's tr.*).

Full of excitement at the advent of so famous a
warrior, Gunther went out to meet Siegfried, and
politely inquired the cause of his visit. He was therefore not a little dismayed when Siegfried replied that he
had come to test the Burgundian's vaunted strength, for
which purpose he proposed a single combat, in which
the victor might claim the lands and allegiance of the
vanquished. Knowing the great strength of his visitor,
Gunther recoiled from such a proposal. Then, as none
of his warriors seemed inclined to accept the challenge,
he and his brother hastened to disarm Siegfried's haughty
mood by their proffers of unbounded hospitality. Thus
Siegfried sojourned for nearly a year at Gunther's court,
displaying his skill in all martial exercises.

Kriemhild Watches Siegfried

All this time he never caught a glimpse of the fair
maiden Kriemhild ; yet she often admired his strength
and manly beauty from behind the palace lattice.

SIEGFRIED'S EXPEDITION

But at last a day came when the games were interrupted by the arrival of a herald, who announced that Ludeger, King of the Saxons, and Ludegast, King of Denmark, were about to invade Burgundy. These tidings filled Gunther's heart with terror, for he knew full well that both of these sovereigns were famous for the number and prowess of their warriors. In the midst of this dilemma, however, Hagen came forward with the suggestion that no doubt Siegfried would help them, since he had lived so long at the court.

Gunther seized the suggestion eagerly, and hastened to ask Siegfried if he would be willing. The answer of the other was short but decisive. He declared that if Gunther would only give him one thousand brave men he would undertake to repel the foe. This offer was accepted joyfully, and Gunther hastily assembled a chosen corps, in which were his brothers Gernot and Giselher, Hagen and his brother Dankwart, Ortwine, Sindolt, and Volker, all of them being men of distinguished courage. Delighted to command such a noble company, Siegfried took leave of his generous host, saying :

"' Sir king, . . . here sit at home and play,
While I and your vassals are fighting far away ;
Here frolic with the ladies and many a merry mate,
And trust to me for guarding your honour and estate.' "
Nibelungenlied (*Lettsom's tr.*).

Siegfried's Expedition on behalf of Gunther

Then the little force, only one thousand strong, marched bravely out of Worms, passed through Hesse, and entered Saxony. Here they encountered the enemy, who numbered no less than twenty thousand valiant fighting men. The battle was immediately begun, and a great struggle soon raged. Every knight fought bravely, yet none did such wonders as Siegfried, for not only did he make both kings prisoners, but he routed their host, and finally returned triumphant to Worms, with much spoil and many captives.

Meanwhile a messenger had preceded him thither to announce the success of the expedition. No sooner did Kriemhild hear of the approach of this herald than she summoned him secretly to her side, so anxious was she to learn news of Siegfried. Then, in her joy at hearing that her hero was not only victorious, but unhurt, she loaded the messenger with presents and sent him away with gladness in his heart.

> " Then spake she midst her blushes, ' Well hast thou earn'd thy
>   meed,
> Well hast thou told thy story, so take the costliest weed,
> And straight I'll bid be brought thee ten marks of ruddy gold.'
> No wonder, to rich ladies glad news are gladly told."
>
> Nibelungenlied (Lettsom's tr.).

Siegfried's Return

Soon the streets resounded with the noise of trumpets which told of the approach of the warriors. Eagerly Kriemhild hastened to her window, from whence she witnessed her hero's triumphant entrance, and heard the people's acclamations of joy. The wounded were cared for, the captive kings hospitably entertained and afterwards duly released, and splendid festivities held to celebrate the glorious victory. Amongst these entertainments was a great tournament, to which Ute, Kriemhild, and all the court ladies were invited to view the prowess of the men-at-arms. It was thus that Siegfried first beheld Kriemheld, and as he saw her his passion rose still higher, for he saw that she was fairer than he could ever have supposed.

> " As the moon arising outglitters every star
>   That through the clouds so purely glimmers from afar,

E'en so love-breathing Kriemhild dimm'd every beauty nigh.
Well might at such a vision many a bold heart beat high."
Nibelungenlied (*Lettsom's tr.*).

His cup of happiness was therefore full to overflowing when he found himself appointed to escort the princess back to the palace. For a moment he was tongue-tied in the presence of her whom he loved, yet by-and-by he plucked up courage and strove to interest and amuse her by his talk. Meanwhile Kriemhild's fair face was covered with blushes as she timidly thanked him for the great service he had just rendered to her brother, Gunther. These words made the heart of Siegfried beat with happiness, and he gave her a solemn promise that as long as he lived he would always help him in every way that he could.

" ' Ever,' said he, ' your brethren I'll serve as best I may,
Nor once, while I have being, will head on pillow lay
Till I have done to please them whate'er they bid me do;
And this, my Lady Kriemhild, is all for love of you.' "
Nibelungenlied (*Lettsom's tr.*).

Then as Kriemhild again murmured her thanks, the two parted; and as they separated each knew of the love of the other, though it was but their first meeting together.

At last the festivities were ended, and Gunther bestowed many gifts on the guests about to return to their own land. Siegfried, too, would also have departed, but that Gunther entreated him to remain at Worms. To this the champion assented gladly, as he was by now deeply in love with the fair Kriemhild, whom he was privileged to see every day.

Brunhild

Scarcely had the excitement consequent on the festivities subsided in Worms when King Gunther declared his desire to win for his wife Brunhild, a princess of Issland, who had vowed to marry none but the man who could surpass her in casting a spear, in throwing a stone, and in jumping.

In vain Siegfried, who knew all about Brunhild, tried to dissuade him ; Gunther insisted upon departing. But at the same time he begged that Siegfried would also accompany him, and promised him Kriemhild's hand as a reward for his assistance as soon as the princess of Issland should be won. Such an offer was not to be refused, and Siegfried immediately accepted it. At the same time he advised Gunther not to go in state, but to take only Hagen and Dankwart as his attendants.

Gunther and Brunhild

After seeking the aid of Kriemhild for a supply of rich clothing suitable for a prince going to woo a maiden, Gunther and the three knights embarked on a small vessel. The sails soon filled, and bore them rapidly down the Rhine and over the sea to Issland. As soon as they were within sight of its shores Siegfried bade his companions be careful to represent him to the strangers as Gunther's vassal only, for he did not wish his true position known. No sooner had the boat landed than it was seen by some inquisitive damsels who were peering out of the windows of the castle. They reported the matter to Brunhild, who immediately and joyfully concluded that Siegfried had come to seek her hand in marriage. But when she heard that he held another man's stirrup to enable him to mount she frowned angrily, wondering why he came as a menial instead of as a king. Afterwards, when the strangers entered her hall, she would have greeted Siegfried first, had he not modestly drawn aside, declaring that the honour was due to his master, Gunther, King of Burgundy, who had come to Issland to woo her.

Annoyed at finding that Siegfried was not a suitor, Brunhild haughtily bade her warriors make all the necessary preparations for the coming contest. Meanwhile Gunther, Hagen, and Dankwart apprehensively watched the movements of four warriors staggering beneath the weight of Brunhild's ponderous shield. Their gloom grew greater when they saw three others equally overpowered by her spear ; while as for the stone she was wont to cast, twelve sturdy servants could scarcely move it.

The Great Contest

Trembling with fear for their master, since he was doomed to die in case of failure, Hagen and Dankwart began to mutter that some treachery was afoot, and openly regretted that they had consented to lay aside their weapons upon entering the castle. Their remarks were at last heard by Brunhild, and succeeded in rousing her bitter scorn. Contemptuously she bade her servants bring the strangers their arms again, since they were clearly men of craven heart.

> " Well heard the noble maiden the warriors' words the while,
> And looking o'er her shoulder, said with a scornful smile,
> ' As he thinks himself so mighty, I'll not deny a guest ;
> Take they their arms and armour, and do as seems them best.
>
> " ' Be they naked and defenceless, or sheath'd in armour sheen,
> To me it nothing matters,' said the haughty queen.
> ' Fear'd yet I never mortal, and, spite of yon stern brow
> And all the strength of Gunther, I fear as little now.' "
> *Nibelungenlied* (*Lettsom's tr.*).

While these preparations were taking place, Siegfried

had gone down to the ship which was riding at anchor. Here, all unseen, he donned his magic cloud-cloak, and so hastened back to the scene of the coming contest. Invisible to every one, he entered the hall and whispered in the ear of Gunther:

> " ' I am Siegfried, thy trusty friend and true ;
> Be not in fear a moment for all the queen can do.'
>
> " Said he, ' Off with the buckler, and give it me to bear;
> Now what I shall advise thee, mark with thy closest care.
> Be it thine to make the gestures, and mine the work to do.' "
> *Nibelungenlied (Lettsom's tr.).*

Siegfried's Help

In obedience to these directions, Gunther merely made the motions, depending upon the invisible Siegfried to parry and make all the attacks.

And now Brunhild was ready. Lifting her gigantic spear, she poised it for a moment, then flung it with such force that both heroes staggered and almost fell. But before she could cry out victory, Siegfried had caught the spear, turned it butt end foremost, and flung it back with such violence that the princess fell, and was obliged to acknowledge herself outdone.

Brunhild's Prowess

Nothing daunted, however, by this first defeat, she caught up the massive stone, tossed it far from her, and then, leaping after it, alighted beside it. But even while she was inwardly congratulating herself, and confidently cherishing the belief that the stranger could not surpass her, Siegfried caught up the stone, flung it farther still, and, grasping Gunther by his broad girdle, bounded through the air with him and landed far beyond it. Amazed, Brunhild acknowledged her defeat. Yet in her heart she was exultant that at last she had met a man who could outdo her in feats of strength. Generously she congratulated the winner, and, calling to her subjects, bade them henceforth acknowledge themselves as the liegemen of the mighty stranger.

> " Then all aloud fair Brunhild bespake her courtier band,
> Seeing in the ring at distance unharm'd her wooer stand :
> ' Hither, my men and kinsmen, low to my better bow.
> I am no more your mistress ; you're Gunther's liegemen now.' "
>
> *Nibelungenlied* (*Lettsom's tr.*).

Impressed by the spectacle which they had witnessed, the warriors all hastened to do her bidding, and escorted their new lord to the castle. Hither, under pretext of fitly celebrating her marriage, Brunhild by-and-by summoned all her retainers from far and near. This rally roused the secret terror of Gunther, Hagen, and Dankwart, for they suspected some act of treachery on the part of the dark-browed queen. Nor was Siegfried himself altogether free from their fears. Therefore he stole away, secretly promising his comrades to return before long with a force sufficient to overawe Brunhild and quell all attempt at foul play.

Having thus hastily embarked upon the little vessel, Siegfried swiftly sailed away to the Nibelungen land, where he arrived in an incredibly short space of time. Here he presented himself at the gates of his castle, and forced an entrance by conquering the giant porter, and Alberich, the dwarf guardian of his treasure. Then, making himself known to his followers, the Nibelungs, he chose out a thousand from among them to accompany him back to Issland to support the Burgundian king.

The Marriage of Gunther and Brunhild

The arrival of this unexpected force greatly surprised

Brunhild. She questioned Gunther as to its meaning, but received only the careless reply that they were but a few of his followers, who had come to make merry at his wedding. Seeing that resistance was hopeless, she prepared herself for the nuptials, which took place in due time. When the usual festivities had taken place, and the wonted largesses had been distributed, Gunther bade his bride prepare to follow him back to the Rhine, together with her maidens, who numbered no less than a hundred and sixty-eight.

Full of reluctance, Brunhild bade farewell to her own country, and, escorted by the thousand Nibelung warriors, set out for the land of her husband. After they had journeyed on their way nine days Gunther suddenly bade Siegfried spur ahead and announce his safe return to his family and subjects. Offended by the tone of command which Gunther had assumed, Siegfried at first proudly refused to obey. But when the king begged it as a favour, in the name of Kriemhild, he immediately relented, and set out.

> " Said he, ' Nay, gentle Siegfried, do but this journey take,
> Not for my sake only, but for my sister's sake ;
> You'll oblige fair Kriemhild in this as well as me.'
> When so implored was Siegfried, ready at once was he.

> " ' Whate'er you will, command me ; let naught be left unsaid;
> I will gladly do it for the lovely maid.
> How can I refuse her who my heart has won ?
> For her ,whate'er your pleasure, tell it, and it is done.' "
> *Nibelungenlied (Lettsom's tr.).*

Siegfried's Return

Most gladly did Kriemhild welcome Siegfried back again, and many were the fair words spoken between them. The news of her brother's marriage, too, filled her heart with joy, and she gave immediate orders for a magnificent reception of the new queen, after which she went down to the river to welcome her in the most cordial and affectionate manner.

Marriage of Siegfried and Kriemhild

A great tournament, followed by a splendid banquet, then ensued. But as they were about to sit down to the feast, the impatient Siegfried ventured to remind Gunther of his promise that he would give him the hand of Kriemhild. In spite of a low-spoken remonstrance from Brunhild, who could not bear the thought that the king should give his only sister in marriage to a menial, Gunther sent for Kriemhild, who blushingly expressed her readiness to marry Siegfried if her brother wished. The marriage was thereupon celebrated immediately, and the two bridal couples sat side by side. But while Kriemhild's fair face was radiant with joy, Brunhild's dark brows were drawn together in an unmistakable and ominous frown.

The Humiliation of Gunther

The banquet over, Gunther and Siegfried withdrew with their brides. Yet when Gunther, now for the first time alone with his wife, would fain have embraced her, she seized him, and, in spite of his vigorous resistance, bound him fast with her long girdle, and so suspended him from a nail in the corner of her apartment. Then, notwithstanding his piteous entreaties, she let him remain there all night long, releasing him only a few moments before the attendants entered the nuptial chamber in the morning. Naturally all were greatly surprised to see Gunther's lowering countenance, which contrasted oddly with Siegfried's radiant mien. For the latter had won a loving wife, and the two were as happy as only lovers can be. Moreover, to show his great love for his bride, Siegfried had given her as wedding gift the great Nibelungen hoard.

71

In the course of the day Gunther managed to draw Siegfried aside, and secretly confided to him the shameful treatment he had received at the hands of his wife. No sooner did Siegfried hear this than he offered to don his cloud-cloak once more, enter the royal chamber unperceived, and force Brunhild to recognise her husband as her master, against whom she would never again make use of her strength.

Brunhild Subdued by Siegfried

In pursuance of this promise Siegfried suddenly left Kriemhild's side at nightfall, and stole unseen into the queen's room. Then when she and Gunther had closed the door he blew out the lights and wrestled with Brunhild until she begged for mercy, promising never to bind him again. For as Siegfried had remained invisible throughout the struggle she thought it was Gunther who had conquered her.

> "Said she, ' Right noble ruler, vouchsafe my life to spare ;
> Whatever I've offended, my duty shall repair.
> I'll meet thy noble passion ; my love with thine shall vie.
> That thou canst tame a woman, none better knows than I.' "
> *Nibelungenlied (Lettsom's tr.).*

Still unperceived, Siegfried now took her girdle and ring, and stole out of the apartment, leaving Gunther alone with his wife. True to her promise, Brunhild ever after treated her husband with due respect, and having once for all been conquered, she entirely lost the fabulous strength which had been her proudest boast, and was no more powerful than any other member of her sex.

After fourteen days of rejoicing Siegfried and Kriemhild journeyed off to Xanten, on the Rhine, where Siegmund and Siegelind received them joyfully, and even abdicated in their favour.

QUARREL OF BRUNHILD AND KRIEMHILD

Ten years passed away very rapidly, during which Siegfried became the father of a son, whom he named Gunther, in honour of his brother-in-law, who had called his heir Siegfried. Meanwhile, shortly after the birth of the little Gunther, his grandmother, Siegelind, died. Then Siegfried, with Kriemhild, his father, and his son, went to the Nibelungen land, where they tarried two years.

- In the meanwhile Brunhild, who still imagined that Siegfried was only her husband's vassal, secretly wondered why he never came to court to do homage for his lands. Finally she suggested to Gunther that it would be well to invite his sister and her husband to visit them at Worms. Gunther seized this suggestion gladly, and immediately sent one of his followers, Gary, to deliver the invitation, which Siegfried accepted for himself and his wife, and also for Siegmund, his father.

The visit was settled to take place in midsummer, and as the journey was very long Kriemhild speedily began her preparations. On leaving home she cheerfully entrusted her little son to the care of the stalwart Nibelung knights, little suspecting that she would never see him again.

When at last Kriemhild arrived at Worms, Brunhild took pains to greet her with as much pomp and ceremony as had been used for her own reception. But in spite of the amity which seemed to exist between the two queens, Brunhild was secretly angry at what she deemed Kriemhild's unwarrantable arrogance.

The Quarrel of Brunhild and Kriemhild

Thus it happened that one day, when the two queens were sitting together, Brunhild grew weary of hearing Kriemhild's constant praise of her husband. Her exasperation grew greater and greater, till at last when

73

Kriemhild innocently declared that Siegfried was without a peer in the world Brunhild cuttingly remarked that since he was Gunther's vassal he must necessarily be his inferior. This reply called forth a retort from Kriemheld, and a dispute was soon raging, in the course of which Kriemhild vowed that she would publicly assert her rank by taking the precedence of Brunhild in entering the church. In hot anger the queens parted to attire themselves with the utmost magnificence. Then, escorted by all their maidens, the two processions met at the church door. There Brunhild bade Kriemhild stand aside and make way for her superior. This order increased the fury of the usually gentle Nibelungen queen, and with great bitterness and vehemence she retorted upon her foe.

Hotter and hotter grew the quarrel, in spite of the place and the onlookers, till in her indignation Kriemhild finally insulted Brunhild grossly by declaring that she was not a faithful wife. In proof of her assertion she produced the ring and the girdle which Siegfried had won in his memorable encounter, and afterwards given imprudently to his wife, to whom he had also confided the secret of Brunhild's wooing.

Hot with indignation, Brunhild peremptorily summoned Gunther to defend her. Full of anger, Gunther then sent for Siegfried, who publicly swore that his wife had not told the truth, and that Gunther's queen had in no way forfeited her good name. Then, to propitiate his host still further, Siegfried declared that the quarrel was disgraceful, and that for his part he was deeply humiliated at the share his wife had taken in it. And, indeed, there was good cause for Siegfried's wrath, for he feared what the consequences might be if ever Brunhild should discover the stratagem by which Gunther had won her as his wife.

With no gentle hand, therefore, he led home the shrinking Kriemhild, and then gave her a cruel beating as a punishment for her wanton speech. But dearly though Gunther would have liked to treat his wife with the same harshness, he by no means dared to do so, for he stood ever in terror of his passionate bride.

Hagen's Sympathy

Meanwhile Brunhild, smarting from the public insult she had received, continued to weep aloud in her vexation, till Hagen came by and inquired the cause of her extravagant sobs. In reply the queen gave him so lurid an account of the encounter that he declared hotly he would see that she was properly avenged.

> " He ask'd her what had happen'd—wherefore he saw her weep ;
> She told him all the story ; he vow'd to her full deep
> That reap should Kriemhild's husband as he had dar'd to sow,
> Or that himself thereafter content should never know."
> *Nibelungenlied* (*Lettsom's tr.*).

Full of thoughts of vengeance, Hagen at last went away to brood over his plans for the humiliation of Siegfried. With this purpose he tried first of all to stir up the anger of Gunther, Gernot, and Ortwine, and prevail upon them to murder Siegfried. But Giselher reproved him for these base designs, and openly took Siegfried's part, declaring wisely :

> "' Sure 'tis but a trifle to stir an angry wife.' "
> *Nibelungenlied* (*Lettsom's tr.*).

But although Giselher succeeded in quelling the attempt for the time being, he was no match for the artful Hagen, who continually reminded Gunther of the insult his wife had received, setting it in the worst possible light, and in this way he so worked upon the

75

king's feelings that finally he consented to a treacherous assault.

Plots against Siegfried

Under pretext that his former enemy, Ludeger, was about to attack him again, Gunther, with every show of kindness, asked Siegfried's assistance. Only too glad to be able to aid his friend, Siegfried willingly assented. At once preparations as if for war were set on foot, and the whole kingdom became astir with excitement. But when Kriemhild heard that her beloved husband was about to rush into danger she was greatly troubled. Vague fears filled her mind, and she spent whole days in gloom. Artfully, Hagen pretended to share her alarm, and so he won her confidence, in which she revealed to him the secret that Siegfried was invulnerable except in one spot, between his shoulders, where a lime leaf had rested and the dragon's blood had not touched him.

" ' So now I'll tell the secret, dear friend, alone to thee
(For thou, I doubt not, cousin, wilt keep thy faith with me),
Where sword may pierce my darling, and death sit on the thrust.
See, in thy truth and honour how full, how firm, my trust !

" ' As from the dragon's death-wounds gush'd out the crimson gore,
With the smoking torrent the warrior wash'd him o'er,
A leaf then 'twixt his shoulders fell from the linden bough.
There only steel can harm him ; for that I tremble now.' "

Nibelungenlied (Lettsom's tr.).

The Hunt

Pretending a sympathy he was far from feeling, and disguising his unholy joy, Hagen bade Kriemhild sew a tiny cross on Siegfried's doublet over the vulnerable spot, that he might the better protect him in case of danger. Then, scarce able to contain himself while he

The Death of Siegfried

The Funeral of Siegfried

listened to her profuse thanks, he dashed off to report
the success of his ruse to the king. Wholly unsuspecting that treachery was afoot, Siegfried joined them
on the morrow, wearing the fatal marked doublet. To
his great surprise he was told that the rebellion had
been quelled without a blow. Yet still no thought of
evil crossed his mind, so that when he was invited to
join in a hunt in the Odenwald instead of the fray he
gladly signified his consent. Full of happiness, he bade
farewell to Kriemhild, who looked after him as he went
with dark forebodings in her heart. But of all this
Siegfried knew nothing, and his laugh rang loud and
long as he scoured the forest, slew several boars, caught
a bear alive, and then playfully let him loose in camp
to furnish sport for the guests while the noonday meal
was being prepared. After this he gaily sat down,
clamouring for a drink. His exertions had made him
very thirsty indeed, and he was sorely disappointed
when he was told that, owing to a mistake, the wine
had been carried to another part of the forest. This
was Hagen's opportunity. Instantly he pointed out a
fresh spring at a short distance, at the sight of which
all Siegfried's wonted good-humour returned. Merrily
he proposed a race thither, offering to run in full
armour, while the others might lay aside their cumber-
some weapons. Hagen and Gunther sprang to accept
the challenge, and the three set off. Although Siegfried
was heavily handicapped, yet he reached the spring
first. But, wishing to show courtesy to his host, he
bade him drink while he disarmed. Then when
Gunther's thirst was quenched Siegfried took his turn,
and so he bent over the stream. As he stooped to the
crystal water Hagen's cruel eyes glittered balefully.
Treacherously he moved from Siegfried's reach all his
weapons except his shield. Then, gliding behind him,

he drove his spear through his body in the exact spot where Kriemhild had embroidered the fatal mark.

Mortally wounded, Siegfried made a desperate effort to avenge himself. But he found nothing save his shield within his reach. Yet he flung this with such force at his murderer that it knocked him down. This last effort exhausted the remainder of his strength, and the hero fell back upon the grass, cursing the treachery of those whom he had trusted as friends.

"Thus spake the deadly wounded : 'Ay, cowards false as hell !
To you I still was faithful ; I serv'd you long and well ;—
But what boots all ?—for guerdon, treason and death I've won.
By your friends, vile traitors ! foully have you done.

"'Whoever shall hereafter from your loins be born,
Shall take from such vile fathers a heritage of scorn.
On me you have wreak'd malice where gratitude was due ;
With shame shall you be banish'd by all good knights and true.'"
Nibelungenlied (Lettsom's tr.).

The Death of Siegfried

Yet even in death Siegfried could not forget his beloved wife. Therefore, laying aside all his anger, he pathetically recommended her to Gunther's care, bidding him guard her well. Scarcely had he gasped out these words when he fell back, dead. Silently the hunters gathered round his corpse, and looked sadly upon the fallen hero, while they took counsel together how they might keep the secret of Hagen's treachery. Finally they agreed to carry the body back to Worms and say that they had found Siegfried dead in the forest, where he had presumably been slain by highwaymen.

"Then many said, repenting, 'This deed will prove our bale ;
Still let us shroud the secret, and all keep in one tale,—
That the good lord of Kriemhild to hunt alone preferr'd,
And so was slain by robbers as through the wood he spurr'd.'"
Nibelungenlied (Lettsom's tr.).

But as for Hagen, although his companions were anxious to shield him, he himself gloried in his dastardly deed, and in his heart he was planning still more sorrow for Kriemhild. Thus he bade the bearers deposit the corpse at her door after nightfall, so that the queen would be the first to see it there when on her way to early mass. This was done, and matters turned out just as the cruel Hagen had hoped. For as Kriemhild opened her chamber door she recognised the dead body of her husband, and fell senseless upon him. No sooner had she recovered from her swoon than she declared with passionate vehemence that her dear husband had been murdered ; nor would anything make her believe that his death had been merely an accident. Thus she lay weeping and saying over and over again :

" ' Woe's me, woe's me for ever ! sure no fair foeman's sword
Shiver'd thy failing buckler ; 'twas murder stopp'd thy breath.
Oh that I knew who did it! death I'd requite with death ! ' "
Nibelungenlied (*Lettsom's tr.*).

By her orders a messenger was sent to break the mournful tidings to Siegmund and the Nibelungs, who still slept. They hastily armed and rallied about her, and would have fallen upon the Burgundians, to avenge their master's death, had she not restrained them, bidding them await a suitable occasion, and promising them her support when the right time came.

The Burial of Siegfried

The preparations for an elaborate funeral were immediately begun, and all lent a willing hand, for Siegfried was greatly beloved at Worms. His body was therefore laid in state in the cathedral, where many came to view it and condole with Kriemhild. But when Gunther drew near to express his sorrow she refused

79

to listen to him until he had promised that all those present at the hunt should touch the body, which would bleed afresh at contact with the murderer's hand. Very reluctantly Gunther was at last obliged to give way, and one by one the warriors drew near and touched the corpse of the slain hero. All stood the test and were honourably acquitted save Hagen, at whose touch Siegfried's blood began to flow.

> "It is a mighty marvel, which oft e'en now we spy,
> That when the blood-stain'd murderer comes to the murder'd nigh,
> The wounds break out a-bleeding ; then too the same befell,
> And thus could each beholder the guilt of Hagen tell."
>
> *Nibelungenlied* (*Lettsom's tr.*).

The sight of this miracle confirmed the suspicions of the sorrow-stricken Kriemhild, and she saw in Hagen the murderer of her dear husband. Yet she restrained the angry Nibelung warriors from taking immediate revenge, and, upheld by Gernot and Giselher, who really sympathised with her grief, she stayed till at last the sad ceremony was over.

But though Siegfried's body had been laid to rest Kriemhild's mourning had only begun, and all her days and nights were spent in bitter weeping. This sorrow was fully shared by Siegmund, who nevertheless at last roused himself from his grief and proposed that the warriors should return home. Kriemhild herself was about to accompany him, when her relatives persuaded her to remain behind in Burgundy. Then the little band which had come in festal array rode silently away in mourning robes, the grim Nibelung knights muttering dark threats against those who had dealt so basely with their beloved master.

> " ' Into this same country we well may come again
> To seek and find the traitor who laid our master low.
> Among the kin of Siegfried they have many a mortal foe.' "
>
> *Nibelungenlied* (*Lettsom's tr.*).

THE NIBELUNG HOARD

Kriemhild Left Alone in Burgundy

Eckewart, the steward, alone remained with Kriemhild, showing a faithfulness which has become proverbial in the German language. With his own hands he prepared for his mistress a dwelling close by the cathedral, so that she might constantly visit her husband's tomb. Here Kriemhild spent three years in complete seclusion, refusing to see either Gunther or the detested Hagen. Meantime these two were busy in their minds with a new scheme. They remembered that the immense Nibelungen hoard had become Kriemhild's by right, and they continually wondered how she could be induced to send for it. Often the subject was discussed by the knights, till at last, after great persuasion, Gunther succeeded in obtaining an interview with the sad queen, his sister. To his joy, he was able, shortly after, to persuade her to send twelve men to claim from Alberich, the dwarf, the fabulous wealth her husband had bestowed upon her as a wedding gift. By-and-by the hoard was brought to the city of Worms, a treasure of such magnificence as had never been seen before:

" It was made up of nothing but precious stones and gold ;
Were all the world bought from it, and down the value told,
Not a mark the less thereafter were left than erst was scor'd.
Good reason sure had Hagen to covet such a hoard.

" And thereamong was lying the wishing-rod of gold,
Which whoso could discover, might in subjection hold
All this wide world as master, with all that dwelt therein.
There came to Worms with Gernot full many of Albric's kin."
Nibelungenlied (Lettsom's tr.).

The Nibelung Hoard

Nearly a hundred waggons were necessary to carry the burden of these sparkling jewels, whose splendour dazzled the eyes of every beholder. Yet Kriemhild would gladly have thrown it all away could she but have seen her husband by her side once more. Quite careless about the gems for her own part, she gave them away on every hand, only bidding all the recipients of her bounty to pray for the soul of Siegfried. So extensive were her largesses that Hagen, who alone did not profit by her generosity, feared in his greed that the treasure might be exhausted before he could obtain a share. Therefore he sought out Gunther and told him that Kriemhild was secretly winning to her side many adherents, whom she would some day urge to avenge her husband's murder by slaying her kindred.

Hagen's Theft

While Gunther was thus trying to devise some plan to obtain possession of the hoard, he was outdone by the cunning Hagen, who boldly seized the keys of the tower where it was kept and secretly removed all the gold. Then to prevent it from falling into any hands but his own he sank it in the Rhine near Lochheim.

> "Ere back the king came thither, impatient of delay,
> Hagen seized the treasure, and bore it thence away.
> Into the Rhine at Lochheim the whole at once threw he !
> Henceforth he thought t' enjoy it, but that was ne'er to be.

> " He nevermore could get it for all his vain desire ;
> So fortune oft the traitor cheats of his treason's hire.
> Alone he hop'd to use it as long as he should live,
> But neither himself could profit, nor to another give."
> *Nibelungenlied (Lettsom's tr.).*

Before very long his theft was discovered, and a great outcry arose. So angry were Gunther, Gernot, and Giselher when they heard what Hagen had done that he deemed it advisable to withdraw from court for a while. At this fresh wrong Kriemhild would fain have left Burgundy for ever, but with much difficulty she was prevailed upon to remain and take up her abode at Lorch, whither Siegfried's remains were, by her order, removed.

In this way thirteen years had passed by since Siegfried's death, when Etzel, King of Hungary, who had lost his beautiful and beloved wife, Helche, bade one of his knights, Rüdiger of Bechlaren, ride to Worms and sue in his master's name for the hand of Kriemhild.

Kriemhild's Second Wooing

Delighted at such an errand, Rüdiger immediately gathered together a suitable train and departed, only stopping on the way to visit his wife and daughter at Bechlaren. Passing all through Bavaria, he arrived at last at Worms, where he was warmly welcomed. Especially warm was the greeting he received from Hagen, who had formerly known him well.

In reply to Gunther's courteous inquiry concerning the welfare of the King and Queen of the Huns, Rüdiger announced the death of the latter, and declared that he had come to sue for Kriemhild's hand.

Rüdiger at Gunther's Court

Gunther gladly received this message, and agreed to do all in his power to win Kriemhild's consent. He promised to see the queen and return the envoy a definite answer within the space of three days. Delighted at his favourable reception, the envoy withdrew, while Gunther went to consult his brothers and nobles as to the advisability of the proposed alliance. He found that all were greatly in favour of it save Hagen, who warned them that if Kriemhild were ever

83

Queen of the Huns she would use her power to avenge her wrongs.

This warning, however, was not heeded by the royal brothers, who went straight away to Kriemhild's presence, and vainly tried to make her accept the Hun's proposal; all she would grant was an audience to Rüdiger. By-and-by the messenger stood before her, eager to plead his master's cause. Passionately he told her of Etzel's desire for her; then he skilfully went on to describe the power of the Huns, and swore they would obey her in all things would she but consent to become their queen. But Kriemhild would have nothing to say to his pleading, till at last the knight played a bold stroke and promised that in return for her consent he would undertake to see that all her wrongs of the past were fully avenged. This consideration roused the apathetic Kriemhild, and for the first time she lent the herald her attention. Seizing his opportunity, the knight went on to make good his suggestion, till at last he had gained his point: the hand of Kriemhild was won.

> " In vain they her entreated, in vain to her they pray'd,
>   Till to the queen the margrave this secret promise made,
>   He'd ' full amends procure her for past or future ill.'
>   Those words her storm-tost bosom had power in part to still."
>   *Nibelungenlied* (*Lettsom's tr.*).

Kriemhild Leaves Worms

The announcement that the queen had consented to become the wife of the powerful King of the Huns gave great satisfaction to Gunther and his knights, who of course knew nothing of the secret agreement upon which the bargain had been made. And now Kriemhild was all haste to set off. Scarcely could she wait till the preparations were complete, so keen was her anxiety. At last all was ready, and the sad-eyed queen rode off with Erkwald, Rüdiger, all her maidens, and five hundred men as a bodyguard. Gernot and Giselher, together with many Burgundian nobles, escorted her to Vergen, on the Danube, where they took an affectionate leave of her, after which they went back to their homes in Burgundy.

From Vergen, Kriemhild and her escort journeyed on to Passau, where they were warmly welcomed and hospitably entertained by good Bishop Pilgrim, brother of Queen Ute. He would gladly have detained them, had not Rüdiger declared that his master impatiently awaited the coming of his bride, whose approach had been duly announced to him.

A second pause was made at Bechlaren, Rüdiger's castle, where Kriemhild was lavishly entertained by his wife and daughter, Gotelinde and Dietelinde. After the usual extravagant distribution of gifts had taken place the procession again swept on across the country and down the Danube, until they met King Etzel. On seeing the man who was about to become her husband Kriemhild strove to lay aside her sadness, and pressed her lips to those of the sovereign as a sign of her willingness to be his wife.

The Marriage of Etzel and Kriemhild

The betrothal was celebrated by tilting and other martial games, and the king and queen then proceeded to Vienna, where a triumphal reception awaited them. Here their marriage was celebrated with all becoming solemnity and great pomp, the very wedding festivities lasting no less than seventeen days. But although all vied in their attempts to please Kriemhild she remained sad and pensive, for she could not forget her beloved Siegfried, and the happy years she had spent with him.

From Vienna the royal couple journeyed on to Gran,

85

which was Etzel's capital. The palace was aglow with excitement at the advent of the new queen, and Kriemhild found innumerable handmaidens ready to do her will. Here the two took up their new life together. For his part, Etzel was very happy and his happiness was further increased by the birth of a little son, who was baptized in the Christian faith, and called Ortlieb.

Although thirteen years had now elapsed since Kriemhild had left her native land, the recollection of her wrongs was as vivid as ever, her melancholy just as profound, and her thoughts were ever busy planning how best to lure Hagen into her kingdom in order to work her revenge.

> "One long and dreary yearning she foster'd hour by hour;
> She thought, 'I am so wealthy and hold such boundless power,
> That I with ease a mischief can bring on all my foes,
> But most on him of Trony, the deadliest far of those.
>
> "'Full oft for its beloved my heart is mourning still;
> Them could I but meet with, who wrought me so much ill,
> Revenge should strike at murder, and life atone for life;
> Wait can I no longer.' So murmur'd Etzel's wife."
>
> *Nibelungenlied (Lettsom's tr.).*

Kriemhild's Revenge

More and more she pondered on these things, till at last she resolved to be idle no longer, but to take steps towards bringing about her desire. She therefore decided to persuade Etzel to invite all her kinsmen for a midsummer visit. This he willingly did, not dreaming of any evil purpose. Two minstrels, Werbel and Swemmel, were thus sent with the most cordial invitation. Before they departed Kriemhild instructed them to be sure and tell all her kinsmen that she was blithe and happy, and not melancholy as of yore, and to use every effort to bring not only the kings, but also Hagen, who, having been at Etzel's court as hostage in his youth could best act as their guide.

The minstrels were warmly received at Worms, where their invitation created great excitement. All were in favour of accepting the kindness except Hagen, who pointed out that Kriemhild had good cause for anger and would surely seek revenge when they were entirely in her power.

> " 'Trust not, Sir King,' said Hagen, 'how smooth soe'er they be,
> These messengers from Hungary ; if Kriemhild you will see,
> You put upon the venture your honour and your life.
> A nurse of ling'ring vengeance is Etzel's moody wife.' "
> *Nibelungenlied* (*Lettsom's tr.*).

Her Invitation Accepted

But all his objections were set aside with the remark that he alone had a guilty conscience ; and the kings bade the minstrels return to announce their coming. In vain Ute, who had a lurking fear of Kriemhild, tried to keep them at home : her entreaties were useless. Gunther was resolved to go. Then Hagen, who was no coward, seeing them determined to set off, grimly prepared to accompany them. At the same time he prevailed upon them to don their strongest armour for the journey, and thus prepared they rode off.

It was a brave company that passed out of the city that day. At the head rode Gunther, accompanied by his two brothers, Hagen and Dankwart, Volker (his minstrel), Gary, and Ortwine, and followed by a thousand picked men as escort. Before leaving he entrusted his wife, Brunhild, and his son to the care of Rumolt, his squire, and, bidding farewell to his people, set out for Hungary, whence he was never to return.

In the meanwhile the Hungarian minstrels had hastened back to Gran to announce the approach of the guests. For a moment in Kriemhild's eyes there flashed

87

a fierce light; then she turned and questioned the messengers closely as to Hagen, and if he were coming. "In sooth, he is coming," replied the heralds, "yet sorely against his will. For indeed we heard him mutter, 'This jaunt's a jaunt to death.'"

The Prophecy of the Swan Maidens

The Burgundians, who in this part of the story are frequently called Nibelungs, because they now held the great hoard, reached the Danube on the twelfth day. As they found neither ford nor ferry, Hagen, after again prophesying all manner of evil, volunteered to go in search of a boat or raft to cross the rapid stream.

He had not gone very far before he heard the sound of voices, and, peeping through the bushes, saw some swan maidens, or "wise women," bathing in a neighbouring fountain. Stealing up unperceived, he secured their plumage, which he consented to restore only after they had predicted the result of his journey. To obtain her garments, one of the women, Hadburg, prophesied great good fortune. But when the pilfered robes were restored, another, called Siegelind, foretold much woe.

"'I will warn thee, Hagen, thou son of Aldrian;
My aunt has lied unto thee her raiment back to get;
If once thou com'st to Hungary, thou'rt taken in the net.

"'Turn while there's time for safety, turn, warriors most and least;
For this, and for this only, you're bidden to the feast,
That you perforce may perish in Etzel's bloody land.
Whoever rideth thither, Death has he close at hand.'"

Nibelungenlied (*Lettsom's tr.*).

Then the maiden went on to add that the chaplain alone would return alive to Worms; yet if, in spite of her words, Hagen must needs cross the ferry, he would find a boatman on the opposite side of the river, farther down, but that he would not obey his call unless he declared his name to be Amelrich.

At this Hagen left the wise women and hastened down the bank of the river. Here he soon saw the ferryman's boat, anchored to the opposite shore. At first he tried to make him come over for a promised reward, but when he failed as the swan maiden had foretold, he cried out that his name was Amelrich. Immediately the ferryman caught up his oars and crossed. But when Hagen sprang into his boat he detected the fraud and began to fight. Although gigantic in size, this ferryman was no match for Hagen, who, after slaying him, took possession of his boat, and so skilfully ferried his masters and companions across the river.

In hope of giving the lie to the swan maiden, Hagen paused once in the middle of the stream to fling the chaplain overboard, thinking he would surely drown. To his surprise and dismay, however, the man struggled back to the shore, where he stood for awhile alone and unharmed, then, turning his back on the river, he slowly wended his way back to Burgundy. This circumstance filled Hagen with fear, for he now knew that the prophecy of the swan maiden was one destined to be fulfilled, and the thought caused him many forebodings. Nevertheless he kept on his way, and at last landed on the opposite shore. Once out of the boat, he bade the main part of the troop ride on ahead, leaving him and Dankwart to bring up the rear, for he fully expected that Gelfrat, master of the murdered ferryman, would pursue them to try to avenge the latter's death. These previsions were soon verified, and in the bloody encounter which ensued Hagen came off victor, with the loss of but four men, while the enemy left more than a hundred dead upon the field.

From the field of battle Hagen hurried on to join the main body of the army once more, after which he passed on with it to Passau, where Bishop Pilgrim was as glad to see his nephews as he had been to welcome his niece. From thence they journeyed to the frontiers of Bechlaren. Here they met with an open warning. For they found Eckewart, who had been sent by Rüdiger to advise them not to advance any farther, as he suspected that some treachery was afoot.

> " Sir Eckewart replied :
> ' Yet much, I own, it grieves me that to the Huns you ride.
> You took the life of Siegfried ; all hate you deadly here ;
> As your true friend I warn you ; watch well, and wisely fear.' "
> *Nibelungenlied* (*Lettsom's tr.*).

But the Burgundians would have deemed themselves for ever disgraced were they now to withdraw from their purpose, so they refused to listen to this warning, and instead entered Rüdiger's castle, where they were warmly received by him and his family. Giselher, seeing the beauty of the maiden Dietelinde, fell deeply in love with her, and prevailed upon the margrave to consent to their immediate marriage, promising, however, to claim and bear away his bride only upon his homeward journey. Once more gifts were lavished with mediæval profusion, Gunther receiving a coat of mail, Gernot a sword, Hagen a shield, and the minstrel Volker many rings of red gold, after which the strangers rode off. As they rode they were escorted by Rüdiger, who accompanied them until they met the brave Dietrich von Bern.

The Second Warning

Again the warriors received a solemn warning from von Bern, who told them that their visit was fraught with danger, for Kriemhild had by no means forgotten the murder of the husband of her youth.

Kriemhild's Greeting

His evil prognostications were also of no avail, and seeing this he sadly accompanied them until they met Kriemhild, whose coldness was at once seen in that she embraced Giselher only. Then, turning suddenly upon Hagen, she inquired aloud, in the presence of all the people, whether he had brought her back her own, the Nibelung hoard. Nothing daunted by this sudden query, Hagen haughtily answered that the treasure still lay deep in the Rhine, where he fancied it would rest until the Judgment Day.

> " ' I' faith, my Lady Kriemhild, 'tis now full many a day
> Since in my power the treasure of the Nibelungers lay.
> In the Rhine my lords bade sink it ; I did their bidding fain,
> And in the Rhine, I warrant, till doomsday 'twill remain.' "
> *Nibelungenlied* (*Lettsom's tr.*).

Brushing aside Hagen's reply, the queen turned her back contemptuously upon him, and invited her other guests to lay aside their weapons, for none might enter the great hall armed. This Hagen refused to allow them to do, saying that he feared treachery. Then the queen, pretending great grief, inquired who could have filled her kinsmen's hearts with such unjust suspicions. Upon this Sir Dietrich, who had no love for the relentless queen, boldly stepped forward to defy her, declaring that it was he who had bidden the Burgundians be thus on their guard.

> " ' 'Twas I that the warning to the noble princes gave,
> And to their liegeman Hagen, to whom such hate thou bear'st.
> Now up, she-fiend ! be doing, and harm me if thou dar'st ! ' "
> *Nibelungenlied* (*Lettsom's tr.*).

The Compact of Hagen and Volker

This retort made the bosom of Kriemhild swell with fury and resentment. But she dared not as yet make any reply. For Dietrich was greatly feared and respected by all his men, who recognised both his integrity and his courage. Therefore she quickly concealed her anger, while Etzel advanced in his turn to welcome his guests, and especially singled out Hagen, the son of his old friend. Then while many of the Burgundians accompanied the king into the hall, Hagen drew Volker aside, and, sitting down on a stone seat near Kriemhild's door, the two entered into a life-and-death alliance together. By-and-by, as Kriemhild looked out of her window, she saw them there. Then her lust for Hagen's death rose to its height, and she bade her followers go out and slay him. But although they numbered four hundred, they hung back from the dastardly enterprise. Seeing their hesitation, the queen thought it must be because they doubted her assertions, so she volunteered to descend alone and wring from Hagen a confession of his crimes, while they lingered within earshot inside the building. Then Volker, seeing the queen approach, proposed to Hagen to rise and show her the customary respect. But the latter, declaring that she would ascribe this sign of courtesy to fear alone, grimly bade him remain seated. Thus they awaited her approach. No sooner had the baleful queen drawn near to Hagen than she began to accuse him with the murder of Siegfried. Boldly the Burgundian acknowledged that he alone had slain the great hero.

> " Said he, ' Why question further ? that were a waste of breath.
> In a word, I am e'en Hagen, who Siegfried did to death.

. . . . . .

ETZEL'S HOSPITALITY

> " ' What I have done, proud princess, I never will deny.
> The cause of all the mischief, the wrong, the loss, am I.
> So now, or man or woman, revenge it whoso will ;
> I scorn to speak a falsehood,—I've done you grievous ill.' "
>
> *Nibelungenlied* (*Lettsom's tr.*).

But although the warriors had heard every word he
had said, when the queen again urged them on to attack
her foe they one and all withdrew. For they feared
to make any assault on one of such evident courage.
This episode, however, was enough to show the Burgundians very plainly the hostility to them that reigned
at court. Hagen and Volker were specially alive to
the danger, and though they soon went back and rejoined
their companions, yet they kept ever side by side, and,
following their agreement, where one went the other
followed.

> " Howe'er the rest were coupled, as mov'd to court the train,
> Volker and Hagen parted ne'er again,
> Save in one mortal struggle, e'en to their dying hour."
>
> *Nibelungenlied* (*Lettsom's tr.*).

Etzel's Hospitality

Meanwhile Etzel invited his guests to a sumptuous
feast, after which they were led to their appointed
quarters, far remote from those of their squires. Yet
the Burgundians bore themselves bravely, and when it
happened that the Huns began to crowd them, Hagen
again frightened them off with one of his black looks.
At last the hall where they were to sleep was reached,
and all the knights lay down to rest, except Hagen
and Volker, who mounted guard. Soon the latter drew
out his fiddle to beguile the hours, and thus the night
wore on.

Once, in the middle of the night, these self-appointed
sentinels saw an armed troop draw near. But when they
loudly challenged the foremost men they beat a hasty

retreat. At dawn of day the knights arose to go to mass. By Hagen's advice they wore their arms, and kept well together, so that they presented such a threatening aspect that Kriemhild's men dared not attack them.

In spite of all these signs, Etzel, whose heart was full of the kindliest intentions, remained entirely ignorant of his wife's evil designs. He had no idea of her deep-seated hate, and so he continued to treat the Burgundians like friends and kinsmen, while all the time his wife was planning their destruction. Had he known, it is quite certain he would have prevented the carrying out of her fell design, for he was a just as well as a brave sovereign.

Mass over, a tournament was announced, and the knights all hurried off to the lists. Two of the most valorous of the Huns, Rüdiger and Dietrich, courteously refrained from taking any share in the contest, for fear lest, if they should prove victors, the chagrin of the strangers might be roused and the smouldering embers of discord burst into flame. In spite of all these precautions, however, the threatened disruption nearly occurred when Volker accidentally slew a Hun. Only King Etzel's prompt interference prevented open hostilities from following.

This accident was duly reported to Kriemhild, who vainly tried to use it as an excuse to bribe Dietrich, or his man Hildebrand, to slay her foe. Finally she won over Blödelin, the king's brother, by promising him a fair bride. To earn this reward the prince went with an armed host to the hall where the Burgundian squires were feasting under Dankwart's care, and there he treacherously slew them all, Dankwart alone escaping to the king's hall to join his brother Hagen.

In the meanwhile Etzel was entertaining his mailed

Hagen slays Ortlieb

The Burgundians and the Huns

guests, and had called for his little son, whom he placed in Gunther's lap, telling him that he would soon send the boy to Burgundy to be educated among his mother's kin.

The Attack

All admired the graceful child except Hagen, who gruffly remarked that the boy appeared more likely to die early than to live to grow up. He had just finished this rude speech, which filled Etzel's heart with dismay, when Dankwart burst into the room, exclaiming that all his companions had been slain, and calling to Hagen for aid.

> "'Be stirring, brother Hagen; you're sitting all too long.
> To you and God in heaven our deadly strait I plain:
> Yeomen and knights together lie in their quarters slain.'"
>
> *Nibelungenlied* (*Lettsom's tr.*).

The moment Hagen heard these tidings he sprang to his feet, and, drawing his sword, he bade Dankwart guard the door and prevent the ingress or egress of a single Hungarian. Then with relentless savagery he struck off the head of the child Ortlieb, which bounded into Kriemhild's lap. Slashing out wildly he then cut off Werbel's hand, and continued hewing right and left among the Hungarians. His example was speedily followed by his companions, and soon the great hall was a scene of bloodshed and riot.

Dismayed at this sudden turn of affairs, the aged King Etzel sat in mortal anguish helplessly watching the massacre, while Kriemhild shrieked aloud to Dietrich to protect her from her foes. Moved to pity by her evident terror, Dietrich blew a resounding blast on his horn, and Gunther paused in his work of destruction to inquire how he might serve the man who had ever shown himself a friend. Dietrich answered by asking for a safe-conduct out of the hall for himself and his followers, which was immediately granted.

" ' Let me with your safe-conduct this hall of Etzel's leave,
And quit this bloody banquet with those who follow me ;
And for this grace for ever I'll at your service be.' "

Nibelungenlied (*Lettsom's tr.*).

The Massacre in the Hall

Dietrich von Bern then passed out of the hall unmolested, leading the king by one hand and the queen
by the other, and closely followed by all his retainers.
This same privilege was granted to Rüdiger and his five
hundred men. But when these had all passed out the
Burgundians renewed the bloody fight, nor paused until
every Hun in the hall had been slain and everything
was reeking with blood.

Full of fury and anguish, the Burgundians gathered
up the corpses and flung them heavily down the stair-
case, at the foot of which stood Etzel, helplessly wringing his hands, and vainly trying to discover some means
of stopping the fight.

In the meanwhile Kriemhild was actively employed
in gathering men, and promising large rewards to any
one who would attack and slay Hagen. Urged on by
her, Iring attempted to approach the hall, but he was
soon driven back. Again he tried to force an entrance.
But this time he met his doom, for Hagen ruthlessly
slew him.

Then Irnfried the Thuringian, and Hawart the Dane,
seeing him fall, rushed impetuously upon the Burgundians to avenge him ; but both fell under the
mighty blows of Hagen and Volker, while one by one
their brave followers, in spite of their numbers, were all
slain by the Burgundians.

Terrible was the sight that filled the noble hall which
had so lately resounded to the sound of harp and song.
Blood stained the walls and the floor, and the very
dishes that had stood upon the table. Fierce cries rose

in the place of laughter, and wickedness shone in the eyes of those who till now had mingled together as kinsmen and allies. Woe and anguish hung in the air, yet still the slaughter went on. Troop after troop of brave men marched to show their courage in fight. But, alas! of all those who thus ventured few returned. For the vigour and relentlessness of the Burgundians made them proof against every attack.

The Truce

Meanwhile Etzel, the Noble-hearted, was mourning bitterly over the dead, and for the time the attacks were relinquished. The weary Burgundians removed their helmets and rested, while Kriemhild continued to muster new troops to attack her kinsmen, who were still strongly entrenched in the great hall.

" 'Twas e'en on a midsummer befell that murderous fight,
When on her nearest kinsmen and many a noble knight
Dame Kriemhild wreak'd the anguish that long in heart she bore,
Whence inly griev'd King Etzel, nor joy knew evermore.

" Yet on such sweeping slaughter at first she had not thought;
She only had for vengeance on one transgressor sought.
She wish'd that but on Hagen the stroke of death might fall;
'Twas the foul fiend's contriving that they should perish all."

Nibelungenlied (*Lettsom's tr.*).

Kriemhild's Cruelty

Sick at the sight of the carnage round them, the Burgundians sent out a message that they would treat with King Etzel for a safe-conduct. Obdurate at first, the old king would have yielded at last, had not Kriemhild advised him to pursue the feud to the bitter end unless her brothers would consent to surrender Hagen to her tender mercies. This Gunther absolutely refused to do. Therefore Kriemhild went to work, and gave secret orders that the hall in which the enemy was entrenched should be set on fire. Surrounded by bitter foes, blinded by smoke, and overcome by the heat, the Burgundians still held their own. In their desperation they slaked their burning thirst by drinking the blood of the slain, and took refuge from the flames under the stone arches which supported the ceiling of the hall.

Thus they managed to survive that terrible night, though with what sufferings none can say. But when morning dawned and the queen heard that they were still alive she bade Rüdiger go forth and fight them. At first he refused, but then she reminded him of the solemn oath he had sworn to her in Worms to induce her to consent to accompany him back to Hungary, and for the sake of his honour he agreed.

Yet before his promise crossed his lips Rüdiger made one last desperate effort to avoid the contest. In this he was the more eager because his word and protection had been pledged to both Kriemhild and the Burgundians. Therefore he begged the queen to absolve him from his oath, and take instead the whole of his personal goods. But the vindictive queen only laughed at the idea of such a bargain. " You swore," she reiterated again and again, till at last, goaded to madness, he yielded to her entreaties. With a sinking heart he summoned his warriors, and led the way to the hall where the enemy lay. So strong was the confidence of the Burgundians in the good faith of Rüdiger that at first they could not believe that he had any hostile intentions. But when he pathetically informed them that he had no choice save to fight, and recommended his wife and daughter to their care in case he should fall, they silently allowed him and his followers to enter the hall, and then grimly renewed the bloody conflict.

GUNTHER AND HAGEN PRISONERS

Once more the hall rang with the din of battle ; once more brave knights fell on every side. As for Rüdiger, after slaying many foes, he encountered Gernot, wielding the sword he had given him. Then these two doughty champions closed in strife with such vehemence that finally each slew the other. The sight of the two slain heroes maddened the rest of the combatants and they fought in such deadly earnest that soon not one was left living of those who had entered the hall. Quickly the news of the terrible disaster spread, till at last it came to the ears of Kriemhild, whose grief at the sight of the dead body of Rüdiger was fearful to behold. Soon the whole town was ringing with sorrow at the death of their hero, and finally the story was told to Dietrich von Bern, who bade his man Hildebrand go and claim the corpse from his Burgundian friends.

Gunther and Hagen Taken Prisoner

Immediately Hildebrand went thither with an armed force, and would doubtless readily have been given what he sought, had not some of his men unfortunately begun to bandy words with the Burgundians, which soon brought about an impetuous fight. In the ensuing battle all the Burgundians fell except Gunther and Hagen, while Hildebrand escaped sore wounded to his master, Dietrich von Bern. When this hero heard that his nephew and vassals were all slain he quickly armed himself, and, after vainly imploring Gunther and Hagen to surrender, fell upon them with an armed force. The two sole remaining Burgundians were now so exhausted that Dietrich soon managed to take them captive. Thus he led them bound to Kriemhild, and implored her to have pity upon them and spare their lives.

" ' Fair and noble Kriemhild,' thus Sir Dietrich spake,
'Spare this captive warrior, who full amends will make
For all his past transgressions ; him here in bonds you see;
Revenge not on the fetter'd th' offences of the free.' "

Nibelungenlied (Lettsom's tr.).

Death of Gunther, Hagen, and Kriemhild

But in spite of the terrible slaughter she had caused
Kriemhild's lust was not yet appeased. She would
promise nothing except that for the present their lives
were safe ; after which she had them confined, each in a
separate cell. There she soon sought out Hagen, and
promised him his liberty if he would but reveal the
place where her treasure was concealed. But Hagen,
mistrusting her, declared that he had solemnly sworn
never to reveal the secret as long as one of his masters
breathed. Kriemhild, whose cruelty had long passed
all bounds, left him only to have her brother Gunther
beheaded. Then she soon returned carrying his head,
which she showed to Hagen, commanding him to
speak. But he still refused to gratify her, and replied
that since he was now the sole depository of the secret
it should perish with him, for he cried mockingly :

" ' So now, where lies the treasure none knows save God and me,
And told it shall be never, be sure, she-fiend, to thee ! ' "

Nibelungenlied (Lettsom's tr.).

This defiant answer so exasperated Kriemhild that
she seized the sword hanging by his side—which she
recognised as Siegfried's favourite weapon—and with
her own hands cut off his head before Etzel or any of
his courtiers could interfere. Hildebrand, seeing this
act of treachery, could no longer restrain his exasperation, but springing impetuously forward he drew
his sword and slew her who had brought untold misery
into the land of the Huns.

KRIEMHILD SLAIN

" The mighty and the noble there lay together dead ;
For this had all the people dole and drearihead.
The feast of royal Etzel was thus shut up in woe.
Pain in the steps of Pleasure treads ever here below.

" 'Tis more than I can tell you what afterwards befell,
Save that there was weeping for friends belov'd so well ;
Knights and squires, dames and damsels, were seen lamenting all.
So end I here my story.   This is the Nibelungers' Fall."
                                    Nibelungenlied (*Lettsom's tr.*).

Thus ended the career of Kriemhild, once the gentlest
of maidens and most loving of wives, but turned by
long brooding over a sore wrong into a monster of
cruel rapacity.

At this point the "Nibelungenlied" proper ends,
but an appendix, probably by another hand, called the
"Lament," continues the story, and relates how Etzel,
Dietrich, and Hildebrand in turn extolled the high
deeds and bewailed the untimely end of each hero.
Then this poem, which is throughout as mournful as
monotonous, describes the departure of the messengers
sent to bear the evil tidings and the weapons of the
slain to Worms, and their arrival at Passau, where more
tears were shed, while Bishop Pilgrim celebrated a solemn
mass for the souls of all the fallen.

From thence the funeral procession slowly travelled
on to Worms, where the sad news was imparted to the
remaining Burgundians, who named the son of Gunther
and Brunhild as their king.   Yet never did the memory
of that fatal ride to Hungary fade from the minds of the
people, and long after they had passed away from this
world their children told of the terrible deeds which
they had heard related by their parents.   Nor was the
word "Hun" ever mentioned among them without a
shudder running through the company.

CHAPTER V : THE LANGOBARDIAN CYCLE

The Langobards and Gepidæ

ALTHOUGH the following tales of mythical heroes have some slight historical basis, they have been so adorned by the fancy of mediæval bards, and so frequently remodelled with utter disregard to all chronological sequence, that the kernel of truth is very hard to find. The stories must therefore be considered as depicting customs and times rather than as describing actual events. They are recorded in the "Heldenbuch," or "Book of Heroes," edited in the fifteenth century by Kaspar von der Rhön from materials which had been embellished by Wolfram von Eschenbach and Heinrich von Ofterdingen in the twelfth century. The poem of "Ortnit," for instance, is known to have existed as early as the ninth century.

According to the poets of the Middle Ages, the Gepidæ and the Langobards settled in Pannonia (Hungary and the neighbouring provinces), where they were respectively governed by Thurisind and Audoin. The sons of these two kings, having quarrelled for a trifle, met in duel soon after, when the Langobardian prince slew his companion, and took possession of his arms, with which he proudly returned home.

But when, flushed with victory, he would fain have taken his seat at his father's board with the men-at-arms, Audoin gravely informed him that it was not customary for a youth to claim a place beside tried warriors until some foreign king had distinguished him by the present of a complete suit of armour. Angry at being thus publicly repulsed, Alboin, the prince, strode out of his father's hall, resolved to march into Thurisind's palace and demand of him the required weapons.

ALBOIN'S CRUELTY

When the King of the Gepidæ saw his son's murderer boldly enter his palace his first impulse was to put him to death. But, respecting the rights of hospitality, he forebore to take immediate vengeance, and even bestowed upon him the customary gift of arms as he departed on the morrow. Yet he warned him never to return, lest he should lose his life at the warriors' hands. Thus Alboin rode off, bearing with him the arms he was well content to possess, and also another treasure, the loss of which the king little suspected. This was the image of little Rosamund, Thurisind's fair granddaughter, whom he solemnly swore he would claim as wife as soon as she was of marriageable age.

Proudly Alboin re-entered his father's hall and flung down the arms he had brought, at the sight of which the Langobards gladly sprang up to recognise him as a full-fledged warrior. Moreover, on the death of his father some little time later they willingly hailed him as king.

Alboin's Cruelty

Shortly after Alboin's accession to the throne a quarrel arose between the Gepidæ and the Langobards, or Lombards, as they were eventually called. In the end war was declared and a decisive battle fought, in which Thurisind and his son perished, while all their lands fell into the conqueror's hands. . With true heathen cruelty the Lombard king had the skulls of the Gepidæ mounted as drinking-vessels, which he delighted in using on all state and festive occasions. Then, pushing onwards, Alboin took forcible possession of his new realm and of the tearful young Rosamund, whom he forced to become his wife, although she shrank in horror from the murderer of all her kin and the oppressor of her people.

103

Yet, powerless to resist, she followed him home, concealing her fears ; and although she never seemed blithe and happy, she obeyed her husband so implicitly that he fancied her a devoted wife. He was so accustomed to Rosamund's ready compliance with his every wish that one day, after winning a great victory over the Ostrogoths, and conquering a province in Northern Italy (which in time came to bear the name of his race from the fact that he took up his abode there), he bade her fill her father's skull with wine and pledge him by drinking first out of this repulsive cup.

The Revolt of Rosamund

The queen hesitated, but, impelled by Alboin's threatening glances and his mailed hand raised to strike her, she tremblingly filled the cup and raised it to her lips. Then, instead of humbly presenting it to her lord, she dashed it haughtily at his feet, and left the hall, saying that though hitherto she had obeyed him she would never again live with him as his wife—a declaration which the warriors present secretly applauded, for they all thought that their king had been wantonly cruel toward his beautiful wife.

The Murder of Alboin

While Alboin was pondering how he might conciliate her without owning himself in the wrong, Rosamund summoned Helmigis, the king's shield-bearer, and finding that he would not execute her orders to murder his master in his sleep, she secured the services of the giant Perideus.

Perideus did not hesitate to obey her command, and soon found a way of robbing his sovereign of life. The news of the tragedy caused little concern, for the tyrannical king had been much hated by his subjects.

Alboin and Rosamund

Ortnit and Alberich

As for Rosamund herself, she was only too glad to be rid of so hateful a lord. She therefore set about securing her position as queen, and for that purpose summoned round her all her adherents, of whom she had many. After this she took pains to seize the treasure belonging to the crown ; then, well satisfied with her efforts, she began her reign. But before long the nobles bade her marry a man to succeed their king, who had left no heirs, whereupon she declared that her choice lay in Helmigis.

Flight of Rosamund

Indignantly the Langobardian nobles refused to recognise an armour-bearer as their king. Then Rosamund, fearing their resentment, fled by night with her treasures, and took refuge with Longinus, the viceroy of the Eastern emperor, who was entrenched in Ravenna. Captivated by the fugitive queen's exquisite beauty no less than by her numerous treasures, Longinus proposed that she should poison Helmigis and marry himself. Already weary of Helmigis, Rosamund obediently handed the deadly cup to that faithful adorer. But he drank only half its contents, when, perceiving that he had been poisoned, he forced her at the point of the sword to drink the remainder, thus making sure that she would not long survive him.

Longinus, thus deprived of a beautiful bride, managed to console himself for her loss by appropriating her treasures, while the Langobardian sceptre, after having been wielded by different kings, fell finally into the hands of Rother, the last influential monarch of a kingdom which Charlemagne had conquered in 774.

King Rother

Rother established his capital at Bari, a great seaport in Apulia. But although his wealth was unbounded and his kingdom extensive he was far from happy, for he had neither wife nor child to share his home. Perceiving his loneliness, one of his courtiers, Duke Berchther, or Berchtung, of Meran, the father of twelve stalwart sons, advised him to seek a wife. In reply Rother declared that he knew of no princess fair enough to please his fastidious taste. Hearing this, the courtier produced the portrait of Oda, daughter of Constantine, Emperor of the East. No sooner had Rother's glance fallen upon the picture than he fell desperately in love with the princess. In vain Berchther warned him that the emperor had the unpleasant habit of beheading all his daughter's would-be suitors ; Rother declared that he must make an attempt to secure this peerless bride, and only with great difficulty was he persuaded to resign the idea of wooing in person.

At last Berchther succeeded in prevailing upon him to send an imposing embassy of twelve noblemen, richly apparelled, and attended by a large suite. Eagerly Rother asked who would undertake the mission. But to his astonishment all the warriors maintained silence, until seven of Berchther's sons volunteered their services, after which five other noblemen signified their readiness to accompany them.

Embassy to Constantinople

To speed them on their way Rother escorted them to the port, and, standing on the pier, he composed and sang a marvellous song. He bade them remember the tune, and promised them that whenever they heard it they might be sure their king was very near.

Arrived at Constantinople, the ambassadors made known their errand, upon which they were immediately cast into prison, in spite of the intercession of the empress on their behalf. Here the knights languished month after month in a foul dungeon, while Rother impatiently watched for their return. When a whole year had elapsed without his having heard any tidings, he resolved to go in disguise to Constantinople to ascertain the fate of his men and win the lovely princess Oda for his bride.

On hearing this decision Berchther vowed that he too would accompany him. Others of the knights also begged to be allowed a place in the mission, for they all loved their eager King Rother. Yet, fearing for their safety, Rother took only a few of the strongest among them, one of whom was Asprian, or Osborn, king of the northern giants, with eleven of his tallest men.

Rother in Constantinople

With this little train Rother impatiently embarked, and set sail for the sunny capital, Constantinople. As the ship ploughed on her way the king sat on deck playing such sweet tunes on his harp that the mermaids rose from the deep to sport around the vessel. According to a prearranged plan, the king presented himself before Constantine as a fugitive and outlaw, complaining bitterly of the King of the Lombards, who, he declared, had banished him and his companions. Pleased with the appearance of the strangers, Constantine gladly accepted their proffered services, and invited them to a banquet, during which he carelessly described how he had received Rother's ambassadors, who were still languishing in his most loathsome dungeons. This boastful talk gradually roused the anger of the giant Asprian, who was but little accustomed to hide his feelings ; and when the emperor's pet lioness came into the hall and playfully snatched a choice morsel out of his hand he impetuously sprang to his feet, caught her

107

in his powerful grasp, and hurled her against the wall, thus slaying her instantly.

Constantine was somewhat dismayed when he saw the strength, and especially the violence, of the new servants he had secured. But he wisely took no notice of the affair, and when the banquet was ended he dismissed Rother and his followers to the apartments which had been assigned them. On the morrow the Lombard king freely distributed the immense treasures he had brought with him, and thus he secured many adherents at court. They sang his praises so loudly that at last the princess Oda became very anxious to see this noted outlaw.

Rother and Oda

Her curiosity at last grew so great that she bribed Herlind, one of her handmaidens, to serve her secretly, and sent her to Rother to invite him to visit her. The maiden cleverly conveyed the message, but did not meet with the reply she expected. For the Langobardian monarch, pretending exaggerated respect, declared that he would never dare to present himself before her beautiful mistress, to whom, however, he sent many rich gifts, among which were two shoes, one of gold and one of silver. Taking the gifts with her, Herlind returned to her mistress. But when Oda would fain have put on the shoes she discovered that they were both for the same foot. She then feigned a resentment she was far from feeling, and bade the handmaiden order her father's new servant to appear before her without delay, bringing a shoe for her other foot, unless he wished to incur her lasting displeasure. Overjoyed at this result of his ruse, which he had foreseen, Rother entered the apartments of the princess unnoticed, and proffered his most humble apologies. Then he fitted a pair of golden shoes on her tiny feet, and, taking advantage of his position as he bent on one knee before her, declared his love and rank, and won from Oda a solemn promise that she would be his wife.

Thus secure in their love the two spent some very happy hours together in intimate exchanges of confidence, and ere Rother left the apartment he had prevailed upon the princess to use her influence on behalf of his imprisoned subjects. Therefore she told her father that her peaceful rest had been disturbed by dreams, in which heavenly voices announced that all manner of evil was about to come upon her unless Rother's ambassadors were taken from prison and hospitably entertained. Oda then wrung from Constantine a promise that the men should be temporarily released, and feasted at his own board that self-same evening. This promise was duly redeemed, and the twelve ambassadors, freed from their chains, and refreshed by warm baths and clean garments, were sumptuously entertained at the emperor's table. Then while they sat there feasting Rother entered the hall, and hiding behind the tapestry hangings near the door, he played the tune they had heard on the day of their departure. Gently the notes sounded through the hall, and at the sound the hearts of the captives bounded with joy. For they knew that their king was near and would soon effect their release.

War with Imelot

In this way several days passed, till the young ambassadors had fully recovered their health and strength. Meanwhile Constantine had been greatly dismayed by learning that Imelot, King of Desert Babylonia, was about to make war against him. Harassed by anxiety, he began to consider how he could best fight against a foe so universally dreaded. Rother, seeing his perplexity, immediately volunteered his services. Moreover, he added that if Constantine would liberate the ambassadors, who were all mighty men of valour, he need have no doubt of coming off conqueror in the war. Only too pleased at such a solution, the emperor followed this advice, and soon set out with Rother and all his companions. Thus one evening the two armies came within sight of and encamped opposite each other, intending to begin the fight at sunrise. During the night, however, Rother and his companions stole into the enemy's midst and slew Imelot's guards. Then, having bound and gagged the prince, Asprian carried him bodily away from the camp, while his Langobardian companions routed all the mighty Babylonian host.

Flushed with victory and worn out by their struggles, they returned a few hours later to the camp of Constantine, and lay down to rest. Soon the rising sun reddened the sky in the east, and the emperor, entering the tent where the Langobards lay, reproached them for their laziness. But even as the words fell from his lips his eyes lighted upon the captive Imelot. Startled, he asked how he came there, and in return he heard from them the story of their night's work. Amazed, he readily consented to allow the allies to return to Constantinople to announce the victory, while he and his army remained to take possession of Desert Babylonia and of all of Imelot's vast treasures.

Rother's Strategy

Meanwhile Rother and his companions returned in haste to Constantinople and rushed into the palace. But instead of announcing a victory, they told the empress and Oda that Constantine had been defeated, that Imelot was on the way to seize the city, and that the emperor had sent them on ahead to convey his wife and daughter to a place of safety, with their most valuable treasures.

Full of alarm, the empress and Oda easily credited their tale, and made immediate preparations for departure. Soon they were joined by Rother on the pier, where his fast sailing vessel was ready to start. All the Langobardians had already embarked, when at last Rother escorted the princess on board, bidding the empress wait on the quay until he returned for her. But as soon as he and his fair charge set foot upon deck the vessel was pushed off, and Rother called out to the distressed empress that he had deceived her in order to carry away her daughter, who was now to become the Langobardian queen.

Constantine's Counter-move

On his return Constantine was naturally very angry at having been so cleverly duped, and vainly tried to devise some plan for recovering the daughter whom he loved so well. Yet though he sat long and deep in thought he could concoct no scheme that seemed to promise success. Therefore when a magician came who offered to execute his wishes, he gladly provided him with a vessel and crew to sail to Bari. Thus equipped, the magician set off, leaving behind him the king, anxious, yet full of hope.

Immediately on putting into port the intriguer, disguised as a peaceful merchant, spread out his wares and invited inspection from the passers-by. His odd assortment of gaily coloured goods soon attracted a good many buyers, from whom, by dint of artful questioning, the magician quickly learned that Rother was absent, and that Oda was at home, carefully guarded by the principal nobles of the realm. When he also learned that one of these noblemen had a crippled child, the magician informed the people who visited his vessel to inspect his wares that the most precious treasure in his possession was a magic stone, which, in a queen's hands, had the power of restoring cripples.

Before long the rumour of this miraculous stone reached the court, as the magician had intended it should. Eagerly the knights persuaded the kind-hearted queen to go down to the vessel to try the efficacy of the stone. The heart of the magician bounded when he saw her approach, and he bade his men be ready to set off at any moment. All unsuspecting, Oda set foot on the vessel, only to find she was being rapidly carried away from her husband. On and on went the boat, till at last Oda saw she was back in her father's home, where she was welcomed with great demonstrations of joy.

As for Rother, when he got back from the war and heard the tidings black despair filled his mind. Immediately he prepared a vessel to go in pursuit of his queen, and selected his giants and bravest noblemen to accompany him. Once more they landed at a short distance from Constantinople, and Rother bade his men hide in a thicket, while he went into the city, disguised as a pilgrim, carrying under his robe a hunting-horn, which he promised to sound should he at any time find himself in danger.

No sooner had he entered the city than, to his surprise, he noticed that all the inhabitants seemed to be greatly depressed. He questioned them concerning their evident sadness, and learned in reply that Imelot, having effected his escape from captivity, had invaded the kingdom, and vowed that he would not retreat unless Oda married his ugly and hunchbacked son without delay.

Oda in Danger

These tidings made Rother press on to the palace, where, thanks to his disguise, he effected an easy entrance. Slipping unnoticed to his wife's side, he dropped into the cup beside her a ring upon which his name was engraved. In a flash Oda recognised the jewel, and tried to hide it away. But her hunchbacked suitor, sitting beside her, had also caught sight of it. He pointed out the intruder, cried that he was Rother in disguise, and bade his guards seize him and hang him. Rother, seeing that he was discovered, boldly stepped forward, declared that he had come to claim his wife, and challenged the craven hunchback. His cowardly opponent, however, merely repeated his orders, and accompanied his guards to a grove outside the city to see his captive executed. Then just as they were about to fasten the fatal noose round his neck, Rother blew a resounding blast upon his horn.

Her Rescue

The effect was magical. Instantly his followers sprang out of their ambush, and falling upon the guards slew them to a man; after which they killed both Imelot and the hunchback, and so recovered possession of Oda. Then, marching back to their ship, they sailed home in triumph to Lombardy. Here Oda bore her husband a daughter called Helche, or Herka, who was afterwards famous for her beauty, and eventually married Etzel (Attila), King of the Huns.

Ortnit

Another renowned Lombardian king was Ortnit, or Otnit, whose realm included not only all Italy from the Alps to the sea, but also the island of Sicily. He had won this domain by his fabulous strength, which, we are told, was equivalent to that of twelve vigorous men.

Yet in spite of all outward prosperity Ortnit was

lonely and unhappy. Now it happened that one day while he was strolling along the seashore at sunset he saw a misty castle rise slowly out of the waves. On its topmost tower he beheld a fair maiden, with whom he fell deeply in love at first sight. As he was gazing spellbound at the lady's beauty, both castle and maiden suddenly vanished. Marvelling what it could mean, Ortnit asked his uncle, Ylyas, or Elias, Prince of the Reussen, to explain this fantastic vision. Whereupon he learned that the castle was the exact reproduction of the stronghold of Muntabure, and the maiden a phantom of Princess Sidrat, daughter of the ruler of Syria, all of which he had been permitted to see through the kindness of the Fata Morgana, or Morgana the fay.

> " As the weary traveller sees,
>   In desert or prairie vast,
> Blue lakes, overhung with trees,
>   That a pleasant shadow cast ;
>
> " Fair towns with turrets high,
>   And shining roofs of gold,
> That vanish as he draws nigh,
>   Like mists together rolled."
>   *Longfellow* (*Fata Morgana*).

On hearing this Ortnit at once vowed that he would go and ask the maiden's hand in marriage ; and although his uncle warned him that Machorell, the girl's father, was wont to behead all his daughter's suitors, and use their heads as decorations for his fortifications, the young king persisted in his resolve.

Ortnit's Great Enterprise

The question of the journey now occupied his mind entirely, and he set about making all the preparations necessary for a long sea voyage. Meanwhile his mother, distracted at the thought of the perilous mission, used every kind of persuasion to turn her son from his purpose. But nothing that she could say could alter his determination, and seeing this she at last resigned herself to what was inevitable. Her next anxiety was to do all she could to help Ortnit to win his way back in safety. For this reason she slipped a ring on to his hand, and bade him ride out of town in a certain direction, and dismount under a lime-tree, where a great wonder would be shown to him.

> " ' If thou wilt seek the adventure, don thy armour strong ;
> Far to the left thou ride the towering rocks along.
> But bide thee, champion, and await, where grows a linden tree ;
> There, flowing from the rock, a well thine eyes will see.

> " ' Far around the meadow spread the branches green ;
> Five hundred armed knights may stand beneath the shade, I ween.
> Below the linden tree await, and thou wilt meet full soon
> The marvellous adventure ; there must the deed be done.' "
>
> *Heldenbuch* (*Weber's tr.*).

The Dwarf Alberich

Full of curiosity as to what this marvel could be, Ortnit obeyed her instructions, and rode off in search of the lime-tree. Having found it, he dismounted at a spot that seemed strangely familiar. Then, gazing inquisitively around him, he became aware of the presence of a lovely sleeping infant. But when he attempted to take the child in his arms he found himself sprawling on the ground, knocked over by a single blow from the babe's tiny fist. Furious at his overthrow, Ortnit grappled with his small assailant, and there followed the most strange of all wrestling matches, one between a full-grown warrior and a seemingly help-less babe. Yet the child was no foe to be easily conquered, and it was only after a long and arduous struggle, in which Ortnit had to exercise his full strength, that he succeeded in pinning down his tiny opponent.

Unable to free himself from Ortnit's powerful grasp, the child now confessed that he was Alberich, king of the dwarfs. He then promised Ortnit a marvellous suit of armour, and the sword Rosen, which had been tempered in dragon's blood, and was therefore considered invulnerable, if he would only let him go.

> " ' Save me, noble Otnit, for thy chivalry ! •
> A hauberk will I give thee, strong, and of wondrous might ;
> Better armour never bore champion in the fight.

> " ' Not eighty thousand marks would buy the hauberk bright.
> A sword of mound I'll give thee, Otnit, thou royal knight ;
> Through armour, both of gold and steel, cuts the weapon keen ;
> The helmet could its edge withstand ne'er in this world was seen.
> *Heldenbuch* (*Weber's tr.*).

To these terms the king consented, and thus he relaxed his hold. But his kindness was ill requited, for the moment he set the dwarf free he felt him snatch the ring his mother had given him off his hand, and saw him mysteriously and suddenly disappear in the shadows, whence his voice sounded tauntingly now on this side, now on that. Some parley ensued before the dwarf would restore the ring, which was no sooner replaced on the hero's hand than he once more found himself able to see his antagonist.

The Secret of Ortnit's Birth

Alberich now gravely informed Ortnit that in spite of his infantile stature he was very old indeed, having lived more than five hundred years. He then went on to tell him that the king, whom Ortnit had until then considered his father, had no claim to the title of parent, for he had secretly divorced his wife, and given her in

116

marriage to Alberich. Thus the dwarf was Ortnit's true father, and he declared himself ready now to acknowledge their relationship and to protect his son.

Too much bewildered to comprehend the full meaning of all the dwarf said, Ortnit gladly accepted the promised armour and the sword Rosen. Then, after directing him to turn the magic ring if ever he needed a father's aid, Alberich vanished. Still dazed and bewildered, Ortnit returned to town, where he informed his mother that he had seen his father. This caused her no surprise, for she guessed how matters would turn out. But she gave him her blessing and called him her good son, after which he set sail for Suders, or Tyre. Following the usual custom of people wishing to preserve a disguise, Ortnit entered the harbour as a merchant, and exhibited his wares to the curious people. Meanwhile Alberich, at his son's request, bore a challenge to Machorell, threatening to take Tyre and the castle of Muntabure unless he were willing to accept Ortnit as son-in-law.

The dwarf acquitted himself nobly of his task, and when Machorell scornfully dismissed him he hastened back to Tyre, bidding Ortnit lose no time in surprising and taking possession of the town. This advice was so well carried out that Ortnit soon found himself master of the city, and, marching on to Muntabure, he laid siege to the castle. His magic ring was of inestimable value to him in this encounter, for by it he restored all his men as soon as they had been wounded. Alberich, who was invisible to all but Prince Ortnit, was allowed to lead the van and bear the banner, which thus seemed to flutter aloft as if by magic. Moreover, the dwarf took advantage of this invisibility to scale the walls of the fortress unseen, and hurl down the ponderous machines used to throw stones, arrows, boiling pitch, and oil. His help was thus of the greatest service to Ortnit, who in the meanwhile was performing such unheard-of deeds of valour that they gradually excited the admiration of Princess Sidrat, who was watching him from her tower.

Princess Sidrat and Ortnit

Observing her evident delight, Alberich stole softly to her elbow, where he whispered into her ear that if she would fain meet the hero all she need do would be to go to the postern gate early on the morrow. The princess gave no definite reply, but the light in her eye seemed to promise acquiescence. Therefore, with a heart beating with hope and excitement, Ortnit hurried thither at early dawn. By-and-by, gliding through the morning mist came the form of the lovely Sidrat. Modestly she listened while Ortnit pleaded his cause ; and such was his passion and eloquence that she yielded to his entreaties and fled with him to his home in Lombardy. Here she became his beloved queen, and, having been initiated into the Christian faith, by baptism she received his name of Liebgart, by which she was ever afterward known.

An Evil Present

So deeply in love were Ortnit and Liebgart that their happiness seemed full to overflowing. Only one thing troubled the mind of the gentle princess, and that was the breach between her husband and her father's court. But soon even this slight cloud seemed about to be removed, for a giant and his wife came from King Machorell's court bringing conciliatory messages, and a promise that the sovereign would visit his daughter in the early spring. They also brought countless valuable presents, among which were two huge eggs. These the giants declared to be priceless, as from them could be hatched magic toads with lodestones in their foreheads. Liebgart's curiosity was naturally much excited by this gift, and learning from the giant couple that they would see to the hatching of the eggs and the bringing up of the toads if a suitable place were provided for them, she sent them into a mountain gorge near Trient, where the climate was hot and damp enough for the hatching.

The Dragons

Time passed, and the giantess Ruotze hatched from the huge eggs, not toads, but dragons or lind-worms. These animals grew with alarming rapidity, and soon the governor of the province sent word to the king that he could no longer provide food enough for the monsters, which had become the terror of the whole countryside. Finally they proved too much even for the giants, who were obliged to flee in hot haste. When Ortnit learned that ordinary weapons had no effect upon these dragons he knew that he was the only man who could slay them. Therefore he donned his magic armour, and, seizing his sword Rosen, he bade Liebgart a tender farewell, telling her that if he did not return she must marry none but the man who wore his ring. Then amidst the lamentations of all his courtiers the brave king sallied forth to deliver his people from the ravenous monsters whom he had thoughtlessly allowed in their midst.

Ortnit's Fight

After a long and perilous journey Ortnit at last reached the mountain region where the fearful monsters lay. His advance was barred by the guardian giant and his wife, but with one swing of his sword Ortnit cut off both their heads. To his surprise he now encountered the dwarf Alberich, who warned him that he would fall a victim to the pestilent dragons, which had bred a number of young ones, destined, in time, to infest all Europe.

The Death of Ortnit

In spite of these warnings Ortnit declared that he must do his best for the sake of his people, and, having given the magic ring back to Alberich, he continued on his way. All day long he vainly sought the monsters in the trackless forest, until, sinking down exhausted at the foot of a tree, he soon fell asleep. This slumber was so profound that it was like a lethargy, and even the wild barking of his dog failed to waken him. Thus all unseen the terrible dragon made its stealthy approach. With one sudden dart forward the monster caught the sleeping king in his powerful claws, and dashed him against the rocks until every bone in his body was broken into bits, and this in spite of the fact that the magic armour itself remained quite whole.

After thus glutting its rage the dragon conveyed the corpse to his den to give to his young. Yet in vain the horrible creatures tried to get at the king to eat his flesh ; the impenetrable armour withstood all their efforts.

Liebgart's Great Grief

In the meantime Liebgart was anxiously awaiting the return of her beloved husband, and fearfully counting the days as they passed. But when she saw his dog steal into the palace in evident grief she knew that Ortnit was dead. Full of anguish, she bemoaned her loss, and cried aloud, " Ortnit, Ortnit," till the hearts of her subjects bled to hear her. In course of time, as Ortnit had left no heir to succeed him, the nobles began to crowd round the queen, imploring her to marry one of them and make him King of Lombardy. Yet she ever refused to listen to their wooing.

Angry at her resistance, the noblemen then took possession of her treasure, her palace, and her kingdom, and left poor Liebgart so utterly destitute that she was forced to support herself by spinning and weaving. Slowly the years passed by, but she carried on these occupations patiently, waiting and watching for the coming of that knight of whom Ortnit had spoken ; he who should come wearing the magic ring, and through whom she would at last regain her former position as Queen of Lombardy.

CHAPTER VI : THE AMELINGS

Hugdietrich

WHILE Ortnit's ancestors were ruling over Lombardy, Anzius was Emperor of Constantinople. This monarch, when about to die, confided his infant son, Hugdietrich, to the care of Berchther of Meran, the very knight who had once accompanied Rother on his journey to Constantinople.

By-and-by Hugdietrich became of an age to marry, and his faithful guardian straightway set about finding a princess for him. One princess only, Hildburg, daughter of Walgund of Thessalonica, seemed to unite all the required advantages of birth, beauty, and wealth. But unfortunately the father of this princess was averse to her marrying, and to prevent her from having any lovers he had locked her up in an isolated tower, where none but women were ever admitted.

Berchther having informed his ward of his plan, and of the difficulties concerning its fulfilment, Hugdietrich immediately made up his mind to bring it about, even if he had to resort to stratagem in order to win his bride. Therefore, after much deep thinking, he let his hair grow, learned all about woman's work and ways, donned feminine garments, and journeyed off to Thessalonica, where he presented himself before the king as a princess in distress, who had come to claim his chivalrous protection. Suspecting no stratagem, Walgund welcomed the pretended princess warmly, and accepted her gifts of gold and embroidery. This latter was very beautiful, and no sooner had the king shown it to his wife and daughter than they expressed a lively desire to see the stranger and let her teach them also how to do such exquisite work.

This message gave Hugdietrich the greatest delight,

and he gladly assented to teach the queen and the princess all that he knew in the art of embroidery. Thus he gained easy admittance to the tower, where he set to work to instruct the young princess, and at the same time win her affections. Before very long Hildburg discovered with alarm that the pretended princess was a suitor in disguise. Nevertheless she yielded to the earnest entreaty of the prince and kept his identity a secret till he had wooed her so successfully that she not only allowed him to take up his abode in the tower, but also consented to a secret union. All went on well for some time, but finally Hugdietrich felt it his duty to return to his kingdom. With bitter tears his young wife clung to his neck as he parted from her, solemnly promising to return ere long to claim her openly.

Birth of Wolfdietrich

But events were not to run so smoothly as Hugdietrich hoped, and on reaching home he found himself unexpectedly detained by a war which had just broken out. Of this Hildburg knew nothing, and while her husband was away fighting the poor young bride was looking out daily for his return. Month after month passed by without any news of the prince, till Hildburg, in her lonely tower, gave birth to a little son, whose advent was, however, kept secret by the ingenuity and devotion of his nurse.

Nevertheless even her watchfulness was one day taken unawares, when the queen unexpectedly presented herself at the door. Full of agitation, the servant hastily carried the child out of the building, and set him down on the grass in the moat, intending to come and get him in a few moments. She was prevented in her design, however, as the queen kept her constantly beside her, and prolonged her visit to the next day.

" In the moat the new-born babe meanwhile in silence lay,
  Sleeping on the verdant grass, gently, all the day.
  From the swathing and the bath the child had stinted weeping ;
  No one saw, or heard its voice, in the meadow sleeping."

Heldenbuch (Weber's tr.).

Meanwhile the faithful nurse was enduring agonies of mind about her charge. At the first possible moment of escape she rushed out to the moat. But the babe, who could creep about, was nowhere to be seen. Not daring to confide the truth to Hildburg, she informed her that she had sent the child out to nurse.

A few days later Berchther of Meran arrived at Thessalonica, saying that Hugdietrich had fallen in love with Hildburg on hearing a description of her charms from the exiled princess, his sister, and openly suing in his name for her hand. Instead of giving an immediate answer to this proposal, Walgund invited the ambassador to hunt with him in a neighbouring forest on the morrow. A willing assent was given, and in the morning a gay company rode off into the woods.

Walgund and the Babe

Now it happened that during the hunt Walgund and Berchther became accidentally separated from their followers, and so drew near to the lonely tower where the princess dwelt. Soon some strange sounds caught their ear, and peering through the underbrush to discover their meaning they saw a beautiful little boy sitting on the grass, playfully handling some young wolf cubs, whose struggles he seemed not to mind in the least. While the two men were gazing spellbound at this strange sight they saw the mother wolf draw near, ready to spring upon the innocent child and tear him limb from limb. As Berchther skilfully flung his spear past the child and slew the wolf Walgund sprang for-

Wolfdietrich and the Cubs

Rauch-Else and Wolfdietrich

ward and caught the babe in his arms, exclaiming that if he were only sure his grandchildren would be as handsome and fearless as this little boy he would soon consent to his daughter's marriage.

As the child was so small that he still required a woman's tender care, Walgund next proposed to carry him to the tower, where his daughter and her attendants could watch over him until he was claimed. Berchther endorsed this proposal, which was therefore immediately carried out. Overjoyed at seeing her child again, Hildburg revealed by her emotion that the child was her very own. The secret thus being out, she told her father all about her secret marriage with Hugdietrich, whom Walgund now graciously accepted as his son-in-law.

In memory of this adventure the baby rescued from the beast of prey was called Wolfdietrich, and he and his mother, accompanied by a nobleman named Sabene, were escorted in state to Constantinople, where Hugdietrich delightedly welcomed them. Here they dwelt in peace for several years, at the end of which, a war having again broken out, Hugdietrich departed to the battlefield. Ere he went he confided his wife and son to the care of Sabene, who now cast aside all his pretended virtue. After insulting the queen most grossly, he began to spread lying reports about the birth of the young heir, until the people, doubting whether he might not be considered a mere foundling, showed some unwillingness to recognise him as their future prince.

Then, the war being over, Hugdietrich returned home, full of delight at seeing again his wife and his little son, and quite unaware of what people had been saying. But by-and-by some of these malicious remarks floated to his ear, and he too began to cherish suspicions. Therefore, instead of keeping Wolfdietrich at court, he sent him to Meran, where Berchther brought him up with his twelve stalwart sons, every one of whom was outshone by the young prince in beauty, courage, and skill in all manly exercises.

In the meanwhile Hildburg had borne two other sons, Bogen and Waxmuth, to Hugdietrich. Then, seeing that Sabene was still trying to poison people's minds against the absent Wolfdietrich and deprive him of his rights, the spirited queen finally sought her husband, and revealed the baseness of Sabene's conduct. Aghast at the tale his wife had to tell, Hugdietrich lost no time in banishing the wicked Sabene from his dominions. A few short months after this a great woe fell upon Queen Hildburg, for her husband fell ill, and soon afterwards died. Yet before he breathed his last Hugdietrich divided his property among his three sons, leaving the sovereignty of Constantinople to Wolfdietrich, and making his two younger sons kings of lands which he had conquered in the south.

But no sooner had Hugdietrich been buried than the nobles of the land, who had all been won over by Sabene's artful insinuations, declared that they would never recognise Wolfdietrich as their ruler, but would recall Sabene to watch over the two younger kings and exercise the royal power in their name. In spite of Hildburg's vigorous resistance these measures were carried out, and Sabene returned in triumph, and basely avenged himself by banishing Hildburg. Thus turned out of the imperial palace at night, the queen was forced to make her way alone and on foot to Meran, where her son Wolfdietrich received her gladly, and promised to protect her with his strong right arm.

Furious on behalf of his dead father's honour, Wolfdietrich now got together a small troop composed of Berchther and his sons, with whom he marched to Constantinople to oust Sabene. But in spite of all the valour of the little company they soon found themselves defeated, and were forced to retreat to the castle of Lilienporte. Here the prince entrenched himself, rejoicing at the sight of the strong battlements, and especially at the provisions stored within its enclosure, which would suffice for all the wants of the garrison for more than seven years.

Scarcely had the great gates clanged behind them when Sabene arrived with a great army. Thereupon began one of the greatest and most famous of sieges. In vain Sabene exercised his greatest skill; in vain he constructed huge engines of war: the fortress held out month after month, till at last three years were gone. Then, at the end of the third year, Wolfdietrich, seeing that their provisions would not hold out for ever, resolved to make his escape alone, and go in search of allies to save his trusty friends. He laid his scheme before Berchther and his mother, and having obtained their consent he set about looking for an opportunity. This soon came, and while a skirmish was going on one day, Wolfdietrich escaped through the postern gate. Then, riding into the forest, he rapidly disappeared in the direction of Lombardy, where he intended to ask the aid of Ortnit. As he went through the deserts of Roumelia, where his guardian had bidden him beware of the enchantments of the witch Rauch-Else, he shared his last piece of bread with his faithful steed; then, faint with hunger and almost perishing with thirst, he plodded painfully on.

Rauch-Else

But at last neither horse nor rider could go on any further. With a groan Wolfdietrich dropped to the barren ground, where he lay in a swoon. From this he was suddenly roused by the appearance of a hideous, bearlike female, who gruffly inquired how he dared venture upon her territory. The unhappy Wolfdietrich recognised by the description his guardian, Berchther, had given him that this could be none other than Rauch-Else herself. Could he have fled, he would quickly have done so, but in his faint, weak state this was impossible.

All he could do, therefore, was to gasp out an appeal for something to eat. Upon this Rauch-Else immediately produced a peculiar-looking root, of which he had no sooner tasted than he felt as strong and rested as ever before. By the witch's advice he gave the remainder of the root to his horse, upon whom it produced the same magic effect. But when he would fain have expressed his gratitude and ridden away Rauch-Else told him that he belonged to her by decree of fate, and asked him to marry her.

Not daring to refuse this proposal, which, however, was very distasteful indeed, Wolfdietrich reluctantly assented, expressing a wish that she were not quite so repulsive. No sooner were the words fairly out of his mouth than he saw her suddenly transformed into a beautiful woman, who declared that she was Sigeminne, Queen of Old Troy, and that the evil spell which had hitherto bound her had now been broken by Wolfdietrich.

Full of happiness, the two slowly proceeded to the sea-shore, where they embarked in a waiting galley, and sailed directly to Sigeminne's kingdom. Here they lived together in such happiness that Wolfdietrich never once gave a thought to his mother, his tutor, or his companions, who were vainly awaiting his return with an army who should deliver them.

> "By the hand she led Wolfdietrich unto the forest's end ;
> To the sea she guided him ; a ship lay on the strand.
> To a spacious realm she brought him, hight the land of Troy."
> *Heldenbuch (Weber's tr.).*

Evil days, however, were in store for Wolfdietrich ; and his happiness was not to endure much longer. The first of these sorrows which fell upon him was the loss of his wife. For while he was pursuing a stag which Sigeminne bade him secure for her, a magician named Drusian suddenly presented himself before the queen and spirited her away.

Overcome with grief on finding his wife gone, Wolfdietrich resolved to go in search of her, nor to rest until he had found her. Then, knowing that nothing but cunning could prevail against the magician's art, he donned a magic silken vest his wife had woven for him, which could not be penetrated by weapon or dragon. Covering this with a pilgrim's garb, he travelled on until he came within sight of the castle of Drusian.

Worn out by his long journey, the prince sat down for a moment to rest ere he began the ascent of the steep mountain upon which the castle stood. Alas ! he soon fell into a fatal sleep, from which he was roughly awakened by a giant, who bore him off as a prisoner to the fortress. Nevertheless, in spite of his helpless condition his heart bounded within him when inside the grim palace Wolfdietrich saw his loved Sigeminne.

Fearing every moment lest he should be detected, he shrank back into his corner and endeavoured to conceal his face in the depths of his cowl. Thus the day wore on, and the pilgrim still sat there. Then when supper was spread on the table and the giant had taken his seat, he turned to the sorrowful queen and unfeelingly declared she had spent enough time in mourning for her husband, and that now she must lay aside her sad garments and marry himself. This proposal proved too much for the blood of Wolfdietrich. Forgetful of

his cowl and his pilgrim's garb, he sprang to his feet
and fell upon his foe. Nor would he by any means
let him go till the other had agreed to a fair fight in
chosen armour. Hereupon many coats of mail were
brought out and laid before the bold stranger, who
chose an iron suit in preference to the richer ones
of silver and gold. Thus prepared, the two closed in
fight, and so boldly did Wolfdietrich acquit himself that
at last the giant fell beneath his blows. Sigeminne,
restored to her husband's arms, then returned with
him to Old Troy, where they ruled happily together
until she died.

When the princess had thus breathed her last,
Wolfdietrich, delivered from the spell she had cast
upon him by making him partake of the magic root,
suddenly remembered his mother, Berchther, and his
faithful companions. Filled with compunction, he
hastened off to help them. On his way he passed
through many lands, till finally he came to a fortified
town, whose walls were adorned with human heads set
up on spikes. Having inquired of a passer-by what
this singular decoration might mean, he learned that
the city belonged to a heathen king, Belligan, who
made it a practice to slay every Christian who entered
his precincts.

Shuddering with horror at the idea of such a tyrant,
Wolfdietrich immediately resolved to rid the earth of
this monster. Boldly he rode into the city, where
he cried that he was ready to meet the king in his
favourite game of dagger-throwing. This challenge
was promptly accepted, and every preparation speedily
made. But although the heathen king was protected
by his daughter's magic spells, he could not withstand
the Christian knight, who pierced him through and
through and at last left him dead.

WOLFDIETRICH AND LIEBGART

" Speedily Wolfdietrich the third knife heaved on high.
Trembling stood Sir Belligan, for he felt his death was nigh.
The pagan's heart asunder with cunning skill he cleft ;
Down upon the grass he fell, of life bereft."

Heldenbuch (*Weber's tr.*)

Yet though he had slain Sir Belligan, Wolfdietrich was by no means to escape without further disaster. As he attempted to leave the castle, waves suddenly surrounded him on all sides, and would speedily have drowned him had he not suspected that this phenomenon was produced by the magic arts of the king's daughter. Feeling sure that this was the case, he seized the baleful witch in his strong grasp and held her head under water until she died. Upon this the waves at once subsided and permitted the prince to escape unharmed.

Continuing his journey, Wolfdietrich next came to some mountains, where he encountered a giantess, who told him the story of Ortnit's death. This so roused his compassion for the unfortunate Liebgart that he straightway vowed he would slay the dragon and avenge all her wrongs. His resolve greatly delighted the giantess, and to enable him to reach his destination sooner she bore him and his horse fifty miles over the mountains in one day, and set him down near Garden (Guarda), where he saw Liebgart and her sole remaining attendant sadly walking up and down.

Struck by Liebgart's resemblance to the dead Sigeminne, Wolfdietrich stood quietly in the shade long enough to overhear her sigh and say how much she wished the brave Wolfdietrich would come that way and avenge her husband's death.

Wolfdietrich and Liebgart

In answer to these words the hero presented himself impetuously before her, swore he would do all in his power to fulfill her wishes, and having received from her fair hand a ring, which she declared would bring the wearer good luck, he hastened off to the mountain gorge to encounter the dragons. On the way thither he met Alberich, who cautioned him not to yield to the desire for slumber if he would overcome the foe. With this caution fresh in his mind, he pressed on, in spite of almost overpowering lassitude, and so he met the dragon.

Wolfdietrich in the Cave of Dragons

In spite of vigorous resistance, the prince at last found himself conquered by the gigantic strength of the loathly beast, and little time elapsed ere he was borne off to the monster's cave, and flung down as food for the young lind-worms. With horrible eagerness the creatures fell upon him, and would certainly have devoured him had he not been protected by Sigeminne's magic shirt, which, to their fury, they could not pierce.

Meanwhile, in spite of his terror, Wolfdietrich was looking eagerly about him for some weapon with which to defend himself. Suddenly he saw Ortnit's ring and his sword Rosen. In a moment he seized the treasures, and thus equipped he fell on his foes to such good purpose that he slew every one of the dragons. He then cut out their tongues, which he packed in a bag brought to him from Alberich by the dwarfs, and triumphantly he' rode off to find Liebgart and tell her of his success. Then as he went yet another misfortune fell upon him, for he lost his way in the forest. It was thus several days before he reached the town where the princess dwelt. As he rode through the gates his joy was turned to indignation, for he heard that Liebgart was about to marry a knight by the name of Gerhart, who had slain the dragon, brought home its head, and claimed the

132

fulfilment of an old promise that she would marry her husband's avenger. Indignant at this base deception, Wolfdietrich spurred onward, and entered the castle in hot haste. Here he denounced the imposter Gerhart, and proved the truth of his assertions by producing the tongues of the dragons. Then, turning to the queen, he stretched out his hand to her, and humbly asked her if she would marry him. At that moment Liebgart saw Ortnit's ring glittering on his finger, and, remembering her husband's last words, she immediately signified her consent.

Marriage of Wolfdietrich and Liebgart

Thus a whole year went by, which the happy couple spent in restoring order, peace, and prosperity to the Lombards. Then, bidding his dear wife a loving farewell, Wolfdietrich set off at last to succour the companions whom he had neglected so long. Landing with his army near Constantinople, he disguised himself as a peasant and made his way into the city. Here he learned that Berchther and his sons had been put into prison, where the former had died. The others, however, were still languishing in captivity, and looking in vain for a deliverer. Dismayed at the sad fate of his old comrades, Wolfdietrich bribed the gaoler to bear them a cheering message and strengthening food, after which he led his army against Sabene, whom he utterly routed.

In this way Wolfdietrich recovered possession of Constantinople, from which foul slanders had driven him forth. Yet in spite of the base behaviour of his brothers, who had believed all the evil reports they had heard, he showed great magnanimity of heart by the ready forgiveness which he granted them both.

His next thought was to behead Sabene and liberate the sons of brave Berchther These things he did, and then returned to Lombardy, whence he set out with Liebgart to Romaburg (Rome), where he was duly crowned emperor.

Nor did Wolfdietrich in his prosperity forget to reward his old followers. To Herbrand, Berchther's eldest son, he gave the city of Garden and all its territories. Later this realm was inherited by Herbrand's son, Hildebrand, a hero whom we shall have further occasion to describe.

Hache, another of Berchther's sons, received as his share all the Rhine land, which he left to his heir, the trusty Eckhardt (Eckewart), who ever and anon appears in Northern literature to win mortals back to virtue and point out the road to honour. As for Wolfdietrich and Liebgart, they became the happy parents of a son whom they called Hugdietrich, after his grandfather. This king's second son, Dietmar, was the father of the famous Dietrich von Bern, the hero of the next chapter of this volume.

CHAPTER VII : DIETRICH VON BERN

The Parentage of Dietrich

DIETRICH VON BERN, whose name is spelt in eighty-five different ways in the various ballads and stories written about him, has been identified with the historical Theodoric of Verona, whose " name was chosen by the poets of the early Middle Ages as the string upon which the pearls of their fantastic imagination were to be strung."

This hero is one of the principal characters in the ancient German "Book of Heroes." His adventures are recorded in many ancient manuscripts, but more especially in the Wilkina saga.

According to most authorities, Dietrich was the son of Dietmar, who was himself the second son of Hugdietrich. Other accounts of the parentage of Dietmar are also to be found, but it is generally accepted that he was the son of Hugdietrich. Be this as it may, in due time Dietmar became the independent ruler of Bern, or Verona. No doubt his high position puffed up his pride, for on his accession he refused to recognise his elder brother, Ermenrich, Emperor of the West, as his liege lord. The young prince had married Odilia, the heiress of the conquered Duke of Verona, who bore him a son called Dietrich. Gentle and generous when all went according to his wishes, this child was uncontrollable when his anger was roused. So terrible, indeed, was the breath which then came from his lips that it became literally a fiery torrent, scorching his opponent, and consuming all that it touched. For this reason there were few who dared to provoke this fearful wrath.

When Dietrich was but five years of age his training was entrusted to Hildebrand, son of Herbrand, one of the Volsung race ; and so well did the tutor acquit himself of this task that he soon made his pupil as accomplished a warrior as himself. Their tastes were, moreover, so similar that they speedily became inseparable friends, and their attachment has become as proverbial among Northern nations as that of David and Jonathan, Damon and Pythias, or Orestes and Pylades.

One day there came news that a giant named Grim, and Hilde, his wife, were committing great depredations in a remote part of the territories belonging to Dietmar, nor had any as yet been found strong enough to overthrow the ferocious pair. Gripping his sword in his firm right hand, Dietrich declared he would be the one to slay them. Hildebrand nodded approval, and instantly the two were off on their way to find the giants. Their path lay through a darksome forest, where before very long they became aware of the presence of a tiny dwarf. This was Alberich, otherwise known as Alferich, Alpris, or Elbegast. Pouncing upon him, the two held him fast, vowing never to let him go till he had pointed out to them the secret place in which the giants lurked.

Seeing that resistance was useless, the dwarf hastened to tell them all that they wanted. Then he showed his eager desire to help them by giving Dietrich the magic sword Nagelring, which alone could pierce the skin of the giants. After this he led both the heroes to the cave where Grim and Hilde were gloating over a magic helmet which they had made and called Hildegrim. Peering through a fissure of the rock, Hildebrand was the first to catch a glimpse of the foe. The sight heated his blood, and in his eagerness to make the attack he braced his shoulder against the huge mass of stone, and, forcing it apart, thus made a passage for himself and his impetuous young pupil.

No sooner did Grim see the sword that Dietrich was

bearing than he recognised it as the blade which had been stolen from him. Snatching a blazing brand from the fire, he rushed with it against the prince ; but his strength could not prevail against the cunning of Nagelring, and after a brief but fierce encounter he succumbed to its magic strokes.

Meantime Hildebrand had been attacked by Hilde, and Dietrich was only just in time to save his master from the blade which the giantess sought to plunge into his heart. With a single stroke of Nagelring, Dietrich cut her in two, but in a trice, to his utter amazement, the severed portions of her huge body knit together and Hilde promptly renewed the combat. Another stroke, however, and again the giantess lay in halves upon the floor. Dietrich was now prepared to meet the magic, and remembering the power of steel to counteract such arts, he laid his blade between the severed parts of the body, and so left it until all power to unite was gone and Hilde lay dead. Glowing with pride and satisfaction the two heroes then returned home, bearing in triumph the two famous trophies, Nagelring and Hildegrim. These Dietrich took as his share of the spoil, leaving to Hildebrand an immense treasure of gold, which made him the richest man of his day. This wealth enabled Hildebrand to marry the noble Ute (Uote, or Uta), who helped her husband to bring up his young brother, who was then but a babe.

But although the young prince of Bern imagined in his excitement that he had exterminated all the giants in his land, he was quickly undeceived. For Sigenot, Grim's brother, coming down from the Alps to visit the giant, found him slain, and vowed to avenge his death. Then the brave prince, hearing that Sigenot was terrorising all the neighbourhood, immediately set out to attack him, followed at a distance by

Hildebrand and the latter's nephew, Wolfhart, who was always ready to undertake any journey, provided there was some prospect of a fight at the end.

Hastening on his way, Dietrich presently came to a forest. Here, feeling hungry, he slew an elk, and proceeded to roast some of its flesh upon a spit. While he was thus engaged he heard shrill cries, and looking up he saw a giant brandishing a dwarf, whom he was about to devour. Ever ready to succour the feeble or the oppressed, Dietrich caught up his sword and attacked the ruffian, who made a brave but fruitless defence. The dwarf, seeing his tormentor dead, then advised Dietrich to fly in haste, lest Sigenot, the most terrible of all the mountain giants, should come to avenge his companion's murder. But instead of following this advice Dietrich persuaded the dwarf to show him the way to the giant's retreat.

Capture of Dietrich by the Giant Sigenot

Following his tiny guide, Dietrich climbed up the snow-clad mountains, where, in the midst of the icebergs, the ice-queen, Virginal, suddenly appeared to him. She too advised him to retreat, as his venture was perilous in the extreme. Equally undeterred by this second warning, Dietrich pressed on. But when he came at last to the giant's abode he was so exhausted by the ascent that, in spite of all his courage, he was defeated, put in chains, and dragged into the den of his enemy. Here he remained in deep gloom and misery, turning over in his mind plan after plan for revenge.

Meanwhile Hildebrand, who had followed his pupil as far as the foot of the mountain, waited in great anxiety throughout eight days. Then, seeing no sign of his lost companion, he concluded that some dire trouble had befallen him. Full of uneasy fear, therefore, he strode quickly up the mountain. The giant, who had watched his approach, no sooner saw him draw near than he went out and fell upon him. With one blow he struck Hildebrand to the ground, after which he dragged his new prisoner within his den. Thinking him senseless, he began leisurely to select chains with which to bind him fast. Hildebrand, however, sprang up noiselessly, seized a weapon that was lying near, and stealing behind a pillar, which served him as a shield, he attacked Sigenot and stretched him lifeless at his feet.

The Rescue of Dietrich

A moment later he heard Dietrich calling to him from the depths of the cave. To spring forward and free his pupil from his chains was the work of a moment. Then, following the dwarf, who openly rejoiced at the death of his foe, the two heroes visited the underground kingdom. There they were hospitably entertained, their wounds were healed, and the king of the dwarfs gave them the finest weapons that they had ever seen.

Thus again the two returned home from an expedition which brought them glory and riches. Shortly after this encounter they were hunting together in the Tyrolian mountains, when Dietrich confided to Hildebrand that he had fallen in love with the ice-fairy, Virginal, and longed to see her again. Scarcely had this confidence left his lips when both knights were startled by the sudden appearance of a dwarf, who presented himself as Bibung, the unconquerable protector of Queen Virginal. In the same breath he bewailed that she had fallen into the hands of the magician Ortgis, who kept her imprisoned in one of her own castles.   Moreover, at every new moon he forced her to surrender one of the snow-maidens, her lovely attendants, whom he kept in prison intending to devour by-and-by.

When Dietrich heard of the unhappy plight of the lady who had won his heart his eyes flashed with anger ; and, bidding the dwarf show him the way, he forthwith set out to rescue her.   They had not gone very far before they beheld the ice-queen's palace, glittering far above their heads.   Then as they climbed eagerly upward to reach it they heard cries of terror, and saw a beautiful girl rush down the pathway, closely pursued by the magician and his mounted train.

Ortgis the Magician

Swift as a flash of lightning Dietrich stood aside while the maiden passed him ; then he stepped boldly into the middle of the path to meet her pursuer. Ortgis the magician made a bold attempt at resistance, but Dietrich and Hildebrand were too strong for him, and ultimately they succeeded in slaying him and all his men.   Jambas, the son of Ortgis, alone effected his escape.   But Dietrich and his master closely pursued him, took forcible possession of his castle, set the captive snow-maidens free, and fearlessly slew all the monsters which Jambas conjured up to destroy them. Then, resuming their interrupted journey, Dietrich and Hildebrand quickly came face to face with the dwarf Bibung, who had named himself the guardian of the fair ice-queen.   During the fray Bibung had wisely remained in hiding, but now he implored them to hasten forward, as his mistress was besieged by Jambas, who was anxious to secure Virginal and all her maidens ; but above all longed to appropriate the great carbuncle which shone in the queen's crown, for this gem gave the possessor full power over the elements, the mountains, and all who ventured within reach of them.

Thus urged to greater speed, the heroes toiled upward, faster and faster, till they came near to the glittering castle of Jeraspunt. As they approached, the besiegers were on the point of overpowering the garrison and gaining possession of the queen, who stood on the battlements wringing her hands in despair. The moment Dietrich perceived her, he rushed impetuously forward, crying that he had come to save her. He struck right and left, and did such execution with his sword that the mountains shook, the icebergs cracked, and great avalanches rolled down into the abysses, carrying with them the bodies of the slain which Dietrich had hurled down from the drawbridge.

Rescue of the Ice-Queen

Thus it happened that in a very short time the enemy was completely routed, and Dietrich was joyfully welcomed by Virginal. Thereupon he poured out the story of his love for the ice-queen so hotly that the princess, happy in the thought of so great a devotion, consented to forsake her glittering castle and relinquish her sway over the mountains, and follow him down into the green valley. Meanwhile Dietrich was impatient to obtain his bride, so their wedding was straightway celebrated in Jeraspunt, which was all hung in bridal white. The whole scene was one of dazzling splendour, for the ice-queen and her maidens wore misty veils and crowns of glittering diamonds, which sparkled and flashed and lit up the whole scene with fairy-like brilliance. In this way was the marriage celebrated, after which the two set off happily into the fair country that lay at the base of the frowning mountain. Here it may be supposed they lived together with great joy, though it is also true that some ballad-singers tell that the queen soon grew homesick down in the green valley, and, deserting her hero husband, returned to her palace on the mountain-top, where she still rules supreme.

Heime and Dietrich

Meanwhile the numerous and splendid adventures of Dietrich became the theme of the wandering bards and minstrels, and thus the rumour of his courage came to the ears of Heime, the son of the Northern stud-keeper Studas. Already Heime was distinguished at home for slaying a dragon, and now at the news of the marvellous prowess of Dietrich he longed to match swords with the champion. For this purpose he got from his father the wonderful weapon Blutgang, with which he set out to test Dietrich's courage, vowing that he would serve him for ever if conquered by him.

> " King Tidrick sits intill Bern ;
>   He rooses [boasts] him of his might ;
> Sae mony has he in battle cow'd,
>   Baith kemp [rough] and doughty knight."
>   *The Ettin Langshanks (Jamieson's tr.).*

Soon Heime reached Bern, where he lost no time in boldly challenging Dietrich. Delighted to find so brave an opponent, Dietrich entered with zest into the match, and speedily overthrew the stranger. Whereupon Heime kept his vow and entered his service. His first good office was to procure for his master the matchless steed Falke, which could carry even Dietrich without showing signs of fatigue. Mounted on this, Dietrich rode up and down the country for many a year, performing many wonderful exploits.

Wittich

By-and-by the rumour of Dietrich's courage also came to Heligoland, where Wieland (Wayland, or Völund), the smith, dwelt with his son Wittich (Witig). Then the latter, determined to try his strength against the hero of Bern, persuaded his father to give him the celebrated sword Mimung, by the help of which he hoped to overcome every foe. Wieland also fashioned a complete suit of armour for his son, gave him much good advice, and parted from him, bidding him prove himself worthy of his ancestors. He also advised him to beseech the help of his grandmother, the mermaid Wachilde, if he were ever in great distress.

Thus instructed, Wittich departed, and on the way to Bern fell in with Hildebrand, Heime, and Hornbogi, another of Dietrich's noted warriors. Perceiving that the stranger was bound on some great errand, the three concealed their names and encouraged their companion to talk. By these means they very quickly learned both where he was going and for what purpose. Then Hildebrand, hearing of the magic sword, and anxious to preserve his pupil from its blows, allowed Wittich to fight single-handed against twelve robbers in a mountain pass. The affair turned out as he had anticipated, for the youth disposed of them all without receiving a scratch. Seeing this, Hildebrand watched for an opportunity, and at last contrived one night, while Wittich was peacefully sleeping at an inn, to substitute his own sword-blade for that which the latter owned. This exchange remained unnoticed until Wittich arrived in Bern. There, while fighting with Dietrich, the blade suddenly snapped in two.

Angry at the way the weapon had played him false, Wittich loudly reproached his father for having provided him with such an unreliable weapon. Then

143

he turned to Hildebrand, intending to announce himself conquered. But when Hildebrand saw what had happened he realised that he had not acted honourably, and handed him back his own blade. A second encounter then followed, in which Dietrich, to his surprise and dismay, found himself conquered.

Full of chagrin, he yet acknowledged readily that he owed his life only to the mercy of Wittich. Then the Northern hero, not to be outdone in magnanimity, confessed in his turn that had it not been for his magic sword he would have been obliged to yield to Dietrich ; after which he voluntarily offered his services to him. Dietrich gladly accepted the offer, and Wittich became one of his most trusted knights.

> " Sae gladly rode they back to Bern ;
> But Tidrick maist was glad ;
> And Vidrich o' his menyie a'
> The foremost place aye had."
> *The Ettin Langshanks (Jamieson's tr.).*

The next adventure of Dietrich, which is recorded in the " Eckenlied," was with the giant Ecke, who held Bolfriana, the widowed Lady of Drachenfels, and her nine daughters in his power. In this encounter the hero of Bern came upon the giant by night. The danger of combating with his powerful foe made him wish that the meeting had chanced any time but then ; yet, not choosing to own himself daunted, he prepared to defend himself against the blows of his adversary. He was, however, about to succumb, when his steed, Falke, scenting his danger, broke loose from the tree to which it had been tied, and, rushing upon Ecke, trampled him to death.

Full of gratitude to his faithful steed, Dietrich now rode on to Drachenfels, where he encountered Fasolt, Ecke's brother. Him he also defeated, and thus delivering the captive ladies he went back to Bern, where Fasolt joined his chosen warriors. Yet this was not the end of all the exploits he achieved. For he went to the rescue of the knight Sintram, whom he saved from the jaws of a dragon, and made him one of his followers. Then, having appropriated Ecke's sword, the great Eckesax, Dietrich was about to give Nagelring to Heime. His resolve was, however, changed on hearing that the latter had stood idly by while Wittich fought single-handed against twelve robbers. Without waiting to hear any more, therefore, Dietrich indignantly banished him from his presence, bidding him never return until he had atoned for his dishonourable conduct by some generous deed.

Incensed at this dismissal, Heime sulkily withdrew to the Falster wood, on the banks of the Wisara, or Weser. Here he became chief of a body of brigands, who ruthlessly pillaged travellers, and by their ill-gotten spoil thus daily increased the hoard which their chief was piling up in one of his strongholds.

But although Dietrich thus lost one of his bravest warriors his band was presently reinforced by Hilde-brand's brother Ilsan, a man who had devoted himself to the life of a monk, but whose great strength and daring made him much more fitted for the battlefield than the cloister. There also came later to Bern to join his forces Wildeber (Wild Boar), a man noted for his immense strength, which he owed to a golden bracelet given him by a mermaid in order to recover her swan plumage, which he had secured.

Thus when Dietrich looked round upon his men he might well be proud of the brave show they made, for nowhere in the country could there be found knights of greater stature or daring.

Together they all set out one bright morning for

Rome to visit Ermenrich, who was uncle to Dietrich. On the way they fell in with Dietlieb the Dane, who willingly offered himself as an escort. His services were accepted, and with his company thus augmented Dietrich proceeded till at last Rome was reached. Here Dietlieb found to his disgust that though ample preparation had been made for Dietrich, yet his suite was but scantily provided for. This by no means pleased the Dane, who was fond of the good things of life. To secure these, therefore, he gave in pledge not only his own horse and weapons, but also those belonging to his leader and to Hildebrand. In this way he was enabled to live luxuriously in Rome, and for the time being all went well.

But when the time of departure came, and Dietrich called for his steed, Dietlieb was forced to confess what he had done. Then the story came to Ermenrich's ears, and he felt called upon to pay the required sum to release the weapons and steeds of his two guests. Angry at the trick, he contemptuously inquired whether Dietlieb were good at anything besides eating and drinking, wherein he evidently excelled. Enraged by this taunt, Dietlieb challenged the champion warrior at Rome, Walther von Wasgenstein (Vosges), and beat him at spear- and stone-throwing. He next performed feats hitherto unheard of, and won such applause that, quite appeased by his gallant deeds, Ermenrich not only paid all his debts, but also gave him a large sum of money. But no sooner did Dietlieb receive this money than, with his usual extravagance, he immediately spent it all in feasting the men-at-arms.

When at last he left the court he was followed by Isung, the imperial minstrel, whose heart had been won by the careless gaiety of the fickle youth. From Rome Dietlieb journeyed to the court of Etzel (Attila), King

of the Huns. Afraid to place too much reliance on
the good services of a knight who was known to flit
from court to court, yet not daring to incur displeasure
by refusing his help altogether, Etzel gave the province
of Styria into the hands of the newcomer, and bade him
defend it against all invasion.

The Dwarf Laurin

For a time Dietlieb held to his work ; then he returned in sorrow to his old master, for his only sister,
Kunhild (Similde, or Similt), had been carried away by
Laurin (Alberich), king of the dwarfs, and was now
detained prisoner in the Tyrolian mountains, not far
from the vaunted Rose Garden. This latter place
was surrounded by a silken thread, and guarded most
jealously by Laurin himself, who exacted the left foot
and right hand of any knight who ventured to enter his
garden or break off a single flower from its stem.

Immediately Dietrich heard the sad story he promised
to set out and rescue the fair Kunhild, and took with
him as companions Dietlieb, Hildebrand, Wittich, and
Wolfhart. Then as they came to the Rose Garden the
wrath of the heroes got the better of them, and they all,
save Dietrich and Hildebrand, after breaking the silken
cord, proceeded to trample on the dainty blossoms.

> " Wittich, the mighty champion, trod the roses to the ground,
> Broke down the gates, and ravaged the garden far renowned ;
> Gone was the portal's splendour, by the heroes bold destroyed ;
> The fragrance of the flowers was past, and all the garden's pride."
> *Heldenbuch* (*Weber's tr.*).

Their raid was not unobserved by the dwarf Laurin,
who only waited to seize his weapons before going out
to the attack. In spite of his insignificant stature, the
dwarf was an opponent to be dreaded. Round his
waist he wore a glittering girdle which gave him the

power of twelve men, and in his hand he brandished a sword which had been tempered in the blood of dragons and could therefore cut through iron and stone. Besides these, he put on his hand the ring of victory, and pulled over his head Tarnkappe, or Helkappe, the magic cap of darkness. Then, thus prepared, he sallied out to the foe. But he found that this time, in spite of all his equipment, he was no match for the knights.

After a severe struggle Dietrich, who had acted upon Hildebrand's instruction, became possessed not only of the magic cap, but also of the girdle and the ring. Moreover, his anger moved him to use the dwarf so roughly that Laurin fled to Dietlieb for protection, promising to restore Kunhild, unless she preferred to remain with him as his wife.

In Laurin's Palace

This amicable agreement having been made, Laurin led the knights down into his subterranean palace, which was illuminated by carbuncles, diamonds, and other precious stones. Here Kunhild and her attendant maidens, attired with the utmost magnificence, welcomed them hospitably and presided at the banquet.

> " Similt into the palace came, with her little maidens all ;
> Garments they wore which glittered brightly in the hall,
> Of fur and costly ciclatoun, and brooches of the gold ;
> No richer guise in royal courts might mortal man behold."
> *Heldenbuch* (*Weber's tr.*).

Yet, in spite of his promise, Laurin was not above taking an advantage of his visitors. Spitefully he ordered the wines to be drugged, so that the brave knights soon sank into a stupor. Then Laurin, seeing their helplessness, deprived them of their weapons, bound them fast, and had them conveyed into a large

The Dwarf Laurin

The Huns

prison. Dietlieb was placed in a chamber apart, where, as soon as he recovered his senses, Laurin told him that he and his companions must die on the morrow.

It was not until midnight that Dietrich awoke. Feeling himself bound, his wrath burned hot within him, and his breath grew so fiery that it consumed the ropes with which he was pinioned. Freeing himself, his first thought was for his companions, whom he speedily released. Then, while they were bewailing their lack of weapons, Kunhild stealthily opened the door. Noiselessly she conducted them into the great hall, and bade them resume possession of their arms. To each she then handed a golden ring, of dwarf manufacture, by wearing which they would be able to see their tiny foes, who were else invisible to all of mortal birth.

Joined by Dietlieb, who had also been liberated by Kunhild, the knights now roused Laurin and his host of giants and dwarfs. An encounter followed, in which it seemed at first as if the knights would scarcely get the better of their foes, but after some sharp and desperate fighting Laurin's men were at last completely routed. As for Laurin, he was made prisoner and carried in chains to Bern, where Kunhild, now full of compassion for him, prevailed upon Dietrich to set him free, provided he would forswear all his malicious propensities and spend the remainder of his life in doing good.

When this promise had been given Laurin was at once set at liberty, whereupon he persuaded the gentle Kunhild, with whom he was deeply in love, to consent to marry him. The ceremony quickly took place, after which the dwarf king and his new queen went to live in the underground palace in the beautiful Rose Garden, which peasants and simple-hearted Alpine hunters have often seen, but which the worldly wise and sceptical have always sought in vain.

The Rose Garden at Worms

The mere fact of having come off victor in one Rose Garden affair made Dietrich hail with joy the tidings brought by a wandering minstrel that at Worms, on the Rhine, Kriemhild, the Burgundian princess, had a similar garden. This was guarded by twelve brave knights, ever ready to try their skill against an equal number of warriors, the prize of the victor being a rose garland and a kiss from the lips of the princess who owned the bower.

Eager to accept this challenge, Dietrich selected Hildebrand, Wittich, Wolfhart, and five other brave men. Then as he could think of no others worthy to share in the adventure, Hildebrand suggested that Rüdiger of Bechlaren, Dietlieb of Steiermark, and his own brother, the monk Ilsan, would be only too glad to help them. This little band rode boldly into Worms, where Dietrich and his men covered themselves with glory by defeating all Kriemhild's champions, and so winning the promised reward.

The Folly of Ilsan

The jocular monk Ilsan was the only one of the company who found the undertaking an occasion for ribaldry. So little did he care for the lovely wreath that had been his reward that he carried the roses back to the monastery, where he pressed them down upon the monks' bald pates, laughing aloud when he saw them wince as the sharp thorns pierced them.

On his way home Dietrich visited Etzel, King of the Huns, and further increased his train by accepting the services of Amalung, Hornbogi's son, and of Herbrand, the great traveller. On his arrival at Bern he found that his father, Dietmar, was dead, and thus he himself became King of Italy, or the Amaling land.

Campaign against the Wilkina Land

Shortly after his accession to the throne he went to help Etzel, who was warring against Osantrix, King of the Wilkina land, now known as Norway and Sweden. With none but his own followers, the knight boldly rode to the seat of war, and throughout the glorious campaign that followed old Hildebrand rode ever ahead, bearing aloft his master's standard, and dealing many memorable blows.

In one of these encounters Wittich was thrown from his horse and stunned, upon which Heime, who had joined the army, taking him for dead, snatched the sword Mimung out of his nerveless grasp and bore it triumphantly away. Wittich, however, was only in a swoon, from which he by-and-by recovered, only to find himself made prisoner by Hertnit, Earl of Greece, Osantrix's brother, who carried him back to the capital, where he put him in prison.

When the campaign against the Wilkina men was ended, Dietrich and his army returned to Bern, leaving Wildeber in Hungary to ascertain whether Wittich were really dead, or whether some dire trouble had befallen him from which he might be rescued by his comrades.

Left to follow out his own plan of attack, Wildeber resolved to make use of strategy. Therefore he slew and flayed a bear, and donned its skin over his armour. Thus disguised, he bade the minstrel Isung lead him to Hertnit's court.

Wittich Rescued by Wildeber

This cunning plan was carried out successfully, and when the minstrel and dancing bear appeared before the court they were hailed with joy. The deception appeared to rouse no suspicion, and the two conspirators were beginning to feel confident, when to Isung's dismay Hertnit insisted upon baiting his hunting hounds against the bear. Nevertheless, so well did Wildeber play his part that he strangled them all, one after another, without seeming to feel their sharp teeth. Furious at the loss of all his pack, Hertnit sprang down into the pit with drawn sword ; but all his blows glanced aside on the armour concealed beneath the rough skin. Meanwhile Wildeber was only watching for an opportunity. Suddenly the pretended bear stood up, caught the weapon which the king had dropped, and struck off his head. Then, joining Isung, he rushed through the palace and delivered the captive Wittich. Whereupon, before any could be found to stop them, they all three rode out of the city, having first seized swords and steeds from the terrified citizens.

The Return to Bern

Their reappearance in Bern was the signal for great rejoicing. Warmly Dietrich welcomed them back and praised Wildeber for his clever scheme. Then, upon the suggestion of Dietrich, Heime returned to Wittich the sword Mimung, which he had taken when its real owner lay apparently dead. This act was loudly applauded, and words of kindness and good-fellowship passed between the two knights. The brave warriors were not long allowed to remain inactive, however, for they were asked to help Ermenrich against his revolted vassal Rimstein. Willingly assenting, they besieged the recalcitrant knight in his stronghold of Gerimsburg, which was given to Walther von Wasgenstein, while Wittich was rewarded for his services by the hand of Bolfriana, the Lady of Drachenfels, and thus became the vassal of Ermenrich.

SIBICH

The estates of Ermenrich were so extensive and so difficult to govern that he was very glad indeed to secure as his chief adviser a capable nobleman named Sibich. This Sibich had a remarkably beautiful wife, whom unfortunately the emperor had once insulted during her husband's absence. As soon as Sibich returned from his journey his wife told him all that had occurred, and the emperor's conduct so enraged the minister that he vowed that he would take a terrible revenge.

The better to accomplish his purpose, Sibich concealed his resentment, and so artfully poisoned Ermenich's mind that the latter ordered his eldest son to be slain. Yet even this did not satisfy the cruel mind of the angry courtier. He resolved to get rid of the second prince also. To accomplish this he therefore induced him to embark in a leaky vessel, which sank when he was out at sea. Thus were two of the princes done to death. Yet, still unsatisfied with the result of his cruelty, Sibich cast round for some reason for getting rid of the third son, Randwer. His opportunity came when he noticed the prince paying innocent attentions to his fair young stepmother, Swanhild, daughter of Siegfried and Kriemhild, and so maliciously did he distort the affair that Ermenrich ordered the prince to be hanged, and his own young wife trampled to death under the hoofs of wild horses.

In this way the wicked Sibich deprived the emperor of both wife and children. His next step was to set about removing from him all others of his kin, so that he might eventually murder the sovereign and take undisputed possession of the empire. With this purpose in view he forged letters which incited the emperor to war against his nephews, the Harlungs. These two young men, who were orphans, dwelt at Breisach, under the guardianship of their tutor, the faithful Eckhardt. During the struggle which followed both of the princes were cruelly slain, and the disconsolate tutor fled to the court of Dietrich, little thinking that Ermenrich would soon turn upon this his last male relative also.

Herbart and Hilde

Meanwhile Dietrich, having been forsaken by Virginal, was anxious to marry again. He therefore sent his nephew Herbart to Arthur's court in the Bertanga land, or Britain, to sue for the hand of Hilde, his fair young daughter. But the idea of sending his child so far away was displeasing to Arthur, and he would not at first permit the young ambassador to catch a glimpse of her face. The strictest measures were taken to prevent his orders from being disobeyed, so that even when the princess was going to church she was guarded by no less than ten warriors, ten monks, and ten duennas. Yet in spite of all these safeguards Herbart was ingenious enough to succeed in seeing the princess. One glance only was enough to show that she was very beautiful, wherefore he lost no time in begging for an interview. This was at last granted, and so Herbart stood before the fair princess. Full of eagerness, he pleaded his master's cause, urging his goodness, his bravery, his renown as inducements to favour his suit. But Hilde was not to be won so easily. She put question after question to Herbart, and at last ended by asking for a portrait of Dietrich. Putting his hand in his pocket, the messenger drew out a picture, which he humbly handed to Hilde. But the princess, being hard to please, cast but one glance upon the face of the portrait before she declared that she would never marry a man who had so little in the way of good looks. Then, turning to Herbart, she looked at him so amorously that he was emboldened

154

to give voice to his own love for her. This time the princess listened graciously, and so successfully did Herbart carry on his wooing that eventually the two fled together from Arthur's court.

Dietrich in Exile

Meanwhile Dietrich had scanty time for mourning the loss of his expected bride, for the imperial army suddenly marched into the Amaling land, and invested the cities of Garden, Milan, Raben (Ravenna), and Mantua. Dietrich was naturally greatly alarmed at the rapidity and ease with which the enemy secured his strongholds, and he guessed there must have been treachery at work. Nor was he mistaken in his supposition, as he very soon after discovered. Nevertheless, for the moment his affairs stood in a sorry plight, and to obtain the release of Hildebrand and a few other faithful followers, who had fallen into the enemy's hands, he was forced to surrender Bern and himself go off into exile.

The humiliation of his banishment was rendered more tolerable by the eagerness with which his followers accompanied him. But indeed they might well do so, since Dietrich had relinquished his very kingdom to obtain their freedom. Together they went to Susat, where they were warmly welcomed by Etzel and Helche (Herka), his wife, who promised to care for Diether, the brother of Dietrich, and have him brought up with her own sons.

There were in those days not a few foreigners at Etzel's court, for he had secured many hostages. Among these were Hagen of Tronje, from the Burgundians ; the Princess Hildegunde, from the Franks ; and Walther von Wasgenstein, from the Duke of Aquitaine.

Walther of Aquitaine and Hildegunde

During the twenty years which Dietrich now spent in the land of the Huns fighting for Etzel, peace was concluded with Burgundy, and Hagen was allowed to return home. Walther of Aquitaine (or von Wasgenstein), whose adventures are related in a Latin poem of the eighth or ninth century, had fallen in love with Hildegunde. Seeing that Etzel, in spite of his promises to set them both free, had no real intention of doing so, he and his lady cleverly effected their escape, and fled to the Wasgenstein, or Vosges, where they paused in a cave to recruit their exhausted strength.

Then Gunther, King of Burgundy, and Hagen of Tronje, his ally, hearing that Walther and Hildegunde were in the neighbourhood, and desirous of obtaining the large sum of gold which they had carried away from Etzel's court, set out to attack them with a force of twelve picked men. But Hildegunde, who was watching while Walther slept, saw them draw near, and quickly gave her lover the alarm. Infuriated at the mere thought of losing his bride, Walther attacked his foe with such irresistible fury that at length all lay dead except Gunther and Hagen. Then these two knights, seeing that all hope was gone, saved themselves by flight.

They did not dare, however, to return to Worms, but lay in ambush beside the road. Then when Walther and Hildegunde passed by, all unsuspicious of danger, their enemies rushed out and attacked them with great fury ; yet in spite of the odds against him Walther triumphantly defeated them both, putting out one of Hagen's eyes and cutting off one of Gunther's hands and one of his feet.

The conflict ended, Hildegunde came forward and bound up the wounds of the three combatants. Then,

156

laying aside all hostility, they sat down together to share a meal, over which they found much cause for mirth because of their wounds. The meal being over, they parted amicably and sought their respective homes. Having thus asserted his prowess, Walther took his bride to Aquitaine, where they were joyously welcomed by their relatives, and, after being duly married, they ruled together for many a long year.

In the meantime Dietrich had been engaged in warring against Waldemar, King of Reussen, which comprised both Russia and Poland. In this war he fought on behalf of Etzel, who, however, forsook him in a cowardly way, and left him in a besieged fortress in the midst of the enemy's land with only a handful of men. In spite of all his courage, Dietrich would have been now forced to surrender had not Rüdiger of Bechlaren come to his rescue. By their combined efforts Waldemar was slain, and his son was brought captive to Susat.

Dietrich and Queen Helche

As for Dietrich and his noble prisoner, they were both seriously wounded. Queen Helche herself tenderly cared for the young prince of Ruessen, who was her kinsman, but the unhappy Dietrich lay neglected and alone in a remote part of the palace. Meanwhile the young prince, being cured, took advantage of Etzel's absence to escape, although Helche implored him not to do so, assuring him that when her husband returned she would have to pay for his absence with her life.

In her distress Helche now thought of Dietrich, and went to beseech his help. Ever ready to do all he could for those in distress, Dietrich, though still weak and ill, rose from his couch, pursued the fugitive, overtook and slew him, and brought his head back to her. The Queen of the Huns never forgot that she owed her life to this brave help, and many times afterwards she proved her gratitude to the knight.

Twenty years had passed since Dietrich had left his native land, and now his soul burned to return thither. He therefore made his desire known to the king, who freely granted him permission to go. Then Helche, in her gratitude for all that Dietrich had done, promised him the aid of her sons, Erp and Ortwine, and also a thousand men. This generous behaviour stirred up Etzel so that he too offered his aid. Thus Dietrich marched back to the Amaling land with all his companions, and an army commanded by the two Hun princes and Rüdiger's only son, Nudung.

On its way, the van of the army took Garden and Padauwe (Padua), and with Dietrich at its head made a triumphant entrance into Bern. Then, hearing that Ermenrich was coming against him, Dietrich went to meet him, and fought a terrible battle near Raben in 493. Here the hero of Bern greatly distinguished himself in the fray, until, hearing that Nudung, the two Hun princes, and his young brother, Diether, had all been slain, he became almost insane with grief.

In his fury he wildly pursued Wittich, his former servant and the murderer of Diether, and would have slain him had not the latter saved himself by plunging into the sea. Then as the waters closed above the knight, the swan-maiden Wachilde, his ancestress, took charge of him, and conveyed him to a place of safety. Thus Dietrich won the victory ; yet his heart was heavy within him as he discovered that he had no longer enough men left to maintain himself in his reconquered kingdom. Full of sadness, he turned and mournfully made his way once more to Susat with the bodies of the slain.

HILDEBRAND AND HADUBRAND

The Marriage of Dietrich

During a second sojourn at the court of the Huns Dietrich married Herrat, or Herand, Princess of Transylvania. Three years later Etzel married Kriemhild, the widow of Siegfried.

Now occurred the fall of the brave Nibelung knights, recorded in the " Nibelungenlied." Dietrich, as we have seen, took an active part in the closing act of this tragedy, and joined in the final lament over the bodies of the slain. Ten years after the terrible battle which had taken place at Raben the prince again resolved to make an attempt to recover his kingdom. With this purpose in view he therefore set out, but with very few followers. On his arrival he found that Ermenrich was dead, having been killed by the swords of Swanhild's brothers or by poison secretly administered by the traitor Sibich. The people were glad to see Dietrich again, and joyfully offered him the crown, which he as joyfully accepted.

Hildebrand and Hadubrand

After a time the lost cities were recovered, one by one, till Dietrich held them again as before. During one of these struggles Hildebrand encountered his son Hadubrand, who, having grown up during his absence, failed to recognise him, and thus challenged him to fight. Mighty blows were exchanged between father and son, each of whom in the pauses of the combat anxiously besought the other to reveal his name. It was only when the strength of either was exhausted that Hadubrand revealed who he was, upon which father and son, dropping their bloody swords, embraced with tears.

> " So spake Hadubrand,
> Son of Hildebrand :
> ' Said unto me
> Some of our people,

Shrewd and old,
Gone hence already,
That Hildebrand was my father called,—
I am called Hadubrand.
Erewhile he eastward went,
Escaping from Odoaker,
Thither with Theodoric
And his many men of battle,
Here he left in the land,
Lorn and lonely,
Bride in bower,
Bairn ungrown,
Having no heritage.' "
Song of Hildebrand (*Bayard Taylor's tr.*).

Hildebrand then rejoined his wife, Ute ; and Dietrich, having slain the traitor Sibich, who had made an attempt to usurp the throne, then marched on to Rome, or Romaburg, where he was crowned Emperor of the West, under the name of Theodoric. Some time after his accession Dietrich lost his good wife Herrat, and such deep grief did this cause him that his sorrow endured even till the last day of his life. Yet there are other authorities also who state that before he died he married again, taking as wife Liebgart, widow of Ortnit.

As for Etzel, he met with an unhappy fate. For, having been lured by Aldrian, Hagen's son, into the cave where the Nibelungen hoard was kept, he was locked up there, and died of hunger with his eyes upon the gold he had coveted. His estates then became the property of Dietrich, who thus became undisputed ruler of nearly all the southern part of Europe.

Dietrich and the Coal-black Steed

In his old age Dietrich, weary of life and embittered by its many trials, ceased to take pleasure in anything except the chase. One day while he was bathing in a

The Tomb of Theodoric

The Emperor Charlemagne

DIETRICH AND THE COAL-BLACK STEED

limpid stream his servant came to tell him that there was a fine stag in sight. Immediately the king called for his horse, but for the moment it was not at hand. In his impatience he sprang upon a coal-black steed standing near, and was borne rapidly away.

As fast as possible the servant tried to follow, but he could never overtake his master, who thus disappeared for ever from sight. And, indeed, among the peasants it is commonly averred that the king now leads the Wild Hunt upon the same sable steed, which he is doomed to ride until the Judgment Day.

In spite of this fabulous account, however, the tomb of Theodoric is still to be seen near Verona. Yet history demonstrates the impossibility of the story of Dietrich von Bern, by proving that Theodoric was not born until after the death of Attila, the unmistakable original of the Etzel in the " Heldenbuch."

CHAPTER VIII : CHARLEMAGNE AND HIS PALADINS

The Position of Charlemagne in History

ONE of the favourite heroes of early mediæval literature is Charlemagne, whose name is connected with countless romantic legends of more or less antique origin. The son of Pepin and Bertha the "large-footed," this monarch took up his abode near the Rhine for the purpose of repressing the invasions of the Northern barbarians, whom he hoped to awe into submission, and then gradually induce to accept the teachings of the missionaries he sent to convert them.

Meanwhile the exploits of the sovereign everywhere brought him fame and renown. Especially was this so amongst those who professed Christianity, since the principal warfares in which Charlemagne engaged were waged against the upholders of paganism. Thus he destroyed the Irminsul, razed heathen temples and groves, and abolished the forms of worship sacred to Odin which were practised by the Druids. Besides all this he undertook, at the request of the Pope, to wage war against the Lombards. In this he was at last successful, and so returned home with all the glory of having won a victory for the head of the Romish Church. The conquest was followed up by another successful exploit, this time directed against the Saracens, who had overrun Spain. By this means Charlemagne naturally came to be regarded as the champion of the Christian Church, and as such his name has been handed down in the chronicles of his day.

Moreover, as is commonly the case with a hero of any prominence, all the heroic enterprises of his predecessors were soon attributed to him. Thus when these legends were turned into popular epics, in the tenth and eleventh centuries, he became the principal hero of France. The great deeds of his paladins, Roland, Oliver, Ogier the Dane, Renaud de Montauban, and others, were also the favourite theme of the poets, and in this way they soon became current in every European tongue. One of the oldest versions now extant of the fabulous adventures of Charlemagne is the Latin chronicle, falsely attributed to Bishop Turpin, Charlemagne's prime minister, but which dates in reality from 1095. It contains the mythical account of the battle of Roncesvalles (or the Valley of Thorns), told with infinite repetition and detail, which gives it an appearance of reality.

Chanson de Roland

The real foundation for the story is furnished from a fragment by Einhard, the son-in-law and historian of Charlemagne, who records a partial defeat in the Pyrenees in 777–778, in which encounter Hroudlandus was slain. From this bald statement arose the mediæval "Chanson de Roland," which was still sung at the time of the battle of Hastings. The probable author of the French metrical version is Turoldus ; but the poem, numbering originally four thousand lines, has gradually been lengthened, until now it includes more than forty thousand. There are early French, Latin, German, Italian, English, and Icelandic song versions of the adventures of Roland, and these in the fourteenth and fifteenth centuries were turned into prose, and formed the basis of the "Romans de Chevalerie," which were popular for so many years. Numerous variations can, of course, be noted in these tales, which have been worked over again by the Italian poets Ariosto and Boiardo, and even treated by Buchanan in our day.

It would be impossible to include in this work a

complete synopsis of all the *chansons de gestes* referring to Charlemagne and his paladins. All that can be done is to give an abstract of those that are most notable, together with the legends which are found in them, and that have gradually been woven round those famous names and become connected with certain localities.

Charlemagne and the Angel

Like many other heroes of mythical fame, Charlemagne was not without visions from heaven. One of the most famous of these is that which came to him on the first night he spent within a magnificent palace he had built for himself near the Rhine. Worn out with excitement and toil, the king was sleeping soundly, when suddenly he felt the light touch of an angel's hand. Straining his ears to catch the message, Charlemagne was startled to hear a sweet voice bidding him go forth and steal. Thrice the message was repeated, till, springing from his couch, the king pulled on his armour, and, creeping softly from his palace, he saddled a horse and set off on his strange mission. Still musing over the command, he went on his way till he met an unknown knight, evidently bound on the same errand. Like a flash the king challenged the other, and after a short fight he unhorsed his opponent. On inquiring the name of his antagonist, Charlemagne learned it was Elbegast, or Alberich, the notorious highwayman. Thereupon he promised to let him go free on condition that he would help him to steal something that night.

Charlemagne as a Robber

Quite unsuspicious as to the identity of his antagonist, Elbegast willingly gave the promise. Thus they rode off together, these two, the king and the highwayman, each as famous as the other, though for very different reasons. Guided by his strange companion, who was well versed in the art of marauding, Charlemagne presently arrived within the castle of one of his ministers, and all unseen penetrated into his very bedroom. Here, as he crouched in the dark, he learned that treachery was afoot. For the knight, believing himself alone with his wife, whispered to her a plot to murder the king on the morrow. Patiently biding his time until they were sound asleep, Charlemagne picked up a worthless trifle, and then noiselessly made his way out, and so returned home unseen. Then, on the morrow, profiting by the knowledge thus obtained, he cleverly outwitted the conspirators, whom he restored to favour only after they had solemnly sworn future loyalty. Moreover as a result of this expedition Charlemagne also won another and most vigorous knight. For Elbegast was so delighted with the prowess of the only man who had ever overthrown him that he renounced his practice of highway robbery, and instead entered the service of the emperor.

In gratitude for the heavenly vision vouchsafed him, the emperor then named his new palace Ingelheim, or Home of the Angel, a name which the place has borne ever since. This thieving episode is often alluded to in the later romances of chivalry. Knights called upon to justify their unlawful appropriation of another's goods found it useful to remind the emperor that he too had once gone about as a thief.

Frastrada and the Magic Ring

Fortunate in warfare, Charlemagne was unfortunate at home. For, married three times, his wives died one after the other. Upon this he married a beautiful Eastern princess by the name of Frastrada, who, aided by a magic ring, soon won his most devoted affection.

The new queen, however, did not long enjoy her power, for a dangerous illness soon overtook her. Then as she lay at the point of death, fearful lest her ring should be worn by another while she was buried and forgotten, Frastrada slipped the magic circlet into her mouth just before she breathed her last.

Solemn preparations were made to bury her in the cathedral of Mayence (where a stone bearing her name could still be seen a few years ago), but the emperor refused to part with the beloved body. Neglectful of all matters of state, he remained in the mortuary chamber day after day. His trusty adviser, Turpin, suspecting the presence of some mysterious talisman, slipped into the room while the emperor, exhausted with fasting and weeping, was wrapped in sleep. After carefully searching for the magic jewel, Turpin discovered it at last in the dead queen's mouth.

> " He searches with care, though with tremulous haste,
> For the spell that bewitches the king ;
> And under her tongue, for security placed,
> Its margin with mystical characters traced,
> At length he discovers a ring."
>
> *King Charlemain* (*Southey*).

Turpin's Discovery and Theft

To secure this ring and slip it on his finger was but the affair of a moment. Then just as Turpin was about to leave the room the emperor awoke. With a shuddering glance at the dead queen, Charlemagne flung himself passionately upon the neck of his prime minister, declaring that he would never be quite inconsolable as long as he was near.

Taking advantage of the power thus secured by the possession of the magic ring, Turpin led Charlemagne away and forced him to eat and drink. The funeral was speedily carried out, after which Turpin succeeded in inducing the emperor to resume the reins of government. From this time the king lavished on Turpin so many declarations of endless affection that at last the minister was heartily sick of his position. But ardently though he longed to get rid of the ring, yet he dared neither hide it nor give it away, for fear it should fall into unscrupulous hands. Thus day by day it became a greater and greater burden to him.

Although advanced in years, Turpin was now forced to accompany Charlemagne everywhere, even on his hunting expeditions. At night, too, the devotion of the emperor would not suffer his minister to leave his side ; together they shared a tent. So one night, while the moon shone brightly, the unhappy minister stole noiselessly out of the imperial tent, and wandered alone in the woods, cogitating how to dispose of the unlucky ring. As he walked thus he came to a glade in the forest, and saw a deep pool, on whose mirror-like surface the moonbeams softly played. Suddenly the thought struck him that the waters would soon conceal the magic ring for ever in their depths. Drawing it from his finger, he threw it into the pond with a sigh of relief, after which he retraced his steps, and soon fell asleep. On the morrow he was delighted to perceive that the spell was broken, and that Charlemagne had returned to the old undemonstrative friendship which had bound them for many a year.

> " Overjoy'd, the good prelate remember'd the spell,
>   And far in the lake flung the ring ;
>   The waters closed round it ; and, wondrous to tell,
>   Released from the cursed enchantment of hell,
>   His reason return'd to the king."
>
> *King Charlemain (Southey).*

The Pool in the Forest

But although the priest had escaped from the enthralment of the ring its influence still haunted the emperor.

All that day he was full of restlessness, and wandered about the palace from room to room, unable to fix his attention on any occupation. At last he called for his horse and went out with his men to hunt in the forest. As if by instinct he turned aside in the direction of the little glade wherein lay the pool containing the magic ring. Eagerly the king drew near to the limpid waters; then, flinging himself from his horse, he stretched himself on the ground and declared he was so enchanted with the spot that he would like nothing so much as to pass the rest of his life there. So he lay and mused, while each moment his admiration of his surroundings grew greater and greater. Yet never once did a shadow of suspicion as to the real cause for his sudden infatuation present itself to his mind. Night-time at last forced the emperor to withdraw from the magic pool. Reluctantly he betook himself homewards, declaring loudly that he would have a palace built in the glade that had charmed him so greatly. No sooner had he conceived this idea than he actually had it carried out, and soon a fair palace stood in the place that so shortly before had been only a leafy forest glade. True to his assertion, the emperor spent most of his days here, and thus, according to tradition, the palace became the nucleus of Aix-la-Chapelle.

> " But he built him a palace there close by the bay,
>   And there did he love to remain ;
>   And the traveller who will, may behold at this day
>   A monument still in the ruins at Aix
>   Of the spell that possess'd Charlemain."
>   *King Charlemain (Southey).*

Charlemagne and Bertha

The character of Charlemagne was above all imperious. For this reason he was supremely annoyed when his sister Bertha not only asserted her love for a brave young knight named Milon, but even persisted in marrying him. Rejected by the emperor, and therefore scorned by all, the young couple lived in obscurity and poverty. Yet they were very happy in their love for each other, and cared little that they were ignored by the court. This happiness was further intensified by the birth of a little son, Roland, who even as a baby showed signs of marvellous courage and strength.

Charlemagne and Roland

Numerous stories are told of the way in which Roland first attracted the attention of the great emperor, his uncle. Of these the most popular is that which relates how Milon, attempting to ford a stream, had been carried away and drowned, while his poor half-famished wife at home was thus left to perish of hunger. Seeing the signs of such acute distress around him, the child went boldly to the banqueting-hall near by, where Charlemagne and his lords were feasting. Casting his eyes round for a suitable dish to plunder, Roland caught up a platter of food and fled. His fearless act greatly amused the emperor, who forbade his servants to interfere. Thus the boy carried off his prize in triumph, and soon set it before the startled eyes of his mother.

Excited by the success of his raid, a few minutes later the child re-entered the hall, and with equal coolness laid hands upon the emperor's cup, full of rich wine. Challenged by Charlemagne, the boy then boldly declared that he wanted the meat and wine for his mother, a lady of high degree. In answer to the emperor's bantering questions, he declared that he was his mother's cupbearer, her page, and her gallant knight, which answers so amused Charlemagne that he sent for her. He saw her to be his own sister, and, stricken with remorse, he asked for her forgiveness and treated

169

her with kindness as long as she lived, and took her son into his service.

Another legend relates that Charlemagne, hearing that the robber knight of the Ardennes had a priceless jewel set in his shield, called all his bravest noblemen together, and bade them sally forth separately, with only a page as escort, in quest of the knight. Once found, they were to challenge him in true knightly fashion, and at the point of the lance win the jewel he wore. A day was appointed when, successful or not, the courtiers were to return, and, beginning with the lowest in rank, were to give a truthful account of their adventures while on the quest.

All the knights departed and scoured the forest of the Ardennes, each hoping to meet the robber knight and win the jewel. Among them was Milon, accompanied by his son Roland, a lad of fifteen, whom he had taken as page and armour-bearer. Milon had spent many days in vain search for the knight, when, exhausted by his long ride, he dismounted, removed his heavy armour, and lay down under a tree to sleep, bidding Roland keep close watch during his slumbers.

Roland and the Jewel

For a while Roland watched faithfully ; then, fired by a desire to distinguish himself, he donned his father's armour, sprang on his steed, and rode off into the forest in search of adventures. He had not gone very far when he saw a gigantic horseman coming to meet him, and by the dazzling glitter of a large stone set in his shield he recognised him to be the invincible knight of the Ardennes. Afraid of nothing, however, the lad laid his lance in rest when challenged to fight, and charged so bravely that he unhorsed his opponent. A fearful battle on foot ensued, each striving hard to accomplish the death of the other. But at last the fresh young energy of Roland conquered, and his terrible foe fell to the ground in agony. A minute later his corpse lay stiff on the field, leaving the victory in the hands of Roland.

Hastily wrenching the coveted jewel from the shield of the dead warrior, the boy hid it in his breast. Then, riding rapidly back to his sleeping father, he laid aside the armour and removed all traces of a bloody encounter. Soon after Milon awoke and resumed the quest, when he came upon the body of the dead knight. He was disappointed indeed to find that another had won the jewel, and rode sadly back to court, to be present on the appointed day.

In much pomp Charlemagne ascended his throne amid the deafening sound of trumpets. Then, seating himself, he bade the knights appear before him and relate their adventures. One after another strode up the hall, followed by an armour-bearer holding his shield. Each in turn told of finding the knight slain and the jewel gone. Last of all came Milon. Gloomily he made his way to the throne to repeat the story that had already been told so often. But as he went, there followed behind him, with a radiant face, young Roland, proudly bearing his father's shield, in the centre of which shone the precious jewel. At the sight of this all the nobles started, and whispered to one another that Milon had done the deed. Then when he dismally told how he too had found the knight dead a shout of incredulity greeted him. Turning his head, he saw to his amazement that his own shield bore the dazzling gem. At the sight of it he appeared so amazed that Charlemagne set himself to question Roland, and thus soon learned how it had been obtained. In reward for his bravery in this encounter Roland was knighted and allowed to take his place among the paladins of the emperor. Nor was it long before he further distinguished himself, becoming, to his father's delight, the most renowned of all that famous company.

According to the old *chanson de geste* entitled "Ogier le Danois," Charlemagne once made war against the King of Denmark, and, defeating him, received as hostage his son Ogier, otherwise known as Olger, or Holger, Danske. The young Danish prince was favoured by the fairies from the time of his birth, six of them having appeared to bring him gifts while he was in his cradle. The first five promised him every earthly bliss; while the sixth, Morgana, foretold that he would never die, but would dwell with her in Avalon.

Ogier the Dane

Not long after this the young prince Ogier was thrown into prison at St. Omer, since the King of Denmark had wantonly violated the treaty he had made with the emperor. There he beguiled the weariness of captivity by falling in love with and secretly marrying the governor's daughter Bellissande. Shortly after this Charlemagne, being about to depart for war, and wishing for the hero's help, released him from his captivity. At last the contest was over, and Ogier returned again to France, where he heard that Bellissande had borne him a son, and that, his father having died, he was now the lawful king of Denmark.

This news made him hasten at once to the emperor and beg for permission to return to his native land. As a reward for the gallant service he had rendered Charlemagne graciously granted the request, after which Ogier went back to Denmark, where he spent several years, reigning so wisely that he was adored by all his subjects. Such is the admiration of the Danes for this hero that the common people still declare that he is either in Avalon or sleeping in the vaults of Elsinore, and that he will awaken, like Frederick Barbarossa, to save his country in the time of its direst need.

> " ' Thou know'st it, peasant ! I am not dead ;
> I come back to thee in my glory.
> I am thy faithful helper in need,
> As in Denmark's ancient story.' "
>
> *Holger Danske* (*Ingemann*).

Ogier and Charlemagne

Years went by, and at last Ogier returned to France. This visit was, however, embittered by the behaviour of his son, by this time grown up, who quarrelled with Prince Charlot over a game of chess. The quarrel at last ran so high that, snatching up the chessboard, the prince dealt his opponent such a blow that he died. Ogier, indignant at the murder, and unable to find redress at the hands of Charlemagne, lost control or himself and insulted him grossly, after which he fled to the court of Didier, King of Lombardy, with whom the Franks were then at feud.

The news of the approach of Ogier was very welcome to King Didier. In his eagerness to greet his guest he even mounted to his tower, where he stood anxiously looking for his coming. At last the stranger came in sight, and Didier hastened down to grasp his hand. Full of excitement, he drew Ogier within his palace, and bade him tell him all he knew about the famous emperor Charlemagne.

> " Olger the Dane, and Desiderio,
> King of the Lombards, on a lofty tower
> Stood gazing northward o'er the rolling plains,
> League after league of harvests, to the foot
> Of the snow-crested Alps, and saw approach
> A mighty army, thronging all the roads
> That led into the city. And the King

Said unto Olger, who had passed his youth
As hostage at the court of France, and knew
The Emperor's form and face, ' Is Charlemagne
Among that host ? ' And Olger answered, ' No.' "
Tales of a Wayside Inn (Longfellow).

Faithfully Ogier related all the preparations Charlemagne had been making for his attack on the King of Lombardy, against whom he was even now marching. Then, taking up his post by the king on the tower, the Dane set himself to watch for the approach of the foe. Soon they came within sight, a great array of warriors and their steeds. Shading his eyes with his hand, Ogier pointed them out to his host, mentioning the names of the knights whom he recognised by their arms. Long before the near approach of the army the King of Lombardy was in terror, and would willingly have hidden himself away underground. Still the brave company came on, till at last the figure of Charlemagne himself was to be seen, clad in iron mail and brandishing aloft his invincible sword, Joyeuse. At the sight of the emperor, magnificent in his war equipment, Ogier himself was struck with fear and trembled where he stood.

" This at a single glance Olger the Dane
Saw from the tower ; and, turning to the King,
Exclaimed in haste : ' Behold ! this is the man
You looked for with such eagerness ! ' and then
Fell as one dead at Desiderio's feet."
Tales of a Wayside Inn (Longfellow).

Ogier and the Angel

The struggle that followed was short and decisive. Charlemagne soon overpowered the Lombard king, and assumed the iron crown, while Ogier escaped from the castle in which he was besieged. Shortly after, however, when asleep near a fountain, the Danish hero was surprised by Turpin. Then, on being led before Charlemagne, he obstinately refused all proffers of reconciliation, and insisted upon Charlot's death, until an angel from heaven suddenly appeared, who forbade him to ask any further for the life of Charlemagne's son. Awed by this message from heaven, Ogier gave up his desire for revenge, and became reinstated in the good graces of the emperor, who had a warm affection for his well-tried warrior. After this reconciliation, according to Adenet, Ogier succeeded in overthrowing a famous Saracen giant, and in reward for his services received the hand of Clarice, Princess of England, and so became king of that realm.

Ogier in the East

Weary of a peaceful existence, Ogier finally left England, and journeyed to the East, where he successfully besieged Acre, Babylon, and Jerusalem. On his way back to France the ship was wrecked on the famous lodestone rock which appears in many mediæval romances. Then, all his companions having perished, the king wandered alone on the shore. There he came to an adamantine castle, invisible by day, but radiant at night, where he was received and sumptuously entertained by Papillon, a magic horse far-famed for skill and wisdom. On the morrow a yet more remarkable adventure befell him, for as he wandered across a flowery meadow he encountered Morgana the fay, who gave him a magic ring. Then happened a marvellous thing, for although Ogier was by now a hundred years old he no sooner put this ring on than he became young once more. Overcome with joy at this transformation, he donned the golden crown of oblivion, and straightway forgot all about home. He now joined Arthur, Oberon, Tristan, and Lancelot, with whom he spent two hundred years in unchanged youth, enjoying constant jousting and fighting.

At the end of that time, his crown having accidentally dropped off, Ogier suddenly remembered the past, and instantly returned to France, riding on Papillon. He reached the court during the reign of one of the Capetian kings. He was, of course, greatly amazed at the changes which meanwhile had taken place. But, heroic as ever, he bravely helped to defend Paris against an invasion by the Normans.

Ogier Carried to Avalon

Shortly after this his magic ring was playfully drawn from his finger and put upon her own by the Countess of Senlis, who, before returning it, discovered that it restored her youth, and she longed to wear it for ever. Wherefore she sent thirty champions to wrest it from its owner, who, however, defeated them, and so triumphantly retained his ring.

And now the prophecy that he would never die came to pass. On the death of the King of France Ogier married his widow, and would have ascended the throne, but Morgana the fay in a fit of jealousy spirited him away in the midst of the marriage ceremony and bore him off to the Isle of Avalon, whence he, like Arthur, will return only when his country needs him.

Roland and Oliver

Another *chanson de geste*, a sort of continuation of "Ogier le Danois," is called "Meurvin," and purports to give a faithful account of the adventures of a son of Ogier and Morgana, an ancestor of Godfrey of Bouillon, King of Jerusalem. In "Guérin de Montglave" we find that Charlemagne, having quarrelled with the Duke of Genoa, proposed that each should send a champion to fight in his name. Charlemagne selected Roland, while the Duke of Genoa chose Oliver as his defender. The battle, according to some authorities, took place on an island in the Rhône. Here the two champions closed in fight, and grappled hard with each other. High in the air glittered Durandana, the famous sword of Roland; high in the air glittered Altecler, the weapon of which Oliver boasted. So well matched were the champions and so equal the force of the blows that they dealt that "giving a Roland for an Oliver" has become a proverbial expression.

For a whole day the fight went on, with only intermissions to gain breath and interchange boasts and taunts; yet at the end neither had gained any advantage. Probably the two champions would have continued the struggle indefinitely, however, had not an angel from heaven interfered and bidden them embrace and become fast friends. Meanwhile Charlemagne had so little hope of the victory of Roland, when he saw the strength of Oliver, that he vowed a pilgrimage to Jerusalem should his nephew escape alive.

Charlemagne's Pilgrimage to Jerusalem

This vow was solemnly carried out, as is recorded in "Galyen Rhetoré." Profiting by their disguise, Charlemagne and his peers reached Jerusalem safely, but here their anxiety to secure relics soon betrayed their identity. Thereupon the King of Jerusalem, Hugues, entertained them sumptuously, after which, hoping to hear many praises of his hospitality, he concealed himself in their apartment at night. The eavesdropper, however, only heard the vain talk of Charlemagne's men, who, unable to sleep, beguiled the hours in making extraordinary boasts. Roland declared that he could blow his horn Olivant so loudly that it would bring down the palace ; Ogier, that he could crumble the principal pillar to dust in his grasp ; and Oliver, that he would marry the princess in spite of her father.

The king, angry at hearing no praises of his wealth and hospitality, revealed what he had heard next morning, and insisted upon his guests fulfilling their boasts, under penalty of death. He was satisfied, however, by the news that Oliver had won the heart of the princess, and the marriage ceremony was speedily celebrated. Soon after this the knight returned to France, but for the meantime the princess remained behind with her father instead of going with her husband. In time a little son, Galyen, was born, who when he grew up to manhood joined his father in the valley of Roncesvalles, just in time to receive his blessing ere he died. Then, having helped Charlemagne to avenge the slaughter of his men in the dread Valley of Thorns, Galyen returned to Jerusalem, where he found his grandfather dead and his mother a captive. His first act was, naturally, to free his mother, after which he was crowned King of Jerusalem, and his adventures came to an end.

Charlemagne's Desire for Peace

By this time Charlemagne had gained many conquests and gathered together much wealth. In none of his encounters, however, had riches or glory been his object. At all times he had striven to spread abroad everywhere the one true faith, and to this he had bent all his energies. Therefore, seeing around him on all hands proofs of his mighty work, he resolved to withdraw from combat and pass the rest of his lifetime in meditation, and so remain at peace with all men. Nevertheless his desire was not to be granted, for a heavenly message bade him continue the strife.

THE VISION OF ST. JAMES

The Miracle of the Stars

Thus it happened that one night as he lay in slumber upon his gorgeous couch he found himself suddenly wide awake. Then as he looked up through the casement he beheld a strange marvel in the sky, for behold, the stars stretched in a string right across the heavens ! As the king lay and pondered upon the marvel he saw that one end of the line lay by the Friesian Sea, while the other stretched away through Germany and France into Galicia, where lay the body of St. James. But though Charlemagne thought much and deeply upon the prodigy he could find no explanation.

The Vision of St. James

Again the next night the same marvel was repeated, and again the king lay awake and pondered over it. Then suddenly there appeared in a vision before him the radiant figure of a man, who pointed to the king as he said : " What dost thou, my son ? " Startled by this sudden apparition, the emperor replied : " Who art thou, I pray thee ? " Whereupon the other made answer : " I am James, the Apostle of Jesus Christ, the son of Zebedee and the brother of John, who was sent to preach the Gospel and perished by the sword. Now, behold, my body lies among heathen, where it is treated with villainous scorn ! I marvel, indeed, that, being so great a champion of the Christian faith, thou hast not ere now wrested my land from the grip of the Saracens. Yet now do as God desires : follow the line which the stars show thee and get thee into Spain to deliver my country. Thus shalt thou get yet more glory and overcome more foes. Moreover, do thou also visit that place where my body lies, and raise there a church to my name." On three different occasions

179

the same marvellous vision appeared to the emperor, and on each occasion the words of St. James were the same.

The Campaign in Spain

Therefore, not daring to disobey so definite a command, Charlemagne gathered together his troops and set out for Spain. Here he laid siege to the city of Pamplona, which nevertheless at the end of two months held out as firmly as before. Baffled on every hand, Charlemagne prayed earnestly to heaven, whereupon a great miracle happened, for the walls fell down even as those of ancient Jericho. Free pardon was granted to all those who embraced the Christian faith, but the rest of the inhabitants were put to the sword. Full of gratitude for the help that had been thus vouchsafed to him, Charlemagne pushed on to the tomb of St. James at Compostela to pay his devotions at the shrine. From thence he resumed his march to Petronium, where he stuck his spear in the ground, since for the time he could go no further. Meanwhile great crowds flocked round the good Bishop Turpin, who willingly administered baptism to all who desired it.

Thus Charlemagne at last prepared to return from the campaign, full of renown, having captured thirty cities in all.

The Idol with the Key

Following up his conquests, Charlemagne afterwards proceeded still further into the country across Europe, till he reached Arabia, where he resolved to strike a fatal blow at the faith of the Saracens. For here, in the city of Salancadys, was a famous idol, said to have been made by Mohammed during his lifetime, and the Prophet had enclosed within it certain demons, so that no one could destroy it, nor could any Christian approach it without being bereft of life. Meanwhile those of the Saracen faith who drew near for purposes of adoration remained unhurt, though the power of the demons was so great that did a bird but perch upon the image it fell lifeless to the ground. This marvellous idol stood upon a gigantic stone pillar, richly carved with many a strange device. The image itself was like the figure of a man, standing upright, with its face turned to the south, and holding in its right hand a key. This, the Saracens maintained, was a sign that one day a King of France should be born who would come to attack the country on behalf of the Christian faith. The time of his approach would be readily discerned, for before he drew near the city the key would drop from the hand of the idol as a sign that the heathen rule was over. This was the city upon which Charlemagne now made ready for an attack. Then as he came near it happened even as had been foretold, for the key fell to the ground with an ominous clang. Terrified at the miracle, the inhabitants hastily gathered up their gold and silver and treasures of every kind and rushed out of the city, not daring to await the coming of so powerful a conqueror. By-and-by Charlemagne reached the walls, to find the town deserted and the gates open. Thus it came to pass even as it had been prophesied, and without a blow the standard of the Christian faith was raised on high.

War against Aigolandus

A triumphant march through the country then ensued, and Charlemagne returned to France, thinking the Saracens subdued. He had scarcely crossed the border, however, when Aigolandus, one of the pagan monarchs, revolted, and soon recovered nearly all the territory his people had lost. These tidings filled Charlemagne with alarm, and he straightway sent back an army, commanded by Milon, Roland's father, who perished gloriously in the campaign. The emperor himself then speedily followed his brother-in-law with great forces, and again besieged Aigolandus in Pamplona. An attempt to make peace was mooted, and the two monarchs met in conference.

But nothing resulted from their meeting, and hostilities went on as before. Several severe encounters followed, in which many knights won for themselves honour and renown. Foremost among these was Roland, whose fame grew daily greater.

> " On stubborn foes he vengeance wreak'd,
>   And laid about him like a Tartar ;
> But if for mercy once they squeak'd,
>   He was the first to grant them quarter
> The battle won, of Roland's soul
>   Each milder virtue took possession ;
> To vanquish'd foes he o'er a bowl
>   His heart surrender'd at discretion."
>   *Orlando Furioso* (*Ariosto*) (*Dr. Burney's tr.*).

At last the war was brought to a close by the death of Aigolandus, after which Charlemagne carried the war into Navarre, where he was challenged by the giant Ferracute, or Ferragus, to meet him in single combat. Although the metrical " Romances " describe Charlemagne as twenty feet in height, and declare that he slept in a hall, his bed surrounded by a hundred lighted tapers and a hundred knights with drawn swords, the emperor felt himself no match for the giant, of whose powers it was said :

> " So hard he was to-fond [proved],
>   That no dint of brond
>   No grieved him, I plight.
> He had twenty men's strength ;
>   And forty feet of length
>   Thilke [each] paynim had ;

And four feet in the face
Y-meten [measured] on the place ;
And fifteen in brede [breadth].
His nose was a foot and more ;
His brow as bristles wore ;
(He that saw it said)
He looked lothliche [loathly],
And was swart [black] as pitch ;
Of him men might adrede ! "
Roland and Ferragus.

Roland and Ferracute

After convincing himself of the danger of meeting this adversary, Charlemagne sent Ogier the Dane to fight him. With dismay he saw his champion not only unhorsed, but borne away like a parcel under the giant's arm, fuming and kicking with impotent rage. On the next day Renaud de Montauban met Ferracute, with the same fate. Several other knights next volunteered, but they one and all met in turn with the same ignominious treatment. Finally Roland took the field, and although the giant pulled him down from his horse he continued the battle all day. Next morning the contest was renewed, and in the meantime, seeing that his sword Durandana had no effect upon Ferracute, Roland armed himself with a club.

In the pauses of the battle the combatants talked together, and Ferracute, relying upon his adversary's keen sense of honour, even laid his head upon Roland's knee during their noonday rest. While resting thus he revealed that he was vulnerable in only one point of his body. When called upon by Roland to believe in Christianity he declared that he could never accept the doctrine of the Trinity.

Roland Expounds the Christian Faith

Roland, in answer, demonstrated that an almond is but one fruit, although composed of rind, shell, and

183

kernel ; that a harp is but one instrument, although it consists of wood, strings, and harmony ; while the very sun has a threefold nature in heat, light, and splendour. These arguments having satisfied Ferracute concerning the Trinity, he removed his doubts concerning the Incarnation by equally forcible reasoning. The giant, however, utterly refused to believe in the Resurrection, although Roland, in support of his creed, quoted the mediæval belief that a lion's cubs are born into the world dead, but come to life on the third day at the sound of their father's roar, or under the warm breath of their mother. But Ferracute would by no means accept this doctrine ; therefore he sprang to his feet and proposed a continuation of the fight, and so the struggle was renewed.

> "Quath Ferragus : 'Now ich wot
> Your Christian law every grot ;
> Now we will fight ;
> Whether law better be,
> Soon we shall y-see,
> Long ere it be night.'"
>
> *Roland and Ferragus.*

Death of Ferracute

In this encounter Roland, weary with his previous efforts, almost succumbed beneath the giant's blows, and in his distress he had recourse to prayer. He was immediately strengthened and comforted by an angelic vision and a promise of victory. Thus encouraged, he dealt Ferracute a deadly blow in the vulnerable spot. The giant fell, calling upon Mohammed as he breathed his last. Full of joy, Roland turned to announce his victory, amid shouts of praise from his comrades.

Sir Otuel

By-and-by, the news of the slaying of Ferracute came to the ears of his nephew, Sir Otuel, who straightway rode after Roland to avenge the death of his uncle. Soon the two knights came together, and a fearful struggle followed, the while Roland by his persuasions endeavoured to win the Saracen to the Christian faith. While Sir Otuel hesitated, in answer to a prayer for its appearance, a snowy dove alighted suddenly on Roland's shield. Upon seeing this marvel the heathen no longer doubted, but declared himself convinced. Whereupon, full of joy, Roland cast down his weapons and warmly grasped his antagonist by the hand, after which Sir Otuel joined the service of Charlemagne, and became one of his most devoted followers.

Charlemagne, having thus won Navarre, carried the war to the south of Spain. Here the Saracens gained an advantage by frightening the horses of the enemy by beating drums and waving banners. Having suffered a partial defeat on account of this device, Charlemagne had the horses' ears stopped with wax and their eyes blindfolded before he resumed the battle. Thanks to this precaution, he succeeded in conquering the Saracen army. The whole country had now been again subdued, and Charlemagne was preparing to return to France, when he remembered that Marsiglio, or Marsilius, a Saracen king, was still entrenched at Saragossa.

> " Carle, our most noble Emperor and King,
>   Hath tarried now full seven years in Spain,
>   Conqu'ring the highland regions to the sea ;
>   No fortress stands before him unsubdued,
>   Nor wall, nor city left, to be destroyed,
>   Save Sarraguce, high on a mountain set.
>   There rules the King Marsile, who loves not God,
>   Apollo worships, and Mohammed serves ;
>   Nor can he from his evil doom escape."
>   *Chanson de Roland* (*Rabillon's tr.*).

Battle of Roncesvalles

After some thought the emperor decided to send an embassy to him to arrange the terms of peace. Roland eagerly offered, but he was refused because of his impetuosity. Then, following the advice of Naismes de Bavière, "the Nestor of the Carolingian legends," he selected Ganelon, Roland's stepfather, as ambassador. The choice proved to be an unhappy one ; for Ganelon was a traitor, and accepted a bribe from the Saracen king to betray Roland and the rearguard of the French army into his power. Advised by this knight, Charlemagne departed from Spain at the head of his army, leaving Roland to bring up the rear. The main part of the army passed through the Pyrenees unmolested, but the rearguard of twenty thousand men, under Roland, was attacked by a superior force of Saracens in ambush as it was passing through the defiles of Roncesvalles. There followed a fearful slaughter, which has since been recounted a hundred times in rhyme and prose.

> " The Count Rollànd rides through the battlefield
> And makes, with Durendal's keen blade in hand,
> A mighty carnage of the Saracens.
> Ah ! had you then beheld the valiant Knight
> Heap corse on corse ; blood drenching all the ground ;
> His own arms, hauberk, all besmeared with gore,
> And his good steed from neck to shoulder bleed ! "
>
> *Chanson de Roland* (*Rabillon's tr.*).

Into the gloomy valley rode the brave knights, little suspecting that they would never reissue. Darker and darker grew the twilight as they passed along the narrow pathway, twisting its way among the jagged rocks. Yet still there was nothing but silence around them, nothing to rouse their alarm. But suddenly

186

there rose a cry, and in a flash there sprang out from behind those treacherous, fair-seeming rocks man after man of the enemy, brandishing, as they dashed forward, gleaming swords and glittering daggers. Then began one of the most terrible slaughters that history has ever recorded. Caught unawares, Roland's brave men fell swiftly beneath the rush of the foe. Not without a struggle did they succumb, not without an effort to retort did they sink dying to the ground. But at last the grim work was done, and of all the fair company which had entered the valley in hope none save Roland and one or two followers emerged from that shadow of death. In his savage grief Roland then bound a Saracen captive to a tree, and wrung from him a confession of the dastardly plot. Thus discovering where Marsiglio was to be found, he rushed into the very midst of the Saracen army and slew him. The Saracens, terrified at the apparition of the hero, beat a hasty retreat, little suspecting that their foe had received a mortal wound and would shortly breathe his last.

Towards the close of the battle, yielding to Oliver's entreaty, Roland sounded a blast on his horn Olivant. Fearing lest his nephew was calling for aid, Charlemagne would fain have gone back, had he not been deterred by Ganelon, who assured him that Roland was merely pursuing a stag.

> " Rollànd raised to his lips the olifant,
> Drew a deep breath, and blew with all his force.
> High are the mountains, and from peak to peak
> The sound re-echoes ; thirty leagues away
> 'Twas heard by Carle and all his brave compeers.
> Cried the king : ' Our men make battle ! ' Ganelon
> Retorts in haste : ' If thus another dared
> To speak, we should denounce it as a lie.'
> Aoi."
> *Chanson de Roland* (*Rabillon's tr.*).

Death of Roland

In despair at receiving no help, and both wounded and faint, Roland now slowly dragged himself to the entrance of the pass of Cisaire. Here he took leave of his faithful steed Veillantif, which he slew with his own hand, to prevent it from falling into the hands of the enemy.

"'Ah, nevermore, and nevermore, shall we to battle ride !
Ah, nevermore, and nevermore, shall we sweet comrades be !
And Veillantif, had I the heart to die forgetting thee ?
To leave thy mighty heart to break, in slavery to the foe ?
I had not rested in the grave, if it had ended so.
Ah, never shall we conquering ride, with banners bright unfurl'd,
A shining light 'mong lesser lights, a wonder to the world.'"

Death of Roland (*Buchanan*).

The Sword Durandana Destroyed

Then, turning away from his dead horse, the hero gazed upon his sword Durandana, which had served him faithfully for so many years, and this too he was loth to picture falling into the hands of the pagans ; therefore he set himself to dispose of it also. This he did either by sinking it deep into a poisoned stream, where it is still supposed to lie, or by breaking it between his own strong hands, after having failed even to bend it on the hard rocks around him.

"And Roland thought : ' I surely die ; but, ere I end,
Let me be sure that thou art ended too, my friend !
For should a heathen hand grasp thee when I am clay,
My ghost would grieve full sore until the judgment day ! '
Then to the marble steps, under the tall, bare trees,
Trailing the mighty sword, he crawl'd on hands and knees,
And on the slimy stone he struck the blade with might—
The bright hilt, sounding, shook, the blade flash'd sparks of light ;
Wildly again he struck, and his sick head went round,
Again there sparkled fire, again rang hollow sound ;
Ten times he struck, and threw strange echoes down the glade,
Yet still unbroken, sparkling fire, glitter'd the peerless blade."

Death of Roland (*Buchanan*).

Charlemagne at the Healing Spring at Aachen

Rogero delivering Angelica

THE SWORD DURANDANA DESTROYED

Having thus disposed of both horse and sword, the dying hero summoned his last strength, and again put his marvellous horn Olivant to his lips. Then such a blast did he blow that the sound re-echoed far and near, to be caught up again and again by the hollow rocks. Even such a blast as this may still be heard in that valley at times, as the pale ghost of the dead warrior rides past in the gloom, blowing his horn as he goes.

Yet even as he blew this last mighty blast Roland fell dead to the ground with the effort. Thus he died, this most famous of ancient heroes, full of glory and renown, heartbroken for the valiant men he had led into the treacherous valley of Roncesvalles.

Many stories are told of the last moments of Roland's life. Some say that when he blew his famous blast on his horn, Theodoricus, the last knight surviving from the Roncesvalles disaster, came quickly to his side. But he found himself too late to be of any use to his loved master, save to hear his last prayer and then reverently close his eyes. Then as the knight knelt by the side of the hero, Bishop Turpin came to his aid. Solemnly he celebrated mass over the body, and chanted a requiem hymn. As he did so he saw a wonderful thing, for he beheld a vision in which he caught a glimpse of the soul of Marsiglio being conveyed on its way to hell, while an angelic host carried the happy spirit of Roland to heaven.

At once the bishop hurried back to the emperor and told him what had happened. "Alas that I paid any attention to that rogue Ganelon!" exclaimed the king. "Even as I heard the horn I felt in my heart that Roland was in need. Would I had hastened to his help!" Then, not daring to stay longer to lament, Charlemagne pushed back to Roncesvalles. Here another miracle happened, for the sun stayed its course till the emperor had routed the foe and found the dead body of his much-loved nephew. With many tears and every expression of love and sorrow the dead hero was conveyed to Blaive, and there buried amid great pomp.

Yet other writers assert that it was not the good knight Theodoricus, but Bishop Turpin himself, who hastened to obey the last call of Roland's horn, and so was the means of seeing the hero as his soul passed away. Be this as it may, it matters little. Indeed, it is possible that the last story of all, the French " Chanson de Roland," is nearest to the truth, which asserts that ere Roland died he stumbled, sorely wounded, over the battlefield till he came across the body of his faithful friend Oliver, at which sight the injured warrior paused, while he cried aloud in his anguish :

> " ' Alas for all thy valour, comrade dear !
> Year after year, day after day, a life
> Of love we led ; ne'er didst thou wrong to me,
> Nor I to thee. If death takes thee away,
> My life is but a pain.' "
> *Chanson de Roland* (*Rabillon's tr.*).

Then, turning aside from the cold body of his dead comrade, Roland painfully dragged himself to the top of a slope, and there lay down to die. Yet before he drew his last breath he gave his soul in prayer to God, and held up his glove in sign of surrender. Nevertheless, even with so many and varying versions as these, there is no reason for believing any of them false, save in the most unimportant details, while above and before all there glows the fact of the love in which Roland was held, and the sorrow that his death caused to his people. Thus ended the life of Roland, in the midst of warfare, on a field strewn with the lifeless bodies of many a brave knight.

> " His right-hand glove he offered up to God ;
> Saint Gabriel took the glove.—With head reclined
> Upon his arm, with hands devoutly joined,

EXECUTION OF GANELON

He breathed his last.   God sent his Cherubim,
Saint Raphael, *Saint Michiel del Peril.*
Together with them Gabriel came.—All bring
The soul of Count Rollànd to Paradise.
                                   Aoi."
                         Chanson de Roland (Rabillon's tr.).

.   .   .   .   .

"Here endeth Otuel, Roland, and Olyvere,
And of the twelve dussypere,
That dieden in the batayle of Runcyvale :
Jesu lord, heaven king,
To his bliss hem and us both bring,
To liven withouten bale ! "

                                   Sir Otuel.

Execution of Ganelon

With a sad heart Charlemagne returned to France,
his company sadly diminished.   On his return he had
reason to suspect Ganelon of treachery, and therefore he
caused him to be tried by twelve peers.   These, unable
to decide the question, bade him prove his innocence in
single combat with Roland's squire, Thiedric.   Then
Ganelon, taking advantage of the usual privilege to have
his cause defended by a champion, selected Pinabel, the
most famous swordsman of the time, never dreaming
but that he would be successful.   In spite of all his
valour, however, this champion was defeated, and the
"judgment of God" was declared to be in favour of
Thiedric.   The unhappy Ganelon was thus convicted
of treason, and sentenced to be drawn and quartered, a
punishment which, after the barbarous custom of those
days, he duly suffered at Aix-la-Chapelle.

"Ere long for this he lost
Both limb and life, judged and condemned at Aix,
There to be hanged with thirty of his race
Who were not spared the punishment of death.
                                   Aoi."
                         Chanson de Roland (Rabillon's tr.).

LEGENDS OF THE MIDDLE AGES

Roland and Aude

Now it had happened that at the siege of Viane, which had taken place some little time before this, Roland, who was then living, had seen Aude, the sister of Oliver, and straightway fallen in love with her beauty. At first she resisted his appeals, but when Roland and Oliver had sworn friendship after their famous duel, Aude shyly consented to accept Roland as a lover. Their betrothal was speedily announced, but ere the marriage could take place the hero had had to hasten off to Spain, from whence he never returned. For some time the fair lady Aude remained in ignorance of her great loss, but when at last it was discovered to her she wept so long and so bitterly that she died. Out of pity for her sad fate her remains were then carried to Blaive and laid tenderly by the side of her hero.

" In Paris Lady Alda sits, Sir Roland's destined bride,
  With her three hundred maidens, to tend her, at her side ;
  Alike their robes and sandals all, and the braid that binds their hair,
  And alike the meal, in their Lady's hall, the whole three hundred share.
  Around her, in her chair of state, they all their places hold ;
  A hundred weave the web of silk, and a hundred spin the gold,
  And a hundred touch their gentle lutes to soothe that Lady's pain,
  As she thinks on him that's far away with the host of Charlemagne.
  Lulled by the sound, she sleeps, but soon she wakens with a scream ;
  And, as her maidens gather round, she thus recounts her dream :
  ' I sat upon a desert shore, and from the mountain nigh,
  Right toward me, I seemed to see a gentle falcon fly ;
  But close behind an eagle swooped, and struck that falcon down,
  And with talons and beak he rent the bird, as he cowered beneath my gown.'
  The chief of her maidens smiled, and said : ' To me it doth not seem
  That the Lady Alda reads aright the boding of her dream.

Thou art the falcon, and thy knight is the eagle in his pride,
As he comes in triumph from the war, and pounces on his bride.'
The maiden laughed, but Alda sighed, and gravely shook her head.
' Full rich,' quoth she, ' shall thy guerdon be, if thou the truth hast
    said.'
'Tis morn ; her letters, stained with blood, the truth too plainly
    tell,
How, in the chase of Ronceval, Sir Roland fought and fell."
                    Lady Alda's Dream (Sir Edmund Head's tr.).

Legend of Roland and Hildegarde

A later legend, which has given rise to sundry poems, connects the name of Roland with one of the most beautiful places on the Rhine. According to popular tradition, Roland sought shelter one evening in the castle of Drachenfels, where he fell in love with Hildegarde, the beautiful daughter of the Lord of Drachenfels. The sudden outbreak of the war in Spain forced him to bid farewell to his betrothed, but he promised to return as soon as possible to celebrate their wedding. During the campaign many stories of his courage came to Hildegarde's ears, till finally, after a long silence, she heard that her lover had perished at Roncesvalles.

Broken-hearted, the fair bride-to-be spent her days and nights in tears, till at last she prevailed upon her father to allow her to enter the convent on the island of Nonnenwörth, in the middle of the river, and within view of the gigantic crag where the castle ruins can still be seen.

" The castled crag of Drachenfels
    Frowns o'er the wide and winding Rhine,
Whose breast of water broadly swells
    Between the banks which bear the vine,
And hills all rich with blossomed trees,
    And fields which promise corn and wine,
And scattered cities crowning these,
    Whose fair white walls along them shine."
                    Childe Harold (Byron).

With much reluctance the Lord of Drachenfels at last gave his consent, and had his daughter conveyed to the retreat she coveted. With pallid cheeks and tear-dimmed eyes Hildegarde now spent her life either in her tiny cell or in the convent chapel, praying for the soul of her beloved. And as she prayed she all the time longed that death might soon come to set her free to join him. Yet, according to this particular legend, Roland was not really dead, as she supposed, but sorely wounded at Roncesvalles.

As soon as he was able to travel, therefore, Roland painfully made his way back to Drachenfels, where he presented himself late one evening, eagerly calling for Hildegarde. A few moments later the joyful light left his eyes for ever, for he learned that his beloved betrothed had taken irrevocable vows, and was now the bride of Heaven.

That selfsame day Roland left the castle of Drachenfels, and, riding to an eminence overlooking the island of Nonnenwörth, he gazed long and tearfully at a little light twinkling in one of the convent windows. Something seemed to suggest that it illumined Hildegarde's lonely cell, and therefore he watched it all night long. When morning came a long procession of nuns issued from the convent on their way to the chapel, and Roland's eager glance soon recognised the form of his beloved.

Rolandseck

This view of his dear lady seemed a slight consolation to the hero, who built a retreat on this rock, which is known as Rolandseck. Here he spent his days in penance and prayer, his eyes fixed ever on the island at his feet and the swift stream which parted him from Hildegarde.

Then one wintry day, many years after he had taken up his abode on the rocky height, Roland missed the

194

graceful form he watched for, and, instead of the usual psalm, he heard a dirge for the dead. Startled, he watched with intense anxiety, till he saw that six of the nuns were carrying a coffin, which they lowered into an open tomb.

Full of terrible fears, Roland gazed at their every movement, and then sank again in prayer, from which he was roused at eveningtide by the convent priest, who gently announced that Hildegarde was at rest. Calmly Roland listened to these tidings, and begged the priest to hear his confession as usual. Then when he had received absolution he expressed a desire to be buried with his face turned toward the convent where Hildegarde had lived and died.

Only too willing to grant such an easy request, the priest readily promised. Then, fearing no evil, he departed. But when he came on the morrow he found Roland dead. Thus these two faithful lovers were joined in death ; and as the monks laid the body of the knight reverently to rest they buried him on the very spot which bears his name, with his face turned toward Nonnenwörth, where Hildegarde sleeps.

Angelica and Rogero

Another later cycle of legends concerning Charlemagne and Roland is to be found in the " Orlando Innamorato " of Boiardo and the " Orlando Furioso " of Ariosto. These poems, written at the end of the fifteenth and beginning of the sixteenth centuries, are full of romantic interest, and one of the picturesque incidents in the latter which has often attracted the artist recalls the Greek myth of Perseus and Andromeda. Angelica, a princess of Cathay, with whom Roland was said to be in love, was sent by Charlemagne on a mission to Bavaria, where she was seized for an offering to a fabulous sea-monster. She was bound naked to a rock, and when it seemed that nothing could save her she was rescued from her perilous position by the Paladin Rogero.

Charlemagne's Sorrow for Roland

The news of the death of Roland was a heavy blow to the old emperor, whose hair was by this time white with age and sorrow. With a sinking heart he realised that presently his turn to depart must also come. Therefore he set about putting his things in order, resolved that when at last death should overtake him it should not find him unprepared. Wherefore he summoned his sons round him, and divided among them his possessions, appointing Louis, the youngest, the successor to his crown.

All this took place at Aix-la-Chapelle, which was the place among all others dear to the heart of the emperor. Here he had long ago built for himself a palace, which he esteemed more than any other he possessed ; here, too, he had built to the Virgin a church, which, though small in size, was filled with the richest of treasures and adorned with every kind of beautiful work.

The Vision Seen by Turpin at Vienna

Meanwhile the good Bishop Turpin, who was away at Vienna, beheld a wonderful vision. For it happened that as he stood there before the altar chanting a psalm he was interrupted by an innumerable host of demons of a black and loathsome appearance.

"Whither are ye bound ?" cried the bishop, startled at the hideous sight.

"To Aix-la-Chapelle, to the bedside of Charlemagne," replied one of the demon host.

"And wherefore ?" demanded Turpin.

"Because the emperor is even now dying," was the

answer, "and we go to strive for his soul, if by chance we may yet bear it to Hell."

Then cried Turpin in his anger and indignation : "I adjure you by the name of Christ that ye return to me without fail on your way hither after your errand."

With a flapping of ghostly wings the swarthy crew departed from the church, and Turpin resumed his psalm.

Yet ere he had got to the end he was interrupted again by the same loathly host.

"Returned ?" cried Turpin, surprised at their swift reappearance. "Then tell me, have ye accomplished your purpose ?"

"By no means," replied the devils sullenly ; "for St. James of Compostella, ever a friend to Charlemagne, who built to his memory a church yonder in Spain, drew near with so many stones, bits of wood, and what not, which he declared were taken from the churches the king had erected throughout the country, that our arguments were of no avail. Thus we left, since we might by no chance have his soul."

"Praise be to God !" ejaculated the bishop, and turning again to the altar he resumed his psalm in a yet more jubilant tone, while the demons fled rapidly back to the depths from which they had emerged. Meanwhile in Aix-la-Chapelle (or Aachen) the emperor grew weaker and weaker, till finally he breathed his last, being then well over his threescore years and ten.

With bitter tears his people heard the news of his death, and prepared to give his body honourable burial. The tomb itself was made magnificent with every kind of gem, and above it was raised an arch of gold, within which was put the embalmed figure of the emperor, clad in his richest robes and seated upon a chair of gold. On his knee were placed copies of the Gospel, which his right hand lightly touched, while his left hand grasped a sceptre. Thus he sat, looking like a great judge, wearing a crown of gold of such huge proportions that it reached up to the arch itself. Moreover, so that his head should not incline either to this side or that, it was made secure by a necklet of gold, fastened at the back to an upright cross, also of gold, which was stuck firmly into the ground. Then the tomb was filled with fair spices and aromatic herbs, and the great doors fastened together, leaving the king alone, still looking as if he were judging the nations.

Such is the story of the old chronicles of the burial of the mighty emperor. Yet it is more probable that the real body of Charlemagne was actually buried, while the figure seated on the chair was only an effigy carved in stone. Nevertheless so the story stands, true or not as it may be, yet a story often repeated among the people, who handed on to their children marvellous tales of an emperor upon whose like we shall not look again.

The Peers of Charlemagne

These were twelve in number, and they were also called Paladins, but this name has been borne by some who were not amongst the twelve. The list of the peers varies in the later *chansons de gestes;* in the "Roland" they are : Roland, Oliver, Ivon, Ivory, Oton, Berenger, Samson, Anseïs, Gerin, Gerier, Engelier, and Gerard de Rousillon. Among those who are sometimes included with the twelve peers may be named : Archbishop Turpin, Ogier the Dane, Ganelon, Renaud, Astolpho, and Aymon.

The Burial of Charlemagne

Satan pursues Malagigi

CHAPTER IX : THE SONS OF AYMON

Aymon and Charlemagne

THE different *chansons de gestes* relating to Aymon and the necromancer Malagigi, or Malagis, probably arose from popular ballads commemorating the struggles of Charles the Bald and his feudatories. These ballads are at least as old as the events which they were intended to record, but the *chansons de gestes* based upon them, and entitled " Duolin de Mayence," " Aymon, Son of Duolin de Mayence," " Maugis," " Rinaldo de Trebizonde," " The Four Sons of Aymon," and " Mabrian," are of much later date, and were particularly admired during the fourteenth and fifteenth centuries.

One of the most famous of Charlemagne's peers was the noble Aymon of Dordogne. For this reason, when the war against the Avars in Hungary had by his bravery been successfully closed, his adherents besought the king to bestow some reward on their chief. Charlemagne, whom many of these later *chansons de gestes* describe as mean and avaricious, refused to grant any recognition, declaring that were he to add still further to his vassal's already extensive territories Aymon would soon become more powerful than his sovereign.

War between Aymon and Charlemagne

This unjust refusal displeased Lord Hug of Dordogne, who had pleaded for his kinsman. Therefore he ventured a retort, which so incensed the king that he slew him then and there. Then Aymon, learning of the death of Lord Hug, and aware of the failure of his last embassy, haughtily withdrew to his own estates, whence he lost no time in beginning to wage war against the emperor.

But though hostilities were thus declared there was

no open battle. Instead, a sort of guerilla warfare was carried on, in which, thanks to his marvellous steed Bayard, which his cousin Malagigi, the necromancer, had brought him from Hell, Aymon always had the advantage. For several years the desultory struggle lasted, till, resolved to end it once and for all, Charlemagne collected a large host, and came to lay siege to the castle where Aymon had entrenched himself with all his adherents.

The Loss of Bayard

Then a great disaster befell Aymon, for he awoke one morning to find that his beloved steed had vanished. But Malagigi, hearing him bewail his loss, bade him be of good cheer, and promised he would himself restore Bayard ere long, though he were forced to go to Mount Vulcanus, the mouth of Hell, to get him. Thus comforted, Aymon turned his mind towards repelling the enemy, while Malagigi set to work to fulfil his promise. It happened that a brisk wind was blowing from the castle towards the camp ; therefore he flung upon the breeze some powdered hellebore, which caused a violent sneezing throughout the army. Then, while his foes were wiping their streaming eyes, the necromancer, who had learned his black art in the famous school of Toledo, slipped through their ranks unseen, and journeyed on to Mount Vulcanus, where he encountered the sovereign of Hell.

Far too cunning to assert what his true errand was, Malagigi offered his services to Satan. These were gladly accepted, and Satan bade his guest keep good watch over Bayard, a horse he had recently stolen. The magician repeated his wish to be useful, whereupon he was led to the place where Bayard was to be found. Full of excitement at the success of his plan, Malagigi lulled Satan to sleep with a drugged potion, after which he hastened to Bayard. The angry steed was pawing the ground of his prison, but when Malagigi drew near and whispered the name of his master into his ear the result was magical. All Bayard's evil humour vanished, and, springing on to his back, Malagigi rode swiftly away.

The joyful whinny of the flying steed roused the lord of Hades from his stupor. Furious at the trick, he immediately mounted upon a storm-cloud and started in pursuit, hurling a red-hot thunderbolt at Malagigi to check his advance. But the wizard muttered a magic spell and held up his crucifix, so that the bolt fell short ; while as for the Devil, losing his balance, he fell to the earth, and thus for ever lamed himself.

Bayard Restored by Malagigi

Meanwhile Count Aymon had been so severely attacked that he had been obliged to flee from his besieged castle, mounted upon a sorry steed instead of his fleet-footed horse. No sooner was his flight detected by the enemy than they set out in pursuit. To make sure he should not escape from their grasp they let loose their bloodhounds, which were just about to overtake and slay him when Malagigi suddenly appeared with Bayard. Then, bounding on to the back of his horse, Aymon drew his famous sword Flamberge, the work of the smith Wieland, and charged into the midst of his foes. So terrible was the shock of this sudden encounter that his enemies shrank back in terror. Relentlessly Aymon hewed about him, till not one of his foes was left, though he himself remained quite unharmed. Flushed with victory, he gathered together many followers, with whose help he soon won back all the castles and fortresses he had lost.

Alarmed at the news of Aymon's successes, Charlemagne finally sent Roland, his nephew and favourite,
bidding him offer a rich ransom to atone for the
murder of Lord Hug, and instructing him to secure
peace at any price. At first Aymon refused these overtures, but at last he consented to cease the feud upon
receipt of six times Lord Hug's weight in gold, and
the hand of the king's sister, Aya, whom he had long
loved.

After some demur these demands were granted, and
peace was concluded. Then Aymon, having married
Aya, led her to the castle of Pierlepont, where they
dwelt most happily together, and became the parents of
four brave sons, Renaud, Alard, Guiscard, and Richard.
Inactivity, however, was not enjoyable to an inveterate
fighter like Aymon, so he left home to journey into
Spain, where the bitter enmity between the Christians
and the Moors afforded him opportunity to fight to his
heart's content.

Years now passed by, during which the knight
covered himself with glory. For, mounted on Bayard,
he was the foremost in every battle, and always struck
terror into the hearts of his foes by the mere flash of
his blade Flamberge. Thus he fought until his sons
had attained to manhood. As for Aya, she had long
thought him dead, and therefore she was very much
startled when one day a messenger came to Pierlepont, telling them that Aymon lay ill in the Pyrenees,
and wished to see his wife and his children once
more.

Full of gladness to hear again from her lord, yet sad
at the thought of his dying condition, Aya hastened
southward. There she found her husband old and
worn, yet not so changed but that she could recognise
him. Aymon, sick as he was, rejoiced at the sight or

his manly sons. To the three eldest he gave the spoil he had won during those many years of warfare, while he promised Renaud (Reinold) his horse and sword, if he could successfully mount and ride the former.

Renaud's Victory over Bayard

Renaud, who was a skilful horseman, was inclined to be scornful at the simplicity of the task. But when he made the attempt and found himself caught by the teeth of the animal and tumbled into the manger he was overcome with surprise. Undismayed by one failure, however, he watched his opportunity, and so sprang boldly upon Bayard. Then, in spite of all the efforts of the horse to throw him, he kept his seat so well that his father formally gave him the promised mount and sword.

All this time Aya had been lavishing such tender care upon her sick husband that at last he was fully restored, and returned in happiness with his family to his home. Then, hearing that Charlemagne had returned from his coronation journey to Rome, and was about to celebrate the majority of his heir, Aymon went to court with his four sons.

As usual, a tournament was held to mark the festive occasion, when Renaud, to the delight of his father, unhorsed every opponent, and even defeated the prince himself. This success roused the anger of Charlot, or Berthelot, as he is called by some authorities, and made him vow revenge. He therefore set about discovering some spiteful thing he could do. Soon he discovered that Renaud was particularly attached to his brother Alard, so he wickedly resolved first to harm the latter. Advised by the traitor Ganelon, Charlot therefore challenged Alard to a game of chess, and insisted that the stakes should be the players' heads.

Charlot's Revenge

This proposal was very distasteful to Alard, for he knew that he would never dare lay any claim to the head of the prince even if he should win the game, while he feared to lose his own if he failed to win. Compelled to accept the challenge, however, he began the game, and played so well that he won five times in succession. Then Charlot, angry at being so completely checkmated, suddenly seized the board and struck his antagonist such a cruel stroke that the blood began to flow. With great magnanimity Alard curbed his wrath and simply withdrew. Nor was it until Renaud had questioned him very closely that he told how the quarrel had occurred.

Renaud's Complaint against Charlot

Indignant at the insult offered his brother, Renaud went to the emperor with his complaint. Reluctantly the umpires testified that the prince had forfeited his head, and declared that the sentence must be carried out. Therefore, drawing his sword, Renaud at one blow bereft the prince of life. Crimson with fury at the assault, the emperor sprang to his feet and darted after the knight, who nevertheless contrived to escape, together with his father and his brothers. But at last, being closely pursued by the imperial troops, Aymon and his sons were brought to bay, when they fought so bravely that they slew many of their assailants. At last, seeing that all their horses except the incomparable Bayard had been slain, Renaud bade his brothers mount behind him, and they dashed away. Meanwhile the aged Aymon had fallen into the hands of the emperor's minister Turpin, who solemnly promised that no harm should befall him. But in spite of this oath, and of the remonstrances of all his peers, Charlemagne prepared to have him publicly hanged, and consented to release him only upon condition that Aymon would promise to deliver his sons into the emperor's hands, were it ever in his power to do so.

The four young men, knowing their father safe, and unwilling to expose their mother to the hardships of the siege which would have followed had they remained at Pierlepont, now journeyed southward, and entered the service of Saforet, King of the Moors. Under his banner they won many victories, till, seeing at the end of three years that this monarch had no intention of giving them a promised reward, they slew him, and offered their swords to Iwo, Prince of Tarasconia.

Marriage of Renaud and Clarissa

Afraid of these warriors, yet wishing to bind them to him by indissoluble ties, Iwo gave Renaud his daughter Clarissa in marriage, and helped him build an impregnable fortress at Montauban. Scarcely was this stronghold finished when Charlemagne came up with a great army to besiege it. But at the end of a year's fruitless attempts, the emperor reluctantly withdrew, leaving Montauban still in the hands of his enemies.

The Return Home of Renaud and his Brothers

Seven years had now elapsed since the four young men had seen their mother. Anxious to embrace her once more, they went disguised in pilgrims' robes to the castle of Pierlepont. Here the chamberlain recognised them and betrayed their presence to Aymon, who, compelled by his oath, prepared to bind his four sons fast and take them captive to his sovereign. Aghast at their father's treatment, the young men nevertheless defended themselves bravely, and, having secured their father, they sent him instead in chains to Charlemagne. But while they were thus engaged misfortune was coming quickly upon them. For Charlemagne was much nearer to them than any of them conceived. Hastening onward, the emperor entered the castle before they had even become aware of his approach, and thus secured three of them. The fourth, Renaud, aided by his mother, escaped in pilgrim's garb, and returned to Montauban. Here he found Bayard, and, without pausing to rest, he rode straight to Paris to deliver his brothers from the emperor's hands.

Overcome by fatigue after this hasty journey, Renaud dismounted shortly before reaching Paris, and fell asleep. Alas! when he awoke he found that his precious steed had vanished, so that he was forced to continue his journey on foot, begging his way. As he went he was joined by his cousin, Malagigi, who also wore a pilgrim's garb. Full of excitement, Renaud poured out his story, whereupon Malagigi promised to aid him not only in freeing his brothers, but also in recovering Bayard.

Malagigi's Stratagem

Unnoticed, the beggars threaded their way through the city of Paris till they came to the palace. There a great tournament was to be held, and the emperor had promised to the victor of the day the famous horse Bayard. To stimulate the knights to greater efforts by a view of the promised prize, the emperor bade a groom lead forth the renowned steed. The horse seemed restive, but suddenly paused beside two beggars with a whinny of joy. The groom, little suspecting that the animal's real master lay hidden under the travel-stained pilgrim's robe, laughingly commented upon Bayard's bad taste. Then Malagigi, the second beggar, suddenly cried aloud that his poor companion was lame and that he had been told that he would never recover from his lameness unless he were once allowed to bestride the famous steed. Anxious to witness a miracle, the emperor gave orders that the beggar should be placed upon Bayard. After some difficulty Renaud was lifted on to the animal, where he at first pretended to be unable to keep his seat. Then, suddenly straightening himself on the saddle, he gripped the reins and dashed away before any one could stop him.

As for Malagigi, having wandered among the throng unheeded, he remained in Paris until evening. Then, making his way into the prison by means of the magic charm "Abracadabra," which he continually repeated, he delivered the other sons of Aymon from their chains. He next entered the palace of the sleeping emperor, and so mesmerised the monarch that he willingly handed over both his sceptre and crown, which Malagigi then bore triumphantly away.

Treachery of Iwo

But when Charlemagne awoke on the morrow he found that his prisoners were gone, and that which had seemed a dream only too true. For the very insignia of royalty had vanished ! Then the full fury of his anger burst forth, till the listeners trembled to hear him. More than ever before he now longed to take the sons of Aymon ; and he spent all his time thinking how best he could secure them. For this purpose he bribed Iwo, with whom the brothers had taken refuge, to send them to him. But Clarissa, suspecting her father's treachery, implored Renaud not to believe him. Nevertheless the reckless champion, relying upon Iwo's promise, set out without arms to seek the emperor's pardon. Soon the treacherous plot became apparent, for on the way the four sons of Aymon fell into an ambuscade, whence they would scarcely have escaped alive had not one of the brothers drawn from under his robe the weapons Clarissa had secretly given him.

The sight of such famous weapons made even the emperor's warriors afraid of the valour of these doughty brethren. Therefore they withdrew to a safe distance, whence they could watch the young men and prevent their escape. Suddenly, however, Malagigi came dashing up on Bayard, for Clarissa had warned him of his kinsmen's danger, and implored him to go to their rescue. Without delay Renaud mounted his favourite steed, and brandishing Flamberge, which his cousin had brought him, he charged so gallantly into the midst of the imperial troops that he speedily put them to flight.

Renaud and Roland

Baffled once again, the emperor grew yet more angry, and setting about to find some one to blame, he declared that Iwo had warned his son-in-law of the danger and provided him with weapons. Not waiting to find out the truth of this, in his wrath he had Iwo seized and sentenced to be hanged. Then Renaud, seeing Clarissa's tears, vowed that he would save his father-in-law from such an ignominious death. With the bravery for which he was famous, he rode boldly against the executioners, and unhorsed the valiant champion Roland. During this encounter Iwo effected his escape, with Renaud following closely behind him. Roland meanwhile had slowly picked himself up and prepared to go after his antagonist and once more try his strength against him.

On the way to Montauban Roland met Richard, one of the four brothers, whom he had carried captive to Charlemange. On hearing this the emperor at once ordered the young knight to be hanged, and bade some of his most noble followers stay to see the sentence executed. To his amazement they one and all refused, for they declared that death on the gallows was too ignominious a punishment for a knight.

Lengthy discussions were thus begun, which consequently delayed the execution, and so enabled Malagigi to warn Renaud of his brother's imminent peril. Mounted upon Bayard, Renaud, accompanied by his two other brothers and a few faithful men, rode straight to Montfaucon. There they camped under the gallows, to be at hand when the guard should come to hang the prisoner on the morrow. Yet even Renaud would have been conquered on this occasion, so soundly did he and his companions sleep, had not the intelligent Bayard awakened his master by his eager pawing of the ground. Springing to his feet, Renaud roused his companions ; then, vaulting upon his steed, he charged the guard. His sudden attack was completely successful, and he straightway delivered his captive brother and carried him off in triumph, after hanging the knight who had volunteered to act as executioner.

Montauban Besieged by Charlemagne

More and more anxious to seize and punish these refractory subjects, Charlemagne now collected an army and began again to besiege the stronghold of Montauban. For years the struggle continued, during which many a brave knight lost his life. Nevertheless the castle still held out, through the clever generalship of Renaud. Within was a scene of desolation. Want and anxiety had robbed the men of their strength, and with pale, wan faces they watched their provisions growing daily less and less. Yet they still held on in their struggle,

and never once did their courage flicker. Then Malagigi, seeing the dire plight in which they stood, resolved
to effect their rescue. He knew that a number of
waggons loaded with food were expected in the camp
of the enemy. Therefore he advised Renaud to make
a bold sally and carry them off, while with his magic
arts he himself would dull the senses of the imperial
army by scattering one of his sleeping-powders in the
air. Arrived at the camp, he had just begun his spell
when Oliver perceived him, and, pouncing upon him,
carried him off to the emperor's tent. Shrewdly suspecting his mission, Oliver never once relinquished his grasp,
though the magician tried hard to make him do so by
throwing a pinch of hellebore in his face.

Sneezing loudly the while, the knight told how he had
caught the magician, and the emperor vowed that the
rascal should be hanged the very next day. When he
heard this decree Malagigi implored the emperor to
give him a good meal, since this was to be his last
night on earth, pledging his word not to leave the
camp unless the emperor were with him. This promise
so reassured Charlemagne that he ordered a sumptuous
repast, charging a few knights to watch Malagigi, lest
after all he should effect his escape. The meal over,
the wizard again used his magic art, by which he soon
plunged the whole camp into a deep sleep. Then,
proceeding unmolested to the imperial tent, he bore off
the sleeping emperor to the gates of Montauban, which
flew open at his well-known voice.

On awaking Charlemagne was overcome with chagrin and alarm to find himself in the hands of his
foes. Yet so magnanimously did Renaud behave that
he gallantly gave him his freedom without exacting
any pledge or ransom in return. Then when Malagigi heard of this foolhardy act of generosity he grew

Charlemagne and the Wife of Aymon

Huon before the Pope

full of fury, and set about burning up his papers, boxes, and bags. When asked why he was acting thus he replied that he was about to leave his mad young kinsmen to their own devices, and take refuge in a hermitage, where he intended to spend the remainder of his life in repenting of his sins. Soon after this he disappeared, and Aymon's sons, escaping secretly from Montauban just before it was forced to surrender, took refuge in a castle they owned in the Ardennes.

Here the emperor pursued them, and kept up the siege until at last the sorrowful Aya sought him and implored him to forgive her sons and to cease from persecuting them. Won over by her gentle words and evident distress, Charlemagne yielded at last to her entreaties, and promised to grant the sons of Aymon full forgiveness provided the fairy steed Bayard were given over to him to be put to death.

Gladly acquiescing to this condition, Aya hastened to Renaud to tell him the joyful news. Breathless from eagerness, she panted out that by the sacrifice of Bayard only a full pardon would be given to Renaud and all his brothers. But instead of seeing gladness flash across Renaud's face she saw only gloom and grim determination. Nothing, he declared, could ever make him give up his faithful horse, which had on so many occasions been the means of saving his life.

Hardly able at first to comprehend all that his answer meant, Aya cried out passionately: "Then do you rate the lives of your brothers—aye, and that of your mother also—so low that you are not willing to sacrifice one horse to save so many? Away with you if such an idea be in your mind!" Torn with grief at her words, Renaud shivered with anguish. Then, recovering himself, he replied in a low, uneven voice: "Take the horse, then, and make peace."

Scarcely had the words left his lips when his mother darted forward to caress him for his deed ; but with a groan Renaud thrust her aside, saying : " I have said it ; see that it is done. Yet now leave me, for I would be alone."

Closing the door softly behind her, Aya hastened back to the emperor with the tidings. A treaty was at once drawn up, and with this precious paper in her hand Aya crept timidly into Renaud's room.

Death of Bayard

A scratch of the pen was all that was needed : Bayard's death-warrant was signed and the sons of Aymon were free ! How small a thing to do, yet how much it meant ! What it cost Renaud to make that fateful mark none could guess, though his mother saw from the anguish in his face that her son was overwhelmed with sore bitterness. Then Charlemagne, fearing lest Renaud should even now change his mind, gave orders for the horse to be brought out and his hoofs heavily weighted. This was speedily done, and the magnificent animal was then led to the middle of a bridge over the Seine. Here, in the midst of Charlemagne and his knights, and the unhappy Renaud, who had been compelled to come to witness the tragedy, the noble horse was driven into the river, and there left to drown. Twice, in spite of the manacles on his feet, the splendid steed rose to the surface, each time casting an agonised look upon his master. This was too much for Renaud ; with a bursting heart he groaned aloud in his sorrow, and so sank on the ground. Yet again the form of Bayard rose above the waters ; but, missing his master's form among the onlookers, he succumbed to the waves, and rose no more. Then as the dark blue waters of the Seine closed for the last time over the steed, silence fell upon the company that watched, and something like a shudder ran among them as they turned away from the scene.

Renaud in the Holy Land

As for Renaud, maddened by the needless cruelty of the act, he tore up the treaty and flung it at the emperor's feet. Then he broke his sword Flamberge and cast it into the Seine, declaring that he would never more wield such a weapon. After this, alone and on foot, he returned to Montauban. In deep gloom he committed his wife and children to the loyal protection of Roland, and bade them a loving farewell as he set out for the Holy Land. Here he fought valiantly against the infidels, being careful to use nothing but a club as a defence, in order to preserve his vow. Yet even with such a weapon his strength was so great that he was offered the crown of Jerusalem as a reward for the great services he had rendered. But Renaud was in no mood for caring for any glory the world could give him; therefore he passed on the title to Godfrey of Bouillon. Then, returning home, he found that Clarissa had died, after having been persecuted for years by the unwelcome attentions of many suitors, who would fain have persuaded her that her husband was dead.

Death of Renaud

Not very long after Renaud's own death took place. Exactly how or where this happened is uncertain. It is said that he died as a hermit, known everywhere for his holy life; yet again it is asserted that, having come to Cologne, he found there the cathedral in process of being built, whereupon the knight offered his services as a mason, and laboured both day and night in his task of love. But his very enthusiasm at last caused his death. For his fellow toilers, exasperated by his constant activity, which put them all to shame, slew him, and flung his body into the Rhine. Strange to relate, however, his body was not carried away by the strong current, but lingered near the city, until it was brought to land and interred by some pious people.

Yet even in death the influence of Renaud did not cease. Many miracles took place near the spot where he was buried, till at last the emperor gave orders that his remains should be conveyed either to Aix-la-Chapelle or to Paris. The body was therefore laid upon a cart, which moved of its own accord to Dortmund, in Westphalia, where it stopped ; nor could it be moved again. Here a church was erected to his memory in 811, and the saintly warrior's remains were laid to rest within the precincts of the building which still bears his name. In Cologne, too, may be seen a chapel dedicated to the valiant hero, and supposed to stand on the very spot where he was so treacherously slain after his long and brilliant career as a knight.

CHAPTER X : HUON OF BORDEAUX

The Influence of the Ballad

IT is usually supposed that this *chanson de geste*, "Huon de Bordeaux," was first composed in the thirteenth century. But the version which has come down to us must have been written shortly before the discovery of printing. During the Middle Ages the poem was deservedly a favourite composition, and it is therefore a little curious that no manuscript copy of it now exists. So universal was the admiration that it excited that it was even translated into English by Lord Berners, under Henry VIII. In modern times it has been the theme of Wieland's finest poem, and of one of Weber's operas, both of which works are known by the title of "Oberon." It is from this work that Shakespeare undoubtedly drew some of the principal characters for his *Midsummer Night's Dream*, where Oberon, king of the fairies, plays no unimportant part.

Charlot and Huon

Now it happened that the hero of this poem, Huon of Bordeaux, and his brother Girard, were on their way from Guienne to Paris to do homage to Charlemagne for their estates. Their approach was known to Charlot, the monarch's eldest son, a man of infamous reputation, and notorious for his cruelty. For no reason except pure wantonness he resolved to waylay the brothers and put them both to death. Attempting this he succeeded only in slaying Girard ere he was himself killed by Huon. Meanwhile Huon, quite unconscious of the illustrious birth of his assailant, calmly proceeded on his way.

By-and-by the news of the prince's death followed Huon to court, who confessed his entire ignorance as to the identity of his assailant. Nevertheless Charlemagne, in his anger, vowed that he would never pardon him until he had proved his loyalty and repentance by journeying to Bagdad, where he was to cut off the head of the great Bashaw, to kiss the Sultan's daughter, and bring back a lock of the mighty potentate's grey beard and four of his best teeth.

> " ' Yet hear the terms ; hear what no earthly power
> Shall ever change ! ' He spoke, and wav'd below
> His sceptre, bent in anger o'er my brow.—
> ' Yes, thou may'st live ;—but, instant, from this hour,
> Away ! in exile rove far nations o'er ;
> Thy foot accurs'd shall tread this soil no more,
> Till thou, in due obedience to my will,
> Shalt, point by point, the word I speak fulfil ;
> Thou diest, if this unwrought thou touch thy native shore.

> " ' Go hence to Bagdad ; in high festal day
> At his round table, when the caliph, plac'd
> In stately pomp, with splendid emirs grac'd,
> Enjoys the banquet rang'd in proud array,
> Slay him who lies the monarch's left beside,
> Dash from his headless trunk the purple tide.
> Then to the right draw near ; with courtly grace
> The beauteous heiress of his throne embrace ;
> And thrice with public kiss salute her as thy bride.

> " ' And while the caliph, at the monstrous scene,
> Such as before ne'er shock'd a caliph's eyes,
> Stares at thy confidence in mute surprise,
> Then, as the Easterns wont, with lowly mien
> Fall on the earth before his golden throne,
> And gain (a trifle, proof of love alone),
> That it may please him, gift of friend to friend,
> Four of his grinders at my bidding send,
> And of his beard a lock with silver hair o'ergrown.' "
>
> *Oberon* (*Wieland*) (*Sotheby's tr.*).

Huon's Quest

Dismayed at the difficulty of his task, and sorrowful at leaving his native land, Huon prepared to begin this apparently hopeless quest. On his way he visited his uncle, the Pope, in Rome, and tried to secure heavenly assistance by a pilgrimage to the holy sepulchre. After this he set out for Babylon, or Bagdad, which, with the usual mediæval scorn for geography evinced in all the *chansons de gestes*, are considered interchangeable names for the same town. But as the knight was journeying by way of the Red Sea he lost his way and stumbled into a thick forest. Here he was quite unable to find a path, though he searched up and down in all directions. Nor was there a human being of any kind to be seen, nor any sign of animal life. To increase his difficulties, darkness soon began to fall, and still the knight knew not where he was. In this dilemma he went blindly on, leading his horse by the bridle, till at last he caught a glimpse of a tiny light in the distance. Hither he directed his way, with all the eagerness of new hope.

> " Not long his step the winding way pursued,
> When on his wistful gaze, to him beseems,
> The light of distant fire delightful gleams.
> His cheek flash'd crimson as the flame he view'd.
> Half wild with hope and fear, he rushed to find
> In these lone woods some glimpse of human kind,
> And, ever and anon, at once the ray
> Flash'd on his sight, then sunk at once away,
> While rose and fell the path as hill and valley wind."
>
> *Oberon* (*Wieland*) (*Sotheby's tr.*).

Sherasmin the Cave-dweller

Scratched and torn by the briars and sharp pebbles, Huon at last reached the cave from whence shone the light. Here he found a gigantic old man, all covered with hair, which was his sole garment. After trying for a few moments to speak in the language of the country, Huon impetuously spoke a few words in his mother tongue. To his intense surprise the uncouth inhabitant of the woods answered him fluently! Startled at this fact, Huon was yet more surprised when he discovered, after a few rapid questions, that the man was Sherasmin, or Gerasmes, who had once been a servant to his father. Taken prisoner by a band of Saracens, the old man had escaped from the hands of his captors, and had taken refuge in these woods, where he had already dwelt many years. His delight at meeting with one belonging to his old country knew no bounds, and he eagerly begged Huon to stay and tell him of all that had been happening. Anxious to go on his journey, yet loth to leave the old man's curiosity unsatisfied, Huon lingered for a while in the cave, telling stories of the court of Charlemagne and the brave deeds that were being done in the world. To all this Sherasmin listened with evident delight. After which Huon begged him in return to point out the road to Bagdad. To his surprise he learned that there were two roads, one very long and comparatively safe, even for an inexperienced traveller, and the other far shorter, but leading through an enchanted forest, where countless dangers awaited the venturesome intruder.

Not at all daunted by the thought of adventures, the young knight decided to travel along the most perilous way. Then, accompanied by Sherasmin, who offered his services as guide, he set out early on the morrow to continue his quest. Thus they fared forth together, these two, the gallant young knight in his fair array, and the dishevelled, gaunt old man, making as they went a strange sight for the eyes of any who might chance to meet them. Three days they journeyed without adventure, but on the fourth they saw a Saracen struggling single-handed against a band of Arabs. With a few well-directed strokes from his mighty sword Huon soon put the whole company to flight, and so the two went on as before. After pausing for a rest and a meal, Huon bade Sherasmin lead the way into the neighbouring forest. Again the old man strove to dissuade him from crossing it, asserting that the forest was haunted by a goblin who could change men into beasts. The hero, who was on his way to insult the proudest ruler on earth, was not to be deterred by a goblin. Then, as Sherasmin still refused to enter first, Huon plunged boldly into the enchanted forest. Reluctantly Sherasmin followed him, finding cause for alarm in the very silence of the dense shade, and timorously glancing from side to side in the gloomy recesses, where strange forms seemed to glide noiselessly about.

> "Meanwhile the wand'ring travellers onward go
> Unawares within the circuit of a wood,
> Whose mazy windings at each step renew'd,
> In many a serpent-fold, twin'd to and fro,
> So that our pair to lose themselves were fain."
>
> *Oberon (Wieland) (Sotheby's tr.).*

Oberon and the Travellers

Further and further into the dimness of the forest they went, so that they lost their way entirely and were guided only by chance, till at last they came to a little glade. Here they flung themselves gladly on the soft turf near to a mighty oak. Then as they sat at their ease and rested they suddenly caught a glimpse of a marvellous vision. For they saw the golden castle of Oberon, king of the fairies, and son of Julius Cæsar and Morgana the fay. Then as they gazed spell-bound at the wonderful sight they beheld the glittering gates of the palace roll back as the king drove through them in a chariot of silver, drawn by leopards, himself appearing in the guise of the God of Love. Thus he advanced in the direction of the travellers.

Then Sherasmin, intoxicated at the appearance of this

radiant creature, and under the influence of wild, un-reasoning fear, seized the bridle of Huon's steed, and in spite of all his remonstrances dragged him into the midst of the forest. Nor did he for a second pause till he thought himself safe from further pursuit ; then, breathless, he sank to the ground, and relaxed his hold of his master.

The Storm in the Forest

But if Sherasmin had only known it, he had done the very worst thing possible by taking to flight ; for he had roused the anger of the king of the fairies, who was determined to punish him for his discourtesy. Thus scarcely had the travellers recovered breath when a fear-ful storm broke over their heads, almost threatening to destroy them. More and more terrified, Sherasmin tried to hurry away from the fury of the elements ; but the farther he went the worse grew the storm.

> " A tempest, wing'd with lightning, storm, and rain,
> O'ertakes our pair : around them midnight throws
> Darkness that hides the world : it peals, cracks, blows,
> As if the uprooted globe would split in twain ;
> The elements in wild confusion flung,
> Each warr'd with each, as fierce from chaos sprung.
> Yet heard from time to time amid the storm,
> The gentle whisper of th' aerial form
> Breath'd forth a lovely tone that died the gales among."
>
> *Oberon* (*Wieland*) (*Sotheby's tr.*).

The fact that this tempest had been called up by Oberon against Huon and Sherasmin was soon made clear. For as the two fell in with a company of monks and nuns, who had been keeping a festival in the woods, the storm suddenly abated its strength. With such com-panions Sherasmin fancied no harm could befall himself or his master, so he gladly followed them to the convent yard. Yet even here another marvel happened, for the

"Oberon appeared like a brilliant **Meteor**"

Huon and Angoulaffre

radiant king suddenly appeared in their midst, looking like a splendid meteor.

> " At once the storm is fled ; serenely mild
> Heav'n smiles around, bright rays the sky adorn,
> While beauteous as an angel newly born
> Beams in the roseate dayspring, glow'd the child.
> A lily stalk his graceful limbs sustain'd,
> Round his smooth neck an ivory horn was chain'd ;
> Yet lovely as he was, on all around
> Strange horror stole, for stern the fairy frown'd,
> And o'er each sadden'd charm a sullen anger reign'd."
>
> *Oberon* (*Wieland*) (*Sotheby's tr.*).

But if the wrath of Oberon was easily roused it vanished as quickly. Therefore, now satisfied at the power he had exhibited to the strangers, he contented himself with arresting the storm by a soft strain blown from his horn. So seductive was the strain that he played that immediately monks, nuns, and Sherasmin, forgetting their age and calling, began to dance in the wildest abandon. Huon alone remained uninfluenced by the music, for he had no wish to avoid an encounter with Oberon.

Oberon's Promise to Huon

Meanwhile the king of the fairies was not unaware of the presence of the knight, and he now revealed to Huon that as his life had been pure and his soul true he would help him in his quest. At a wave from the lily wand the magic music ceased, the charm was broken, and the dancers sank upon the grass. Then Oberon, seeing that Sherasmin was well-nigh exhausted, graciously forgave him his offence, and offered him a golden beaker of wine, bidding him drink without fear. Nevertheless Sherasmin was of a suspicious nature, and though he dared not refuse the draught he drank with fear.

221

Nor was it until he had found that the wine had greatly refreshed him that he completely dismissed his alarm.

The Magic Horn

Then, turning to Huon, Oberon declared that he was fully aware of the peculiar nature of the quest he had undertaken, and that he wished him well. After this he gave him the golden beaker, assuring him that it would always be full of the richest wine for the virtuous, but would burn the evildoer with a devouring fire. He also bestowed his magic horn upon him, telling him that a gentle blast would cause all the hearers to dance, while a loud one would bring to his aid the king of the fairies himself.

> " ' Does but its snail-like spiral hollow sing,
> A lovely note soft swell'd with gentle breath,
> Though thousand warriors threaten instant death,
> And with advancing weapons round enring ;
> Then, as thou late hast seen, in restless dance
> All, all must spin, and every sword and lance
> Fall with th' exhausted warriors to the ground.
> But if thou peal it with impatient sound,
> I at thy call appear, more swift than lightning glance.' "
>
> *Oberon* (*Wieland*) (*Sotheby's tr.*).

Full of gratitude for these precious gifts, Huon knelt before the king to do him obeisance. His action pleased the monarch, who smiled sweetly upon him ; after which, with a wave of his lily wand, the king of the fairies disappeared, leaving a subtle fragrance behind him. Indeed, so suddenly did the radiance of his presence vanish that had it not been for the golden beaker and the ivory horn which Huon still held he might have been tempted to consider the whole occurrence a dream.

THE GIANT ANGOULAFFRE

The Journey to Bagdad

In a more hopeful spirit the two travellers now resumed their journey to Bagdad, until they reached Tourmont, where they found that it was governed by one of Huon's uncles, who, captured in his youth by the Saracens, had turned Mussulman, and had thus gradually risen to the highest dignity. Seeing Huon refresh some of the Christians of his household with a draught of wine from the magic cup, the ruler asked to be allowed to drink from it too. But no sooner had he taken hold of it than he was unmercifully burned, for he was a renegade, and the magic cup refreshed only believers in the Christian faith.

The Giant Angoulaffre

Incensed at what he fancied a deliberate insult, the governor of Tourmont planned to slay his nephew at a great banquet. Nevertheless his cruel intention came to nothing, for the knight defended himself so bravely that he slew several antagonists, one after the other. Then he cunningly disposed of the others by breathing a soft note upon his magic horn, which set them all dancing wildly until they sank breathless and exhausted upon their divans.

Meanwhile Huon, taking advantage of their exhaustion, dashed from the palace on a swift steed, and in this way soon reached the castle of the giant Angoulaffre. This giant it was who had stolen from Oberon a magic ring which made the wearer invulnerable. With this on his finger, therefore, the wicked Angoulaffre had committed countless crimes with impunity. Even as Huon came near the castle he met an unfortunate knight who piteously informed him that the giant had captured his promised bride, whom he now detained in a dungeon together with several other helpless damsels.

Like a true knight-errant, Huon vowed speedily to deliver these helpless ladies, and in spite of the armed guards at every doorway he was enabled, by the use of Oberon's gifts, to pass unmolested into Angoulaffre's chamber. There he found the huge form of the hideous giant plunged in a lethargy. Hurriedly searching the chamber, Huon found the fair bride whom he had come to deliver. In a few hurried sentences she told him that her captor constantly forced his unwelcome attentions upon her; but that, owing to the protection of the Virgin, a trance overtook him and made him helpless whenever he tried to force her inclinations and take her to wife.

> " ' As oft the hateful battle he renews,
>   As oft the miracle his force subdues ;
>   The ring no virtue boasts whene'er that sleep assails.' "
>   *Oberon (Wieland) (Sotheby's tr.).*

Angela and Alexis

Prompted by this fair princess, whose name was Angela, Huon secured the stolen ring, and donned a magic hauberk hanging near. But as he scorned to take any further advantage of a sleeping foe, he patiently awaited the giant's awakening to engage in one of those combats in which knights of old so often distinguished themselves. After a great struggle Huon was victorious, and slew his horrible foe. Then he restored the fair Angela to her lover, Alexis, and gave a magnificent banquet, which was attended by the fifty rescued damsels, and by fifty knights who had come to help their comrade, fair Angela's lover. Full of gratitude for their deliverance, the knights and their ladies begged Huon to stay with them. But he refused, for he had still far to go and many things to do. Therefore he pressed on with as much haste as he could, till at last exhaustion forced him to take rest beneath a tree. Here, as he slept, another marvel happened ; for Oberon caused a tent to shelter him to be raised above him by invisible hands. Happy thoughts flitted softly through the sleeper's mind, and he dreamt of a beautiful princess whom he should one day win for his wife. Yet he also dreamt of the perils that he must undergo before he could hope to obtain her hand.

Awakening full of hope and courage, Huon continued his way, together with the faithful Sherasmin. Everywhere they went they were made aware of the help of the powerful king of the fairies, who even sent one of his spirits, Malebron, to carry them across the waters of the Red Sea. Thus they travelled through burning wastes of sand, refreshed and strengthened by occasional draughts from the magic goblet, till they came at last to a forest, where they saw a Saracen about to succumb beneath the attack of a monstrous lion. Immediately Huon flew to his rescue, and slew the lion. Then, having drunk deeply from his magic cup, he handed it to the Saracen, on whose lips the refreshing wine turned to liquid flame.

> " With evil eye, from Huon's courteous hand,
>   Filled to the brim, the heathen takes the bowl—
>   Back from his lip th' indignant bubbles roll !
>   The spring is dried, and hot as fiery brand,
>   Proof of internal guilt, the metal glows.
>   Far from his grasp the wretch the goblet throws,
>   Raves, roars, and stamps."
>   *Oberon* (*Wieland*) (*Sotheby's tr.*).

Stung by the heat, the Saracen flung aside the cup with an oath. Then, seeing that his own steed had been slain by the lion, he sprang unceremoniously upon

Huon's horse, and rode rapidly away before he could be pursued.

Princess Rezia

Thus, with only one horse to serve both their needs, Huon and Sherasmin were obliged to proceed more slowly to Bagdad. Yet at last they got to the great city, but only to find every hostelry full. Inquiring the reason for the assembly of such great crowds, Huon was told that the Princess Rezia was about to be married to Babican, King of Hyrcania, and therefore the people were anxious to see the nuptials. Somewhat distressed upon hearing this news, Huon and his companion redoubled their efforts to obtain a lodging, till at last they discovered one in the hut of a very old woman. Their hostess, who was none other than the mother of one of the maidens of the princess, amused her visitors by telling them that the bride was most unwilling to marry. She also told them that Rezia had lately been troubled by a dream, in which she had seen herself in the guise of a hind, pursued through a pathless forest by Babican. In this dream she was saved and restored to her former shape by a radiant personage, who rode in a glistening silver car, drawn by leopards. He was accompanied by a fair-haired knight, whom he presented to her as her future bridegroom.

> " The shadow flies ; but from her heart again
> He never fades—the youth with golden hair ;
> Eternally his image hovers there,
> Exhaustless source of sweetly pensive pain,
> In nightly visions, and in day-dreams shown."
>
> *Oberon* (*Wieland*) (*Sotheby's tr.*).

More and more excited as the story went on, Huon listened in breathless rapture, for he now felt assured that the Princess Rezia was the lovely princess he had

226

seen in his dream, and that Oberon intended them for
each other. He therefore assured the old woman that
the princess should never marry the detested Babican.
Then, although Sherasmin pointed out to him that the
way to a lady's favour seldom consists in cutting off the
head of her intended bridegroom, depriving her father
of four teeth and a lock of his beard, and kissing her
without any permission, the young hero persisted in his
resolution to visit the palace on the morrow.

Oberon again to the Rescue

Thus they withdrew to their chamber, where they
passed the night in sleep. In the palace, too, the
princess laid herself to rest, and fell into a deep
slumber. Then as they slept, Huon in the dingy
hut and Rezia in her splendid palace, both were visited
by fair dreams, in which Oberon, their guardian spirit,
promised them his aid. Thus it happened that while
the princess was arraying herself for her nuptials on the
morrow the old woman rushed into her apartment and
announced that a fair-haired knight, who was evidently
the promised deliverer, had slept in her humble dwelling the night before. Comforted by these tidings,
Rezia made a triumphant entrance into the palace hall,
where her father, the bridegroom, and all the principal
dignitaries of the court awaited her appearance.

> " Emirs and viziers, all the courtly crowd
>   Meantime attendant at the Sultan's call,
>   With festal splendour grace the nuptial hall.
>   The banquet waits, the cymbals clang aloud.
>   The grey-beard caliph from his golden door
>   Stalks mid the slaves that fall his path before ;
>   Behind, of stately gesture, proud to view,
>   The Druse prince, though somewhat pale of hue,
>   Comes as a bridegroom deck'd with jewels blazing o'er."
>   *Oberon* (*Wieland*) (*Sotheby's tr.*).

In the meantime Huon, awaking at early dawn, found a complete suit of Saracenic apparel at his bedside. Joyfully he donned the gift, and thus entered the palace unchallenged. Here he passed into the banqueting hall, where he perceived the grey-bearded caliph, and recognised in the bridegroom at his left the Saracen whom he had delivered from the lion, and who had so discourteously stolen his horse. Without wasting any time in cautious thought, Huon strode forward, and with one flash of his curved scimitar smote off the head of the Saracen. Thus was fulfilled the first part of Charlemagne's command, though by no means the whole. Indeed, as Huon stood there, alone in the midst of an alien race, it seemed very unlikely that he would ever be able to carry out all the conditions Charlemagne had imposed. Meanwhile the thud of the head as it fell to the ground caused Huon to turn round and his turban to fall off. But as for the princess, seated at the caliph's right, she gazed, as if she were spell-bound, straight before her at the knight, whose golden locks fell in rich curls about his shoulders.

Huon's Success

Exactly what happened at this point it is hard to say, but the most popular story states that Huon, taking advantage of the first moments of surprise, kissed Rezia thrice, and slipped on her finger, in sign of betrothal, the magic ring which he had taken from Angoulaffre. Then, seeing the caliph's guards about to fall upon him, he gently breathed soft music on his magic horn, and set caliph and court a-dancing.

> " The whole divan, one swimming circle, glides
> Swift without stop : the old bashaws click time,
> As if on polish'd ice ; in trance sublime
> The iman hoar with some spruce courtier slides.

FLIGHT OF REZIA

Nor rank nor age from capering refrain ;
Nor can the king his royal foot restrain !
He too must reel amid the frolic row,
Grasp the Grand Vizier by his beard of snow,
And teach the aged man once more to bound amain ! "
Oberon (Wieland) (Sotheby's tr.).

Flight of Rezia

Forced to dance whether they would or not, the unhappy courtiers spun round and round, while Huon
led Rezia to the door, where Sherasmin was waiting
for them with fleet steeds, and Fatima, the princess's
favourite attendant.   Leaving the princess for a moment
in the care of Sherasmin, Huon hastened back to the
palace hall, where he found that the caliph, completely
exhausted, had sunk upon a divan.   Carefully obeying
the prescribed ceremonies, Huon politely craved a lock
of his beard and four of his teeth as a present for
Charlemagne.   This impudent request so incensed the
caliph that he shouted aloud to his guards to slay the
stranger.   In this dire plight Huon was forced to defend
himself with a curtain-rod and a golden bowl, until,
feeling he needed help, he suddenly blew a resounding
peal upon his magic horn.   Scarcely had the great blast
died on the air when the earth shook, the palace rocked,
and Oberon appeared in the midst of rolling thunder
and flashing lightning.   With a wave of his lily wand
the god of the fairies plunged caliph and people into a
deep sleep.   Then he bade Huon take his silver car and
hasten with his bride and attendants to Ascalon, where he
would find a ship waiting to take them back to France.

" ' So haste, thou matchless pair !
On wings of love my car, that cuts the air,
Shall waft you high above terrestrial sight,
And place, ere morning melt the shades of night,
On Askalon's far shore, beneath my guardian care.' "
Oberon (Wieland) (Sotheby's tr.).

Oberon's Warning

Only too glad to hurry off with the lovely Rezia, Huon hastened to obey, knowing full well that Oberon would in the meantime look after his interests in Bagdad. Nor was his hope disappointed, for as the two lovers were about to embark at Ascalon Oberon suddenly appeared to claim his silver chariot. Then in return he handed the knight a magnificent golden casket sparkling with jewels, in which lay the teeth of the caliph and a lock of his beard. Overcome with gratitude, Huon stammered out his thanks for the generous way in which the fairy god had helped him. "One thing only do I ask of you," said Oberon, as he stood watching them get ready to start; "that is that you do not celebrate your marriage until you have been to Rome to be blessed by the Pope."

"Willingly, willingly," cried the two in one breath, ready in their mutual joy to promise anything.

After a solemn warning by Oberon that if this pledge were rashly broken it would be visited by his swift vengeance, the vessel containing the happy lovers glided slowly seaward.

> " ' And deep, O Huon ! grave it in your brain !
> Till good Sylvester, pious father, sheds
> Heaven's holy consecration on your heads,
> As brother and as sister chaste remain !
> Oh, may ye not, with inauspicious haste,
> The fruit forbidden prematurely taste !
> Know, if ye rashly venture ere the time,
> That Oberon, in vengeance of your crime,
> Leaves you, without a friend, on life's deserted waste ! ' "
>
> *Oberon* (*Wieland*) (*Sotheby's tr.*).

Thus the happy knight and his still happier bride journeyed gaily on their way, till at last they got to Lepanto. Here Huon insisted that his companion

230

DISOBEDIENCE AND PUNISHMENT

Sherasmin should take passage on another vessel, which was sailing direct to France, that by this means he might hasten ahead, lay the golden casket at Charlemagne's feet, and announce the approach of Huon with his Eastern bride.

Reluctantly Sherasmin departed, for he was much averse from the thought of leaving his master to accomplish the rest of the journey unguided. Yet he dared not disobey. Then when the old man had left their vessel, Huon expounded the Christian faith to Rezia, who was not only converted, but also baptized by a priest on board. He gave her the Christian name of Amanda in exchange for her pagan name of Rezia, or Esclarmonde. This same priest also consecrated their marriage ; and though Huon had certainly intended to await the Pope's blessing ere he claimed Amanda as his wife, his good resolutions were soon forgotten, and the last injunction of Oberon disregarded.

Disobedience and Punishment

This disobedience to so small a request on the part of one who had done so much did not go unpunished. Huon was soon made aware that the king of the fairies was very angry indeed. For a fearful tempest suddenly arose, which threatened to destroy the vessel and all on board. Full of superstitious fears, the sailors cast lots to decide who should be sacrificed to allay the fury of the storm. Fearfully Huon plunged in his hand, only to draw the fatal number. Crying aloud in her grief, Amanda declared that her lover should never perish alone, and she flung herself with him into the tumultuous waves. Then as the lovers vanished overboard the storm was suddenly appeased, and instead of drowning together, the two were drifted by the magic of the ring which the princess wore to a volcanic island. Yet here their condition was but little better, for they almost perished from hunger and thirst.

Hand in hand they wandered disconsolately over the rocks, looking eagerly for something to eat. Then suddenly they spied what they thought were apples. But alas! when they put the fruit into their mouths it crumbled away into ashes, for these were the apples of Sodom. Disheartened by this disappointment, they still struggled on, till at last they were encouraged by finding some dates. These they swallowed greedily in their hunger, so that soon there were no more left.

Desperate at the wan face of his fair wife, Huon left her in a place of safety, and with infinite toil ploughed his way over a mountain till he came to a fertile valley on the further slope. This was the home of Titania, queen of the fairies, who had quarrelled with Oberon, and was waiting here until she should be recalled to Fairyland.

But Huon was unaware of her presence, and unable to discover a single inhabitant of the valley, save a hermit, who welcomed him gladly. After hearing about the misfortunes of the knight and his bride, the hermit pointed out to Huon a short and easy way by which he could return to bring the princess. At the same time he urged him to appease the anger of Oberon by living for a time by himself and spending the days in prayer and fasting.

> " ' Blest,' says the hermit, ' blest the man whom fate
> Guides with strict hand, but not unfriendly aim!
> How blest! whose slightest fault is doom'd to shame!
> Him, trained to virtue, purest joys await,—
> Earth's purest joys reward each trying pain!
> Think not the fairy will for aye remain
> Inexorable foe to hearts like thine:
> Still o'er you hangs his viewless hand divine;
> Do but deserve his grace, and ye his grace obtain."
> *Oberon (Wieland) (Sotheby's tr.).*

NEPTUNE

The Holy Grail

AMANDA AND THE PIRATES

Huon's Penance

Only too willing to undergo any penance which would bring about their escape from the island, Huon hastened back to Amanda, and told her all that the hermit had said. Without a murmur she agreed that it should be as her husband desired. Thus they made their way together to the green valley by means of the short road that the hermit had pointed out.

Once arrived, Huon set to work and built a small hut for Amanda's own use. As for himself, he dwelt with the hermit in his cell, some little distance from the cot of the princess. Thus days and weeks passed by, which Huon spent in tilling the soil for their sustenance and in listening to the teachings of the holy man.

Time passed, till one day Amanda wandered a little way up the mountain, and fell asleep in a lovely grotto, which she now for the first time discovered. When she awoke from a blissful dream she found herself clasping her new-born babe, who during her slumbers had been cared for by the elves who owned Titania's sway.

Full of joy, the princess pressed her babe to her bosom, while for the first time for many a day happiness filled her heart. Then when the babe was a little more than a year old the aged monk died, and Huon and Amanda, despairing of release from the desert island, were weary of living apart. Hereupon Titania, who foresaw that Oberon would send new misfortunes upon them to punish them in case they did not stand the second test, carried little Huonet off to Fairyland, lest he should suffer for his parents' sins.

Amanda and the Pirates

In the meantime Huon and Amanda searched frantically for the missing babe, fancying he had wandered off into the woods. During their search they became separated, and while Amanda was walking along the sea-shore she was seized by pirates, whose intention was to carry her away and sell her as a slave to the Sultan. Huon heard her cries of distress, and rushed to her rescue. But in spite of his utmost efforts to join her he saw her borne away to the waiting vessel, while he was bound to a tree in the woods, and left there to die.

> "Deep in the wood, at distance from the shore,
> They drag their victim, that his loudest word
> Pour'd on the desert air may pass unheard.
> Then bind the wretch, and fasten o'er and o'er
> Arm, leg, and neck, and shoulders, to a tree.
> To heaven he looks in speechless agony,
> O'ercome by woe's unutterable weight.
> Thus he—the while, with jocund shout elate,
> The crew bear off their prey, and bound along the sea."
>
> *Oberon (Wieland) (Sotheby's tr.).*

Oberon Relents

Then, and only then, Oberon had pity upon the unfortunate knight, and sent one of his invisible servants, who not only unbound him, but transported him with miraculous rapidity over land and sea, till he deposited him at the door of a gardener's house in Tunis.

Meanwhile the aged Sherasmin had not been without adventures. After parting from his master at Lepanto he travelled on until he came to the gates of the palace with his precious casket. Not till then did he realise that Charlemagne would never credit his tale unless Huon were there with his bride to vouch for its truth. Therefore, instead of entering the royal abode, he hastened back to Rome, where for two months he awaited the arrival of the young couple. At last, seeing no sign of their coming, the faithful Sherasmin, sure that some terrible misfortune had overtaken his master and his bride, donned a pilgrim's robe and set out to find them. In this way he wandered from place to place seeking them, until finally he came to Tunis, where Fatima, Amanda's maid, had been sold into slavery. Here too he sorrowfully learned of his master's death.

In order to be near Fatima, Sherasmin took a gardener's position in the Sultan's palace. Thus it happened that when he opened the door of his humble dwelling one morning he was overjoyed to find Huon, who had been brought there by the messenger of Oberon. The story was long in the telling, but at last it was done, and the two consulted together as to finding Amanda. Following Sherasmin's advice, Huon, under the assumed name of Hassan, became his assistant in the Sultan's gardens, and thus the two were always together.

The pirates, in the meanwhile, hoping to sell Amanda to the Sultan himself, had treated her with the utmost deference ; but as they neared the shore of Tunis their vessel had suffered shipwreck, and all on board had perished miserably, save only the princess, who was miraculously washed ashore at the feet of the Sultan. Charmed by her beauty, the sovereign conveyed her to his palace, where he would immediately have married her had she not told him that she had made a vow of chastity which she was bound to keep for two years.

Huon and Amanda Reunited

Then Huon, unconscious of Amanda's presence, worked in the garden daily, till the daughter of the Sultan saw him and fell in love with him. But in spite of all her efforts to win a smile from her gardener she was unsuccessful. In high dudgeon at her failure, the princess resolved to take her revenge, which she shortly afterwards tried to do in a very cruel manner. For in the meantime Fatima had discovered Amanda's presence in the palace. Joyfully she ran to tell Huon, who, unable to control his eagerness, made a desperate effort to reach her. His desire was, however, discovered by the jealous princess, and since Huon would not love her she was determined that he should not love another. She therefore artfully laid her plans, and accused him of a heinous crime, for which the Sultan, finding appearances against him, condemned him to death. Amanda, who was warned by Fatima of Huon's danger, rushed into the Sultan's presence to plead for her husband's life ; but when she discovered that she could obtain it only at the price of renouncing him for ever and marrying the Sultan she declared that she preferred to die, and elected to be burned with her beloved. The flames were already rising around them both when Oberon, touched by their sufferings and their constancy, suddenly appeared, and again hung his horn about Huon's neck.

Rapturously the knight put the magic horn to his lips and blew a soft note, which instantly set all the hearers dancing. Yet even in his agony Huon was merciful to the people who were around him ; for he played only a gentle note, and not a loud blast, which would have set the time at a gallop.

> " No sooner had the grateful knight beheld,
>   With joyful ardour seen, the ivory horn,
>   Sweet pledge of fairy grace, his neck adorn,
> Than with melodious whisper gently swell'd,
>   His lip entices forth the sweetest tone
>   That ever breath'd through magic ivory blown :
> He scorns to doom a coward race to death.
> ' Dance ! till ye weary gasp, depriv'd of breath—
> Huon permits himself this slight revenge alone.' "
>   *Oberon* (*Wieland*) (*Sotheby's tr.*).

Huon and Amanda in Fairyland

Then while all were dancing, much against their will, Huon and Amanda, Sherasmin and Fatima, gaily stepped into the silvery car which Oberon placed at their disposal, and were rapidly transported to Fairyland. Here their happiness rose to its height, for they found little Huonet in perfect health. Great was the happiness that reigned in Fairyland on that day. For not only were the troubles of Huon and Amanda over, but Queen Titania herself had become reconciled to King Oberon. This she had accomplished by presenting him with the ring of the giant Angoulaffre, which she had found on the sandy shore where Amanda had dropped it in her struggles with the pirates. Gratified by the gift, and pleased with the great devotion of the faithful Huon and Amanda, Oberon not only took the knight back into his favour, but also reinstated Titania in her true place as queen of his realm. Thus Huon and Amanda lingered in Fairyland, full of happiness and peace, till at last Huon declared it was time they should return to the court of the emperor. Anxious to help him in every way, Oberon wafted him in his car to the gates of Paris. There Huon arrived just in time to win, at the point of his lance, his patrimony of Guienne, which Charlemagne had offered as prize at a tournament. Bending low before his monarch, the hero then revealed his name, presented his wife, and gave him the golden casket containing the lock of hair and the four teeth, saying that thus he had accomplished his quest.

> " Our hero lifts the helmet from his head ;
> And boldly ent'ring, like the god of day,
> His golden ringlets down his armour play.
> All, wond'ring, greet the youth long mourn'd as dead,
> Before the king his spirit seems to stand !
> Sir Huon with Amanda, hand in hand,

Salutes the emperor with respectful bow—
'Behold, obedient to his plighted vow,
Thy vassal, sovereign liege, returning to thy land !

" ' For by the help of Heaven this arm has done
What thou enjoin'dst—and lo ! before thine eye
The beard and teeth of Asia's monarch lie,
At hazard of my life, to please thee, won ;
And in this fair, by every peril tried,
The heiress of his throne, my love, my bride ! '
He spoke ; and lo ! at once her knight to grace,
Off falls the veil that hid Amanda's face,
And a new radiance gilds the hall from side to side."

Oberon (*Wieland*) (*Sotheby's tr.*).

Scarcely able to credit his hearing, Charlemagne inquired minutely how the hazardous quest had been achieved ; in reply to which Huon narrated all the adventures that had befallen him since he first set out. Marvelling at the strange recital, the king gladly restored him to favour, and gave a great feast in his honour. Then after staying a short time at court, Huon and Amanda travelled southward to Guienne, where their subjects received them with every demonstration of extravagant joy. Here they spent the remainder of their lives together in happiness and comparative peace.

An Earlier Version of the Story

Though this is the most popular version of the story, there is an earlier one which tells how the princess Esclarmonde, whom the pirates intended to convey to the court of her uncle, Yvoirin of Montbrand, was wrecked near the palace of Galafre, King of Tunis. This sovereign respected her vow of chastity, but obstinately refused to give her up to her uncle when he claimed her. Then Huon, delivered from his fetters on the island, was borne by Malebron, Oberon's servant, to Yvoirin's court, where he immediately offered himself as champion to defy Galafre and win back his beloved wife at the point of the sword. The challenge was accepted, and when Huon appeared in martial array at Tunis Galafre selected as his champion Sherasmin, who had also been shipwrecked off his coast, and had thus become his slave. Thus Huon and Sherasmin met in combat, till, recognising each other after a few moments' struggle, they suddenly embraced, and, joining forces, slew the pagans and carried off Esclarmonde and Fatima. After this they embarked upon a swift sailing vessel, and soon arrived at Rome, where Huon related his adventures to the Pope, who gave him his blessing.

Yet as Huon was on his very way to Charlemagne's court treachery befell him, for Girard, a knight who had taken possession of Huon's estates, stole the golden casket from Sherasmin, and sent Huon and Esclarmonde in chains to Bordeaux. Then, going himself to court, he informed Charlemagne that although Huon had failed in his quest he had dared to return to France. Furious at this news, Charlemagne, whose anger had not yet cooled, proceeded to Bordeaux, where he tried Huon, and condemned him to death. But just as the knight was about to perish Oberon suddenly appeared, and, flinging the emperor and Girard into fetters, he only consented to restore them to freedom when Charlemagne promised to reinstate Huon.

The humiliated emperor unwillingly consented, whereupon Oberon produced the missing casket and revealed Girard's treachery. Then, after seeing the real traitor punished, the king of the fairies bore Huon and Esclarmonde off to Fairyland. Here they spent the remainder of their lives in happiness, while in due time Huon reigned in Oberon's stead.

LEGENDS OF THE MIDDLE AGES

Equally marvellous adventures are also told about his renowned daughter, Claretie, who forms the subject of another but minor *chanson de geste*, in which she is asserted to be the ancestress of all the Capetian Kings of France.

CHAPTER XI : TITUREL AND THE HOLY GRAIL

The Origin of the Legend

OF all the romances of chivalry the most mystical and spiritual is undoubtedly the legend of the Holy Grail. Rooted in the mythology of all primitive races is the belief in a land of peace and happiness, a sort of earthly paradise, once possessed by man, but now lost, and only to be attained again by the virtuous. The legend of the Holy Grail, which some authorities declare was first known in Europe by the Moors, and Christianised by the Spaniards, was soon introduced into France, where Robert de Borron and Chrestien de Troyes wrote lengthy poems about it. Other writers took up the same theme, among them Walter Map, Archdeacon of Oxford, who connected it with the Arthurian legends. It soon became known in Germany, where, in the hands of Gottfried von Strassburg, and especially of Wolfram von Eschenbach, it assumed its most perfect and popular form. The " Parzival " of Eschenbach also forms the basis of the much-discussed last opera of the great Wagner.[1]

The story of the Grail is thus naturally confused, owing to the many changes made by the different authors. The account here given, while mentioning the most striking incidents of other versions, is in general an outline of the " Titurel " and " Parzival " of von Eschenbach.

The Holy Grail

Thus it happened that when Lucifer was cast out of Heaven one stone of great beauty was detached from the marvellous crown which sixty thousand angels

[1] *See* " Stories from Wagner," by J. W. McSpadden.

had tendered him. This stone fell upon earth, and from it was carved a vessel of great beauty, which came, after many ages, into the hands of Joseph of Arimathea. He offered it to the Saviour, who made use of it in the Last Supper. When the blood flowed from the Redeemer's side, Joseph of Arimathea caught a few drops of it in this wonderful vessel. Owing to this circumstance it was thought to be endowed with marvellous powers. "Wherever it was there were good things in abundance. Whoever looked upon it, even though he were sick unto death, could not die that week ; whoever looked at it continually, his cheeks never grew pale, nor his hair grey."

Once a year, on the anniversary of the Saviour's death, a white dove brought a fresh host down from Heaven, and placed it on the vessel, which was borne by a company of angels, or by spotless virgins. The care of it was at times entrusted to mortals, who, however, had to prove themselves worthy of this exalted honour by leading unblemished lives. This vessel, called the "Holy Grail," remained after the crucifixion in the hands of Joseph of Arimathea. Then the Jews, angry because Joseph had helped to bury Christ, cast him into a dungeon, and left him there for a whole year without food or drink. Their purpose in doing so was to slay Joseph, as they had already slain Nicodemus, so that should the Romans ever ask them to produce Christ's body they might declare that it had been stolen by Joseph of Arimathea. Yet they little suspected that Joseph, having the Holy Grail with him, could suffer no lack.

By-and-by Vespasian, the Roman emperor, heard the story of Christ's passion as related by a knight who had just returned from the Holy Land. The story greatly excited him, and he sent a commission to Jerusalem to

242

investigate the matter and bring back some holy relic to cure his son Titus of leprosy.

In due time the ambassadors returned, giving Pilate's version of the story, and bringing with them an old woman who after her death became known as St. Veronica. Full of reverent awe, Veronica drew forth the cloth with which she had wiped the Lord's face, and upon which His likeness had been plainly left. Eagerly the king hastened to bear it before his stricken son, who instantly recovered at the mere sight of the holy relic. Then, together with Vespasian, Titus proceeded to Jerusalem. There they vainly tried to compel the Jews to produce the body of Christ, until one of them revealed, under pressure of torture, the place where Joseph was imprisoned. Determined to get at the truth, Vespasian himself went to the dungeon, where he was hailed by the saint, who was perfectly well and strong. Amazed at this miracle, Vespasian had Joseph set free, who, fearing further persecution from the Jews, soon departed with his sister, Enigée, and her husband, Brons, for a distant land. The pilgrims found a place of refuge near Marseilles, where the Holy Grail supplied all their needs until one of them committed a sin. Then Divine displeasure became manifest by a terrible famine.

As none knew who had sinned, Joseph was instructed in a vision to discover the culprit by the same means with which the Lord had revealed the guilt of Judas. Still following Divine commands, Joseph made a table, and directed Brons to catch a fish. The Grail was placed before Joseph's seat at table, where all who implicitly believed were invited to take a seat. Eleven seats were soon occupied, and only the place of Judas remained empty. Then Moses, a hypocrite and sinner, attempted to seat himself in the empty place, but the earth opened wide beneath him and engulfed him.

In another vision Joseph was now told that the vacancy would only be filled on the day of doom. At the same time he was also told that a similar table would be constructed by Merlin. Here the grandson of Brons would honourably occupy the vacant place, which is designated in the legend as the " Siege Perilous," because it proved fatal to all for whom it was not intended.

In the " Great St. Grail," one of the longest poems on this theme, there are countless adventures and journeys, " transformations of fair females into foul fiends, conversions wholesale and individual, allegorical visions, miracles, and portents. Eastern splendour and Northern weirdness, angelry and devilry, together with abundant fighting and quite a phenomenal amount of swooning, make up a strange medley of Celtic, pagan, and Christian legends, which alternate in a kaleidoscopic maze that defies the symmetry demanded by modern æsthetic canons in every artistic production."

The later history of the Holy Grail is variously related. But it is held by many that it was carried by Joseph of Arimathea to Glastonbury, where it long remained visible, and whence it vanished only when men became too sinful to be permitted to retain it in their midst.

Birth of Titurel

Another legend relates that a rich man from Cappadocia, named Berillus, followed Vespasian to Rome, where he won great estates. He was a virtuous man, and his good qualities were inherited by all his descendants. One of these, called Titurisone, was full of sorrow because he had no son to continue his race. Then, following the advice of a wise soothsayer, he made a pilgrimage to the holy sepulchre, and there laid a crucifix of pure gold upon the altar. To his great joy, on his return he was rewarded for his pilgrimage by the birth of a son, whom he called Titurel.

By-and-by this child grew to manhood, and spent all his time in warring against the Saracens, which was the name given to all pagans in these metrical romances. The booty he won he gave either to the Church or to the poor, and his courage and virtue were only equalled by his piety and extreme humility.

One day, when Titurel was walking alone in the woods musing upon holy things, he suddenly saw an angel standing before him. In musical tones the heavenly visitant announced that he had been chosen as the guardian of the Holy Grail, which he would find upon Montsalvatch. Therefore the angel warned him to set a watch over his lips and guard well his way of living, since none but the pure might even catch so much as a glimpse of the holy vessel.

The thought of the great charge to be put in his hand filled Titurel with awe, and he hastened home, pondering as to where Montsalvatch might be. For he did not know; neither to this day has any one discovered the exact spot of the mystical place, though some assert it to have been in Spain. Meanwhile Titurel, obeying the voice of the angel, sold all that he possessed, save only his armour and his sword. Then he again returned to the place where he had first seen the vision, for he knew not what he was to do next.

But as he stood gazing up into the blue sky and longing earnestly to follow his Master a mysterious white cloud seemed to beckon him onwards. Instinctively the gazer turned to follow it, and so guided he passed through vast solitudes and impenetrable woods, till he began to climb a steep mountain, whose ascent at first seemed impossible. Clinging to the rocks, and gazing ever ahead at the guiding cloud, Titurel came at last to the top of the mountain, where, in a beam of refulgent light, he beheld the Holy Grail, borne in the air by invisible hands. He raised his heart in passionate prayer that he might be found worthy to guard the emerald-coloured wonder which was thus entrusted to his care, and in his rapture hardly heeded the welcoming cries of a number of knights in shining armour, who hailed him as their king.

The vision of the Holy Grail, which was as evanescent as beautiful, soon disappeared. But Titurel, knowing that the spot was holy, guarded it with all his might against the infidels who would fain have climbed the steep slope. Several years went by without the Holy Grail coming down to earth ; therefore Titurel conceived the plan of building a temple suitable for its reception. The knights who helped to build and afterwards guarded this ple were called "Templars." Their first effort was to clear the mountain-top, which they found was one single onyx of enormous size. This they levelled and polished until it shone like a mirror, and upon this foundation they prepared to build their shrine.

Temple of the Holy Grail

Then as Titurel was hesitating what plan to adopt for the building he prayed for guidance, and when he arose on the morrow he found the ground plan all traced out and the building materials ready for use. From morning till eve the knights laboured at their holy task, and when they ceased invisible hands continued the work till morning. Thus pushed onward, the building progressed rapidly, and the temple rose on the mountain-top in magnificent splendour. Some idea of its unrivalled loveliness may be faintly gained from the description which tells that "The temple itself was one hundred fathoms in diameter. Around it were seventy-two chapels of an octagonal shape. To every pair of chapels there was a tower six stories high, approachable by a winding stair on the outside. In the centre stood a tower twice as big as the others, which rested on arches. The vaulting was of blue sapphire, and in the centre was a plate of emerald, with the Lamb and the banner of the Cross in enamel. All the altar stones were of sapphire, as symbols of the propitiation of sins. Upon the inside of the cupola surmounting the temple, the sun and moon were represented in diamonds and topazes, and shed a light as of day even in the darkness of the night. The windows were of crystal, beryl, and other transparent stones. The floor was of translucent crystal, under which all the fishes of the sea were carved out of onyx, just like life. The towers were of precious stones inlaid with gold ; their roofs of gold and blue enamel. Upon every tower there was a crystal cross, and upon it a golden eagle with expanded wings, which at a distance appeared to be flying. At the summit of the main tower was an immense carbuncle, which served, like a star, to guide the Templars thither at night. In the centre of the building, under the dome, was a miniature representation of the whole, and in this the holy vessel was kept."

Descent of the Holy Grail

At last the work was finished, and the wonderful temple stood in all its peerless glory. Its consecration was then solemnly carried out by the priests, whose hearts glowed with reverent pride at the sight of the holy edifice. Slowly they walked up and down, singing sweet psalms and waving their censers as they passed along the dim aisles and under the splendid arches. But suddenly one and all paused and gazed with quickened senses at the place where the altar stood. For there, on a beam of light, came the holy cup, stealing noiselessly through the air, till it hovered above the altar itself. Awestruck, the priests hushed their songs and looked rapturously at the marvel before them. Then as they gazed there fell upon their ears a sweet strain sung by a choir of angels, that chanted the praises of the Most High.

With fearful awe Titurel took charge of the vessel which had thus come down to earth. Nor did either he or any of his knights fail in the great undertaking they had vowed to perform : for when they were faint and hungry the holy cup sustained them ; when they were wounded it healed them as they knelt in worship before this token of the favour of Heaven. Moreover, it also became as it were the voice of God himself ; for upon its rim there appeared from time to time a Divine message, written in letters of fire, which burnt themselves into the hearts of the knights who were permitted to read them.

Meanwhile, so marvellous was the power of the Holy Grail, that though by this time Titurel was more than four hundred years old he seemed like a man of forty. Nevertheless he was startled one day when he beheld on the edge of the vessel a message in burning flame which bade him seek a wife, that his race might not be extinguished. Up till now, the care of his precious charge had so occupied his mind that he had given never a thought to any of the matters with which other men are concerned. Therefore the message made him suddenly realise that there were yet other things for him to do. Quickly he summoned all the knights of the temple and bade them read in turn the message that was written. Then as each saw, an exclamation or wonder rose from his lips, for they too had been so absorbed in their work that they had quite forgotten everything else.

The Princess Richoude

Nevertheless the injunction was not to be disobeyed, so one and all set about trying to find a woman worthy to marry so great a knight as their leader. Their choice at last fell upon Richoude, the daughter of a Spaniard, and an imposing embassy was therefore sent to the maiden. The princess had long known of the great deeds Titurel had done, and she at once signified her willingness to become his queen. Joyfully the messengers led her to their king, and the marriage was straightway celebrated.

For twenty years Richoude was a faithful wife, and when she died she left two children—a son, Frimoutel, and a daughter, Richoude—to comfort the sorrowing Titurel for her loss. Both these married in their turn, the children of Frimoutel being two sons, Amfortas and Trevrezent, and three daughters, Herzeloide, Josiane, and Repanse de Joie. As these children grew up Titurel gradually aged, till he became too old to bear the weight of his armour. Therefore he spent all his days in seclusion in the temple watching the mystic verse. Then, one day, as he knelt gazing upon the holy cup he saw letters of fire suddenly flash round the rim, and he read the message that he should name his son Frimoutel king in his stead. Joyfully the old man obeyed, for he felt that the defence of the Holy Grail was a heavier burden than he could now sustain.

Birth of Parzival

Yet although he renounced the throne in favour of his son, Titurel still lived on. In time he witnessed the marriage of Josiane, and bitterly mourned for her when she died in giving birth to a little daughter, called Sigune. This child, being thus left without a mother's care, was entrusted to Herzeloide, who brought her up with Tchionatulander, the orphaned son of a friend. Herzeloide married a prince named Gamuret, and became the happy mother of Parzival, who, however, soon lost his father in a terrible battle.

Fearful lest when her son grew up he should want to follow his father's example and make war against even the most formidable foes, Herzeloide carried him off into the forest of Soltane (which some authors locate in Brittany), and there brought him up in complete solitude and ignorance.

> " The child her falling tears bedew ;
> No wife was ever found more true.
> She teemed with joy and uttered sighs ;
> And tears midst laughter filled her eyes.
> Her heart delighted in his birth ;
> In sorrow deep was drowned her mirth."
> *Parzival* (*Wolfram von Eschenbach*) (*Dippold's tr.*).

While Herzeloide was still living in Soltane her father, Frimoutel, becoming weary of the monotonous life on Montsalvatch, went out into the world. Here he died far away from home beneath the thrust of a knight. Amfortas, his son, who was now crowned in obedience to the command of the Holy Grail, proved equally restless, and went out also in search of adventures. Like his father, he too was wounded by a poisoned lance ; yet instead of dying he lived to return to the Holy Grail. But since his wound had not been received in defence of the holy vessel, it never healed, and caused him untold suffering.

The Sickness of Amfortas

The aged Titurel, seeing his suffering, was touched with pity. Ardently he prayed that his grandson might be released from the pain which embittered every moment of his life. Then at last he saw with joy one day glowing letters on the rim of the Holy Grail which told him that before very long a chosen hero would climb the mountain and ask about the cause of the suffering of Amfortas. At this question the evil spell would be broken, Amfortas healed, and the newcomer appointed king and guardian of the Holy Grail.

This promise of ultimate cure saved Amfortas from utter despair, and all the Templars lived in constant anticipation of the coming hero, and of the question which would put an end to the torment which they daily witnessed.

Parzival's Early Life

Parzival in the meantime was growing up in the forest, where he amused himself with a bow and arrow of his own manufacture. But when for the first time he killed a tiny bird, and saw it lying limp and helpless in his hand, he brought it tearfully to his mother and inquired what it meant. In answering him she said it was God Who gave life, and thus for the first time the child heard the name of the Creator. Eagerly he asked her what she meant, whereupon she replied : " Brighter is God than e'en the brightest day ; yet once He took the form and face of man."

Thus brought up in complete ignorance, it is no wonder that when young Parzival chanced to encounter some knights in brilliant armour in the forest he fell

down and offered to worship them. Amused at the
lad's simplicity, the knights told him all about the gay
world of chivalry beyond the forest, and advised him
to ride to Arthur's court, where, if worthy, he would
receive the order of knighthood, and perchance be
admitted to the Round Table. Bewildered with joy at
hearing of all these marvellous things, and dancing with
eagerness to set out immediately, Parzival returned to
his mother to relate what he had seen, and to implore her
to give him a horse, that he might ride after the knights.

> " ' I saw four men, dear mother mine ;
> Not brighter is the Lord divine.
> They spoke to me of chivalry ;
> Through Arthur's power of royalty,
> In knightly honour well arrayed,
> I shall receive the acolade.' "
>
> *Parzival* (*Wolfram von Eschenbach*) (*Dippold's tr.*).

Herzeloide sighed when she heard his words, for
she feared she would lose her son for ever. Yet she
comforted herself with the thought of the long years
they had passed together in the forest. Nevertheless,
so reluctant was she to agree to his departure that she
prepared for him the motley garb of a fool and gave
him a very sorry nag to ride. In this way she selfishly
hoped that the ridicule he was certain to meet with
would drive him back home.

> " The boy, silly yet brave indeed,
> Oft from his mother begged a steed.
> That in her heart she did lament ;
> She thought : ' Him must I make content,
> Yet must the thing an evil be.'
> Thereafter further pondered she :
> ' The folk are prone to ridicule.
> My child the garments of a fool
> Shall on his shining body wear.
> If he be scoffed and beaten there,
> Perchance he'll come to me again.' "
>
> *Parzival* (*Wolfram von Eschenbach*) (*Bayard Taylor's tr.*).

252

Parzival's Journey into the World

As for Parzival, he was quite careless about the fashion of his clothes, provided only he might set out to explore the wide world. His heart was merry as he mounted his shabby steed, and he never once gave a thought to the curious figure he cut in his odd clothes. Meanwhile his mother heaped upon him all sorts of unpractical advice, thus hoping to make him appear more foolish than ever. Gratefully Parzival accepted it all ; for as yet he knew nothing of the wisdom of the world. Then, jerking his reins, he started his horse, feeling happy in his heart at the thought of the journey he was to go, yet sad at leaving his home. As for Herzeloide, with a heavy heart she accompanied her son part way ; then, straining him to her bosom, she kissed him good-bye and stood aside to watch him set off. Gaily he rode to the bend in the forest, then laughingly turned and waved his hand as the thick trees hid him from view. Little did he think he had looked his last upon his mother. Yet it was even so, for as Parzival disappeared from view in the forest paths the sad heart of Herzeloide broke and she breathed her last.

However, Parzival rode onward till he came to a meadow, in which some tents were pitched. Here he saw a beautiful lady asleep in one of the tents, and, dismounting, he wakened her with a kiss. For this had been one of his mother's injunctions—a kiss for every fair lady he met. He was therefore not a little surprised when the maiden flushed with anger and rebuked him for his rudeness. Therefore he tried to pacify her by telling her that he had often thus saluted his mother, after which she slipped the bracelet from her arm, and bestowed it upon him as a proof that her anger had vanished. Thus rewarded, Parzival rode

253

happily on his way, fearing no evil. But soon Lord
Orilus, the lady's husband, hearing from her that a
youth had come up and kissed her, flew into a towering
rage, and rode speedily after the offender, hoping to
overtake the impudent varlet and punish him.

Parzival in the interval had journeyed on through
the forest till he came upon a maiden weeping over the
body of her slain lover. In answer to his inquiries she
told him that she was his cousin, Sigune, and that the
dead man, Tchionatulander, had been killed in trying
to fulfil a trifling request she had made. For she asked
him to recover her pet dog, which had been stolen, and
in the encounter which followed he had been slain.
Full of astonishment at such cruelty, Parzival promised
to avenge Tchionatulander as soon as possible, and to
remember that the murderer was a Red Knight.

By-and-by he came to a river, and called to a boatman to ferry him over. Having nothing with which to
reward the ferryman, Parzival gave him the bracelet he
had received from the wife of Orilus. Then, hearing
that Arthur was holding his court at Nantes, he proceeded thither without further delay.

On entering the city Parzival encountered the Red
Knight, who mockingly asked him where he was
going. Quite unabashed, Parzival quickly retorted :
" To Arthur's court to ask him for your arms and
steed ! "

Parzival at Arthur's Court

As he rode further into the town the youth's motley
garb attracted much attention, and the town boys began
to jeer at him, until Iwanet, one of the king's squires,
came to inquire the cause of the tumult. Hereupon
he took Parzival under his protection, and conducted
him to the great hall, where, if we are to believe some

Parzival at the Court of King Arthur

Parzival prays for Guidance

accounts, Parzival, in his ignorance, presented himself on horseback. Quite bewildered at the sight of the gay company, the inexperienced youth wonderingly inquired why there were so many Arthurs. With a good-natured laugh Iwanet told him that the wearer of the crown was the sole king. Then Parzival, boldly stepping up to him, asked for the arms and steed of the Red Knight.

Amazed at the request, Arthur turned and gazed at the rash speaker before he replied that he might have them provided he could win them. This was enough for the impetuous stranger, who darted from the hall and sped after the Red Knight. Then, overtaking him, he loudly bade him surrender his weapons and his steed. The Red Knight, thus challenged, had no choice but to fight, even with so ludicrous an enemy. Yet so bravely did Parzival wield his spear, in spite of his inexperience, that soon he slew his opponent. Far too eager to waste a thought in pity for the dead knight stretched at his feet, Parzival hastened to secure the steed. Then as he stood there puzzling as to how to remove the fallen warrior's armour, Iwanet came by. Recognising the odd-looking youth, the knight rode up and inquired into the matter. Then when he saw the Red Knight dead, and learned that he had fallen by Parzival's hand, he quickly helped to unfasten the armour, and assisted the conqueror to don it. Yet because his mother had sent him forth in motley garb Parzival would not have this removed, but pulled on the armour over it. Thus equipped he rode forth determined to do brave deeds.

Far and wide rode Parzival, till he came to the castle of Gurnemanz, a noble knight, with whom he remained for some time. Here he received valuable instruction in all a knight should know, so that when he left this place about a year later he was an accomplished knight, clad as beseemed his calling, and ready to fulfil all the duties which chivalry imposed upon its votaries.

Parzival and Conduiramour

As he was thus longing for a mission upon which to go he heard that Queen Conduiramour was hard pressed in her capital of Belripar by an unwelcome suitor. Pledged by his word to defend all ladies in distress, Parzival immediately set out to rescue this queen. Single-handed he fought with the besiegers one by one, till at last he had overcome them all. Then the citizens of Belripar, to show their gratitude to their deliverer, offered him the hand of Conduiramour, which offer he gladly accepted. But even in this new home Parzival could not forget his sorrowing mother, and he soon left his wife to go in search of Herzeloide and fill her heart with gladness. For he knew not as yet of the death of his gentle parent. Thus he set off, promising his wife, however, that he would return soon, and bring his mother to Belripar to share their joy. In the course of this journey homeward Parzival came to a lake, where a richly dressed fisherman, in answer to his inquiry, directed him to a neighbouring castle, where he might find shelter.

Parzival on Montsalvatch

Now although Parzival did not know it, he had come to the castle on Montsalvatch. At his call the drawbridge was immediately lowered, and richly clad servants bade him welcome with joyful mien. They told him that he had long been expected, and after arraying him in a jewelled garment, sent by Queen Repanse de Joie, they conducted him into a large, brilliantly illumined hall. There four hundred knights were seated on soft cushions, before small tables, each

256

laid for four guests. As they saw him enter a flash of
joy passed over their grave and melancholy faces, as if
they saw in him a deliverer. Wonderingly Parzival
gazed about him, till he noticed that the chief seat in
the hall was occupied by a man wrapped in furs, who
was evidently suffering from some painful disease.
Seeing the gaze of the knight, the king (for he it was)
made a sign to Parzival to draw near, and gave him a
seat beside him. After this he presented him with a
sword of exquisite workmanship, and bade him welcome,
saying he had long been expected. Amazed by all he
heard and saw, Parzival thought he had come into a
palace of marvels. Yet he did not ask any questions,
for he feared to seem inquisitive, and thus make
himself unworthy of being a knight. So he sat and
pondered, while all the time his eager eyes were searching the hall to find some explanation of the mystery.
Soon, however, his amazement was deepened still
further. For suddenly the great doors opened, and a
servant appeared bearing the bloody head of a lance,
with which he silently walked around the hall, while
all gazed upon it and groaned aloud.

The servant had scarcely vanished when the doors
again opened, and a company of beautiful virgins came
marching in, two by two. They bore an embroidered
cushion, an ebony stand, and sundry other articles,
which they laid before the fur-clad king. Last of all
came the beautiful maiden Repanse de Joie, carrying a
glowing vessel ; and as she entered and laid it before
the king Parzival heard the assembled knights whisper
that this was the Holy Grail.

> " Now after them advanced the Queen,
> With countenance of so bright a sheen,
> They all imagined day would dawn.
> One saw the maiden was clothed on

With muslin stuffs of Araby.
On a green silk cushion she
The pearl of Paradise did bear.

  •   •   •

The blameless Queen, proud, pure, and calm,
Before the host put down the Grail ;
And Percival, so runs the tale,
To gaze upon her did not fail,
Who thither bore the Holy Grail."
Parzival (*Wolfram von Eschenbach*) (*Bayard Taylor's tr.*).

The Miracle of the Grail

Full of awe and excitement, Parzival watched while the maidens slowly retired and the knights and squires drew near. And now he saw the greatest of all miracles. For from the shining vessel streamed forth a supply of the daintiest dishes and richest wines, each guest being served with the viands which he liked best. Nevertheless all ate sadly and in silence, while as for Parzival he sat and wondered what it might all mean. Yet desiring to be ever courteous he remained mute. The meal ended, the sufferer rose from his seat, gazed reproachfully at the visitor, who by asking a question could have saved him such pain, and slowly left the room, uttering a deep sigh.

The Disappointment of Amfortas

With angry glances the knights also left the hall, and sad-faced servants conducted Parzival past a sleeping-room, where they showed him an old white-haired man who lay in a troubled sleep. At this Parzival wondered still more, but still he did not venture to ask who it might be. Next the servants took him to an apartment where he could spend the night. The tapestry hangings of this room were all embroidered with gorgeous pictures. Left to himself, the young knight wandered round the
258

room looking at these pictures one by one, till at last he stopped. He was looking at a scene which represented his host borne to the ground by a spear-thrust in his bleeding side. At the sight of this Parzival's curiosity burned within him, and he longed to ask for an explanation. But, scorning to ask a servant what he had not ventured to demand of the master, he went quietly to bed, thinking that he would try to secure an explanation on the morrow.

When he awoke he found himself alone. No servant answered his call. All the doors were fastened except those which led outside, where he found his steed awaiting him. When he had passed the drawbridge it rose up slowly behind him, and a voice called out from the tower : "Thou art accursed ; for thou hadst been chosen to do a great work, which thou hast left undone!" Then, looking upward, Parzival saw a horrible face gazing after him with a fiendish grin, and making a gesture as of malediction.

Parzival and Sigune

Quite unable to understand the meaning of all this, the knight journeyed on sadly till he came to a lonely cell in the desert, where he found Sigune weeping over a shrine in which lay Tchionatulander's embalmed remains. She too received him with curses, and revealed to him that by one sympathetic question only he might have ended the prolonged pain of Amfortas, broken an evil spell, and won for himself a glorious crown.

Horrified now that he knew what harm he had done, Parzival rode away, feeling as if he were indeed accursed. His greatest wish was to return to the mysterious castle and atone for his remissness by asking the question which would release the king from further pain. But alas! the castle had vanished; nor could the knight find the least trace of its whereabouts. Only after many adventures did Parzival at last arrive again within its portals and see again the suffering king.

Meanwhile at times the longing to give up the quest and return home to his young wife was almost unendurable. For he loved her dearly, and his thoughts were ever with her. Everything that he saw about him reminded him of her fairness, till even a drop of blood fallen on the snow brought to his thought the dazzling complexion of Conduiramour, and her sorrow when he departed.

> " 'Conduiramour, thine image is
> Here in the snow now dyed with red
> And in the blood on snowy bed.
> Conduiramour, to them compare
> Thy forms of grace and beauty rare.' "
> *Parzival (Wolfram von Eschenbach) (Dippold's tr.).*

In spite of countless temptations, Parzival remained true to his wife as he rode from place to place constantly seeking the Holy Grail, while his oft-reiterated questions concerning it caused him to be considered a madman or a fool by all he met.

In the course of his journeys he encountered a lady in chains, led by a knight who seemed to take pleasure in torturing her. Taught by Gurnemanz to rescue all ladies in distress, Parzival challenged and defeated this knight. Then only did he discover that it was Sir Orilus, who had led his wife about in chains to punish her for accepting a kiss from a strange youth. Aghast at the thought of the result of his carelessness, Parzival hastened to give an explanation of the whole affair, upon which the defeated knight was appeased, and readily promised to treat his wife with all kindness in future.

GAWAIN'S QUEST

The Renown of Parzival

Meanwhile, as Parzival had ordered all the knights whom he had defeated to journey immediately to Arthur's court and tender him their services, the king had in this way won many brave warriors. Delighted by these constant arrivals, and pleased at the repeated accounts of Parzival's valour, he became very anxious to see him once more.

To gratify this wish several knights were sent in search of the wanderer, and when they finally found him they bade him come to court. Yielding to their entreaties, Parzival obeyed, and was knighted by Arthur's own hand, after which it is said by some that he occupied the "Siege Perilous" at the Round Table. Other versions state, however, that just as he was about to take this seat the witch Kundrie, a messenger of the Holy Grail, appeared in the hall. She vehemently denounced the knight, and related how sorely he had failed in his duty. Then, cursing him, as the gate-keeper had done, for his lack of sympathy, she fled from the hall. Recalled to a sense of his duty by her words, Parzival immediately left the hall to renew the quest, which had already lasted for many months. In this he was closely followed by Gawain, one of Arthur's knights, who greatly admired Parzival, and judged that his failure to release King Amfortas from pain had been caused only by ignorance.

Gawain's Quest

Four years now elapsed—four years of penance and suffering for Parzival, and of brilliant fighting and thrilling adventures for Gawain. Thus the two knights followed hard in the footsteps of each other; yet never did Gawain overtake his friend, though he met many whom Parzival had helped or defeated. At last Gawain decided that his quest would end sooner if he too sought the Holy Grail, the goal of all his friend's hopes, and therefore he bent his energies towards discovering the holy vessel.

Pushing on, therefore, to Montsalvatch, Gawain fell in with a beautiful woman, to whom he made a declaration of love. In reply she merely answered that those who loved her must serve her, and bade him fetch her palfrey from a neighbouring garden. Hastening to do so, Gawain met the gardener, who told him that this lady was the Duchess Orgueilleuse, whose beauty had fired many a knight. He added that many had died for her sake ; and that to win her favour Amfortas, King of the Holy Grail, had braved the poisoned spear which wounded him fatally. Nevertheless, undeterred by this warning, Gawain brought out the lady's palfrey, helped her to mount, and followed her submissively through many lands. Everywhere they went the proud lady stirred up some quarrel, after which she always called upon Gawain to fight the enemies whom she had thus wantonly made. After much wandering Gawain and his fair guide reached the top of a hill, whence they could look across a valley to a gigantic castle, perched on a rock, near which was a pine-tree. Pointing this out, the Lady Orgueilleuse now informed Gawain that the castle belonged to her mortal enemy, Gramoflaus. She bade him bring her a twig of the tree, and conquer the owner of the castle, who would challenge him as soon as he touched it. As a reward she promised that if he obeyed her exactly she would be his faithful wife.

Klingsor's Castle

Then Gawain, emboldened by this promise, dashed down into the valley, swam across the moat, plucked a branch from the tree, and accepted the challenge which Gramoflaus promptly offered. The meeting was appointed to take place eight days later, in front of the castle of King Klingsor, whither Gawain immediately proceeded with the Lady Orgueilleuse. On the way she told him that this castle, which faced her father's, was occupied by a magician, who kept many noble ladies in close confinement, and had even cruelly laden them with heavy chains.

On hearing this Gawain at once vowed that he would punish the magician also. Then, having seen Orgueilleuse safely enter her father's palace, he crossed the river and rode toward Klingsor's castle. It was dusk as he rode, and therefore he noticed the more plainly the brilliant lights which lit up each of the windows of the palace in front of him. Startled, he saw outlined against the radiance pale, wan faces, which looked out into the darkness with wide, pathetic eyes, as if they were seeking a deliverer who never came. Stirred to fury at the thought of these hapless ladies, Gawain hastened on the more, till at last he came within reach of the palace. Then as he strode within the hall a great fear fell on his heart, for though he had been readily admitted, yet within he found both hall and court were deserted. From room to room he wandered, yet he met no one. Then, weary of his vain search, he prepared at last to occupy a comfortable couch in one of the chambers. To his utter amazement, however, the bed retreated as he advanced, until, impatient at this trickery, he sprang boldly upon it. A moment later a rain of sharp spears and daggers fell upon his couch, but they did him no harm, for he had not removed his heavy armour. Then when the rain of weapons was over a gigantic peasant armed with a huge club stalked into the room, closely followed by a fierce lion. Expecting to find the knight dead, the peasant advanced boldly. But when he discovered his enemy was alive and unhurt he beat a hasty retreat, leaving the lion to attack him alone.

A fierce encounter now followed between the knight and the beast ; yet in spite of its size and fury Gawain defended himself so bravely that finally he slew the monster, which was Klingsor in disguise. Then as the lion expired the spell was broken, the captives were released, and the exhausted Gawain was tenderly cared for by his mother and sister Itonie, who were among those whom his courage had set free. The news of this victory was immediately sent to Arthur, who now came to witness the battle between Gawain and a champion who was to appear for Gramoflaus.

Worn out by the terrible struggle he had gone through so recently, Gawain's strength and courage were about to give way before the stranger's terrible onslaught, when Itonie implored the latter to spare Gawain, since his name and valour were so well known. At the sound of this word the knight sheathed his sword, and, raising his vizor, revealed the sad but beautiful countenance of Parzival.

The joy of reunion over, Parzival remained there long enough to witness the marriages of Gawain and Orgueilleuse, and of Itonie and Gramoflaus, and to be solemnly admitted to the Round Table. Yet in the midst of the general gladness he himself remained sad and gloomy, for he thought ever of Amfortas and his grievous wound. As soon as possible, therefore, Parzival again departed, humbly praying that he might at last find the Holy Grail, and right the wrong he had unconsciously done. For the thought of the injury which he had occasioned Amfortas weighed heavily on the heart of the noble knight.

264

Parzival and the Hermit

Some months later, exhausted by constant journeys, Parzival painfully dragged himself to a hermit's hut. There he learned that the lonely penitent was Trevrezent, the brother of Amfortas, who, having also preferred worldly pleasures to the service of the Holy Grail, had accompanied him on his fatal excursion. Then when Trevrezent had seen his brother so sorely wounded he repented of his sins, and, retiring into the woods, spent his days and nights in penance and prayer. Ignorant of the identity of his visitor, Trevrezent poured out to Parzival the story of the expected stranger, whose question would break the evil spell, and related how grievously he and all the Templars had been disappointed when such a man had actually come and gone, but without fulfilling their hopes. Parzival then penitently confessed that it was he who had thus disappointed them, related his sorrow and ceaseless quest, and told the story of his early youth and adventures. No sooner had Trevrezent heard the name of his guest than he exclaimed that they must be uncle and nephew, since the name of his sister had been Herzeloide. Eagerly Parzival asked for news of his mother, only to hear of her death. Bitter sorrow surged in his heart at the words, and his face, always sad, grew yet sadder. Seeing this, Trevrezent tried to comfort the knight, and, laying his hands in blessing upon him, bade him go on in hope in his search for the Holy Grail. Grasping the hermit by the hand, Parzival bade him farewell ; then, with his heart somewhat lightened, he went on his way, till he encountered a knight, who, laying lance in rest, challenged him to fight. In one of the pauses of the battle he learned that his brave opponent was his step-brother, Fierefiss. The two joyfully embraced and flung their weapons aside, while Fierefiss declared his intention of following Parzival on his almost endless quest. In this way they came to a mountain, of a grim and frowning aspect. Painfully they climbed its steep sides, till at last, after much exertion, they found themselves in front of a castle, which seemed strangely familiar to Parzival.

Even as he gazed around him the doors opened, and willing squires waited upon both brothers, and led them into the great hall, where the pageant already described was repeated. Then when Queen Repanse de Joie entered bearing the Holy Grail Parzival, mindful of his former failure to do the right thing, humbly prayed aloud for Divine guidance to bring about the promised redemption. An angel voice now seemed to answer, " Ask ! " Then Parzival bent kindly over the wounded king, and gently inquired what ailed him. At those words the spell was broken, and a long cry of joy arose as Amfortas, strong and well, sprang to his feet.

Amid a buzz of excitement and rejoicing a very aged man, who was none other than Parzival's great-grand-father, Titurel, drew near, bearing the crown, which he placed on the head of the knight as he hailed him as guardian and defender of the Holy Grail. Immediately the cry was taken up by all present, and shouted again and again till the castle itself shook with the sound. Then when the cries of the knights had died away there was heard a chorus of angelic voices singing sweetly :

> " ' Hail to thee, Percival, King of the Grail !
> Seemingly lost for ever,
> Now thou art blessed for ever.
> Hail to thee, Percival, King of the Grail ! ' "
> *Parzival* (*Wolfram von Eschenbach*) (*McDowall's tr.*).

PARZIVAL AND THE HERMIT

But yet another happiness was in store for Parzival, for now the doors opened wide and admitted Conduiramour and her twin sons, summoned thither by the power of the Holy Grail, that Parzival's happiness might be complete. Then throughout the hall there stole a flood of light from the holy vessel, which bathed all present with its refulgent glow. Fierefiss alone remained untouched by the marvellous light, since it never rested on any save those of the Christian faith. Nevertheless, so impressed was he by all that he saw that he professed his faith in the creed of the knights and begged to be baptized.

Full of delight, the others hastened to have the ceremony performed, whereupon Fierefiss too was illumined with the glow from the sacred cup. His connection with the Templars was further strengthened by his marriage with Repanse de Joie, and they thus became the parents of a son named John, who was afterwards a noted warrior, and the founder of the historic order of the Knights Templars.

Hereupon Titurel, having lived to see the recovery of his son, called all his descendants round him and blessed them. He told them, too, that Sigune was happy, for she had joined her lover's spirit in the heavenly abode. Then, passing out of the great hall, the aged knight was never seen again. As for the witch Kundrie, it is said she died of joy on seeing the recovery of Amfortas.

Another version of the legend of the Holy Grail relates that Parzival, having cured his uncle, went to Arthur's court. There he remained until Amfortas died, when he was called back to Montsalvatch to inherit his possessions, among which was the Holy Grail. Arthur and all the knights of the Round Table were present at his coronation, and paid him a yearly visit. When he died, " the Sangreal, the sacred lance, and the silver trencher or paten which covered the

Grail, were carried up to the holy heavens in presence of the attendants, and since that time have never anywhere been seen on earth."

Other versions relate that Arthur and his knights sought the Holy Grail in vain, for their hearts were not pure enough to behold it. Still others declare that the sacred vessel was conveyed to the Far East, and committed to the care of Prester John.

Lohengrin

Yet another legend, the legend of Lohengrin, which is connected with the Holy Grail, tells the following story.

After the happy reunion of Parzival and Conduiramour on Montsalvatch, they dwelt with much happiness in the castle of the Holy Grail. Then when their sons had grown to man's estate Kardeiss, the elder, became ruler of his mother's kingdom of Belripar, while Lohengrin, the younger, remained in the service of the Holy Grail. The office of bearing the sacred cup had by this time passed from the hands of Repanse de Joie, who had married Fierefiss. Instead, it was borne by Aribadale, daughter of Parzival and his queen. The holy vessel was guarded as carefully as before, and the knights watched with eager vigilance for the fiery messages that enwreathed its rim. Moreover, when danger threatened a silver bell could always be heard pealing, as a sign to the knights to be on their guard.

One day the sound of the silvery bell was heard pealing ever louder and louder, till the knights came in haste to the hall. There they read on the vase that Lohengrin had been chosen to defend the rights of an innocent person, and would be conveyed to his destination by a swan. Never had one of the knights of the Grail disputed any of its commands ; therefore the

268

young man immediately donned the armour of silver which Amfortas had worn, and, bidding farewell to his mother and sister, he left the temple. Parzival, his father, then accompanied him to the foot of the mountain, where they saw a snowy swan swimming gracefully over the smooth waters of the lake, drawing after her a little boat.

Bidding his father farewell, Lohengrin received from him a horn, which he was told to sound thrice on arriving at his destination, and an equal number of times when he wished to return to Montsalvatch. Parzival also reminded him that a servant of the Grail must reveal neither his name nor his origin unless asked to do so, and that, having once made himself known, he was bound to return without delay to the holy mountain.

Thus reminded of the custom of all the Templars, Lohengrin sprang into the boat, and was rapidly borne away, to the sound of mysterious music.

Else of Brabant

While Lohengrin was thus being swiftly wafted over the waters, Else, the beautiful Duchess of Brabant, was spending her days in tears. She was an orphan, and as she possessed great wealth and extensive lands many were anxious to secure her hand. Among these suitors her guardian, Frederick of Telramund, was the most importunate. Angry at her repeated refusals, and feeling sure in his heart that she would never consent to marry him, he resolved to obtain her inheritance in a different way.

Meanwhile, one day while Else was wandering alone in the forest she rested for a moment under a tree, where she dreamed that a radiant knight came to greet her, and offered her a little bell, saying that she need but ring it whenever she required a champion. The maiden awoke, and as she opened her eyes a falcon came fluttering gently down from the sky and perched upon her shoulder. Seeing that he wore a tiny bell like the one she had noticed in her dream, Else unfastened it. As if some special purpose had been accomplished, the falcon at once flew away.

Full of wonder, Else looked at the tiny bell in her hand, and then hung it on her rosary. Feeling happier than she had done for a long time, she returned home. Yet if she had known it a terrible misfortune was about to fall upon her. For before many days had passed she had been thrown into prison by Frederick of Telramund, who made several foul charges against her. Exactly what these were perhaps no one knows. Yet some say he charged her with the murder of her brother, and others with admitting the attentions of a man unworthy of her rank. Henry the Fowler, Emperor of Germany, hearing of these accusations, came to Cleves, where, as the witnesses could not agree, he ordered that the matter should be settled by a judicial duel.

Else and the Silver Bell

This decision was received with exultation by Frederick of Telramund, and, proudly confident in his strength, he challenged any man to prove him mistaken at the point of the sword. But no champion appeared to fight for the unhappy Else, who, kneeling in her cell, beat her breast with her rosary until the little silver bell attached to it rang loudly, while she fervently prayed, "O Lord, send me a champion." The faint tinkling of the bell floated out of the window, and was wafted away to Montsalvatch. As it travelled it grew louder and louder, so that this was the very sound that had called the knights into the temple, where Lohengrin received his orders from the Holy Grail.

Lohengrin and Else

The Wizard

ELSE RESCUED BY LOHENGRIN

Days went by, and at last the morning appointed for the duel dawned. Then just as the heralds were sounding the last call for Else's champion to appear, the swan boat glided up the Rhine, and Lohengrin sprang into the lists, after thrice blowing his magic horn.

Else Rescued by Lohengrin

Loud and long rang the cheers of the onlookers as they saw the brave knight prepare for combat. For the people loved Else the Duchess, and were sorely grieved at the accusations against her.

All craned eagerly forward as the two champions closed in battle. Before long the issue was decided and Frederick of Telramund lay in the dust. Here he confessed his guilt, amid the plaudits of the people, who hailed the Swan Knight as victor. Then Else, touched by his prompt response to her appeal, and won by his passionate wooing, consented to become his wife, though she did not so much as know his name. Yet this affected her happiness but little when their nuptials were celebrated at Antwerp, in the presence of the emperor, who had gone with them to witness their marriage.

Meanwhile Lohengrin had cautioned Else that she must never ask his name. For a time she carefully obeyed his order, till there came a day when, harassed by the envious whispers of people, the fatal question sprang from her lips. Regretfully Lohengrin led her into the great hall, where, in the presence of the assembled knights, he told her that he was Lohengrin, son of Parzival, the guardian of the Holy Grail. Then, embracing her tenderly, he told her that "love cannot live without faith," and that he must now leave her and return to the holy mountain. When he had thrice blown his magic horn the sound of faint music again heralded the approach of the swan ; Lohengrin sprang into the boat, and soon vanished, leaving Else alone.

Some versions of the story relate that she did not long survive his departure, but tha* her released spirit followed him to Montsalvatch, where they dwelt happily for ever. Other accounts, however, aver that when Lohengrin vanished Else's brother returned to champion her cause and prevent her from being molested ever again.

CHAPTER XII : MERLIN

The Origin of the Legends

A S Professor Saintsbury has so ably expressed it, "The origin of the legends of King Arthur, of the Round Table, of the Holy Grail, and of all the adventures and traditions connected with these centres, is one of the most intricate questions in the history of mediæval literature." Owing to the loss of many ancient manuscripts, the real origin of all these tales may never be discovered ; and so diversified is the opinion of authorities that whether the legends owe their birth to Celtic, Breton, or Welsh poetry we may never know. These tales, apparently almost unknown before the twelfth century, soon became so popular that in the course of the next two hundred years they had given birth to more than a dozen poems and prose romances, whence Malory drew the materials for his version of the story of King Arthur. Nennius, Geoffrey of Monmouth, Walter Map, Chrestien de Troyes, Robert de Borron, Gottfried von Strassburg, Wolfram von Eschenbach, Hartmann von Aue, Tennyson, Matthew Arnold, Swinburne, and Wagner have all written of these legends in turn, and to these writers we owe the most noted versions of the tales forming the Arthurian cycle. They include, besides the story of Arthur himself, an account of Merlin, of Lancelot, of Parzival, of the love of Tristan and Iseult, and of the quest of the Holy Grail.

The majority of these works were written in French, which was the court language of England in the mediæval ages ; but the story was " Englished " by Malory in the fourteenth century. In every European language there are versions of these stories, which interested all hearers alike, and by exerting a gentle influence upon the rude customs of the age "communicated a romantic spirit to literature" and taught all men courtesy.

The Real Merlin

The first of these romances is that of Merlin the enchanter, written in old French, and ascribed to Robert de Borron. The following is a modified version of the story, supplemented from other sources. The real Merlin is supposed to have been a bard of the fifth century, who served first the British chief Ambrosius Aurelianus, and then King Arthur. The Merlin of this romance lost his reason after the battle of Solway Firth, broke his sword, and retired into the forest, where he was soon after found dead.

A more exciting and interesting career, however, marks the mythical figure, so familiar in all Arthurian stories. This Merlin was of fairy birth, and had magical powers from the first. Now it happened that King Constans, who drove Hengist from England, was the father of three sons—Constantine, Uther, and Pendragon. When dying this king left the throne to his eldest son, Constantine, who chose Vortigern as his Prime Minister. Shortly after Constantine's accession, Hengist again invaded England, and Constantine, deserted by his minister, was treacherously slain. As a reward for his defection at this critical moment Vortigern was offered the throne, which he accepted. In spite of the fact that the two other sons of Constans were still in existence, the usurping Vortigern still hoped to retain the crown.

To defend himself against any army which might try to deprive him of his sovereignty, Vortigern resolved to build a great fortress on the Salisbury plains. But although the masons worked diligently by day and built walls wide and thick, they always found them overturned in the morning. The astrologers, when consulted in reference to this strange occurrence, declared that the walls would not stand until the ground had been watered with the blood of a child who could claim no human father.

Meanwhile Satan, angry at the increasing number of Christian converts, was planning how he could contrive a counter-move. Therefore with hideous cunning he resolved to make a demon child spring from a human virgin. Thus he prepared to carry out his wicked plot by means of a beautiful and pious maiden. Nevertheless, as the maiden went daily to confess her every deed and thought to a holy man, Blaise, he soon discovered the intention of the demons, and resolved to frustrate it.

Birth of the Mythical Merlin

By his advice the girl was locked up in a tower, where she gave birth to her son. Blaise, the priest, more watchful than the demons, no sooner heard of the child's birth than he hastened to baptize him, giving him the name of Merlin. The holy rite annulled the evil purpose of Satan, but, owing to his uncanny origin, the child was gifted with all manner of strange powers, and from the first was marked as a fairy child.

> " To him
> Great light from God gave sight of all things dim,
> And wisdom of all wondrous things, to say
> What root should bear what fruit of night or day ;
> And sovereign speech and counsel above man :
> Wherefore his youth like age was wise and wan,
> And his age sorrowful and fain to sleep."
> *Tristram of Lyonesse (Swinburne).*

Furious at the frustration of their plot, the demons fled back to Hell, while the babe in the tower lay and smiled sweetly at his gentle mother. Seeing him smile, she caught him to her heart and covered him with kisses as she murmured that soon, very soon, she must leave her dear little son, for she would be put to death. Then as she rocked herself to and fro in her anguish she was startled by hearing her baby son speak and declare that she should not die, for he would prove her innocent of all crime. Frightened at the sound of his miraculous speech, his mother said nothing ; but she hugged him the closer to her.

Merlin as a Prophet

Yet five days later, when the trial took place, another and more wonderful miracle happened, for Merlin, who was but a few days old, sat up boldly in his mother's lap and spoke so forcibly to the judges that he soon secured her acquittal. Once when he was five years old, while playing in the street, he saw the messengers of Vortigern. Warned by his prophetic instinct that they were seeking him, he ran to meet them, and offered to accompany them to the king. On the way thither he saw a youth buying shoes, at which sight he laughed aloud. When questioned concerning the cause of his mirth he predicted that the youth would die within a few hours.

> " Then said Merlin, ' See ye nought
> That young man, that hath shoon bought,
> And strong leather to do hem clout [patch],
> And grease to smear hem all about ?
> He weeneth to live hem to wear :
> But, by my soul, I dare well swear,
> His wretched life he shall for-let [lose],
> Ere he come to his own gate.' "
>
> *Merlin (Ellis).*

The Fight of the Dragons

A few more predictions of an equally uncanny and unpleasant nature firmly established his reputation as a prophet even before he reached court. There he boldly told the king that the astrologers, wishing to destroy the demon's offspring, since he was wiser than they, had demanded his blood under pretext that the walls of Salisbury would stand were it only shed. When asked why the walls continually fell during the night, Merlin attributed it to the nightly conflict of two dragons, one white and one red, which lay concealed underground. In obedience to his instructions, search was made for these monsters. They were soon discovered, and the whole court crowded to watch the fearful struggle which followed between the two horrible creatures. Up and down went the dragons, twisting now this way and now that as they trailed their hideous bodies over the ground. Fire broke from their mouths and flashed in and out as they darted at each other with venomous fury, till at last the huge white dragon slew the red one.

> " With long tailis, fele [many] fold,
>   And found right as Merlin told.
>   That one dragon was red as fire,
>   With eyen bright, as basin clear ;
>   His tail was great and nothing small ;
>   His body was a rood withal.
>   His shaft may no man tell ;
>   He looked as a fiend from hell.
>   The white dragon lay him by,
>   Stern of look, and griesly.
>   His mouth and throat yawned wide ;
>   The fire brast [burst] out on ilka [each] side.
>   His tail was ragged as a fiend,
>   And, upon his tail's end,
>   There was y-shaped a griesly head,
>   To fight with the dragon red."
>
> *Merlin (Ellis).*

Suddenly, as if aware of the presence of foes, the victorious dragon glared fearfully round and then dragged its huge length quickly out of sight, so that in this way the king was rid of both the pests. The work of the castle now proceeded without further hindrance. Yet Vortigern was very uneasy, because Merlin had not only said that the struggle of the red and the white dragons represented his coming conflict with Constans' sons, but he had added that he would suffer defeat. This prophecy was soon fulfilled. Uther and his brother Pendragon landed in Britain with the army they had assembled, and Vortigern was burned in the castle he had just completed.

Shortly after this victory there arose a war between the Britons, under Uther and Pendragon, and the Saxons, under Hengist. Merlin, who had by this time become the Chancellor and chief adviser of the British kings, predicted that they would win the victory, but that one of them would be slain. This prediction was speedily verified, and Uther, adding the name Pendragon to his own, remained sole king. Anxious to show every respect to the memory of his brother, he implored Merlin to erect a suitable monument to his memory. Therefore the enchanter conveyed great stones from Ireland to England in the course of a single night, and set them up at Stonehenge, where they can still be seen.

> " How Merlin by his skill, and magic's wondrous might,
> From Ireland hither brought the Stonendge in a night."
> *Polyolbion (Drayton).*

Merlin and the Round Table

From here Merlin went next to Carduel, or Carlisle, where he again showed his favour for Uther Pendragon by building him a splendid castle, in which he established a Round Table. In this he followed the example of Joseph of Arimathea, who had once maintained a similar

Stonehenge

Tintagel

following. Round this board were places for a large number of knights, together with a special seat reserved for the Holy Grail, which had at this time vanished from Britain because of the sinfulness of the people. Nevertheless the knights still hoped to have it restored among them when they had become sufficiently pure.

> " This table gan [began] Uther the wight ;
>   Ac [but] it to ende had he no might.
>   For, theygh [though] alle the kinges under our lord
>   Hadde y-sitten [sat] at that bord,
>   Knight by knight, ich you telle,
>   The table might nought fulfille,
>   Till they were born that should do all
>   Fulfill the mervaile of the Greal."
>
> *Merlin (Ellis).*

When the Round Table was at last ready a great festival was announced, and all the knights came to Carduel, accompanied by their wives. Of these latter the fairest was Yguerne, wife of Gorlois, Lord of Tintagel, in Cornwall, and with her Uther fell desperately in love.

> " This fest was noble ynow, and nobliche y-do [done] ;
>   For mony was the faire ledy, that y-come was thereto.
>   Yguerne, Gorloys wyf, was fairest of echon [each one],
>   That was contasse of Cornewail, for so fair was there non."
>
> *Robert of Gloucester.*

Now Yguerne had already three or four daughters, who afterwards became famous in the Arthurian legends as mothers of illustrious knights, among whom were Gawain, Gravain, and Ywain. By-and-by one of the king's councillors, Ulfin, revealed the king's passion to Yguerne, upon which she told the news to her husband. Furious with indignation at the insult offered him, Gorlois at once left the court, and locked his wife up in the impregnable fortress of Tintagel ; then, gathering together an army, he began to fight against Uther Pendragon.

Meanwhile Merlin, who was always eager to help Uther, changed him into the form of Gorlois, and himself and Ulfin into those of the squires of the Duke of Cornwall. This was on the eve of the day of battle, when Gorlois himself was busy with his troops, not suspecting any trickery. Immediately the three, confident in their disguise, made their way to Tintagel, where Yguerne threw the gates open at their call and received Uther as her husband, without ever suspecting the deception practised upon her.

Birth of Arthur

Nor did she ever discover the fraud. For on the morrow the battle took place, and Gorlois was slain. Then Uther, being free to marry Yguerne, speedily persuaded her to yield to his passion, so that she became his wife. By-and-by a son was born, whom they called Arthur, but who was commonly supposed to be the posthumous child of Gorlois. When the babe was only a few days old Uther handed the boy over to Merlin to be brought up. Then the wizard chose out Sir Hector to be the boy's guardian, and thus Arthur grew up in the company of little Sir Kay, the son of Sir Hector, and none suspected the truth, that he was really of royal birth.

Yet the lineage of the boy might be seen in his face, for by fifteen he was so fair to look upon, so brave in all warlike feats, and so accomplished in all the ways of knighthood, that none could see him without loving him.

> " He was fair, and well agré [agreeable],
> And was a thild [child] of gret noblay.
> He was curteys, faire and gent,
> And wight [brave], and hardi, veramen [truly].
> Curteyslich [courteously] and fair he spac [spake].
> With him was none evil lack [fault]."
>
> *Merlin (Ellis.)*

BIRTH OF ARTHUR

By-and-by Uther died, leaving no heir, for no one counted Arthur as his son, nor did Arthur think that any but Gorlois had been his father. Merlin alone knew of the secret ; but for the time he kept silence, saying that the true king would be at last revealed by a miracle.

When he judged that a fitting time had arrived he made known the real facts about Arthur's birth, and hailed him as king in Uther's stead. His example was quickly followed by the knights, who would have chosen no one more readily than Arthur, for he was beloved by them all. Thus Arthur ascended the throne and ruled over his people. In this he was greatly helped by Merlin, who made himself his chief adviser, and by his wisdom guided him in many a difficult place. Through his help Arthur was always successful in war, so that he conquered twelve kings one after the other, and thus covered himself with great glory.

Now as Merlin could assume any shape he pleased Arthur often used him as a messenger. In this way one of the romances relates that he once went in the guise of a stag to Rome to bear a challenge from the king to meet in single combat Julius Cæsar—not the great conqueror of Gaul, but the mythical father of Oberon. He was also renowned for the good advice which he gave, not only to Vortigern and Uther Pendragon, but also to Arthur, each of whom placed implicit faith in his gift of divination. Moreover, he made numerous predictions concerning the glorious future of England, all of which, if we are to believe tradition, have been strictly fulfilled.

> " O goodly River ! near unto thy sacred spring
> Prophetic Merlin sate, when to the British King
> The changes long to come, auspiciously he told."
> *Polyolbion (Drayton)*.

Merlin as a Builder

But apart from his great wisdom in prophecy, Merlin was also renowned as a builder and architect. Besides the construction of Stonehenge, and of the castle for Uther Pendragon, he is said to have built Arthur's beautiful palace at Camelot, together with not a few magic fountains, which are mentioned in other mediæval romances. One of these is referred to by Spenser in the " Faerie Queene," and another by Ariosto in his " Orlando Furioso."

> " This Spring was one of those four fountains rare,
> Of those in France produced by Merlin's sleight,
> Encompassed round about with marble fair,
> Shining and polished, and than milk more white.
> There in the stones choice figures chiselled were,
> By that magician's god-like labour dight ;
> Some voice was wanting, these you might have thought
> Were living, and with nerve and spirit fraught."
>
> *Orlando Furioso* (*Ariosto*) (*Rose's tr.*).

Many are the stories told about the different objects which Merlin made and invested with magic properties. Amongst these one of the most famous was a cup which never failed to reveal the true character of the drinker. For at the touch of unclean lips the liquid would overflow, no matter how small the drop which the vessel contained. Another of Merlin's triumphs was the manufacture of Arthur's armour, which nothing could pierce, while the magic mirror, in which was always reflected whatever the gazer wished to see, was often the subject of song.

> " It Merlin was, which whylome did excel
> All living wightes in might of magicke spell :
> Both shield, and sword, and armour all he wrought
> For this young Prince, when first to armes he fell."
>
> *Faerie Queene* (*Spenser*).

Merlin and Vivian

Yet though Merlin knew so much and was so much wiser than other people, he was often beguiled by the enticements of his fair mistress, Vivian, the Lady of the Lake. Full of longing to learn all Merlin's secrets, Vivian followed him wherever he went, and made countless efforts to learn his arts and to discover his magic spells. Then, in order to inveigle the aged Merlin into telling her all she wished to know, Vivian pretended great devotion, so that she never left his side, but followed him coaxingly till " Merlin locked his hand in hers " and told her all that her heart desired.

Once, indeed, she even followed him as far as the fairy-haunted forest of Broceliande, in Brittany, where she finally beguiled him into revealing a magic spell by which a human being could be enclosed in a hawthorn tree, in which he would have to dwell for ever.

> " And then she follow'd Merlin all the way,
> E'en to the wild woods of Broceliande.
> For Merlin once had told her of a charm,
> The which if any wrought on any one
> With woven paces and with waving arms,
> The man so wrought on ever seem'd to lie
> Closed in the four walls of a hollow tower,
> From which was no escape for evermore ;
> And none could find that man for evermore,
> Nor could he see but him who wrought the charm
> Coming and going ; and he lay as dead
> And lost to life and use and name and fame."
>
> *Merlin and Vivien* (*Tennyson*).

Then, having won from the wizard this last great secret, Vivian began to grow weary of her aged lover. Therefore she spitefully set about finding some means of ridding herself of him. The idea of the hawthorn bush flashed into her mind, and at once she resolved to make use of Merlin's own art against himself. Coaxingly she lured him into the depths of a gloomy forest, her mind fixed on her unscrupulous purpose. Then, once in the depths of the trees, she uttered the magic words and imprisoned him in a thorn bush, whence, if the tales of the Breton peasants can be believed, his voice can still be heard issuing from time to time.

> " They sate them down together, and a sleep
> Fell upon Merlin, more like death, so deep.
> Her finger on her lips, then Vivian rose,
> And from her brown-lock'd head the wimple throws,
> And takes it in her hand, and waves it over
> The blossom'd thorn tree and her sleeping lover.
> Nine times she waved the fluttering wimple round,
> And made a little plot of magic ground.
> And in that daisied circle, as men say,
> Is Merlin prisoner till the judgment day ;
> But she herself whither she will can rove—
> For she was passing weary of his love."
>
> *Tristram and Iseult* (*Matthew Arnold*).

Then, abandoning the imprisoned magician, Vivian turned lightly homewards.

This is one version of the story, but there is another which relates how Merlin, having grown very old indeed, once sat down on the " Siege Perilous," forgetting that none but a sinless man could occupy it with impunity. Scarcely had he seated himself, however, when he was immediately swallowed up by the earth, which yawned wide beneath his feet. Nor was he ever again seen upon earth.

Yet a third version says that Vivian, through love, imprisoned Merlin in an underground palace, where she alone could visit him. There he dwells, unchanged by the flight of time, daily increasing the store of knowledge by which he won such renown.

CHAPTER XIII : THE ROUND TABLE

Questions of Fact

THE cold hand of history, which is for ever robbing us of some of our oldest and best cherished stories, points rigidly to the fact that no such person as King Arthur ever presided over a Round Table. Be this as it may, romance still hugs her heroes to her heart as possessions to be not willingly let die. Though Arthur may never have lived in real fact, yet his personality has become so vitally fixed in the mind of the people that he may at least be conceded a virtual existence as the figure who embodies the characteristics of the numerous smaller champions who may perhaps claim historic support. And, indeed, "the question of the actual existence and acts of Arthur has very little to do with the question of the origin of the Arthurian cycle."

So many places in Wales, Scotland, and England show traces of Arthurian influence that it is safe to say that, did he exist, Arthur was a Briton. But his fame spread far beyond the borders of his small kingdom, till at last all Europe was saturated with stories concerning his prowess, the popularity of which is evidenced by the fact that they were among the first works printed, and were thus brought into general circulation.

Upon the birth of Arthur, King Uther Pendragon, as we have already seen, entrusted his new-born son to the care of the enchanter Merlin, who carried him to the castle of Sir Hector, or Anton, where the young prince was brought up as a child of the house.

> "Wherefore Merlin took the child,
> And gave him to Sir Anton, an old knight
> And ancient friend of Uther ; and his wife
> Nursed the young prince, and rear'd him with her own ;
> And no man knew."
>
> *The Coming of Arthur (Tennyson).*

LEGENDS OF THE MIDDLE AGES

The Magic Sword

Two years later King Uther Pendragon died, and the noblemen, not knowing whom to choose as his successor, consulted Merlin, promising to abide by his decision. By his advice, therefore, they all assembled in St. Stephen's Church, in London, on Christmas Day, prepared to hear what the wizard had to relate. Then when mass was over they were called to look at a large stone which had mysteriously appeared in the church-yard. This stone was surmounted by a ponderous anvil, in which the blade of a sword was deeply sunk. Drawing near to examine the wonder, they read an in-scription upon the jewelled hilt, to the effect that none but the man who could draw out the sword should dare to take possession of the throne. Delighted at this solution of their difficulty, every knight in turn tried to wrench free the sword, but none succeeded.

Full of disappointment, they turned home, the question of the throne still unsettled. Meanwhile several years passed by ere Sir Hector came to London with his son, Sir Kay, and his foster-son, young Arthur. Sir Kay, who for the first time in his life was to take part in a tournament, was greatly chagrined on arriving at the lists to discover that he had forgotten his sword ; so Arthur volunteered to ride back and get it. He found the house closed ; yet, being determined to secure a sword for his foster-brother, he strode hastily into the church-yard, and easily drew from the anvil the weapon he had heard so much about, and which all had vainly tried to secure.

Arthur Made King

Then as he carelessly handed the famous sword to Sir Kay, Sir Hector saw it. Amazed at the sight, he

286

King Arthur

Queen Guinevere

eagerly inquired how Arthur had secured it. "Even from the anvil in the churchyard," replied Arthur ; "for, being in haste to secure a weapon, I drew this forth." Scarcely able to credit the fact, Sir Hector ran to tell his fellow knights what had happened. Then together they went with Arthur to the churchyard, and watched him first re-insert the weapon in the anvil and then easily draw it forth. Not till then would they be satisfied that he was really their chosen king. But seeing him accomplish both these feats they at once hailed him as their sovereign, and shouted with joy till the old church-yard rang with the noise.

But no sooner was Arthur on the throne than envious tongues began to be busy about the tale of his birth. Some declared that did Merlin choose he could tell them many things about the young king ; for they asserted he was not, as he now declared, the son of Uther Pendragon and Yguerne, but a babe mysteriously brought up from the depths of the sea, on the crest of the ninth wave, and cast ashore at the wizard's feet. Hence many people distrusted the young king, and at first refused to obey him.

> "Watch'd the great sea fall,
> Wave after wave, each mightier than the last,
> Till last, a ninth one, gathering half the deep,
> And full of voices, slowly rose and plunged
> Roaring, and all the wave was in a flame :
> And down the wave and in the flame was borne
> A naked babe, and rode to Merlin's feet,
> Who stoopt and caught the babe, and cried ' The King !
> Here is an heir for Uther !' "
>
> *The Coming of Arthur* (*Tennyson*).

The root of this disaffection was to be found in jealousy. For one look at Arthur was enough to show his kingly descent, so splendid was his bearing, so open his countenance.

Amongst those who nevertheless professed suspicion were some of the king's own kindred, and notably his four nephews, Gawain, Gaheris, Agravaine, and Gareth. Very unwillingly Arthur was therefore obliged to make war against them. The greatest of these foes was Gawain, whose strength increased in a marvellous fashion from nine to twelve in the morning, and from three to six in the afternoon. Yet the king, by following Merlin's advice and taking advantage of his comparatively weak moments, succeeded in defeating him.

Sir Pellinore

Having for the time being defeated his enemies, Arthur, aided by Merlin, ruled over the land wisely and well. He set himself strenuously to redress wrongs and re-establish order and security. For during the long interregnum since Uther Pendragon's death, confusion and rapine had become common. In all this Arthur proved successful, so that his people revered him greatly, and his knights willingly gave him their allegiance. Yet even Arthur sometimes made a mistake, as happened once with Sir Pellinore. For the king, being ill-advised, made a sudden and undeserved attack upon this knight. Whereupon the sword which he held in his hand failed him and broke. Left thus without any means of defence, the king would surely have perished had not Merlin used his magic arts and thrown Sir Pellinore into a deep swoon while he bore away his charge to a place of safety.

Thus deprived of his magic sword, Arthur bitterly bewailed its loss, for he knew not how to procure another like it. But while he stood by a lake wondering what he should do he beheld a white-draped arm rise out of the water, holding aloft a jewelled sword. Startled at the sight, Arthur watched it with fascinated gaze till the Lady of the Lake appeared beside him and told him it was intended for his use.

> " ' Thou rememberest how
> In those old days, one summer noon, an arm
> Rose up from out the bosom of the lake,
> Clothed in white samite, mystic, wonderful,
> Holding the sword—and how I row'd across
> And took it, and have worn it, like a king ;
> And, wheresoever I am sung or told
> In aftertime, this also shall be known.' "
>
> *The Passing of Arthur* (*Tennyson*).

Excalibur

Full of joy at her words, Arthur rowed out into the middle of the lake and secured the sword, which became known by the name Excalibur. The king was then told by the Lady of the Lake that the weapon was gifted with magic powers, and that as long as the scabbard remained in his possession he would suffer neither wound nor defeat.

Thus armed, Arthur went back to his palace, where, hearing that the Saxons had again invaded the country, he went to wage war against them, and won many victories. Shortly after this it also came to his ears that Leodegraunce, King of Scotland, was threatened by his brother Ryance, King of Ireland, who was determined to complete a mantle furred with the beards of kings, and wanted only one more to have what he desired. Indignant at the ferocious whim of the Irish king, Arthur hastened to the help of Leodegraunce. In the encounter that followed Arthur wielded his sword so valiantly that he not only killed the cruel Ryance, but appropriated his mantle and carried it away in triumph as a trophy of his success.

> " And for a trophy brought the Giant's coat away
> Made of the beards of Kings."
>
> *Polyolbion* (*Drayton*).

Arthur's Marriage with Guinevere

Covered with glory and renown, Arthur then returned
to the court of King Leodegraunce, where he fell in
love with the latter's fair daughter, Guinevere.   As for
the princess, she no sooner saw Arthur than she thought
him the bravest and most splendid king in the world,
so that when he asked her to marry him she gladly consented.   The marriage would have taken place at once
had not Merlin decreed that the king must first fight
in a campaign in Brittany.   Therefore Arthur went off
to war more eager than ever to win glory for the sake
of fair Guinevere.   At last he returned to claim his
bride, and the wedding took place amid great pomp.
Having received as the dower of the princess the
Round Table once made for his own father, Arthur
journeyed with his bride to Camelot, or Winchester,
where he bade all his court be present at Pentecost for
a great feast.

" The nearest neighbouring flood to Arthur's ancient seat,
　Which made the Britons' name through all the world so great.
　Like Camelot, what place was ever yet renown'd ?
　Where, as at Carlion, oft, he kept the Table-Round,
　Most famous for the sports at Pentecost so long,
　From whence all knightly deeds, and brave achievements sprong."
　　　　　　　　　　　　　Polyolbion (*Drayton*).

So ended the first part of Arthur's reign, and the
second and more glorious period began.

Knights of the Round Table

When Arthur had once more arrived in Camelot
he conceived the idea of founding an order of knights,
sworn to be loyal to him, who should sit at the
famous table he had brought with him, and be known
as the Knights of the Round Table.   For this purpose he caused to be erected a magnificent castle, with
a banqueting hall reserved especially for the magic

board, round which were placed the seats to be accorded to the knights. How many there were of these is not certain ; the most probable number is twelve, though it is sometimes asserted there were as many as several hundred. Be this as it may, the seats were eagerly coveted, and the knights who succeeded in being awarded a place always adopted a special device on their shields to proclaim the honour they had won.

At last the building of the hall was finished, and the renowned table was put into its place. Round it there stood, within twelve niches in the wall, huge statues of the twelve kings whom Arthur had already overthrown. In the hand of each was a taper, which Merlin foretold would shine brightly until the Holy Grail should appear. Striding into his hall, King Arthur looked about him, and was well pleased at the magnificent spectacle. Full of contentment, he turned to Merlin, saying : "Behold, the hall is made, the table is here, the seats are ready. Do thou now tell me the names of the knights worthy to fill those seats."

So Merlin named them in order one by one, till all the seats save two were occupied. A great banquet followed, and the chosen band sat down together in high ecstasy. Yet their thoughts were by no means fixed on anything save the doing of pure and noble deeds, for the desire of each was to see the Holy Grail.

Later, as the knights arose from their seats, when the banquet was ended, they saw that their names were inscribed in letters of gold on the places they had occupied. Moreover, one of the empty seats was marked " Siege Perilous."

Marvelling as to what this could mean, the nobles eagerly questioned Merlin, who told them that that seat was reserved for a knight who should be absolutely pure, so that did any other adventure himself upon it he would straightway be swallowed up by the yawning earth.

LEGENDS OF THE MIDDLE AGES

Lancelot du Lac

Soon the knights of the Round Table became famous everywhere for their brave and noble deeds, and the name of each one was revered. Yet amongst them all Sir Lancelot du Lac was most beloved by the people. Chrestien de Troyes, Geoffrey de Ligny, Robert de Borron, and Walter Map have all written about this brave warrior, while the fact that his name was given to one of the knaves on the playing-cards invented at about this time proves that he was widely known. Malory, too, in his prose version of the " Morte d'Arthur " has drawn principally from the poems treating of Lancelot.

The early childhood of Sir Lancelot is full of interest. He was said to be the son of King Ban and Helen, who were obliged to flee from their besieged castle in Brittany when their son was but a babe. Before they had gone far, however, the aged Ban, seeing his home in flames, sank dying to the ground. Helen, eager to minister to her husband, laid her baby boy down on the grass near a lake. But alas ! when she again turned her attention to him she saw him in the arms of Vivian, the Lady of the Lake, who plunged with him into the waters.

" In the wife's woe, the mother was forgot.
    At last (for I was all earth held of him
Who had been all to her, and now was not)
    She rose, and looked with tearless eyes, but dim,
In the babe's face the father still to see ;
And lo ! the babe was on another's knee !

" Another's lips had kissed it into sleep,
    And o'er the sleep another watchful smiled ;
The Fairy sate beside the lake's still deep,
    And hush'd with chaunted charms the orphan child !
Scared at the mother's cry, as fleets a dream,
Both Child and Fairy melt into the stream."

King Arthur (*Bulwer Lytton*).

Full of bitter auguish, Helen cried aloud in her grief; but to no avail, for the fairy soon floated out of sight. Thus bereft of both husband and child at one blow, Helen sorrowfully withdrew into a convent, while Lancelot was brought up with his two cousins, Lyonel and Bohort, in the palace of the Lady of the Lake. Here he remained until he was eighteen, when the fairy herself brought him to court and presented him to the king. Captivated by his appearance, Arthur at once made him his friend and confidant, and gave him an honoured place at the Round Table. His arrival was also warmly welcomed by all the other knights, whom he far excelled in beauty and courage.

> " But one Sir Lancelot du Lake,
>   Who was approvèd well,
>   He for his deeds and feats of armes
>   All others did excell."
>
> *Sir Lancelot du Lake* (*Old Ballad*).

Lancelot and Guinevere

Nevertheless, in spite or the fair beginning of his life at court, Lancelot was doomed to much sorrow. For he had no sooner beheld Queen Guinevere than he fell deeply in love with her. Flattered by his attention, the queen grew fond of her devoted knight, and granted him many marks of her favour. Then so strongly did passion get the better of her that she even encouraged him to betray his friend and king on more than one occasion. Lancelot, urged in one direction by passion, in another by loyalty, led a very unhappy life, which made him relapse into wild fits of frenzy, during which he roamed aimlessly about for many years. When the violence of the fits subsided he always returned to court, where he redoubled his energy in accomplishing unheard-of deeds of valour. In all these encounters he was successful, for he ever fought on the side of right. Moreover, he never once wavered from his allegiance to the queen, although many fair ladies tried to make him forget her.

Some poets, anxious to vindicate the queen, declare that there were two Guineveres, one pure, lovely, and worthy of all admiration, who suffered for the sins of the other. Nevertheless all agree as to the unswerving fidelity of Lancelot to her.

Strange to say, though all the court knew of the queen's love for Sir Lancelot, Arthur himself was too pure-minded to suspect such a thing. Nor was it till some time had gone and the secret could by no means be concealed that he saw the truth. Full of sorrow, he bade his queen depart, and she thereupon took refuge with her lover in Joyeuse Garde (Berwick), a castle he had won at the point of his lance to please her. But by-and-by the king, having ascertained that the real Guinevere had been wrongfully accused, reinstated her in his favour, and Lancelot again returned to court, where he continued to love and serve her.

On one occasion, hearing that she had been made captive by Meleagans, her faithful follower rushed after her to rescue her, tracing her on her way by a comb and ringlet she had dropped as she went. But misfortune befell the anxious knight as he rode, for his horse was taken from him by enchantment, so that in order sooner to overtake the queen he rode on in a cart. This was considered a disgraceful mode of progress for a knight, as a nobleman in those days was condemned to ride in a cart in punishment for crimes for which common people were sentenced to the pillory.

Nevertheless, so eager was Lancelot to succour Guinevere that he never once thought of how he was carried thither. At last he succeeded in reaching the castle whither Guinevere had been borne. Eagerly he rejoined the queen after he had slain her captor. But instead of receiving her thanks she turned upon him, and in a fit of anger taunted her lover about his journey in the cart. Frenzied at her taunts, Lancelot fled from her presence and roamed wildly about, until the queen recognised her error, and sent twenty-three knights in search of him. Yet so far had he gone that they journeyed for two whole years without finding him.

> "'Then Sir Bors had ridden on
> Softly, and sorrowing for our Lancelot,
> Because his former madness, once the talk
> And scandal of our table, had return'd;
> For Lancelot's kith and kin so worship him
> That ill to him is ill to them.'"
>
> *The Holy Grail (Tennyson).*

Meanwhile a fair and pious damsel had taken pity upon the distraught knight, and seeing that he had atoned by suffering for all his sins she had him borne into the chamber where the Holy Grail was kept; "and then there came a holy man, who uncovered the vessel; and so by miracle, and by virtue of that holy vessel, Sir Lancelot was all healed and recovered."

Gareth and Lynette

Restored from his madness, Lancelot now returned to Camelot, where he was joyfully welcomed by the king, the queen, and all the knights of the Round Table, so much was he beloved. Here Lancelot knighted Sir Gareth, who, to please his mother, had concealed his true name and had acted as kitchen vassal for a whole year. Immediately the new-made knight started out with a fair maiden called Lynette to deliver her captive sister. Thinking him nothing but the kitchen vassal he seemed, the damsel insulted Gareth in every possible way. He bravely endured her taunts, courageously defeated all her adversaries, and finally won her admiration and respect to such a degree that she bade him ride beside her, and humbly asked his pardon for having so grievously misjudged him.

> " ' Sir,—and, good faith, I fain had added Knight,
> But that I heard thee call thyself a knave,—
> Shamed am I that I so rebuked, reviled,
> Missaid thee ; noble I am ; and thought the King
> Scorn'd me and mine ; and now thy pardon, friend,
> For thou hast ever answer'd courteously.' "
>
> *Gareth and Lynette* (*Tennyson*).

Marriage of Gareth and Lynette

Full of generosity, Gareth willingly granted her full forgiveness, for in spite of her wayward pride he had already come to love her dearly. At her request he now rode at her side, where he fought more bravely still. Then, after defeating many knights and delivering her sister from captivity, he secured Lynette's promise to become his wife as soon as he had been admitted to the Round Table. Hastening back to Arthur's court, he begged for this honour to be given him. Willingly Arthur agreed, for the prowess of the young knight had won the admiration of all. Therefore, full of gladness, he sought out Lynette, and the two were married.

Geraint and Enid

About the same time Gareth's brother, Geraint, had also become a member of the Round Table. He too gained renown for many deeds of valour, after which he married Enid the Fair, the only daughter of an old and impoverished knight, whom Geraint delivered from the tyranny of his oppressor and restored to all his former state. Taking his wife away with him to his lonely manor, Geraint so fulfilled the every wish of his fair bride that at last he laid aside all his former high desires, and spent the days at home dallying in pleasure.

But this devotion was unpleasing to Enid; for her noble mind soon perceived that her husband was neglecting both honour and duty to linger by her side. One day while he lay asleep before her she, in an outburst of wifely love, poured out her heart, and ended her confession by declaring that since Geraint neglected everything for her sake only, she must be an unworthy wife.

Geraint awoke too late to overhear the first part of her speech; but, seeing her tears, and catching the words " unworthy wife," he immediately imagined that she had ceased to love him, and that she was receiving the attentions of another. In his anger Geraint (who is known in French and German poems as Erec) rose from his couch and sternly bade his wife don her meanest apparel and silently follow him through the world.

> " The page he bade with speed
> Prepare his own strong steed,
> Dame Enid's palfrey there beside ;
> He said that he would ride
> For pastime far away :
> So forward hastened they."
>
> *Erek and Enid (Hartmann von Aue)*
> *(Bayard Taylor's tr.).*

Full of a desire to serve the husband whom she so dearly loved, Enid patiently did his bidding. Alone she watched him fight the knights who challenged him by the way ; alone bound up his wounds. Quite unable to understand the reason for his severe coldness towards her, she yet stood all his tests so nobly that at last he saw how greatly he had misjudged her. Full of eager repentance, he confessed his error, and restored her again to her rightful place.

As for the loving Enid, her heart overflowed with happiness, so that they dwelt together in the perfection of mutual love and trust until the day when Geraint fell gloriously while fighting the battles of his lord the king.

Sir Galahad

Now it befell one Whitsuntide, when all the knights were assembled at a great feast about the table at Camelot, that a distressed damsel suddenly entered the hall and implored Lancelot to accompany her to the neighbouring forest.   Asking why it was she desired him to do this, he was told that a young warrior was there who greatly longed to receive knighthood from the hands of Sir Lancelot.   Resolved to help the maiden if possible, Sir Lancelot rose from his seat and went with her into the wood.   There he found her deliverer, whom he straight-way knighted.   This, indeed, was the knight who later, because of his noble life, became known as Sir Galahad the Pure.   Some writers even say he was the son of Lancelot, while others declare that he was not of mortal birth.

Scarcely had Lancelot returned to the hall when he heard that a miracle had occurred, and together the whole company rushed down to the river-side.   There they saw that the rumour was true, for they one and all beheld a heavy stone floating down the stream. Amazed at the sight, they gazed yet more earnestly, till they perceived that a costly weapon was sunk deep in the stone.   At last the stone came to land, and as the knights crowded round it they saw on this weapon an inscription warning all that none but a peerless knight should attempt to draw it out, upon penalty of a grievous punishment.   As they read, the knights of the Round Table modestly drew back from the task, for each in his heart was conscious of some sin.

SIR GALAHAD

When they returned into the hall, full of the sight they had witnessed, an aged man entered, accompanied by Galahad. Fearless in the strength of his innocence, Galahad sat down in the seat "Siege Perilous." For a moment the company watched in terror ; then as they saw his name suddenly appear in letters of gold upon it all knew that he was the knight destined to win the honour. Full of joy, they acclaimed him till the rafters in the great hall shook. Suddenly they noticed that he wore by his side an empty scabbard. Whereupon he declared it had been prophesied that a magic weapon should be given to him. At once the miracle of the sword in the floating stone became clear. Quickly they took their comrade down to the river, and watched him as he gripped the shaft of the mysterious weapon. Immediately it yielded to his grasp, and he easily drew it forth. Whereupon he thrust it into his scabbard, which he found fitted it exactly.

That selfsame night, after evensong, when all the knights were seated about the Round Table at Camelot, they heard a long roll of thunder, and felt the palace shake. The brilliant lights held by the statues of the twelve conquered kings grew strangely dim, and behold ! gliding down upon a refulgent beam of celestial light there came a dazzling vision of the Holy Grail. Covered by white samite, and borne by invisible hands, the sacred vessel was slowly carried round the great hall, while a delicious perfume was wafted throughout the huge edifice. Silent from awe, the knights of the Round Table gazed rapturously at this resplendent vision, till at last it vanished as suddenly and as mysteriously as it had come. A deep sigh floated through the hall as the knights felt the tension relax ; then as each looked down on to the plate that stood on the table before him he saw there the food which he liked best.

Fearing to break the silence, the knights waited motionless until the light sprang bright and clear again from the tapers. Then solemnly they gave fervent thanks for the mercy which had been vouchsafed them, till Lancelot, springing impetuously to his feet, vowed that he would ride forth in search of the Holy Grail, and would know no rest until he had beheld it unveiled. "And I," "And I," cried each of the others in turn; and so the vow was registered by all the knights of the Round Table. Then, hearing these words, Arthur questioned them closely, and thus discovered that none had seen the vessel unveiled. Therefore, though he was sad at the thought of losing so many of his brave followers for so long, yet the king knew that as they had sworn the oath, they must carry it out. So, looking round upon them all, he gave them his blessing and bade them go.

An air of sadness hung in the air that night when the men rose from their seats. Long they lingered ere they turned to bid their leader good-night, for they felt that never again at any feast would they all meet together, an unbroken band. Yet they did not shrink from their resolve, nor wish in their hearts to take back their word.

Quest of the Holy Grail

Then on the morrow they rode rorth on their noble purpose. Some went alone, but others chose a companion; yet never more than two journeyed in company. Thus separated the whole of that goodly band, to roam wide over the world and do many brave deeds in the name of justice and purity. But whether any of them ever saw the Grail save Parzival and Galahad is not known. Some declare that Lancelot saw it, through a veil, faintly; but others maintain that not even Parzival gained this glory; that Sir Galahad the Pure alone saw

The Dream of Sir Launcelot

Elaine

the vision, and then only when, after years of prayer and fasting, his soul was being borne to Heaven.

After many years had gone by in vain, the majority of the knights realised that they were unworthy of so great a boon, and thus they returned to Camelot, where they were bidden to a great feast by the queen. While they were feasting at her table a terrible thing happened, for one of their number, having partaken of a poisonous draught, fell lifeless to the ground. Full of consternation at the deed, the knights sprang to their feet, while some cried out loudly that the queen was guilty of the murder, since the knight who had fallen had sat at her side. " Confess," they cried fiercely, "or prove your innocence in fight." Terrified at their fierceness, the queen consented to their terms, and sought a knight to defend her. Arthur himself was forbidden this, since he was her husband, and therefore debarred by law of the privilege of fighting for her in the lists of Camelot. But alas! no one was forthcoming, and the poor queen would have been condemned to be burned alive for lack of a champion had not Lancelot appeared in disguise and forced her accuser to retract his words.

One of the great features of Arthur's court had been the yearly tournaments he encouraged, where the victor's prize each time was a precious jewel. These jewels, which were highly prized, had come into the possession of the king in a peculiar way. While wandering as a lad in Lyonesse Arthur had found the mouldering bones of two kings. Tradition relates that these monarchs had slain each other, and that as they were brothers the murder seemed so heinous that none dared to touch their remains. There among the rusty armour lay a kingly crown studded with diamonds, which Arthur picked up and carelessly set upon his own head. At that very moment a prophetic voice was heard declaring to him he should some day rule. Startled, but gratified, at the words, Arthur carefully kept the precious crown, and made each jewel set in it the object of a brilliant pageant when the prophecy had been fulfilled.

> " And Arthur came, and labouring up the pass,
>   All in a misty moonshine, unawares
>   Had trodden that crown'd skeleton, and the skull
>   Brake from the nape, and from the skull the crown
>   Roll'd into light, and turning on its rims
>   Fled like a glittering rivulet to the tarn.
>   And down the shingly scaur he plunged, and caught,
>   And set it on his head, and in his heart
>   Heard murmurs,—' Lo ! thou likewise shalt be King.' "
>   *Lancelot and Elaine* (*Tennyson*).

Lancelot's Skill in Jousting

Now at every one of these knightly games Lancelot had been present, and had easily borne away the prize. For his very name was almost enough to secure him the victory. Knowing that some knights attributed his continual success to the lustre which ever surrounded his name, Lancelot pretended, when the last tournament drew near, that he was quite without interest in it. Then, riding off to Astolat, or Guildford, he asked Elaine, the fair maiden who dwelt there, to guard his blazoned shield and give him another in exchange.

Elaine, who had fallen in love with Lancelot at first sight, immediately complied with his request, and even timidly suggested that he should wear her colours in the coming fray. Up till now Lancelot had never worn any favours except those given him by Guinevere, but on this occasion, thinking that it would help to conceal his identity, he accepted the crimson, pearl-embroidered sleeve she offered, and fastened it in his helmet, after the manner of knights in those days. Then as he drove the pin through the crimson silk he turned to Elaine and said :

> " ' Lady, thy sleeve thou shalt off-shear,
> I wol it take for the love of thee ;
> So did I never no lady's ere [before]
> But one, that most hath lovèd me.' "
>
> *Lancelot du Lac (Ellis)*.

Blushing with pleasure at seeing the knight decked out in her colours, Elaine stood watching her guest as he rode off with Sir Lawaine, her brother. Then with a sigh she turned to the castle again as the two disappeared from view. Meanwhile, secure in his disguise, Lancelot rode on to the tournament. Here it turned out as he had hoped ; for, still unknown, he unhorsed every knight and won the prize. His last encounter, however, nearly proved fatal, for in it he received a grievous wound. Then, feeling faint from the injury done him, and wishing still to be unrecognised, Lancelot did not wait to claim the prize, but rode immediately out of the town. Scarcely had he passed the gates when he fell forward in a swoon, and was thus carried to the cell of a neighbouring hermit. Here his wound was dressed, and he was carefully nursed by Elaine, who had heard that a knight had been wounded, and, recognising Lancelot in the description, had immediately set out in search of him.

Lancelot and Elaine

Thus time went by, while Elaine, happy in nursing back to health the knight she loved, grew daily fairer and brighter to look upon. But at last the time of Sir Lancelot's weakness passed, and he longed once more to be out in the field. Therefore he claimed his shield and turned to bid gentle Elaine good-bye. Torn with grief at seeing him go, she unwittingly let fall a hint of the love she bore him. A shadow passed over the knight's strong face at her words ; for he too knew the bitterness of unfulfilled love. Very gently, therefore, he told her that his love was already another's, and so he left her to fight out her grief. But the woe of loving and not being loved soon robbed the cheek of Elaine of its colour, till it was plain to all that the end of the " lily maid of Astolat " was near. Then, feeling her death approach, broken-hearted Elaine dictated a farewell letter to Lancelot, which she made her father promise to clasp in her dead hand. She also directed that her body should be laid in state on a barge, and sent to Camelot in charge of a mute boatman. For she craved at least burial from the hands of Lancelot.

In the meantime the hero of the tournament had been sought everywhere by Gawain, who was the bearer of the diamond won at such cost. Coming to Astolat before Lancelot was cured, Gawain had learned the name of the victor, which in thoughtlessness he immediately proclaimed to Guinevere. The queen, however, hearing a vague rumour that Lancelot had worn the colours of the maiden of Astolat, and was about to marry her, grew so jealous that when Lancelot reappeared at court she received him very coldly. Unable to understand her mood, Lancelot humbly offered her the present he had brought, which was nothing less than a necklace studded with the splendid diamonds he had won at the different tournaments. Carelessly the queen handled the magnificent gift ; then with a swift movement she flung it into the river that ran at the castle's base.

> "She seized,
> And, thro' the casement standing wide for heat,
> Flung them, and down they flash'd, and smote the stream.
> Then from the smitten surface flash'd, as it were,
> Diamonds to meet them, and they passed away."
>
> *Lancelot and Elaine* (*Tennyson*).

THE FUNERAL BARGE

The Funeral Barge

Aghast at her deed, Lancelot leaned out of the window to trace the jewels in their fall, and as he did so he saw a barge slowly drifting down the stream. Its peculiar appearance attracted his attention, and he stood and watched as it drew near. He saw that it bore a corpse ; a moment later with a start he had recognised the features of Elaine. The mute boatman paused at the castle steps, while Arthur directed that the body should be borne into his presence. Tenderly he took the letter from the stiff hand of the Lily Maid, and read it aloud in the midst of the awestruck court. Then Arthur, touched by the story of the girl's love, bade Lancelot fulfil her last request and lay her to rest. Willingly Lancelot accepted the task ; and, turning to those who were assembled there, he told them the maiden's story. His voice quivered as he mentioned her death, and he cried :

> " ' My lord liege Arthur, and all ye that hear,
> Know that for this most gentle maiden's death
> Right heavy am I ; for good she was and true,
> But loved me with a love beyond all love
> In women, whomsoever I have known.
> Yet to be loved makes not to love again ;
> Not at my years, however it hold in youth.
> I swear by truth and knighthood that I gave
> No cause, not willingly, for such a love :
> To this I call my friends in testimony,
> Her brethren, and her father, who himself
> Besought me to be plain and blunt, and use,
> To break her passion, some discourtesy
> Against my nature : what I could, I did.
> I left her and I bade her no farewell ;
> Tho', had I dreamt the damsel would have died,
> I might have put my wits to some rough use,
> And help'd her from herself.' "

Lancelot and Elaine (Tennyson).

Haunted by remorse for this involuntary crime, Lancelot again wandered away from Camelot. Nevertheless, as before, he returned in time to save Guinevere from yet another false accusation. In his indignation at the treatment to which she had been exposed, Lancelot would listen to no one, but bore her off to Joyeuse Garde, where he swore he would defend her even against the king. This action roused Arthur, whose mind had been poisoned by envious courtiers, so that he besieged his recreant wife and knight. But although in the heat of his anger Arthur repeatedly challenged Lancelot to meet him, the knight ever refused to bear arms directly against his king.

Yet the difficulty was by no means settled, and at last it grew so notorious that the Pope himself interfered, and sent messengers to England to inquire into the matter. Then Lancelot, being assured that henceforward Guinevere would be treated with all due respect, surrendered her to the king and retreated to his paternal estate in Brittany. But as Arthur's resentment against Lancelot had not yet cooled he left Guinevere under the care and protection of his nephew Mordred, and then, at the head of a large force, he departed for Brittany.

The Treachery of Mordred

Scarcely had Arthur gone than Mordred, the traitor, immediately took advantage of his uncle's absence to lay claim to the throne. Knowing there was none who could contradict him, he loudly declared that Arthur had been slain, and tried to force Guinevere to marry him. Bitterly the queen repulsed him ; therefore, in revenge, he seized her and kept her a close prisoner, and set her free only when she pretended to agree to his wishes, and asked permission to go to London to buy herself wedding finery.

306

ARTHUR AND MORDRED FIGHT

But the real intentions of Guinevere were quite otherwise. Thus, as soon as she arrived in the city she entrenched herself in the Tower, and sent word to her husband of her perilous position. Without any delay Arthur abandoned the siege of Lancelot's stronghold, and, crossing the Channel, encountered Mordred's army near Dover.

Furious at being out-tricked, Mordred marshalled all his hosts, till at last, after some discussion, it was decided that Arthur and a certain number of knights should meet Mordred with an equal number, and consider the terms of peace. It had been strictly enjoined on both parties that no weapon should be drawn, and all would have gone well had not an adder been lurking in the grass. Taken unawares by the sudden appearance of this reptile, one of the knights drew his sword to kill it, and this unexpected movement proved the signal for one of the bloodiest battles described in mediæval poetry.

> " An addere crept forth of a bushe,
> Stunge one o' th' king's knightes on the knee.
> Alacke ! it was a woefulle chance,
> As ever was in Christientie ;
> When the knighte founde him wounded sore,
> And sawe the wild worme hanginge there,
> His sworde he from the scabbarde drewe ;
> A piteous case, as ye shall heare ;
> For when the two hostes saw the sworde,
> They joyned in battayle instantlye ;
> Till of so manye noble knightes,
> On one side there was left but three."
>
> *King Arthur's Death.*

Arthur and Mordred Fight Together

On both sides the knights fought with the utmost courage till nearly every one had been slain. Then it happened that at last Arthur encountered Mordred. The eyes of each glittered as the two closed together in

307

deadly combat. "It is death for one of us," muttered Mordred. "Then for thee, traitor!" retorted the exhausted king as he dealt his opponent a fatal blow. Yet even as Mordred fell to the ground he thrust fiercely at the king, who reeled beneath his attack, and dropped, dying, to the earth. Thus fell King Arthur by the hand of his treacherous nephew, after a reign of unsurpassed greatness and renown. Yet even now his death would not have occurred had not his magic scabbard been stolen from him by his sister, Morgana the fay, who thus became really responsible for the slaughter of the brave sovereign. That was a terrible field! On all sides were strewn the dead bodies of gallant knights, while the groans of the dying tore the air. Of Mordred's men not one remained alive, while of all Arthur's noble host Sir Bedivere alone had escaped. Full of uncontrollable grief at the sight of his dying master, this knight hastened to kneel at his side.

In faltering accents Arthur now bade him take the brand Excalibur and cast it far from him into the waters of the lake, then return to report what he should see. The knight, thinking it a pity to throw away so valuable a sword, concealed it twice; but the dying monarch detected the fraud, and so besought Sir Bedivere that at last he fulfilled his wishes. Even as the magic blade touched the waters Sir Bedivere saw a hand and arm rise up from the depths to seize it, brandish it thrice, and disappear. Amazed at the sight, he hurried to Arthur, and declared how he had closed his eyes that the rich gems in the hilt should not turn him again from his purpose.

> "'Then with both hands I flung him, wheeling him;
> But when I look'd again, behold an arm,
> Clothed in white samite, mystic, wonderful,
> That caught him by the hilt, and brandish'd him
> Three times, and drew him under in the mere.'"
>
> *The Passing of Arthur (Tennyson).*

The Passing of Arthur

Tristan and Iseult

ARTHUR IN AVALON

As Arthur heard his words he gave a sigh of relief, and after telling his faithful squire that Merlin had declared that he should not die he bade the knight lay him in a barge, all hung with black, which he would find floating in the care of Morgana the fay, the Queen of Northgallis, and the Queen of the Westerlands.

Choking with sorrow at the thought of saying farewell to his king, the knight made haste to obey. Easily he discovered the boat, and therein he laid the monarch in the charge of the three queens. Then, seeing his beloved king about to leave him, Bedivere implored permission to accompany him. This, however, Arthur could not grant, for it had been decreed that he should go alone to the island of Avalon, where he hoped to be cured of his grievous wound, and some day to return to his sorrowing people.

Arthur in Avalon

Thus the ominous barge set off, draped in black, with its strange burden, never to be seen again. Yet because of the hope of his return that Arthur had spoken of, his coming was long eagerly looked for. Nor did people venture to say whether he were living or dead. Yet for the most part it was believed that he was enjoying perpetual youth and bliss in the fabled island of Avalon, whence it was averred he would return when his people needed him. This belief was so deeply rooted in England that Philip of Spain, upon marrying Mary, was compelled to take a solemn oath whereby he bound himself to relinquish the crown in favour of Arthur should he appear to claim it.

> " Still look the Britons for the day
> Of Arthur's coming o'er the sea."
> *Brut (Layamon).*

Other romances and poems relate that Arthur was borne in the sable-hung barge to Glastonbury, where his remains were laid in the tomb, while Guinevere retired into the nunnery at Almesbury. There she was once more visited by the sorrowing Lancelot, who, in spite of all his haste, had arrived too late either to save the king or be reconciled to him. This was a cause of great grief to the knight, for he still loved and revered the name of Arthur. Therefore in his sorrow and remorse he withdrew into a hermitage, where he spent six years in constant penance and prayer. Here he was warned in a vision that Guinevere was no more. Full of apprehension, he hastened to Almesbury, only to find his dream too true. With tender reverence Lancelot had her buried by Arthur's side in the chapel at Glastonbury, after which he again withdrew to his cell. Six weeks later, worn out by abstinence and night watches, the troubled spirit of this famous warrior peacefully passed away. As his spirit left its body a priest who was watching near him said that he had seen the angels receive and bear his ransomed soul straight up to Heaven, where it was greeted by a choir of angels.

But the body of Lancelot was laid at rest at the feet of Arthur, or, as some say, at Joyeuse Garde, where he and the queen had spent so many happy hours together. Beloved in his lifetime, he was bitterly lamented at his death, and Sir Ector de Moris spoke the thoughts of all the knights when he declared : " ' Ah, Sir Lancelot, thou were head of all Christian knights ; and now I dare say, that, Sir Lancelot, there thou liest, thou were never matched of none earthly knight's hands ; and thou were the courtliest knight that ever bare shield ; and thou were the truest friend to thy lover that ever bestrode horse ; and thou were the truest lover of a sinful man that ever loved woman ; and thou were the kindest man that ever struck the sword ; and thou were the goodliest person that ever came among press of knights ; and thou were the meekest man, and the gentlest, that ever ate in hall among ladies ; and thou were the sternest knight to thy mortal foe that ever put spear in rest.' "

CHAPTER XIV : TRISTAN AND ISEULT

The Origin of the Story

THE story of Tristan, which seems to have been current from earliest times, refers, perhaps, to the adventures of a knight the contemporary of Arthur or of Cassivellaunus. The tale seems to have already been known in the sixth century, and was soon seized upon by the bards, who found it a rich theme for their metrical romances. It is quite unknown whether it was first turned into Latin, French, or Welsh verse ; but an established fact is that it has been translated into every European language, and was listened to with as much interest by the inhabitants of Iceland as by those of the sunny plains of Greece.

We know that there are metrical versions, or remains of metrical versions, attributed to Thomas of Ercildoune (the Rhymer), to Raoul de Beauvais, Chrestien de Troyes, Rusticien de Pise, Luces de Gast, Robert and Hélie de Borron, and Gottfried von Strassburg, and that in our day it has been retold by Matthew Arnold and Swinburne, and made the subject of an opera by Wagner. These old metrical versions, recited with manifold variations by the minstrels, were finally collected into a prose romance, like most of the mediæval poems of this kind.

The outline of the story, collected from many different sources, is as follows :

Meliadus, otherwise known as Rivalin, or Roland Rise, was Lord of Lyonesse (Ermonie, or Parmenia). For some time war had been waged between this knight and another named Morgan, but at last a truce for seven years was concluded. Thus secured against the ravages of his enemy, Meliadus set out to visit Mark, King of Cornwall. The real motive for his visit was to be present at a great tournament which had been announced by the Cornish monarch, and by reason of which many knights of tried valour flocked to his capital, Tintagel. With great flourish of trumpets the lists were at last declared open and the jousting began. Then, though many a powerful warrior tried his skill against the stranger, Meliadus, none could succeed in unhorsing him. Such courage did the champion display that the lists rang with his praises. Moreover, won by his gallant bearing, the fair Blanchefleur, sister to King Mark, confessed she had lost her heart to the Lord of Lyonesse. Yet when Meliadus humbly asked Mark to agree to the union he refused in bitter terms. Therefore the young people were secretly married, or, if we are to believe another version of the story, ran away together from the court of King Mark.

Birth of Tristan

According to the first account, Blanchefleur remained at court, until, hearing that her husband had died, she breathed her last in giving birth to a son, whom she called Tristan, or Tristrem, because he had come into the world under such sad circumstances. The second version relates that Blanchefleur died as Morgan entered the castle over her husband's dead body, and that her faithful retainer, Kurvenal, otherwise known as Rohand, or Rual, in order to save her son, claimed him as his own.

The child Tristan thus grew up without knowing his real parentage. Nevertheless Kurvenal took care that he should learn all that a knight was expected to know in the way of hunting and fighting. Moreover, he gained much credit for his skill in playing on the harp. But at last one day an adventure befell him, for as he strolled on board a Norwegian vessel, which had anchored in the harbour near his ancestral home, he accepted the challenge of the Norsemen to play a game of chess for a certain wager.

The Capture of Tristan

As Tristan was as clever at chess as he was skilful upon the harp he soon won the game. Angry at being defeated, and unwilling to pay their forfeited wager, the Norsemen suddenly raised the anchor and sailed away, intending to sell the kidnapped youth as a slave.

> " Ther com a schip of Norway,
>   To Sir Rohandes hold,
>   With haukes white and grey,
>   And panes fair y-fold :
>   Tristrem herd it say,
>   On his playing he wold
>   Tventi schilling to lay,
>   Sir Rohand him told,
>   And taught ;
>   For hauke silver he gold ;
>   The fairest men him raught."
>
> *Sir Tristrem (Scott).*

They had not gone far, however, before a terrible tempest arose, which threatened to sink the vessel and drown all on board. Then the mariners, supposing in their terror that this peril had come upon them because they had acted dishonourably, made a solemn vow to liberate the youth if they escaped.

With miraculous suddenness this vow had no sooner been made than the wind ceased to blow ; whereupon, anchoring in the nearest bay, the Norsemen bade Tristan land, and paid him the sum he had won at chess.

Tristan in Cornwall

Thus Tristan was left alone on an unknown shore with nothing in his hand save his harp and his bow and the money his enemies had just paid him. Neverthe-

314

less, as he watched the ship bearing the Norsemen far
out of sight he felt nothing but gladness to have escaped
alive from their clutches. Shouldering his harp, therefore, and carrying his bow in his hand, he turned away
with a song on his lips to investigate the country that
lay before him. It chanced that his way took him
through a dense and gloomy forest, where he came
upon some huntsmen grouped round a deer which they
had just slain. As Tristan passed by he stopped for a
moment, and skilfully helped them in their labour of
flaying their quarry. In return for his courtesy the
knights took him back with them to the court of their
sovereign, King Mark, where he delighted every one by
his sweet music. Only too pleased to have such a
guest at his banquets, Mark urged the youth to stay
with him as long as he pleased. This kindness naturally
pleased Tristan, who was in no haste to depart. Therefore he lingered at court, winning golden opinions from
one and all.

Meanwhile his foster-father, Kurvenal, had set out to
seek his charge. Far and wide he wandered, till he too
came to the court of King Mark. Here he was overjoyed to find Tristan, the story of whose parentage he
hastened to reveal to the king.

Tristan now for the first time heard the story of
his father's death. Full of indignation at the recital,
he refused to rest until he had avenged the deed. Hot
with anger, therefore, he set out, nor would he be
deterred from his purpose of going at once. Straight
to the castle of Morgan he rode, where he challenged the
knight in combat, and speedily slew him. Then, taking
possession of his father's estate of Lyonesse, he entrusted
it to Kurvenal's care, while he himself went back to Cornwall. On arriving at Tintagel he was surprised to find
all the court plunged in sorrow. Anxiously he inquired

the cause, whereupon he was informed that Morold, brother of the King of Ireland, had come to claim his usual tribute of three hundred pounds of silver and tin and three hundred promising youths to be sold into slavery.

"Tell me," cried Tristan, unable to believe what he heard, "has this vile monarch ever ere now wrung from you this tribute?"

"Aye," replied the knights sadly; "ever since his victory over our king he has been wont to demand it yearly."

"And obtain it?" demanded Tristan excitedly.

"And obtain it," echoed the knights, as if ashamed of the words.

Unable to conceal his incredulity, Tristan walked boldly up to the emissary seeking the royal presence, and, snatching the treaty in his strong young hands, he tore it in two and flung the pieces in the other's face. Then with a haughty air he challenged the Irish stranger to combat.

The challenge was accepted carelessly by Morold, for not only was he a giant of great strength, but he had also with him a famous poisoned sword, which was wont to do deadly work.

A few minutes later the great struggle began, and

> "Sir Morold rode upon his steed,
> And flew against Tristan with speed
> Still greater than is falcon's flight;
> But warlike too was Tristan's might."
> *Gottfried von Strassburg (Dippold's tr.).*

Fearful was the sight of those two champions locked together in strife, terrible the noise of the blows which fell upon their armour. But at last Tristan sank to the ground on one knee, for his opponent's poisoned weapon had pierced his side.

Instantly Morold called upon him to acknowledge

316

himself beaten, promising to obtain a balsam from his sister Iseult (Isolde, Ysolde), who knew a remedy for such a dangerous wound.   But Tristan, remembering that if he surrendered three hundred innocent children would be sold as slaves, made a last despairing effort. Gathering together all his strength, he dealt his antagonist such a blow that he cut clean through his helmet.   With a bitter groan Morold dropped to the ground dying, for so fiercely had Tristan smitten his foe that a fragment of his sword pierced his skull, where it remained firmly embedded.

Hardly able to believe the good news that their cruel enemy was no more, the people of Cornwall acclaimed the name of Tristan, while King Mark himself loudly asserted that since he had no son Tristan should be his heir.   As for the Irish heralds who had accompanied Morold, in deep dejection they returned empty-handed to Ireland, taking with them the dead body of their leader.

Tristan's Wound

Nevertheless, in spite of his great renown, Tristan was far from happy.   For the wound in his side refused to heal, and gradually became so offensive that no one could bear his presence.   Then as none of the court doctors could relieve him he remembered Morold's words, and resolved to go to Ireland to beg Iseult to give him her aid.   Conscious, however, that she would never consent to help him if she suspected his identity, he embarked alone, or with Kurvenal, in a small vessel, taking with him only his harp.   Thus he drifted toward Ireland, which he reached at the end of fifteen days.   Arrived at last at court, Tristan declared that he was a wandering minstrel called Tantris, and bespoke the kind offices of the queen, Iseult.   Charmed

317

by his music, the queen graciously gave him her help, and quickly cured him of his grievous wound.

Still unknown, Tristan now remained at the Irish court for some time, spending many hours with Iseult, the daughter and namesake of the queen, whom he instructed daily in the art of music. Then, after dallying in Ireland for some months, he at last bade his hosts farewell, and returned to Cornwall. Here he related to Mark the story of his cure, and so extolled the beauty of young Iseult that the passion of the king was roused and he became possessed of a desire to marry her. By the advice of the courtiers, who were jealous of Tristan, and who hoped that this mission would cost him his life, the knight was sent back with an imposing retinue to sue for the maiden's hand and to escort her safely to Cornwall.

With much pomp Tristan and his followers landed in Ireland, to find the people there overwhelmed by terrible anxiety. Upon questioning them he learned that a terrible dragon had taken up its station near the city, and was devastating the country. So great was the fear of the people, moreover, that the king had promised the hand of Iseult to the man who should slay the monster. Immediately Tristan concluded that by killing the dragon he would have the best chance of successfully carrying out his uncle's wishes, so he sallied forth alone to attack it.

> " This dragon had two furious wings,
>   Each one upon each shoulder ;
>   With a sting in his tayl as long as a flayl,
>   Which made him bolder and bolder.
>
> " He had long claws, and in his jaws
>   Four and forty teeth of iron ;
>   With a hide as tough as any buff
>   Which did him round environ."
>
> *Dragon of Wantley* (*Old Ballad*).

Tristan and the Dragon

In spite of the fearful appearance of this monster and of the volumes of fire and venom which it belched forth, Tristan encountered it bravely, and finally slew it. Then, cutting out its tongue, he thrust it into his pocket, so that he might have it to show in proof of his victory. Nevertheless he had gone only a few steps when, exhausted by his prolonged conflict, stunned by the poisonous fumes which he had inhaled, and overcome by the close contact with the dragon's tongue, he sank fainting to the ground. A few moments later the butler of the Irish king rode up. He saw the dragon dead, with his conqueror apparently lifeless beside him, and quickly resolved to take advantage of this fortunate chance to secure the hand of the fair princess. He therefore cut off the dragon's head, and, going to court, boasted of having slain the monster. But the princess Iseult and the queen, well aware that the man was a coward, refused to believe his story, and hastened off to the scene of the conflict, where they found the fainting Tristan with the dragon's tongue in his pocket.

Full of compassion for his sore condition, and angry at the deception of the butler, the two Iseults carefully bound up Tristan's wounds and had him conveyed to the palace. Then, while Iseult the younger sat beside her patient, watching his slumbers, she idly drew his sword from the scabbard. Suddenly her eye was caught by a notch in the blade, which she soon discovered was of exactly the same shape and size as the fragment of steel which had been found in her uncle's skull.

> " Then all at once her heart grew cold
> In thinking of that deed of old.
> Her colour changed through grief and ire
> From deadly pale to glowing fire.

With sorrow she exclaimed : ' Alas !
Oh, woe ! what has now come to pass ?
Who carried here this weapon dread,
By which mine uncle was struck dead ?
And he who slew him, Tristan hight.
Who gave it to this minstrel knight ? ' "
Gottfried von Strassburg (*Dippold's tr.*).

At last the truth dawned upon Iseult, and she saw in the slayer of the dragon the murderer of her uncle Morold. Believing it her duty, therefore, to slay her foe as he lay helpless in her care, Iseult was about to strike the blow, when he opened his eyes and disarmed her by a glance. Then when she told the story to her mother, Queen Iseult declared that Tristan had atoned for his crime by delivering the people from the power of the dragon ; therefore his life must be at all costs preserved.

By-and-by Tristan, quite recovered from his wounds, appeared at court, where he offered to prove at the point of his sword that the butler had no claim to the hand of the princess. A duel was arranged, and the butler, disarmed by Tristan, confessed his lie. Hereupon Tristan then produced the dragon's tongue and told his adventures ; but, to the general surprise, instead of suing for Iseult's hand for himself, he now asked it in the name of his uncle, King Mark of Cornwall.

The Love Potion

The young princess was none too pleased at this unexpected turn of affairs. Nevertheless she obediently prepared to accompany the embassy to Tintagel. Her mother, however, wishing to preserve her from a loveless marriage, now sought out all manner of herbs wherewith to brew one of those magic love potions which were popularly supposed to have unlimited powers.

With much loving care and thought the queen thus

Tristan and Iseult

"Brangwaine sorrowed with many Tears"

THE LOVE POTION

prepared the draught which she believed would bring endless happiness to her child. Then when the drink was ready she poured it slowly into a golden cup, and entrusted it to Brangwaine, Iseult's maid. "On the marriage morn of the Princess and King Mark," said Queen Iseult, "do thou hand them this cup to quaff. But till then bear the secret in thine own bosom."

Promising obedience, Brangwaine carefully carried this potion on board ship, and placed it in a cupboard, whence she intended to produce it when the suitable moment came. Meanwhile the princess embarked with the escort sent from Cornwall, and set off to the court of King Mark. Then Tristan, in order to beguile the long, weary hours of the journey, entertained her with all the songs and stories that he knew, till the days had sped by merrily one by one. But, alas! there came a morning when, after singing for some time, he asked his fair young mistress for a drink; and she, going to the cupboard, drew out the magic potion, little guessing its power.

Following the custom in those days, before she offered the wine she first put it to her own lips, and then handed it to the thirsty minstrel, who drained it greedily. No sooner had they drunk, however, than the draught, working with subtle power, suddenly kindled in their hearts a passionate love, destined to last as long as they both lived.

> " Now that the maiden and the man,
> Fair Iseult and Tristàn,
> Both drank the drink, upon them pressed
> What gives the world such sore unrest,—
> Love, skilled in sly and prowling arts,—
> And swiftly crept in both their hearts ;
> So, ere of him they were aware,
> Stood his victorious banners there.
> He drew them both into his power ;
> One and single were they that hour
> That two and twofold were before."
> > Gottfried von Strassburg (*Bayard Taylor's tr.*).

After the first few hours of rapture had passed, the young people, conscious of their guilt, honourably resolved to keep their word and conquer the fatal passion which had overwhelmed them. Therefore they remained apart, in spite of the fiery ardour of the love which consumed them both. In this way the voyage, which had before been a delight, became a torment to each, and both sighed with relief when Cornwall came in view.

A few days later they reached Tintagel, and Iseult was at once married to King Mark. Nevertheless she was not happy in her union, for her heart had been given to Tristan; nor was the unheroic Mark a man likely to win the admiration of so proud a princess.

Brangwaine sorrowed with many tears for the mishap which she had been unable to prevent, and she studied to shield her mistress and to blind the king, since it was in the power of no mortal to quench the fatal passion.

Tristan and Iseult

This story of a love potion whose magic power none could resist, and of the undying love which it kindled in the unsuspecting hearts of Tristan and Iseult, has been treated in many ways by the different poets and prose writers who have handled it.

In many respects the story is a parallel of that of Lancelot and Guinevere, although it contains some incidents which are duplicated in the " Nibelungenlied " only.

Because of his boundless love Tristan is said to have had an intuitive knowledge of Iseult's peril, which enabled him to rescue her from threatened danger. In some of these old romances are picturesque descriptions of scenery and of the signals used by lovers to communicate with each other when forced by adverse circumstances to remain apart. Thus, for instance, there is a poem which tells how Tristan's love messages were written on chips of wood, which he floated down the little stream which flowed past his sylvan lodge and crossed the garden of the queen.

Meliadus

Now the story of the love which Tristan bore for Iseult had been discovered by a knight named Meliadus, who out of jealousy went to inform the king. To his chagrin, Meliadus could not succeed at first in rousing the king to action, but at last by his hints and insinuations he so worked on the monarch that he declared he would test the queen. For this purpose he called upon her to prove her innocence either by undergoing the ordeal of fire or by taking a public oath that she had shown favour to none but him. Haughtily Iseult agreed to the terms. While she was on her way to the place where this ceremony was to be enacted she was carried across a stream by Tristan disguised as a beggar, and, at his request, kissed him in reward for this service.

When called upon to take her oath before the judges and assembled court Iseult could truthfully swear that, with the exception of the beggar whom she had just publicly kissed, no other man than the king could boast of having received any special mark of her favour.

Thus made aware of their danger, the lovers again decided to part, and Tristan, deprived for a time of the sight of Iseult, became possessed of a frenzy, during which he wrought many marvellous deeds; for in the strength of his passion he easily outdid that which another knight only compassed with difficulty. At last, having recovered from his madness, and hoping to forget the fatal passion which had already caused him so much sorrow, he now wandered off to Arthur's court, where he performed many deeds of valour. Thence he went on to various strange lands, distinguishing himself greatly everywhere, until he received from a poisoned arrow a wound which no doctor could heal.

Iseult of Brittany

Afraid to expose himself again to the fascinations of Iseult of Cornwall, Tristan went to Brittany, where another Iseult, Iseult of the White Hands, equally well skilled in medicine, tenderly nursed him back to health. This maiden, as good and gentle as she was beautiful, soon fell in love with the handsome knight, and, hearing him sing a passionate lay in honour of Iseult, she fancied that her affections were returned, and that it was intended for her ear.

> " I know her by her mildness rare,
>   Her snow-white hands, her golden hair ;
>   I know her by her rich silk dress,
>   And her fragile loveliness,—
>   The sweetest Christian soul alive,
>   Iseult of Brittany."
>   *Tristram and Iseult* (*Matthew Arnold*).

With a look of shy gladness in her eyes she listened to the words, and hid them away in her heart. Then by-and-by the brother of this fair Iseult, seeing his sister's love for Tristan, offered him her hand. After a moment's hesitation Tristan accepted the honour, more out of gratitude than love, and in the hope that he might at last conquer his unhappy passion. But in spite of all his good resolutions he could not forget Iseult of Cornwall, and he treated his wife with such polite coolness that finally her brother's suspicions were aroused.

Iseult compelled to undergo the Ordeal of Fire

Sigurd Ring

ISEULT OF BRITTANY

Shortly afterwards Tristan fell upon and conquered a neighbouring giant and magician named Beliagog. In answer to his victim's cry for life Tristan at last yielded, but demanded from him a solemn promise. This was that Beliagog would build a marvellous palace in the forest, and adorn it with paintings and sculptures, true to life and representing all the different stages of the knight's passion for Iseult of Cornwall. Therefore when Ganhardin, Iseult's brother, asked Tristan why he took so little pleasure in the company of his fair young wife the knight led him to this palace and mutely pointed to the pictures. Then as Ganhardin looked he understood, and his heart rose in compassion for the knight who had known such woe. Moreover, captivated by the portrait of Brangwaine, Ganhardin begged Tristan to take him with him to Cornwall, for he was resolved to win her for his wife. Only too pleased to obey, Tristan willingly agreed, and the two set off together. On the way thither they met with many adventures; for they delivered Arthur from the power of the Lady of the Lake, and carried off Iseult, whom the cowardly Mark was ill-treating, to Lancelot's castle of Joyeuse Garde. There she became acquainted with Guinevere, and remained with her until Arthur brought about a general reconciliation.

Turning his back upon Tintagel, Tristan once more returned to Brittany, where his faithful wife welcomed him with loving joy. But as for Tristan, he could find no happiness because of his love for the first Iseult. Therefore he sought to drown his sadness in fighting, and thus he laid low one champion after another, till at last in one great encounter he was so sorely wounded that even Iseult of Brittany could not cure him. His faithful steward, Kurvenal, hoping yet to save him, sailed for Cornwall to bring the other Iseult; and as he left he promised his master to change the black sails of the vessel for white in case his quest were successful.

Eagerly the knight watched to see if he could discern any fair fluttering sails on the sea. But alas! as the vessel came in sight Tristan breathed his last, so that no help either from Iseult of Brittany or Iseult of Cornwall could any more avail him.

Some writers have stated that Iseult of Brittany was guilty of Tristan's death by falsely averring, in answer to her husband's feverish inquiry, that the long-expected vessel was wafted along by black sails; but according to other accounts she remained gentle and lovable to the end.

Miracle of the Plants

Iseult of Cornwall, finding her lover dead, straightway breathed her last upon his corpse. Both bodies were then carried to Cornwall, where they were interred in separate graves by order of King Mark. But from the tomb of the dead minstrel there sprang a creeper, which, finding its way along the walls, descended into Iseult's grave. Thrice cut down by Mark's orders, the plant persisted in growing, thus emphasising by a miracle the passionate love which made this couple proverbial in the Middle Ages. There are in subsequent literature many parallels of the miracle of the plant which sprang from Tristan's tomb, as is seen by the " Ballad of Lord Thomas and Fair Annet," and the " Ballad of Lord Lovel," where, as in later versions of the Tristan legend, a rose and a vine grew out of the respective graves and twined tenderly around each other.

> " And out of her breast there grew a red rose,
>   And out of his breast a briar."
> *Ballad of Lord Lovel.*

CHAPTER XV : RAGNAR LODBROK

Ragnar Lodbrok Saga

RAGNAR LODBROK, who figures in history as the contemporary of Charlemagne, is one of the great Northern heroes, to whom many mythical deeds of valour are ascribed. His story has given rise not only to the celebrated Ragnar Lodbrok Saga, so popular in the thirteenth century, but also to many poems and songs by ancient scalds and modern poets.

> " Last from among the Heroes one came near,
> No God, but of the hero troop the chief—
> Regner, who swept the northern sea with fleets,
> And ruled o'er Denmark and the heathy isles,
> Living ; but Ella captured him and slew ;—
> A king whose fame then fill'd the vast of Heaven,
> Now time obscures it, and men's later deeds."
>
> *Balder Dead* (*Matthew Arnold*).

The material of the Ragnar Lodbrok Saga was probably largely borrowed from the Volsunga Saga and from the saga of Dietrich von Bern, the chief aim of the ancient composers being to connect the Danish dynasty of kings with the great hero Sigurd, the slayer of Fafnir, and thereby to prove that their ancestor was no less a person than Odin.

Now Ragnar, the hero, was the son of Sigurd Ring by his first wife, Alfild. According to one version of the story, Sigurd Ring married Ingeborg, and died, leaving Frithiof to protect his young son. According to another, Sigurd Ring appointed Ragnar as his successor, and had him recognised as future ruler by the Thing before he set out upon his last military expedition.

This was a quest for a new wife named Alfsol, a

princess of Jutland, with whom, in spite of his advanced years, he had fallen passionately in love. Her family, however, having no wish to see the princess married to so aged a man as Sigurd Ring, indignantly refused his request. Then when he urged it at the point of the sword they prepared themselves for battle. In the struggle which followed Sigurd Ring was victorious; whereupon, rather than see Alfsol fall into the hand of the viking, her father made her drink of a poisoned cup. Thus when Sigurd Ring came to claim his bride he found only a dead corpse awaiting him. Full of rage and sorrow, he declared that without her he would no longer suffer life himself. Therefore by his orders Alfsol's body was laid in state on a funeral pyre on his most splendid ship. Then, when the fire had been kindled and the ship cut adrift from its moorings, Sigurd Ring sprang on board, and, stabbing himself, was consumed by the side of the fair maiden he loved.

Thus Ragnar, the son of Sigurd Ring, was called to the throne, though but a boy of fifteen years old. Yet in spite of his youth he was well able to rule, for just as he outshone all his companions in beauty and intelligence, so he could match the bravest heroes in courage and daring. Moreover, he generally escaped uninjured from every battle, owing to a magic shirt which his mother had woven for him.

> " ' I give thee the long shirt,
> Nowhere sewn,
> Woven with a loving mind,
> Of hair —— [obscure word].
> Wounds will not bleed
> Nor will edges bite thee
> In the holy garment ;
> It was consecrated to the gods.' "
> *Ragnar Lodbrok Saga.*

LODGERDA, THE WARRIOR MAIDEN

Anxious to test his prowess abroad, the young monarch led out his men every summer upon some exciting viking expedition, in which the knights could display their courage and supply themselves with plunder. For all the Northern heroes proudly boasted that the sword was their god and gold their goddess.

Lodgerda, the Warrior Maiden

Upon one such occasion Ragnar, having landed in a remote part of Norway, climbed one of the neighbouring mountains, and looked down upon a fruitful valley. This was the country of Lodgerda, a warrior maiden, who delighted in the chase and all athletic exercises, and ruled over all that valley. Excited by the stories of her bravery and beauty, Ragnar immediately resolved to visit this fair princess. Then no sooner did he see her than, overcome by her many attractions, he fell in love with her, and married her. After this she became his constant companion in all his pursuits ; yet so great was her love for her own land that nothing would induce her to leave it and return home with King Ragnar.

After spending three years in Norway with Lodgerda, the young viking became restless and unhappy ; and learning that his kingdom had been raided during his prolonged absence, he parted from his wife in hot haste. He pursued his enemies to Whitaby and to Lym-Fiord, winning a signal victory over them in both places, and then re-entered his capital of Hledra in triumph, amid the acclamations of his joyful people.

He had not been resting long upon his newly won laurels when a Northern seer came to his court, and showed him in a magic mirror the image of Thora, the beautiful daughter of Jarl Herrand of East Gothland.

Considering himself free from any duty to Lodgerda, since she had persistently refused to come to Hledra, Ragnar put many eager questions to the wizard about the princess whose portrait he carried.

Gradually the seer unfolded the whole story to Ragnar. The unhappy princess had once received from her father an egg, which she had had hatched out by a swan. When the egg burst it disclosed a dragon, which at last grew to such an enormous size that it coiled itself round the house where the princess dwelt. Here it watched over her with jealous care, allowing none to approach except the servant who brought Thora her meals and provided an ox daily for the monster's sustenance. Broken-hearted at the fate that had befallen his daughter, Herrand had offered Thora's hand in marriage and immense sums of gold to any hero brave enough to slay this dragon ; but none dared venture within reach of its powerful jaws, whence came fire, venom, and noxious vapours.

As the wizard said the last word he stepped back a pace and looked at King Ragnar for a moment out of his half-closed eyes. The expression on the young monarch's face evidently pleased him, for a smile darted suddenly round the old man's lips.

Then Ragnar, raising himself to his full height, cried in his strong, clear voice : "I will go to slay this dragon and rescue the lovely Princess Thora."

The words had scarcely left his lips before he was making preparations for departure. Choosing a strange garment of leather and wool, smeared all over with pitch, he set out on his great quest, resolved to rid the maiden of her foe, and thus obtain her hand. Nor did he fail in his endeavour, for soon beneath the strokes of his relentless sword the dragon dropped to the earth dead.

ORIGIN OF THE NAME LODBROK

> " ' Nor long before
> In arms I reached the Gothic shore,
> To work the loathly serpent's death.
> I slew the reptile of the heath.' "
>
> *Death Song of Regner Lodbrock* (*Herbert's tr.*).

Origin of the Name Lodbrok

In commemoration of this victory, Ragnar ever after bore also the name of Lodbrok, or Leather Hose, a title which he was proud to bear, though on the day of his victory he hastily laid his odd-looking garment aside and donned royal garb ere he went to receive his prize, the beautiful maiden Thora as his wife.

> " ' My prize was Thora ; from that fight,
> 'Mongst warriors am I Lodbrock hight.
> I pierced the monster's scaly side
> With steel, the soldier's wealth and pride.' "
>
> *Death Song of Regner Lodbrock* (*Herbert's tr.*).

Thora gladly accompanied Ragnar back to Hledra, and lived happily with him for several years, during which she bore him two sturdy sons, Agnar and Erik, who soon gave proof of uncommon courage. Such was Ragnar's devotion to his new wife that he even forbore to take part in the usual viking expeditions to linger by her side. All his love could not long avail to keep her with him, however, for she soon fell ill and died, leaving Ragnar stricken with bitter grief.

Seeing him consumed by his great sorrow, his knights at last urged that he should launch his dragon ship once more and seek for adventures in foreign lands. Not caring whether he went or not, Ragnar gave way to their wishes, and set sail with a goodly following or knights. Over the salt waves sped the ship, till at last they came to the port of Spangarhede. Here Ragnar bade his men carry their flour ashore and ask the people in a hut which he descried there to help them to knead and bake their bread. The sailors obeyed ; but when they entered the lowly hut and saw the filthy old woman who appeared to be its sole occupant they hesitated to bespeak her aid.

Krake

While they were deliberating what they should do, a beautiful girl, poorly clad, but immaculately clean, entered the hut. The old woman, addressing her as Krake (Crow), bade her see what the strangers wanted. Eagerly they told their errand, and admiringly watched her as she deftly fashioned the dough into loaves and slipped them into the hot oven. Then, bidding the sailors watch them closely, lest they should burn, she turned to see about her household duties. But, fascinated by her beauty, the men forgot all about their loaves as they gazed upon her flitting about the house, so that thus their loaves were badly burned.

Laden with their spoilt bread, they returned to the vessel, where Ragnar Lodbrok reproved them severely for their carelessness. Then the men, eager to justify themselves, began describing the maiden Krake in such glowing terms that their king at last expressed a desire to see her. With the view of testing her wit and intelligence as well as her beauty, Ragnar sent a message bidding her appear before him neither naked nor clad, neither alone nor unaccompanied, neither fasting nor yet having partaken of any food.

This singular message was punctually delivered, and Krake, who was as clever as she was beautiful, soon presented herself, with a fish-net wound several times around her graceful form, her sheep-dog beside her, and the odour of the leek she had bitten into still hovering over her red lips.

Ragnar, charmed by her ingenuity no less than by her

Krake

The Valkyrs

extreme beauty, then and there proposed to marry her. But Krake, who was not to be so lightly won, declared that he must first prove the depth of his affection by remaining constant to her for one whole year, at the end of which time she would marry him if he still cared to claim her hand.

Marriage of Ragnar and Krake

The year passed by ; Ragnar returned to renew his suit, and Krake, satisfied that she had inspired no momentary passion, forsook the hut and accompanied the great viking to Hledra, where she became Queen of Denmark.   Here the two lived together in great happiness for some years, during which were born to them four sons—Ivar, Björn, Hvitserk, and Rogenwald.   From their earliest days the four showed themselves full of great courage, and eager to copy the prowess of their father, Ragnar, and of their stepbrothers, Erik and Agnar, who even in their youth were already great vikings.

Nevertheless the Danes, who had never fully approved of Ragnar's last marriage, murmured frequently because they were obliged to obey a low-born queen, and one who bore the vulgar name of Krake.   Little by little these murmurs grew louder, till finally they came to Ragnar's ears while he was visiting Eystein, King of Svithiod, or Sweden.   Craftily the Danish courtiers went to work, urging now this reason and now that, till at last Ragnar was prevailed upon to sue for the hand of a Swedish princess.   His overtures were accepted upon his promise to divorce Krake.   Therefore he turned himself homewards to put away his faithful, lowly wife, and return as soon as he could to Sweden to claim a more nobly born bride.

As Ragnar entered the palace at Hledra Krake came,

333

as usual, to meet him. At the sight of her beauty his conscience smote him, and he answered all her tender inquiries so roughly that she suddenly turned and asked him why he had made arrangements to divorce her and take a new wife. Surprised at her knowledge, for he fancied the matter still a secret, Ragnar Lodbrok asked who had told her. Thereupon Krake explained that, feeling anxious about him, she had sent her pet magpies after him, and that the birds had come home and revealed all.

Aslaug

This answer, which perhaps gave rise to the common expression " A little bird told me," greatly astonished Ragnar. He was about to try to excuse himself when Krake, drawing herself up proudly, declared that while she was perfectly ready to depart, it was but just that he should now learn that her extraction was far less humble than he thought. She then proceeded to tell him that her real name was Aslaug, and that she was the daughter of Sigurd Fafnisbane (the slayer of Fafnir) and the beautiful Valkyr Brunhild. Her grandfather, or her foster-father, Heimir, to protect her from the foes who would fain have taken her life, had hidden her in his hollow harp when she was but a babe. He had tenderly cared for her until he was treacherously murdered by peasants, who had found her in the hollow harp instead of the treasure they sought there.

> " Let be—as ancient stories tell—
> Full knowledge upon Ragnar fell
> In lapse of time, that this was she
> Begot in the felicity
> Swift-fleeting of the wondrous twain,
> Who afterwards through change and pain
> Must live apart to meet in death."
> *The Fostering of Aslaug* (*William Morris*).

SIGURD THE SNAKE-EYED

Conscience-stricken, the unhappy king listened while Krake poured forth her story, and in his heart he reproached himself bitterly that he had not sooner suspected the truth from her bearing and her wit.

" Behold ! " cried Krake, or Aslaug, and thrusting her hand into her bosom she drew forth a ring and a letter which had belonged to her illustrious mother. " And if that be not proof enough," she continued coldly, " the next child I bear shall have in his right eye the image of a dragon, as a sign that he is the grandson of the slayer of Fafnir."

" It is enough," said the king in a humble voice. " I believe." Thereupon the queen's anger suddenly vanished, and the two were happier together than they had been for many a long day.

Then, summoning his nobles together in solemn conclave, Ragnar told them the true story of the birth of their queen, and declared that henceforth she should be no more called Krake, but Aslaug, which was her rightful name.

A cheer went up from the men at the words, and the phrase " Queen Aslaug " passed from mouth to mouth.

After this there was no more talk about the king's marriage with the Swedish princess, but all united in trying to show their devotion to the queen they had hitherto slighted.

Sigurd the Snake-eyed

The truth of the story Krake had told was soon made manifest beyond a doubt by the birth of a fifth son, who, as she had predicted, came into the world with a peculiar birthmark, to which he owed his name—Sigurd the Snake-eyed. As it was then the custom for kings to entrust their sons to some noted warrior to foster, this child was given to the celebrated Norman pirate Hastings, who, as soon as his charge had attained a suitable age, taught him

335

the art of viking warfare, and took him, with his four elder brothers, to raid the coasts of all the southern countries.

Ivar, the eldest of the sons of Ragnar and Aslaug, although crippled from birth, was always ready to join in the fray, into the midst of which he was borne on a shield. From this point of vantage he would shoot arrow after arrow, with fatal accuracy of aim. Moreover, as he had employed much of his leisure time in learning runes[1] and all kinds of magic arts, he was often of great assistance to his brothers, who generally chose him to be leader of their expeditions.

But while Ragnar's five sons were engaged in fighting the English at Whitaby, to punish them for plundering and setting fire to some Danish ships, Rogenwald, the fourth son, fell to rise no more. Thus Ragnar was deprived of the help of one of the strongest of his followers at a moment when he most needed it. For Eystein, the Swedish king, insulted because Ragnar had not come to claim the princess as his bride, fell upon him with a large army. At first Ragnar resolved to go and repel the attack in person, but he was finally persuaded by his two eldest sons, Agnar and Erik, to let them go in his stead.

The Enchanted Cow

Regretfully Ragnar saw them depart, for his blood boiled to take part in the strife. Yet though Agnar and Erik fought with great courage they both fell before the enemy, who were greatly aided by an enchanted cow.

> " ' We smote with swords ; at dawn of day
> A hundred spearmen gasping lay,
> Bent beneath the arrowy strife.
> Egill reft my son of life ;
> Too soon my Agnar's youth was spent,
> The scabbard thorn his bosom rent.' "
>   *Death Song of Regner Lodbrock (Herbert's tr.)*.

[1] *See* "Myths of the Norsemen," Guerber, p. 33.

THE ENCHANTED COW

The news of the slaughter of the princes was at last brought to Ragnar, who was about to sally forth to avenge them, when Hastings and the other sons returned. Then Aslaug prevailed upon her husband to linger by her side and let his sons go out to avenge the death of their brothers. In the battle which followed the magic of Ivar was of the greatest possible use, for by it he slew the famous enchanted cow, which could make more havoc than an army of warriors. Meanwhile his brothers, having slain Eystein and raided the country, sailed off to renew their depredations elsewhere.

The band of vikings then visited the coasts of England, Ireland, France, Italy, Greece, and the Greek isles, plundering, murdering, and burning wherever they went. Assisted by Hastings, the brothers took Wiflisburg (probably the Roman Aventicum), and even besieged Luna, in Etruria.

Then, finding this city too strongly fortified and too well garrisoned to yield to an assault, the Normans (as all the Northern pirates were indiscriminately called in the South) resolved to secure it by stratagem. They therefore pretended that Hastings, their leader, was desperately ill, and induced a bishop to come out of the town to baptize him, so that he might die in the Christian faith. Three days later they again sent a herald to say that Hastings had died, and that his last wish had been to be buried in a Christian church. They therefore asked permission to enter the city unarmed and bear their leader to his last resting-place, promising not only to receive baptism, but also to endow with great wealth the church where Hastings was buried. This was a request that even an enemy found difficult to refuse, and though they hesitated to give an advantage to the Normans, they shrank from ignoring a wish of the dead.

Hastings's Stratagem

Won by these specious promises, the inhabitants of Luna at last opened their gates, and the funeral procession filed solemnly into the city. But treachery soon followed. For in the midst of the mass the coffin lid flew open, and Hastings sprang out, sword in hand, and unscrupulously killed the officiating bishop and priests. This example was followed by his soldiers, who produced the weapons they had concealed upon their persons and slew all the inhabitants of the town.

These lawless invaders were about to proceed to Rome and sack that city also, when they were deterred by a pilgrim whom they met. He told them that the city was so far away that he had worn out two pairs of iron-soled shoes in coming thence. The Normans, believing this tale, which was only a stratagem devised by the quick-witted pilgrim, resolved not to waste time over the attack and, re-embarking in their vessels, they sailed home.

In the meantime Ragnar Lodbrok had not been inactive, but had continued his adventurous career, winning numerous battles, and bringing home much plunder to enrich his kingdom and his subjects.

> " ' I have fought battles
> Fifty and one
> Which were famous ;
> I have wounded many men.' "
>
> *Ragnar's Sons' Saga.*

At last he set out on an expedition against Ella, King of Northumberland, from which he was doomed never to return. From the very outset the gods seemed to have decided that in this contest Ragnar should not prove as successful as usual. The poets tell us that they even sent the Valkyrs, who were the battle-maidens of Northern mythology, to warn him of his coming defeat, and to tell him of the bliss awaiting him in Valhalla.

> " ' Regner ! tell thy fair-hair'd bride
> She must slumber at thy side !
> Tell the brother of thy breast
> Even for him thy grave hath rest !
> Tell the raven steed which bore thee
> When the wild wolf fled before thee,
> He too with his lord must fall,—
> There is room in Odin's Hall ! ' "
>
> *Valkyriur Song* (*Mrs. Hemans*).

Death of Ragnar Lodbrok

Undeterred by this warning, Ragnar went on, for he had ever been a man of great courage. The fight that followed was one of the most fearful ever witnessed, for one by one all Ragnar's brave men fell till not one was left. Ragnar himself would have long since fallen had it not been for the magic shirt which he wore, and which had been given him by his mother. Nevertheless, when the day was over and the shadows were beginning to come down upon the battlefield he was captured by the foe, and led into the presence of their king. "Give us your name," cried the men of Ella roughly. But Ragnar only looked at them coldly, and answered never a word. Then as he remained obstinately silent they finally flung him into a den of snakes, where the reptiles crawled all over him, vainly trying to pierce the magic shirt with their venomous fangs. Ella perceived at last that it was this garment which preserved his captive from death, and had it forcibly removed ; after which Ragnar was then thrust back amid the writhing, hissing snakes. Stung by the venomous reptiles, Ragnar felt that death was near. Therefore he opened his lips and chanted a

triumphant death-song, in which he recounted his manifold battles, and foretold that his brave sons would
avenge his cruel death.

> " ' Grim stings the adder's forkèd dart ;
> The vipers nestle in my heart.
> But soon, I wot, shall Vider's wand,
> Fixed in Ella's bosom stand.
> My youthful sons with rage will swell,
> Listening how their father fell ;
> Those gallant boys in peace unbroken
> Will never rest, till I be wroken [avenged].' "
>
> *Death Song of Regner Lodbrock (Herbert's tr.).*

This heroic strain has been immortalised by ancient
scalds and modern poets. They have all felt the same
admiration for the dauntless old viking, who even amid
the pangs of death gloried in his past achievements and
looked ardently forward to his sojourn in Valhalla.
There, he fancied, he would still be able to indulge
in his favourite pastime, warfare, and daily lead the
einheriar, or spirits of dead warriors, to their daily
battles.

> " ' Cease, my strain ! I hear a voice
> From realms where martial souls rejoice ;
> I hear the maids of slaughter call,
> Who bid me hence to Odin's hall :
> High seated in their blest abodes
> I soon shall quaff the drink of gods.
> The hours of life have glided by ;
> I fall, but smiling shall I die.' "
>
> *Death Song of Regner Lodbrock (Herbert's tr.).*

Founding of London

Meanwhile the sons of Ragnar Lodbrok had reached
home, and were peacefully occupied in playing chess,
when a messenger came to announce their father's sad
end. Bursting with rage and impatience to avenge him,
they started off without waiting to collect a large force,

and in spite of many inauspicious omens. Then Ella, who had made great preparations against them, came out with an immense host, composed not only of all his own subjects, but also of many allies, among whom was King Alfred. In spite of their valour, the Normans were completely defeated by the superior forces of the enemy, and only a few of them survived. Ivar and his remaining followers consented at last to surrender, provided that Ella would atone for their losses by giving them as much land as an ox-hide would enclose. This seemingly trifling request was granted without demur; nor could the king retract his promise when he saw that the ox-hide, cut into tiny strips, enclosed a vast space of land, upon which the Normans proceeded to construct an almost impregnable fortress, called Lunduna Burg, and now the modern London.

Here Ivar took up his permanent abode, while his brothers returned to Hledra. Little by little the stranger alienated the affections of Ella's subjects, and won them over to him by rich gifts and artful flattery. When at last sure of their allegiance, he incited them to revolt against the king; and as he had solemnly sworn never to bear arms against Ella he kept the letter of his promise by sending for his brothers to act as their leaders.

Death of Ella

Surrounded by foes on every hand, Ella was soon made prisoner. Then the fierce vikings stretched him out upon one of those rude stone altars which can still be seen in England, and ruthlessly avenged their father's cruel death by cutting the bloody eagle upon him.[1] After Ella's death Ivar became even more powerful than before, while his younger brothers continued their

[1] See " Myths of the Norsemen," Guerber, p. 86.

viking expeditions, took an active part in all the piratical incursions of the time, and even, we are told, besieged Paris in the reign of Louis the Fat.

Other Danish and Scandinavian vikings were equally venturesome and successful, and many eventually settled in the lands which they had conquered. Among these was the famous Rollo, otherwise known as Rolf Ganger, who, too gigantic in stature to ride on horseback, always went on foot. He settled with his followers in a fertile province in Northern France, which owes to them its name of Normandy.

The rude independence of the Northmen is well illustrated by their behaviour when called to court to do homage for this new fief. Here Rollo was directed to place both his hands between those of the king and take his vow of allegiance. To this he submitted with indifferent grace. But when he was told that he must conclude the ceremony by kissing the monarch's foot he obstinately refused to do so. A proxy was finally suggested, and Rollo, calling one of his Berserkers, bade him take his place. The stalwart giant strode forward, but, instead of kneeling, he grasped the king's foot and raised it to his lips. The king, not expecting such a jerk, lost his balance and fell heavily backward. All the Frenchmen present were, of course, scandalised; but the barbarian refused to make any apology, and strode haughtily out of the place, vowing he would never come to court again.

All the Northern pirates were, as we have seen, called Normans. They did not all settle in the North, however, for many of them found their way into Italy, and even to Constantinople, where they formed the celebrated Varangian Guard, and faithfully watched over the safety of the emperor. It was probably one of these soldiers who traced the runes upon the stone lion which

342

DEATH OF ELLA

was subsequently transferred to Venice, where it now
adorns the Piazza of St. Mark's.

" Rose the Norseman chief Hardrada, like a lion from his lair ;
His the fearless soul to conquer, his the willing soul to dare.
Gathered Skald and wild Varingar, where the raven banner shone,
And the dread steeds of the ocean, left the Northland's frozen zone."

Marri's Vision (Vail).

CHAPTER XVI : THE CID

Ballads of the Cid

THE ballads of the Cid, which number about two hundred, and some of which are of undoubted antiquity, were not committed to writing until the twelfth century, when a poem of about three thousand lines was composed. This poem, descriptive of a national hero's exploits, was probably written about half a century after his death. The earliest manuscript of it now extant bears the date either 1245 or 1345. The Cid was a real personage, named Rodrigo Diaz, or Ruy Diaz. He was born in Burgos, in the eleventh century, and won the name of " Cid " (Conqueror) by defeating five Moorish kings, when Spain had been in the hands of the Arabs for more than three centuries.

> " Mighty victor, never vanquish'd,
> Bulwark of our native land,
> Shield of Spain, her boast and glory,
> Knight of the far-dreaded brand,
> Venging scourge of Moors and traitors,
> Mighty thunderbolt of war,
> Mirror bright of chivalry,
> Ruy, my Cid Campeador ! "
> *Ancient Spanish Ballads* (*Lockhart's tr.*).

Rodrigo was still a young and untried warrior when his aged father, Diego Laynez, was grossly and publicly insulted by Don Gomez, who gave him a blow in the face. Diego was far too feeble to seek the usual redress in fight. Nevertheless the insult rankled so deeply in his heart that it prevented him from either sleeping or eating, and embittered every moment of his life.

> " Sleep was banish'd from his eyelids ;
> Not a mouthful could he taste ;
> There he sat with downcast visage,—
> Direly had he been disgrac'd.

DEFEAT OF THE MOORS

"Never stirr'd he from his chamber ;
With no friends would he converse,
Lest the breath of his dishonour
Should pollute them with its curse."

Ancient Spanish Ballads (Lockhart's tr.).

Don Gomez Slain by Rodrigo

Long he brooded over the shame that had fallen upon him, till at last he confessed his humiliation to his son Rodrigo. Impetuously Rodrigo sprang up and vowed to avenge him. Then, armed with his father's cross-hilted sword, and encouraged by his solemn blessing, he marched into the hall of Don Gomez, and challenged him to fight. In spite of his youth, Rodrigo conducted himself so bravely in this his first encounter that he slew his opponent, and by shedding his blood washed out the stain upon his father's honour, according to the chivalric creed of the time. Then, to convince Diego that he had been duly avenged, the young hero cut off the head of Don Gomez, and triumphantly laid it before him.

"'Ne'er again thy foe can harm thee ;
All his pride is now laid low ;
Vain his hand is now to smite thee,
And this tongue is silent now.'"

Ancient Spanish Ballads (Lockhart's tr.).

Defeat of the Moors

Full of joy at the removal of the blemish on his honour, old Diego again left home, and went to King Ferdinand's court, where he bade Rodrigo do homage to the king. The proud youth obeyed this command with indifferent grace, and with so defiant a bearing that the frightened monarch banished him from his presence. Gathering round him three hundred knights, each as haughty and independent as himself, Rodrigo left the court. Before very long he fell in with the Moors who were invading Castile. At once Rodrigo raised the battle-cry of Spain and rushed upon the foe, with such success that he took five of their kings prisoners. Nor would he agree to release these until they had promised to pay tribute and to refrain from further warfare. Only too glad to obtain their liberty, they readily pledged themselves to do his will, and departed, calling him " Cid," the name by which he was thenceforth known.

Speedily the news of the great exploit which Rodrigo had carried out came to the ears of Ferdinand. Delighted at the signal defeat of his foes, the king sent for the conqueror and received him back into favour, giving him an honourable place among his courtiers. Yet there were not wanting some who were inclined to be jealous of the fame the young knight had so speedily won, and who only bided their time to poison the king's mind against him.

Soon after Rodrigo's triumphant return Doña Ximena, daughter of Don Gomez, also appeared in Burgos, and, falling at the king's feet, demanded justice. Seeing the Cid among the courtiers, she vehemently denounced him for having slain her father, and bade him take her life also, as she had no wish to survive a parent whom she loved so dearly. Pointing her finger scornfully towards the hero, she cried bitterly :

> " ' Thou hast slain the best and bravest
>   That e'er set a lance in rest ;
> Of our holy faith the bulwark,—
>   Terror of each Paynim breast.
>
> " ' Traitorous murderer, slay me also !
>   Though a woman, slaughter me !
> Spare not—I'm Ximena Gomez,
>   Thine eternal enemy !

"Doña Ximena demanded justice"

Envoys of Henry III. and the Pope

MARRIAGE OF THE CID

" ' Here's my throat—smite, I beseech thee !
Smite, and fatal be thy blow !
Death is all I ask, thou caitiff,—
Grant this boon unto thy foe.' "
Ancient Spanish Ballads (*Lockhart's tr.*).

Nevertheless all the maiden's passionate accusations
failed to stir the king against the knight who had done
him such good service. Seeing that her plea was disregarded, the maiden haughtily withdrew. Soon, however, she returned ; but again she was repulsed. A
second time she withdrew, only to reappear shortly after
to make a third appeal. However, as she busied herself
over these constant journeys to and from court, Doña
Ximena heard many tales of the valour and nobility of
the Cid. Won over by the glamour of his deeds, the
injured maiden on her fifth visit to Ferdinand declared
she would consent to forego all further thoughts of
vengeance if the king would give her Rodrigo for a
husband.

" ' I am daughter of Don Gomez,
Count of Gormaz was he hight,
Him Rodrigo by his valour
Did o'erthrow in mortal fight.

" ' King, I come to crave a favour—
This the boon for which I pray,
That thou give me this Rodrigo
For my wedded lord this day.' "
Ancient Spanish Ballads (*Lockhart's tr.*).

Marriage of the Cid

This proposition well pleased the king, who had for
some time past suspected that the Cid had fallen in love
with his fair foe. Therefore he gladly acceded to the
demand, and sent word of it to Rodrigo. With much
pomp the knight re-entered the city with his suite of three
hundred men, declaring that nothing could please him

so much as to wed the fair Ximena. At once the ceremony was arranged, and Rodrigo hastened to put on his finest robes, together with the famous sword Tizona, which he had won from the Moors. With much pomp and rejoicing the nuptials were celebrated, the king giving Rodrigo the cities of Valduerna, Soldaña, Belforado, and San Pedro de Cardeña as a wedding portion. When the marriage feasting was over, Rodrigo, wishing to show his wife all honour, declared that he would not rest until he had won five battles, and only then would he consider himself really entitled to claim her love.

> " ' A man I slew—a man I give thee—
> Here I stand thy will to bide !
> Thou, in place of a dead father,
> Hast a husband at thy side.' "
>
> *Ancient Spanish Ballads* (*Lockhart's tr.*).

The Cid's Piety

His brave words pleased the bride well, and she was quite content to see her husband set off when he went for such a purpose. Yet before he started the Cid remembered a vow he had made, and being anxious above all to keep such a promise, he set out with twenty brave followers on a pious pilgrimage to Santiago de Compostella, the shrine of the patron saint of Spain. On his way thither he frequently distributed alms, and paused to recite a prayer at every church and wayside shrine. Moreover, so courteous did he show himself to every one who passed by, that, meeting a poor, loathly leper, he shared his meat with him, and even slept with him in a village inn. In the middle of the night Rodrigo suddenly awoke to find his bedfellow gone. Then as he puzzled upon the circumstance he was favoured by a vision of St. Lazarus, who praised his charity, and promised him great temporal prosperity and eternal life.

THE CID'S PIETY

" ' Life shall bring thee no dishonour—
Thou shalt ever conqueror be ;
Death shall find thee still victorious,
For God's blessing rests on thee.' "

Ancient Spanish Ballads (Lockhart's tr.).

With a light heart the knight continued his journey, showing himself ever kind and pitiful as he went. Moreover, when his pilgrimage was ended Rodrigo further proved his piety by setting aside a large sum of money for the establishment of a leper-house, which, in honour of the saint who had visited him, was known as "St. Lazarus." Then he hastened off to Calahorra, a frontier town of Castile and Aragon, which was a bone of contention between two monarchs.

While the Cid was still speeding on his way, Don Ramiro of Aragon had arranged with Ferdinand of Castile that their quarrel should be decided by a duel between two knights. Don Ramiro therefore selected as his champion Martin Gonzalez, while Ferdinand entrusted his cause to the Cid, who had meanwhile arrived. Preparations for the duel were made, and the two champions stood up to fight. Then before the combat began Martin Gonzalez began to taunt Rodrigo, telling him that he would never again be able to mount his favourite steed, Babieça, or see his wife, for he was doomed to die.

" ' Sore, Rodrigo, must thou tremble
Now to meet me in the fight,
Since thy head will soon be sever'd
For a trophy of my might.

" ' Never more to thine own castle
Wilt thou turn Babieça's rein ;
Never will thy lov'd Ximena
See thee at her side again.' "

Ancient Spanish Ballads (Lockhart's tr.).

The Duel between Gonzalez and the Cid

This boasting did not in the least dismay the Cid, who fought so bravely that he defeated Martin Gonzalez, and won such plaudits that the jealousy of the Castilian knights was further excited. In their envy they even plotted with the Moors to slay Rodrigo by treachery. This plan did not succeed, however, because the Moorish kings whom he had captured and released gave him a timely warning of the threatening danger.

By-and-by the news of the treachery reached the ears of the king, who was so angry at the plot that he banished the jealous courtiers, and, aided by Rodrigo, defeated the hostile Moors in Estremadura. There the Christian army besieged Coimbra in vain for seven whole months, and were on the point of raising the siege in despair when St. James appeared to a pilgrim and promised his help on the morrow.

Once more full of hope, the soldiers prepared for the battle next day. Eagerly they looked round their ranks as they drew up in full array. Nor was their hope of a deliverer frustrated, for there on a snow-white steed rode the figure of an unknown warrior, who ever led the way into the thickest of the fight.

Battle-cry of the Spaniards

"Who is he?" passed rrom mouth to mouth. But one and all shook their heads silently in reply. Then, as by a sudden impulse, the cry "St. James! St. James!" burst from their lips as the knights charged with renewed fury into the midst of their foes.

From this point the battle turned in their favour, so that ere the day had ended the victory was theirs and the town of Coimbra was taken.

After this magnificent success the renown of Rodrigo

rose higher than ever, while the king and the queen themselves vied in showing him honour. From that day, too, the cry " St. James ! " became the favourite battle-shout among the Spaniards, who remembered gratefully the miraculous help they had received from the stranger on the snow-white steed.

A few minor victories were afterwards gained by the triumphant Cid, who then returned to Zamora, where Ximena, his wife, was waiting for him. Here he received much booty from the five Moorish kings, who sent not only the promised tribute, but rich gifts to their generous conqueror. Although the Cid rejoiced in these tokens, he gave all the tribute and most of the spoil to Ferdinand, his liege lord, for he considered the glory of success a sufficient reward for himself.

While the great conqueror was thus resting after the warfare a great council had been held at Florence, where the Emperor of Germany, Henry III., complained to the Pope that King Ferdinand had not only failed to do homage for his crown, but that he had also refused to acknowledge his superiority. Immediately on hearing this news the Pope sent a message to King Ferdinand asking for homage and tribute, and threatening a crusade in case of disobedience. This arbitrary message greatly displeased the Spanish ruler, and roused the indignation of the Cid, who declared that his king was the vassal of no monarch, and offered to fight any one who dared maintain a contrary opinion. Therefore he constrained the king to send a reply of defiance.

> " ' Never yet have we done homage—
> Shall we to a stranger bow ?
> Great the honour God hath given us—
> Shall we lose that honour now ?

· · · ·

" ' Send then to the Holy Father,
Proudly thus to him reply—
Thou, the king, and I, Rodrigo,
Him and all his power defy.' "
Ancient Spanish Ballads (*Lockhart's tr.*).

Won over by the impetuosity of his powerful subject, Ferdinand sent the challenge to the Pope, who thereupon instructed the emperor to send a champion to meet Rodrigo. Yet even this imperial champion fell beneath the victorious hand of the Cid, who afterwards so grievously routed all the enemies of King Ferdinand that no further demands for tribute were ever made.

Meanwhile old age had fast been falling upon the king, who now became convinced that he must soon die. And, indeed, before very long the monarch breathed his last. At his death he left Castile to his eldest son, Don Sancho, Leon to Don Alfonso, and Galicia to Don Garcia, while his daughters, Doña Urraca and Doña Elvira, received the wealthy cities of Zamora and Toro. Nevertheless, many of his heirs were bitterly disappointed by the careful division which the king had arranged, and Don Sancho made no secret of the fact that he thought the whole kingdom should rightly be his. He took care, however, to induce the Cid to enter his service, for he knew that with such a champion he would be free from all danger of insult. This foresight was soon justified, for on a visit to Rome, when the Cid observed that Don Sancho had been given a less exalted seat than that of the King of France, he protested so violently that the Pope excommunicated him.

Nevertheless the matter of the dispute was investigated and put right. Then when the seats had been made of even height the Cid, who was a good Catholic, humbled himself before the Pope and begged forgiveness. Being fully aware of the great value of the knight as a bulwark against the heathen Moors, the Pope at once granted him full absolution, and peace again reigned on every hand.

> " ' I absolve thee, Don Ruy Diaz,
> I absolve thee cheerfully,
> If, while at my court, thou showest
> Due respect and courtesy.' "
>
> *Ancient Spanish Ballads* (*Lockhart's tr.*).

The Cid Campeador

By-and-by Don Sancho left Rome and returned to Castile, where he found himself threatened by his namesake, the King of Navarre, and by Don Ramiro of Aragon. Both these monarchs shortly afterwards actually invaded Castile, only to be ignominiously repulsed by the Cid. Then as some of the Moors had helped the invaders the Cid next proceeded to punish these rebels ; nor did he give up the siege of Saragossa till the inhabitants made terms with him. This campaign won for the Cid the title of " Campeador " (Champion), which he well deserved, for none was ever readier than he to do battle for his king.

While Don Sancho and his invaluable ally were thus engaged, Don Garcia, King of Galicia, who was also anxious to increase his kingdom, deprived his sister Doña Urraca of her city of Zamora. In her distress the Infanta came to Don Sancho and made her lament, thereby affording him the long-sought pretext to wage war against his brother and rob him of his kingdom.

The news of the intended campaign was unwelcome in the ears of the Cid, who was averse to fighting against those of his own country. Yet, upon the entreaties of Sancho, he reluctantly consented to lend his help, since it seemed at one time that Don Garcia would gain the victory. Once during an action the Cid found himself a prisoner in the midst of Garcia's army, just after

353

Garcia had been captured by the troops of King Sancho. Chafing at the restraint, the Cid asked that his captors should set him free in exchange for King Garcia. Contemptuously the enemy laughed in his face their refusal, whereupon the blood of the Cid so boiled within him that he at once effected his escape.

> " ' Hie thee hence, Rodrigo Diaz,
>   An thou love thy liberty ;
>   Lest, with this thy king, we take thee
>   Into dire captivity.' "
>
> *Ancient Spanish Ballads* (*Lockhart's tr.*).

The immense strength, of the Cid, always ten times greater than that of any other man, was increased yet more by the fury of his passion ; so that, charging into the foe he soon put him to flight, recovered possession of his king, and not only held Don Garcia a prisoner, but also secured Don Alfonso, who had joined in the revolt. Don Garcia was sent in chains to the castle of Luna, where he eventually died, entreating that he might be buried, with his fetters, in the city of Leon.

Alfonso at Toledo

As for Don Alfonso, Doña Urraca pleaded his cause so successfully that he was allowed to retire into a monastery, whence he soon effected his escape and joined the Moors at Toledo. There he became the companion and ally of Alimaymon, from whom he learned many secrets. Thus once, during a pretended nap, he overheard the Moor state that even Toledo could be taken by the Christians, provided they had the patience to begin a seven years' siege, and to destroy all the harvests, so as to reduce the people to starvation. Carefully storing this information away in his mind, Alfonso later found it of great service, for by it he was able to drive the Moors out of the city of Toledo.

In the meantime Sancho, not satisfied with his triple kingdom, robbed Doña Elvira of Toro, and began to besiege Doña Urraca in Zamora, which he hoped to take also, in spite of its almost impregnable position.

> " ' See ! where on yon cliff Zamora
> Lifteth up her haughty brow ;
> Walls of strength on high begird her,
> Duero swift and deep below.' "
> *Ancient Spanish Ballads* (*Lockhart's tr.*).

In this enterprise the Cid openly declared his repugnance against despoiling the princess of her possession, declaring that it was unworthy of a knight to attempt to deprive a woman of her inheritance. Yet in his obstinacy the king insisted that the knight should go himself to Doña Urraca, and summon her to surrender at once.

"Since it is you who ask," replied the hero reluctantly, "I will go. Yet it is an errand by no means to my mind." Thus protesting, he set out to deliver his message, and met the bitter reproaches of the besieged princess. After consulting her assembled people, Urraca dismissed the messenger with the reply that they would die ere they would surrender.

> " ' Then did swear all her brave vassals
> In Zamora's walls to die,
> Ere unto the king they'd yield it,
> And disgrace their chivalry."
> *Ancient Spanish Ballads* (*Lockhart's tr.*).

Siege of Zamora

Slowly the Cid returned to Don Sancho with the unwelcome reply, whereupon the capricious monarch was so angry that he banished his faithful ally. Therefore the latter departed for Toledo, whence, however, he

355

was soon recalled, for his monarch could do nothing without him. Thus restored to favour, the Cid opened the siege of Zamora, which lasted so long that the inhabitants began to suffer all the pangs of famine.

At last a Zamoran by the name of Vellido, or Bellido, or Dolfos, came out of the town in secret, and, under pretence of betraying the city into Don Sancho's hands, obtained a private interview with him. Dolfos availed himself of this opportunity to murder the king, and rushed back to the city before the crime was discovered. He entered the gates just in time to escape from the Cid, who, having mounted hastily, without spurs, could not urge Babieça on to his utmost speed and so overtake the murderer. Then as the great gates clanged upon the assassin the Cid ground his teeth with rage as he cried:

> " ' Cursèd be the wretch! and cursèd
> He who mounteth without spur!
> Had I arm'd my heels with rowels,
> I had slain the treacherous cur.' "
>
> *Ancient Spanish Ballads* (*Lockhart's tr.*).

Very quickly the news of the murder of the king had spread through the camp, filling the soldiers with the greatest grief and dismay. Immediately Don Diego Ordonez sent a challenge to Don Arias Gonzalo, who, while accepting the combat for his son, swore that none of the Zamorans knew of the dastardly deed, which Dolfos alone had planned.

> " ' Fire consume us, Count Gonzalo,
> If in this we guilty be!
> None of us within Zamora
> Of this deed had privity.
>
> " ' Dolfos only is the traitor;
> None but he the king did slay.
> Thou canst safely go to battle,
> God will be thy shield and stay.' "
>
> *Ancient Spanish Ballads* (*Lockhart's tr.*).

This oath was confirmed by the outcome of the duel, and none of the besiegers ever again ventured to doubt the honour of the Zamorans.

Alfonso Made King

The question of the succession was now discussed, for Don Sancho had left no children to inherit his kingdom. Therefore it came by right of inheritance to Don Alfonso, who was still at Toledo, a nominal guest, but in reality a prisoner. Doña Urraca, who was deeply attached to her brother, now managed to convey to him secret information of Don Sancho's death, and Don Alfonso cleverly effected his escape, turning his pursuers off his track by reversing the shoes of his horse. Thus he arrived at Zamora, where he found all were ready to do him homage except the Cid, who proudly held aloof, declaring he would pay no homage until Don Alfonso had publicly sworn that he had not bribed Dolfos to commit the dastardly crime which had called him to the throne.

> " ' Wherefore, if thou be but guiltless,
>   Straight I pray of thee to swear,—
> Thou and twelve of these thy liegemen,
>   Who with thee in exile were,—
> That in thy late brother's death
>   Thou hadst neither part nor share,
> That none of ye to his murder
>   Privy or consenting were.' "
>
> *Ancient Spanish Ballads* (*Lockhart's tr.*).

Unable lightly to incur the disaffection of so powerful a subject, King Alfonso swore the oath. Yet, angry at being thus called upon to answer for his conduct to a mere subject, he viewed the Cid with great dislike, and only awaited a suitable occasion to take his revenge. This came during a war with the Moors, when Alfonso made use of a trifling pretext to banish the hero, allowing him only nine days to prepare for departure. The Cid accepted this cruel decree with dignity, merely saying as he went that he hoped the time would never come when the king would regret his absence or his country need his right arm.

> " ' I obey, O King Alfonso,
>   Guilty though in naught I be,
> For it doth behoove a vassal
>   To obey his lord's decree ;
> Prompter far am I to serve thee
>   Than thou art to guerdon me.
>
> " ' I do pray our Holy Lady
>   Her protection to afford,
> That thou never mayst in battle
>   Need the Cid's right arm and sword.' "
>   *Ancient Spanish Ballads* (*Lockhart's tr.*).

His banishment was the signal for great lamentation among the people, who dearly loved their great champion. Yet they dared not offer him help and shelter, lest they should incur the king's wrath, and so lose their property, and perhaps even forfeit their eyesight. With a heart full of bitter reflections, therefore, the Cid slowly rode away, and camped without the city to make his final arrangements. Here he was cheered by the devotion of one of his followers, who supplied him with the necessary food, remarking that he cared "not a fig" for Alfonso's prohibitions, which remark is probably the first recorded use of this now popular expression.

The Cid in Exile

Money was necessary for the Cid ere he could begin his journey ; therefore he pledged two locked coffers full of sand to some Jews, who, thinking that the boxes contained vast treasures, or relying upon the Cid's promise to release them for a stipulated sum, advanced him six hundred marks of gold. The Cid then took leave of his beloved wife Ximena, and of his two infant daughters, whom he entrusted to the care of a worthy priest, after which, followed by three hundred men, he rode slowly away from his native land, vowing that he would yet return, covered with glory, and bringing great spoil.

> " ' Comrades, should it please high Heaven
> That we see Castile once more,—
> Though we now go forth as outcasts,
> Sad, dishonour'd, homeless, poor,—
> We'll return with glory laden
> And the spoilings of the Moor.' "
>
> *Ancient Spanish Ballads* (*Lockhart's tr.*).

Nor was the boast of the Cid a vain one, for such success attended the little band of exiles that within the next three weeks they won two strongholds from the Moors, and much spoil, among which was the sword Colada, which was second only to Tizona. From the spoil the Cid selected a regal present, which he sent to Alfonso, who in return granted a general pardon to the Cid's followers, and published an edict allowing all who wished to fight against the Moors to join him. A few more victories and another present so entirely dispelled Alfonso's displeasure that he restored the Cid to favour, and, moreover, promised that thereafter thirty days should be allowed to every exile to prepare for his departure.

About this time Alimaymon, King of Toledo, died, leaving Toledo in the hands of his grandson, Yahia, who was generally disliked. Therefore Alfonso thought the time had come for attempting his long-cherished scheme for taking the city. For this purpose he carried out the advice he had once gained from Alimaymon, and devastated all the crops. Then starvation and the great conquests made by the Cid at last forced the people to surrender into the hands of the Christian king. Nevertheless, at the very moment when there should have been nothing but goodwill between Alfonso and his great ally, the Cid, a second disagreement arose, and the king insulted the other. Thereupon the Cid left the army in anger, and, gathering together his own followers, made a sudden attack upon Castile. No sooner had he departed, however, than the Moors regained courage, and fought with such new vigour that they soon became masters of Valencia. Bitterly the king repented of the hot words which had deprived him of the powerful arm of the Cid ! By-and-by the news of the disaster came to the ears of the knight himself, who at once returned and captured the city. Overcome with joy at the sudden change in affairs, the king covered him with thanks, which were redoubled when he heard that the Cid intended to make Valencia his headquarters, and had summoned his wife and daughters thither. At the same time, too, the Cid sent the Jews more than the sum of money upon which they had agreed in redemption of the sealed chests, which now for the first time they learned were filled only with sand.

> " ' Say, albeit within the coffers
>   Naught but sand they can espy,
>   That the pure gold of my truth
>   Deep beneath that sand doth lie.' "
>   *Ancient Spanish Ballads* (*Lockhart's tr.*).

The Counts of Carrion

As the Cid was now master of Valencia and of untold wealth, his daughters were soon sought in marriage by many suitors. Among these were the two Counts of Carrion, whose proposals were warmly encouraged by Alfonso. Seeing how much the king

The Cid and the Lion

The Cid's Last Battle

desired the alliance, the Cid consented to give the hands of his daughters to the lords of Carrion, and thus the marriage of the maidens was soon celebrated. The occasion was signalised by every kind of pomp, of which it has been chronicled : " Who can tell the great nobleness which the Cid displayed at that wedding ! the feasts and the bull-fights, and the throwing at the target, and the throwing canes, and how many joculars were there, and all the sports which are proper at such weddings ! "

Pleased with their sumptuous entertainment, the Infantes of Carrion lingered at Valencia for two years, during which time the Cid had ample opportunity to convince himself that they were not the brave and upright husbands he would fain have secured for his daughters. Indeed, the fact of their cowardice was soon apparent to all. For it happened that a lion broke loose from the Cid's private menagerie, and entered the hall where he was sleeping in the midst of his guests, who were playing chess. Seeing the approach of the beast, the princes straightway fled, one falling into an empty vat in his haste, and the other taking refuge behind the Cid's couch. Awakened by the noise, the Cid seized his sword, twisted his cloak around his arm, and, grasping the lion by its mane, thrust it back into its cage, and then calmly returned to his place, while the trembling lords of Carrion stole forth from their hiding-places.

" Till the good Cid awoke ; he rose without alarm ;
He went to meet the lion, with his mantle on his arm.
The lion was abash'd the noble Cid to meet,
He bow'd his mane to earth, his muzzle at his feet.
The Cid by the neck and mane drew him to his den,
He thrust him in at the hatch, and came to the hall again ;
He found his knights, his vassals, and all his valiant men.
He ask'd for his sons-in-law, they were neither of them there."

Chronicles of the Cid (Hookham Frere's tr.).

This cowardly conduct of the Infantes of Carrion could not fail to call forth some gibes from the Cid's followers, among whom the word "lion" became a popular joke. Smarting with chagrin, the nobles, however, concealed their anger, biding their time till they could take their revenge. Before very long an occasion for displaying courage again arose, for Valencia was besieged by Moors. Yet even here the lords of Carrion proved very inefficient helpers, in no way worthy to be the sons-in-law of the brave Cid. The scorn in which they were held by the soldiers thus deepened daily, till at last the cowardice of the two became a subject of open talk.

Meanwhile, by the strenuous efforts of the Cid, the Moors were driven away from Valencia with great loss, and peace was once more restored. The Infantes of Carrion then asked permission to return home with their brides, and the spoil and presents the Cid had given them, among which were the swords Colada and Tizona. Loth to see his daughters go, yet not wishing to detain the lords of Carrion longer, the Cid gave his consent, and escorted them part way on their journey. Then, bidding farewell to his daughters with much sorrow, he returned alone to Valencia, which appeared deserted without the presence of the children he loved.

> " The Cid he parted from his daughters,
>   Naught could he his grief disguise ;
> As he clasped them to his bosom,
>   Tears did stream from out his eyes."
>   *Ancient Spanish Ballads* (*Lockhart's tr.*).

The Cruelty of the Lords of Carrion

After journeying on for some time with their brides, and also Felez Muñoz, who was acting as escort, the Infantes of Carrion camped near the Douro. Here

362

they resolved to carry out a dastardly revenge upon the Cid. Therefore early the next day they sent all their suite ahead, saying that they themselves would follow with the two princesses. Then, being left alone with the gentle ladies who were their wives, the Infantes of Carrion stripped them of their garments, lashed them with thorns, kicked them with their spurs, and finally left them for dead on the blood-stained ground, while they themselves rode on to join their escort.

Thus deserted, the princesses would undoubtedly soon have perished had not Felez Muñoz cleverly managed to separate himself from the party, and, riding swiftly back to the banks of the Douro, found his unhappy cousins in their sorry plight. Bursting with indignation, Felez Muñoz carefully dressed their wounds, and then carried the unfortunate ladies to the house of a poor man, whose wife and daughters undertook to nurse them, while Felez Muñoz hastened back to Valencia to tell the Cid what had occurred. Then if Felez Muñoz had quivered with rage at the insult, his wrath was as nothing compared with that of the Cid Campeador. Vowing he would be fully avenged, the angry father strode to Alfonso, who had supported the marriage, and demanded redress.

> " ' Lo ! my daughters have been outrag'd !
> For thine own, thy kingdom's sake,
> Look, Alfonso, to mine honour !
> Vengeance thou or I must take.' "
> *Ancient Spanish Ballads* (*Lockhart's tr.*).

Alfonso, who had by this time learned to value the Cid's services, was very angry when he heard how the Infantes of Carrion had insulted their wives, and immediately summoned them to appear before the Cortes, the Spanish assembly, at Toledo, and justify themselves, if it were possible. Hither the Cid was

363

also summoned—a summons which he gladly obeyed. At once he claimed from his cowardly sons-in-law the two precious blades Tizona and Colada, and the large dowry he had given with his daughters; after which he fiercely challenged the knights to meet him in combat. In reply the lords of Carrion endeavoured to defend their conduct on the ground that the daughters of the Cid were of inferior birth, and so not fit to mate with them.

New Suitors

Yet how false was the base excuse was soon made evident by the arrival of an embassy from Navarre, asking for the hands of the Cid's daughters for the Infantes of that kingdom. This message gave great pleasure to the Cid, for the Infantes of Navarre were of far more exalted rank than the lords of Carrion. Therefore he accepted the offer gladly, and made every arrangement for the fitting entertainment of the knights who had borne the message. From these affairs he turned to select three champions who should meet the Infantes of Carrion and their uncle in combat, after which he prepared to depart from Toledo. Yet ere he went, as a proof of his loyalty, he offered to Alfonso his famous steed Babieça. But the king wisely bade him keep that peerless steed for himself, since the best of knights deserved the best of horses.

> " ' 'Tis the noble Babieça that is fam'd for speed and force,
> Among the Christians nor the Moors there is not such another one,
> My Sovereign, Lord, and Sire, he is fit for you alone ;
> Give orders to your people, and take him for your own.'
> The King replied, ' It cannot be ; Cid, you shall keep your horse ;
> He must not leave his master, nor change him for a worse ;
> Our kingdom has been honour'd by you and by your steed—
> The man that would take him from you, evil may he speed.
> A courser such as he is fit for such a knight,
> To beat down Moors in battle, and follow them in flight.' "
>
> *Chronicles of the Cid (Hookham Frere's tr.).*

DEATH OF THE CID FORETOLD

Just before the Cid left for his home the appointed contest took place, in the presence of the king, the Cid, and the assembled Cortes. The issue was evident from the first. Soon the Infantes of Carrion and their uncle were defeated and banished, and the Cid returned in triumph to Valencia. Here the second marriage of his daughters took place, and here, too, he received an embassy bringing him rich gifts from the Sultan of Persia, who had heard of his fame.

Death of the Cid Foretold

Five years later, under the leadership of Bucar, King of Morocco, the Moors returned to besiege Valencia. With his usual daring the Cid was about to prepare to do battle against this overwhelming force when there came upon him a vision of St. Peter. Awestruck, the hero listened while the saint told him that within thirty days he would die. Yet at the same time he comforted him by saying that though he were dead he would still triumph over the enemy whom he had fought against for so many years.

> " ' Dear art thou to God, Rodrigo,
> And this grace He granteth thee :
> When thy soul hath fled, thy body
> Still shall cause the Moors to flee ;
> And, by aid of Santiago,
> Gain a glorious victory.' "
>
> *Ancient Spanish Ballads (Lockhart's tr.).*

Sure in his heart that the words he had heard in the vision would come true, the pious and simple-hearted warrior immediately began to set his affairs in order. He appointed a successor, gave instructions that none should bewail his death lest the news should encourage the Moors, and directed that his embalmed body should be set upon Babieça, and that, with Tizona in his hand, he should be led against the enemy on a certain day, when he promised a signal victory.

> " ' Saddle next my Babieça,
>   Arm him well as for the fight ;
> On his back then tie my body,
>   In my well-known armour dight.

> " ' In my right hand place Tizona ;
>   Lead me forth unto the war ;
> Bear my standard fast behind me,
>   As it was my wont of yore.' "
>
> *Ancient Spanish Ballads (Lockhart's tr.).*

The Cid's Last Battle

Meanwhile the thirty days slipped away one by one ; yet ere the last of these had run its course the Cid had passed away. Then, knowing well the temper of their dead chief, the knights strove to carry out his final wish, even as he would have it done. A sortie was planned, and the grim body of the Cid, strapped to a horse, was placed in the van. In this manner the lifeless chieftain rode again to battle, causing defeat among the foe by his mere presence. For such was the terror which the sight of the hero inspired that the Moors fled before him. And as they fled the Spaniards fell upon them, slaying them nearly all, till Bucar himself beat a hasty retreat, for he thought that seventy thousand Christians, led by the patron saint of Spain, were about to fall upon him and annihilate him utterly.

> " Seventy thousand Christian warriors,
>   All in snowy garments dight,
> Led by one of giant stature,
>   Mounted on a charger white ;

> " On his breast a cross of crimson,
>   In his hand a sword of fire,
> With it hew'd he down the Paynims,
>   As they fled, with slaughter dire."
>
> *Ancient Spanish Ballads (Lockhart's tr.).*

366

THE CID'S LAST BATTLE

Thus the Christians routed the enemy. Yet knowing, as the Cid had told them, that they would never be able to hold Valencia when he was gone, they now marched on into Castile, the dead hero still riding in their midst on Babieça. Then Ximena sent word of their father's death to her daughters, who came quickly to meet him, sobbing as they came. Yet when they saw him ride in upon his well-known steed they could scarce believe him dead, so unchanged was his appearance.

By Alfonso's order the Cid's body was placed in the church of San Pedro de Cardeña, where for ten years it remained seated in a chair of state, and in plain view of all. Such was the respect which the dead hero inspired that none dared lay a finger upon him, except a wanton Jew, who, remembering the Cid's proud boast that no man had ever dared lay a hand upon his beard, once attempted to do so. But before his sacrilegious fingers could touch it a marvel happened, for the hero's lifeless hand clasped the sword-hilt and drew Tizona a few inches from out its scabbard.

> " Ere the beard his fingers touched,
>   Lo ! the silent man of death
>   Grasp'd the hilt, and drew Tizona
>   Full a span from out the sheath ! "
>   *Ancient Spanish Ballads* (*Lockhart's tr.*).

In the face of such a miracle the boaster shrank back in dismay ; nor did any after this venture to lift an insulting finger against the Cid Campeador, mighty even in death. Nor was the body hidden away from view in the grave till long years had gone by and it began to show signs of decay. As for the steed Babieça, it continued to be held in great honour, but no one was ever again allowed to bestride it.

Evacuation of Valencia

Meanwhile the Moors had rallied around Valencia, but feared to enter the city. After hovering near for several days, wondering at the strange silence, they at last ventured to enter the open gates, which they had not dared to cross for fear of an ambuscade, and penetrated into the court of the palace. Here they found a notice, left by the order of the Cid, announcing his death and the complete evacuation of the city by the Christian army. The Cid's sword Tizona became an heirloom in the family of the Marquis of Falies. On it are said to be two inscriptions, the one "I am Tizona, made in era 1040," the other "Hail, Maria, full of grace."

Tomb of the Cid and Ximena at San Pedro de Cardeña

CHAPTER XVII : GENERAL SURVEY OF ROMANCE LITERATURE

Cycles of Romance

IN the preceding chapters an outline has been given of the principal epics which formed the staple of romance literature in the Middle Ages. One characteristic links together these very different stories, the characteristic of hero worship. Every now and then out of the general mass of men there loomed one larger figure, stronger in build, mightier in handling the sword. Gradually this figure became known everywhere for that of a hero, with whose name there became gradually associated all the various legends of minor heroes, now dwarfed by the side of one mightier than they. Thus the one supreme figure drew to itself stories of all sorts of prowess, and these stories eventually formed what is known as a cycle of romance. The various cycles which thus grew up have all a great resemblance to one another, and turn for the most part upon themes connected with chivalry. For, after the glorification of some individual hero, the epics aimed always at lauding knighthood generally. Some of the stories, indeed, such as those of the Holy Grail, were intended to magnify the two most celebrated of all the orders, the Templars and the Knights of St. John.

Other styles of imaginative writing were known at the same time also, yet the main feature of the literature of the age is first the metrical romance, which later was retold in prose, and was the direct outcome of the great national epics.

We have outlined very briefly, as a work of this character requires, the principal features of the Arthurian, Carolingian, and Teutonic cycles. We have also touched somewhat upon the Anglo-Danish and Scandinavian

369

contributions to the literature of the period. Of the extensive Spanish cycle, we have given only a short sketch of the romance, or rather the chronicle, of the Cid, leaving out entirely the vast and deservedly popular cycles of Amadis of Gaul and of the Palmerins. This omission has been intentional, however, because these romances have left but few traces in our literature. As it is seldom that there is an allusion to them, they are not of so great importance to the English student of letters as the Franco-German, Celto-British, and Scandinavian tales. Moreover, the stories of Amadis of Gaul and of the Palmerins are very evident imitations of the principal romances of chivalry which we have already considered. They are formed of an intricate series of adventures and enchantments, and are, if anything, more extravagant than the other mediæval romances. In addition, they are further distinguished by a tinge of Oriental mysticism and imagery, which is easily seen to be the result of the Crusades.

The Italian cycle, which we have not specially referred to because it relates principally to Charlemagne and Roland, is particularly noted for its felicity of expression and richness of description. Like the Spanish writers, the Italians love to revel in magic, which is best seen in the greatest masterpieces of that age, the poems of " Orlando Innamorato " and " Orlando Furioso," by Boiardo and Ariosto.

Mediæval literature includes also a very large and so-called " unaffiliated cycle " of romances. This is composed of many stories, the precursors of the novel and " short story " of the present age. We are indebted to this cycle for several well-known works of fiction, such as the tale of patient Griselda, the gentle and meek-spirited heroine who has become the personification of long-suffering and charity. After the mediæval writers

370

had made much use of this tale it was taken up in turn by Boccaccio and Chaucer, who have made it immortal.

The Norman tale of King Robert of Sicily, so beautifully rendered in verse by Longfellow in his " Tales of a Wayside Inn," also belongs to this cycle, and some authorities claim that it includes the famous animal epic " Reynard the Fox," which has been dealt with in the present volume. This story of Reynard the fox is one of the most important mediæval contributions to the literature of the world, and is the source from which many subsequent writers have drawn the themes for their fables.

Classical Cycle

A very large class of romances, common to all European nations during the Middle Ages, has also been purposely omitted from the foregoing pages. This is the so-called " classical cycle," or the romances based on the Greek and Latin epics, which were very popular during the age of chivalry. Nevertheless they occupy so prominent a place in mediæval literature that their subjects deserve at least a little attention.

In these classical romances the heroes of antiquity have lost many of their native characteristics, and are generally represented as knights-errant, and made to talk and act as such knights would. Christianity and mythology are jumbled up together in the most haphazard fashion, while history, chronology, and geography are set at defiance and treated with the same fine scorn of the probabilities.

The classical romances forming this great general cycle are subdivided into several classes or cycles. The interest of the first is mainly centred upon the heroes of Homer and Hesiod, and thus the best known and most popular of these mediæval works was the " Roman de Troie," relating the siege and downfall of Troy.

Based upon post-classical Greek and Latin writings rather than upon the great Homeric epic itself, the story, which had already undergone many changes to suit the ever-varying public taste, was further transformed by the Anglo-Norman *trouvère* Benoît de Sainte-More, about 1184. He composed a poem of thirty thousand lines, in which he related not only the siege and downfall of Troy, but also the Argonautic expedition, the wanderings of Ulysses, the story of Æneas, and many other mythological tales.

This poet, following the custom of the age, naïvely reproduced the manners, customs, and, in general, the beliefs of the twelfth century. There is plenty of local colour in his work, only the colour belongs to his own time and locality, and not to that of the heroes whose adventures he purports to relate. In his work the old classical heroes are transformed into typical mediæval knights. Thus heroines such as Helen and Medea, for instance, are portrayed as damsels in distress.

This prevalent custom of viewing the ancients solely from the mediæval point of view gave rise not only to grotesque pen-pictures, but also to a number of paintings, among which may be mentioned Gozzoli's *Capture of Helen*. In this representation Paris, in trunk hose, is seen carrying off the fair Helen pickaback, notwithstanding the evident clamour raised by the assembled court ladies, who are attired in very full skirts and mediæval headdresses.

The "Roman de Troie"

Therefore, because of the originality of handling always observed by the translator, and because the whole setting of the Middle Ages has been so minutely described in regard to the customs, dress, festivities, weapons, manners, and landscapes, these romances have been justly regarded as original works. The "Roman de Troie," for instance, was translated into every European dialect, and was quite as popular in mediæval Europe as the "Iliad" had been in Hellenic countries during the palmy days of Greece. There are still extant many versions of the romance in every European tongue, for it penetrated even into the frozen regions of Scandinavia and Iceland. It was therefore recited in every castle and town by the wandering minstrels, *trouvères*, troubadours, *minnesingers*, and scalds, who thus individually and collectively continued the work begun so many years before by the Greek rhapsodists. Thus for more than two thousand years the story which still delights us has been familiar among high and low, and has served to beguile the hours both for old and young.

This cycle further includes a revised and much-transformed edition of the adventures of Æneas and of the early history of Rome. But although all these tales were first embodied in metrical romances, these soon gave way to prose versions of equally interminable length, which each narrator varied and embellished according to his taste and skill.

The extreme popularity of Benoît de Sainte-More's work induced, as a natural consequence, many imitations. Thus numerous *chansons de gestes*, constructed on the same general plan, soon became current everywhere. Certain of the episodes of these tales which were particularly liked were worked over, added to, and elaborated until they assumed the proportions of romances in themselves. Such, for example, was the case with the story of Troilus and Cressida, which was treated by countless mediæval poets, and finally given the form in which we know it best, first by Chaucer in his "Canterbury Tales," and lastly by Shakespeare in his well-known play.

373

"Alexandre le Grant"

Another great romance of the classical cycle is the one known as "Alexandre le Grant." First written in verse by Lambert le Cort, in a metre which is now exclusively known as Alexandrine, because it was first used to set forth the charms and describe the deeds of this hero, it was recast by many poets, till at last it too was turned into a prose romance.

The first poetical version was probably composed in the eleventh century, and is said to have been 22,600 lines long. Mediæval writers still further added to and embellished this heterogeneous material, which had already been drawn from many sources ; for it is not too much to assert that every Greek and Latin writer of the time was more or less occupied with describing the career of the mighty conqueror of the Far East. Therefore, though the romance of " Alexandre le Grant " purports to relate the life and adventures of the King of Macedon, it is scarcely to be viewed as an authentic account. For fancy has been the winner in the race, and left fact far behind, so that the result is a very extravagant picture of deeds of impossible valour.

In the romance as we know it Alexander is described as a mediæval rather than an ancient hero. The early history of Macedon is related, after which the poet tells of the birth of Alexander, which he declares to have been an event due to divine intervention. In vivid colours the matchless courage of the young knight is painted, till at last Philip's death occurs and Alexander is hailed as king. The conquest of the world is in this romance introduced by the siege and submission of Rome, after which the young monarch starts upon his expedition into Asia Minor and the subsequent

374

overthrow of Persia. The war with Porus and the fighting in India are dwelt upon at great length, as are the riches and magnificence of the East. Alexander visits Amazons and cannibals, views all possible and impossible wonders ; and in his fabulous history we find the first mention in European literature of the marvellous "Fountain of Youth," the object of Ponce de Leon's search in Florida many years later.

When, in the course of this lengthy romance, Alexander has triumphantly reached the ends of the earth, he sighs for new worlds to conquer, and even aspires to the dominion of the realm of the air. To wish is to obtain. A magic glass cage, rapidly borne aloft by eight griffins, conveys the conqueror through the aerial kingdom. Here all the birds in turn do homage to him, and he is enabled to understand their language, thanks to the kind intervention of a magician.

But Alexander's ambition is still insatiable, and, earth and air having both submitted to his sway, and all the living creatures therein having recognised him as master and promised their allegiance, he next proposes to annex the empire of the sea. Magic is again employed to gratify this wish, and Alexander sinks to the bottom of the sea in a diving-bell of a peculiar shape. Here, as with the birds in the air, all the finny tribe press round to do him homage. Then, after receiving their oaths of fealty, and viewing all the marvels of the deep, as conceived by the mediæval writer's fancy, Alexander returns to Babylon.

Earth, air, and sea having all been subdued, the writer, unable to follow the course of Alexander's conquests any further, now minutely describes a grand coronation scene at Babylon. There, with the usual disregard for chronology which characterises all the productions of this age, he makes the hero participate in a solemn mass !

The story ends with a highly sensational description of the death of Alexander by poisoning, and an elaborate enumeration of the pomps of his obsequies.

"Rome la Grant"

A third order of romances, also belonging to this cycle, includes a lengthy poem known as "Rome la Grant." Here Virgil appears as a common enchanter. With the exception of a few well-known names, all trace of antiquity is lost. The heroes are now exposed to hairbreadth escapes ; wonderful adventures succeed one another without any pause ; and there is the constant series of enchantments which invariably characterises the works of the Italian poets of the day.

These tales, and those on the same theme which had preceded them, gave rise to a generally accepted theory of European colonisation subsequent to the Trojan War. Thus powerful nobles and every royal family claimed descent from the line of Priam.

Story of Brutus

As the Romans insisted that their city owed its existence to the descendants of Æneas, so the French kings Dagobert and Charles the Bald claimed to belong to the illustrious Trojan race. The same tradition appeared in England about the third century, and from Gildas and Nennius was adopted by Geoffrey of Monmouth. It is from this historian that Wace drew the materials for the metrical tale of Brutus (Brute), the supposed founder of the British race and kingdom. In his poem, which is twenty thousand lines long, Wace relates the adventures and life of Brutus, who was the great-grandson of Æneas.

STORY OF BRUTUS

At the time of the birth of Brutus his parents were fiightened by an oracle, who predicted that their son would be the cause of the death of themselves, and only after long wanderings himself attain the highest pitch of glory. This prophecy was duly fulfilled ; for his mother, a niece of Lavinia, died at his birth, while fifteen years later, when out hunting, the son accidentally slew his father. Thus, expelled from Italy on account of this involuntary crime, Brutus began his wanderings.

In the course of time the knight went to Greece, where he found the descendants of Helenus, one of Priam's sons, languishing in captivity. Offering his help to the revolted Trojans, Brutus headed their army, and after helping them to defeat Pandrasus, King of Greece, obtained their freedom. Hereupon he invited them to accompany him to some distant land, where they could found a new kingdom.

Led by Brutus, who in the meanwhile had married the daughter of Pandrasus, the Trojans sailed away, till, landing on the deserted island of Leogecia, they visited the temple of Diana, and questioned her statue, which gave the following oracle :

> " ' Brutus ! there lies beyond the Gallic bounds
> An island which the western sea surrounds,
> By giants once possessed ; now few remain
> To bar thy entrance, or obstruct thy reign.
> To reach that happy shore thy sails employ ;
> There fate decrees to raise a second Troy,
> And found an empire in thy royal line,
> Which time shall ne'er destroy, nor bounds confine.' "
>
> *Geoffrey of Monmouth (Giles's tr.).*

Thus directed by miracle, Brutus sailed confidently on. As he went he met with many adventures, and twice he landed on the coast of Africa. Then, the

Pillars of Hercules once passed, the travellers beheld the sirens, and, landing once more, they were joined by Corineus, who proposed to go with them as a guide.

Thus accompanied, Brutus coasted along the shores of the kingdom of Aquitaine and up the Loire. But here his men quarrelled with the inhabitants, and so became involved in an unhappy strife. Yet in spite of the unexpectedness of the attack and the great odds against him in regard to numbers, Brutus managed to quell his foes. In this he was aided not a little by the huge strength of Corineus, whose bulk alone was enough to strike terror to the hearts of all beholders. Amongst those who fell on the side of Brutus was his nephew, Turonus, who was buried on the spot on which afterwards rose the city of Tours, itself called after the dead knight.

The combat thus being successfully ended, Brutus made haste again to embark; nor did he loiter till he had reached the shores of the island of Albion. Here his landing was opposed by giants; yet, by the timely help of Corineus, Brutus was again successful, and forced the giants to give them passage. In these references to Corineus lies the first germ of the nursery tale of " Jack the Giant-killer," for Corineus, having chosen Corinea, or Cornwall, as his own province, defeated there the famous Goëmagot. This great giant, who was no less than twelve cubits high, was easily overthrown by the magnificent strength of his antagonist, who further displayed his power by plucking a great oak up by its roots as if it had been a weed. In another encounter with Goëmagot, Corineus made an end once and for all of the giant, for as they wrestled mightily together he seized Goëmagot in his arms and flung him bodily into the sea, at Plymouth, or, as it was then called, Lam Goëmagot.

KING LEIR

The Founding of London

Meanwhile Brutus pursued his way till he came to the Thames, on whose banks he founded New Troy, a city whose name was changed to London in honour of Lud, one of his descendants. Brutus called the newly won country Britain, and his eldest sons, Locrine and Camber, gave their names to the provinces of Locria and Cambria when they became joint rulers of their father's kingdom, while Albanact, his third son, took possession of the northern part, or Scotland, which he called Albania.

Nevertheless Albanact was not allowed to reign in peace, for he was soon called upon to war against Humber, King of the Huns. A sharp combat followed, during which Humber was defeated, and drowned in the stream which still bears his name. Later on Locrine's daughter, Sabrina, also suffered death from drowning, and so gave her name to the Severn.

King Leir

Many vicissitudes thus befell the posterity of Brutus, and there was much fighting both at home and abroad. During all this strife many cities were founded, each of which took the name of some ruler of the line of Brutus. Amongst these was King Leir, the founder of Leicester, whose story, familiarised by Shakespeare's play, was earlier treated by Geoffrey of Monmouth.

The chronicler then resumes the account of the famous descendants of the illustrious Brutus, enumerating them each in turn, and relating their adventures, till the reign of Cassivellaunus and the invasion of Britain by the Romans. Shortly after this, under the reign of Cymbelinus, he mentions the birth of Christ, and then resumes the thread of his fabulous history, till he brings it down to the reign of Uther Pendragon, where it has been taken up in the Arthurian cycle.

This chronicle, which gave rise to many romances, was still considered reliable even in Shakespeare's time, and many poets have drawn freely upon it. The mediæval poets long used it as a quarry, and it has been further utilised by some more recent poets, among whom we must count Drayton, who has made frequent mention of these ancient names in his poem " Polyolbion," also Spenser, who has immortalised many of the old legends in his " Faerie Queene."

There are still many other mediæval tales and romances of interest. Yet these can scarcely be treated in detail in a work which aims at giving a general idea of those great romances which have preserved so vividly the colour and atmosphere of the past, and to which all readers will turn who know the fascination of those stories of

" Old, unhappy, far-off things, and battles long ago."

INDEX TO POETICAL QUOTATIONS

Ariosto, 182

Arnold, Matthew, 284, 324, 327

Beowulf (translations), 1, 2, 3, 4, 6, 8, 9, 10, 11, 14, 16, 17

Buchanan, 188

Bulwer Lytton, 292

Burney, Dr. (translation), 182

Byron, 193

Chanson de Roland (translations by Rabillon), 185, 186, 187, 190, 191

Conybeare (translations), 1, 2, 6, 8, 10, 11, 14, 17

Death Song of Regner Lodbrock (translations by Herbert), 331, 336, 340

Dippold, G. T., 24, 25, 28, 29, 30, 33, 250, 252, 260, 316, 320

Dragon of Wantley, 318

Drayton, 278, 281, 289, 290

Ellis, 276, 277, 279, 280, 303

Ettin Langshanks, The, 142, 144

Geoffrey of Monmouth, 377

Giles (translation), 377

Goethe, 36, 37, 39, 40, 41, 43, 45, 46, 47, 49, 52, 55, 57, 58

Gottfried von Strassburg, 321

Gudrun, 24, 25, 28, 29, 30, 33

Hall, J. L. (translation), 6

Head, Sir Edmund, 193

Heldenbuch (translations by Weber), 115, 116, 124, 128, 131, 147, 148

Hemans, Mrs., 339

Herbert (translations), 331, 336, 340

Hildebrand, Song of (translation by Bayard Taylor), 160

Hookham Frere (translations), 361, 364

Ingemann, 173

Jamieson (translations), 142, 144

Jones, J. C., 10

Keary (translation), 3

King Arthur's Death, 307

Lady Alda's Dream (translation by Head), 193

Layamon, 309

Lettsom (translations), 62, 63, 64, 65, 67, 68, 69, 70, 72, 75, 76, 78, 79, 80, 81, 82, 84, 86, 87, 88, 90, 91, 92, 93, 95, 97, 100, 101

Lockhart, 344, 345, 346, 347, 348, 349, 352, 353, 354, 355, 356, 357, 358, 359, 360, 362, 363, 365, 366, 367

Longfellow, 4, 114, 174

Lord Lovel, Ballad of, 326

McDowall (translation), 266

Metcalfe (translations), 9, 16

Morris, William, 334

Nibelungenlied (translations by Lettsom), 62, 63, 64, 65, 67, 68, 69, 70, 72, 75, 76, 78, 79, 80, 81, 82, 84, 86, 87, 88, 90, 91, 92, 93, 95, 97, 100, 101

Niendorf, 34

Rabillon (translations), 185, 186, 187, 190, 191

Ragnar Lodbrok Saga, 328

Ragnar's Sons' Saga, 338

Robert of Gloucester, 279

Rogers (translations), 36, 37, 39, 40, 41, 43, 45, 46, 47, 49, 52, 55, 57, 58

Roland and Ferragus, 183, 184,

Rose (translation), 282

Scott, Sir Walter, 314

Sir Lancelot du Lake, 293

Sir Otuel, 191

Sotheby (translations), 216, 217, 219, 220, 221, 222, 224, 225, 226, 227, 229, 230, 232, 234, 236, 238

Southey, 166, 167, 168

Spenser, 282

Swinburne, 275

Taylor, Bayard, 160, 258, 297, 321

Tennyson, 283, 285, 287, 289, 295, 296, 302, 304, 305, 308

Vail, 343

Weber (translations), 115, 116, 124, 128, 131, 147, 148

Wieland, 216, 217, 219, 220, 221, 222, 224, 225, 226, 227, 228, 229, 230, 232, 234, 236, 238

Wolfram von Eschenbach, 250, 252, 258, 260, 266

GLOSSARY AND INDEX

A

AA'CHEN. See Aix-la-Chapelle, 197

AB - RA - CA - DAB'RA. Malagigi's charm, 207

ACRE. Besieged by Ogier, 175

ADENET (ä-de-nä'), 175

ÆS'CHE-RE. Attacked by Grendel's mother, 9 ; bewailed by Hygelac, 9 ; avenged by Beowulf, 11

AGNAR. Son of Ragnar Lodbrok, 331 ; death of, 336

AI-GO-LAN'DUS. Pagan monarch besieged by Charlemagne, 181 ; again besieged in Pamplona, 182 ; his death, 182

AIX-LA-CHAPELLE', 168, 196, 197

A'LARD. Parents of, 202; brother of Renaud, 203 ; cruelly attacked by Charlot, 204 ; his magnanimity, 204

AL'BA-NACT. Son of Brutus ; gave name to province of Albania, 379

AL'BER-ICH (see Laurin and Elbegast). Guards Nibelungen hoard, 69 ; receives messengers from Kriemhild, 81 ; reveals himself to Ortnit and struggles with him, 114, 115 ; helps Ortnit, 117 ; counsels Wolfdietrich, 132 ; met by Dietrich, 136 ; assists Charlemagne on a marauding expedition, 164

AL'BOIN. Son of Audoin, 102 ; forces Rosamund to wed him, 103 ; defeats Ostrogoths, 104 ; murder of, 104

AL'DRI-AN. Lures Etzel, 160

AL-EX-AN'DRE LE GRANT. Synopsis of, 374-376

ALEX'IS. Knight, Angela's lover, 224

AL'FER-ICH. Same as Alberich

AL-FON'SO, DON. History of, 354-355 ; made king, 357

ALF-SOL. Story of, 327-328

AL-I-MAY'MON. Reveals secret of capture of Toledo, 354 ; dies, 359

AL'PRIS. See Alberich

AL-TE'CLER. Sword of Oliver, 177

AM'A-LING LAND. Same as Italy, 151, 155, 158

AM'A-LUNG. Son of Hornbogi, 150

A-MAN-DA. See Rezia, 231 ; kidnapped, 234 ; reunited to husband, 235 ; in Fairyland, 237 ; earlier versions of story, 238-240

AM'EL-RICH. Name for Hagen to ferryman, 89

AM'FOR-TAS. Illness of, 251 ; disappointed of hopes in Parzival, 258 ; healed, 266

AN'GE-LA, 224

ANGELICA. A princess of Cathay ; Roland in love with, 195 ; seized as an offering to a seamonster, 195 ; rescued by Rogero, 196

ANGLO-SAXONS. "Beowulf" composed by, 1

AN'GOU-LAFFRE. The giant stealer of Oberon's ring, 223 ; persecutes Angela, 224 ; killed by Huon, 224

ANIMALS, ASSEMBLY OF, 36

AN'ZI-US. Emperor of Constantinople, 122

AQUITAINE. Etzel secures hostages from Duke of, 155; Walther takes bride to, 157

ARABIA. Charlemagne reaches, 180

ARDENNES (är-den'). Robber knight of, 170

AR-I-OS'TO. Italian poet, 163

AR-THUR. Herbart sent to court of, to sue for Hilde, 154 ; Ogier joins, 175 ; origin of legends, 273 ; birth of, 280 ; his sword, 286 ; is made king, 287 ; receives Excalibur from the Lady of the Lake, 289 ; marries Guinevere, 290 ; is wounded, 308 ; his death, 308 ; is borne to Avalon, 309

AS'CA-LON. Huon and his bride go to, 229

GLOSSARY AND INDEX

AS'LAUG. See Krake, 334

AS'PRI-AN. King of northern giants, 107

ATLI. Same as Etzel, 59

AT'TI-LA (see Etzel), 146, 161

AUDE (ōd). Beloved by Roland, 192

AU'DOIN. Governor in Pannonia 102

AV'A-LON. Home of Morgana, 172, 173; Ogier spirited to, 176

A'YA. Marries Aymon, 202; nurses Aymon in the Pyrenees, 203; persuades the emperor to pardon her sons, 211; scene with Renaud, 212

AY'MON. Origin of poem, 199; loses Bayard, 200; his exploits, 201; at court, 203; his oath, 205; treachery of Iwo, 207

B

BAB'I-CAN. King of Hyrcania, 226

BA-BIE'ÇA. Steed of the Cid, 349, 364

BABYLON. Besieged by Ogier, 175. See Bagdad, 216, 217

BABYLONIA. Imelot, king of, 109

BAG-DAD', 216, 217

BA'LI-AN. Hagen borne in safety to court of, 21; city of, 23

BA'RI. Rother's capital, 105, 111

BAU'TA. Memorial stone for Beowulf, 17

BAVARIA. Rüdiger passes through, 83

BAY'ARD. Given by Malagigi, 200; lost by Aymon, 200; captured by Satan, 200; given to Renaud, 203; death of, 212

BECH-LAR'EN, 83, 85, 90, 150, 157

BED'I-VERE. Knight of Arthur, 308

BEE-HUNTER. See Beowulf

BEL-I-A-GOG', 325

BELLIDO (or VELLIDO), 356

BELLIGAN, SIR, 131

BEL-LIS-SANDE. Wife of Ogier, 172

BEL'LYN. Story of, 50–52, 54

BENOÎT DE SAINTE-MORE'S. Popularity of his work, 373

BE'O-WULF. Epic of, 1; sets sail for Heorot, 5; swims against Breka, 5; arrives at Heorot, 6; his vigil, 7; struggle with Grendel, 7; second vigil, 9; fight against Grendel's mother, 10–11; returns to Heorot, 11; sees Hygelac, 12; supports Hardred, 13; made king, 13; last fight, 14; death, 16; burial, 17

BERCH'THER OF MERAN, 122, 124, 126, 127, 133, 134

BERN (or VERONA), 135, 142, 145, 149, 150, 151, 152, 155, 158

BER'NERS, LORD. Translates "Huon of Bordeaux," 215

BER-SERK-ER RAGE, 21

BER-TANGA LAND. Same as Britain, 154

BER-THA. Mother of Charlemagne, 162; sister to Charlemagne, 168; marries Milon, 169

BER-THE'LOT. See Charlot

BI-BUNG. Dwarf protector of Virginal, 139–140

BLAIVE, 192

BLANCHE'FLEUR. Won by Meliadus, 313

BLÖ'DE-LIN, 94

BLUTGANG. Weapon of Studas, 142

BO'GEN. Son of Hildburg, 126

BO-IAR'DO, 163

BOL-FRI-AN-A, 144, 152

BORRON, ROBERT DE, 241, 273, 292

BRANG-WAINE. Iseult's maid, 321; her sorrow over the love potion, 322

BREI-SACH. City of, 153

BRE-KA. Swims against Beowulf, 5

BRITAIN. See Bertanga Land

BRI-SIN'GĀ-MEN. Necklace given to Beowulf, 8

BRONS. Brother-in-law of Joseph of Arimathea, 243

BROWN. The messenger for the assembly of animals, 40–42, 46, 50

BRUN'HILD. Parentage of, 66; wooed by Gunther, 66; contests with Gunther, 67; her pon-

derous shield, 67 ; won by
Gunther, 69 ; subdued by Siegfried, 72 ; quarrel between
Brunhild and Kriemhild, 74 ;
left in care of Rumolt, 87 ;
mother of Krake or Aslaug, 334
BRUTUS, 376–378
BÜCHAN-AN, 163
BURGUNDY. Threatened invasion of, 63 ; Kriemhild remains
in, 80 ; peace concluded with,156
BURGUNDIANS, 79, 88, 90, 91,
92, 94, 96, 97, 98, 101, 155

C

CAMBER. Son of Brutus ; gave
name to province of Cambria,
379
CAMELOT. Palace at, 290, 295;
knights of, 291 ; Gareth and
Geraint at, 296 ; feast at, 298–
300 ; knights set out from, 300;
return to, 301 ; Guinevere's
feast at, 301 ; Elaine's body
arrives at, 305
CAM-PE-A-DOR'. Title of the Cid,
353
CANTERBURY TALES, 373
CA-PE'TIAN. Reign of kings of,
176, 240
CARDUEL, 278
CARLYLE. Comments of, on "Reineke Fuchs," 36
CAR'RION, EARLS OF, 360–365
CHANSON DE ROLAND, 163, 190
CHAR'LE-MAGNE. Parentage of,
162 ; his paladins, 163 ; as a
robber, 164 ; bewitched by
ring, 166 ; sees and forgives
Bertha, 169 ; attacks Didier of
Lombardy, 173 ; sees vision of
stars, 179 ; engages in war
against Aigolandus, 181 ; fights
against Ferracute, 183 ; wars
in Spain, 185 ; sends embassy
to Marsiglio, 186 ; retreat of,
186 ; battle of Roncesvalles,
186 ; hears Roland's horn, 187 ;
returns to Roncesvalles, 189 ;
orders trial of Ganelon, 191 ;
his death, 195 ; his burial, 197 ;
other legends regarding Charle-

magne's death, 197 ; the peers
of, twelve, 198 ; Aymon a peer
of, 199 ; character of, 199 ;
wars against Aymon, 200 ;
treats with Aymon, 202 ; coronation of, at Rome, 203 ; hostility towards the sons of Aymon, 205 ; captures sons of
Aymon, 206 ; bribes Iwo, 207 ;
Richard carried captive to, 208 ;
besieges Montauban, 209 ; Malagigi seized and carried to, 210;
Aya intercedes with, 211 ; demands Bayard's death, 212 ;
Huon does homage to, 215 ;
assigns Huon a three-fold task,
216 ; pardons Huon, 239 ; contemporary of Ragnar Lodbrok,
327 ; Italian Cycle treats of, 370
CHARLES THE BALD. Popular
ballads regarding, 199
CHAR'LOT, 173 ; kills Ogier's
son, 173 ; his death insisted on,
175 ; Renaud's complaints
against, 204
CHRESTIEN DE TROYES (krä-té-an'
deh trwä), poems of, 241, 292
CHRISTIAN FAITH. Attack on behalf of, foretold, 181
CID. Origin of poem, 344 ; at
court, 346 ; marriage, 348 ; his
exploits, 350 ; receives title
Campeador, 353 ; is exiled, 355 ;
his daughters sought in marriage, 360 ; his death, 366 ;
his burial, 367
CI-SAIRE'. Pass in which Roland
kills his steed, 188
CLARICE. Wife of Ogier, 175
CLA-RIS-SA. Wife of Renaud,
205 ; her death, 213
CLARETIE (klä-re-tē'). Ancestress
of Capetian race, 240
CO-LA-DA. Sword belonging to
the Cid, 359 ; given to lords of
Carrion, 364
COM-POS-TEL-LA. Shrine of, 180 ;
St. James of, 196
CON-DUIR-A-MOUR, 256
CONSTANTINE. Emperor in East,
106 ; receives Rother, 107 ;
Rother assists against Imelot,
109

CON-STAN-TI-NO'PLE. Visited by Rother, 107 ; Anzius emperor of, 122 ; Wolfdietrich, king of, 126 ; Wolfdietrich enters, 133

CORNWALL. See story of Tristan and Iseult, 312–326

COW, THE MAGIC, 336–337

D

DAG'O BERT. Claims descent from Trojans, 376

DANES. Beowulf amongst, 6 ; their gratitude, 12 ; their admiration for Ogier, 173

DANK'RAT. King of Burgundy, parent of Gunther, 59 ; is succeeded by Gunther, 59

DANK'WART. Accompanies Gunther, 63, 66 ; watches warriors with Brunhild's shield, 67 ; sees treachery, 67, 69 ; accompanies Gunther out of Worms, 87 ; escapes slaughter, 94

DANSKE. Same as Ogier, 172

DEN'MARK. Hrothgar, king of, 1 ; Beowulf sails to, 5 ; queen of, 8, 333 ; Ludegast, king of, 63 ; Charlemagne wars against king of, 172

DES-I-DE'RI-US. See Didier

DI-A'NA. Brutus in temple of, 377

DID'I-ER. King of Lombardy, 173

DIEGO LAYNEZ (de-ä'go la-nez). Insulted by Gomez, 344 ; witnesses death of latter, 345 ; goes to Ferdinand's court, 345 ; challenge to Don Arias Gonzalo, 356

DIE-TE-LIN'DE. Entertains Kriemhild, 85 ; Giselher falls in love with 90

DIE'THER. Brother of Dietrich, 155 ; slain near Raben, 158

DIET-LIEB. Offers himself as escort to Dietrich, 146 ; lives luxuriously at Rome, 146 ; said by Ermenrich to be a glutton, 146 ; proves his prowess and is rewarded by king, 146 ; journeys to court of Etzel, 147 ; receives Styria, from Etzel 147 ; returns to his old master, 147 ; goes with Dietrich to rescue of his sister, 147 ; is captured, 148 ; released, 149 ; suggested helper of Dietrich, 150

DIET'MAR. Father of Dietrich, 134 ; news of death of, 151

DIE-TRICH VON BERN. Meets the Nibelungs, 90 ; defies Kriemhild, 91 ; claims safe-conduct, 96 ; his parentage, 134, 135 ; meets Alferich, 136 ; slays Grim and Hilde, 137 ; rescues and marries Virginal, 141 ; rides Falke, 142 ; fights with Wittich; 144 ; sets out for Rome, 146 ; meets Dietlieb on the way, 146 ; reaches Rome, 146 ; later called upon by Dietlieb to set out on expedition to rescue sister of latter, 147 ; is captured, 148 ; breaks free, 149 ; sets out for Rose Garden at Worms, 150 ; returns to Bern, 151 ; forsaken by Virginal, 154 ; goes into exile, 155 ; fights for Etzel in land of Huns, 156 ; wars against Waldemar, 157 ; marries Herrat, 159 ; crowned Emperor, 159, 160 ; marries Liebgart, 160 ; leader of Wild Hunt, 161 ; the Saga, 327

DOL'FOS. See Vellido, 356

DORT'MUND. Renaud's body carried to, 214

DRA'CHEN - FELS. 1. Lady of, held prisoner by Ecke, 144 ; delivered by Dietrich, 145 ; given in marriage to Wittich, 152. 2. Lord of, visited by Roland, who falls in love with his daughter, 193, 194

DRAYTON. His poem "Polyolbion," 380

DRUIDS, 162

DRU'SI-AN. A magician ; carries off Sigeminne, 129

DU'O-LIN DE MAY'ENCE. A *chanson de geste*, 199

DUR-AN-DA'NA. Sword of Roland, 177, 183, 188

GLOSSARY AND INDEX

E

EAD'GILS. Son of Othere, and King of Sweden, 13

ECK'E. The giant; holds Bolfriana and her daughter, 144; attacked by Dietrich, 144; killed by Falke, the steed, 144

ECK'EN-LIED. Story of Ecke, 144

ECK'E-SAX. The sword of Ecke, 145

ECK'E-WART. Remains with Kriemhild in Burgundy, 81; prepares dwelling for his mistress, 81; leaves Burgundy with his mistress, 84; brings warning for Burgundians, 90

ECK'HARDT. Rhine land left to him, 134; flees to court of Dietrich, 154; tutor to the Harlungs, 154

EDDA. Story of Hilde in, 18

EIN'HARD. Son-in-law of Charlemagne; founds story of Charlemagne's exploits, 163

E-LAINE'. Gives her love to Lancelot, 303; her death, 305

EL'BE-GAST. See Alberich, 164

E'LI-AS. See Ylyas, 114

EL'LA. King of Northumberland; leads expedition against Ragnar Lodbrok, 338; defeats Ragnar, 339; removes from him his magic shirt, 339; his own defeat foretold by Ragnar, 340; is overthrown by Ivar, 341

EL'SE. Duchess of Brabant, 269–272; spends her days in tears, 269; her guardian, Frederick of Telramund, among her suitors, 269; she dreams of a radiant knight, 269; thrown into prison by Frederick, 270; Lohengrin her champion, 271; later deserted by Lohengrin, 272

EL-SI-NORE'. Ogier sleeping in vaults of, 173

ENGLAND. Vikings visit, 337

E'NID THE FAIR. Story of, 296–298; marries Geraint, 296; does not wish her husband to withdraw from active life, 297; calls herself an unworthy wife, 297; her patience, 298

ENIGEE (ä'nĕ-zhä). Sister of Joseph, 243

E'RIK. Son of Ragnar, 331; goes to fight against Eystein, 336; killed in battle, 336

ER'ME-LYN. Wife of Reynard, 49; helps her husband to attack Lampe, 50; · assists in deception of Bellyn, 51

ER'MEN'RICH. King, 48; his hoard used to subsidise mercenaries, 48; Emperor of West, 135; jeers at his guest Dietlieb as a glutton, 146; pays Dietlieb's debts, 146; Sibich plots against, 153; Dietrich hears of death of, 159

ERP. Son of Helche; his help promised by her to Dietrich, 158

ES-CLAR-MONDE. See Amanda, 238

ET'ZEL. King of Hungary, 59; wooes Kriemhild, 83; marries Kriemhild, 85; his capital, Gran, 85; entertains the Burgundians, 92, 93; holds a banquet, 93; aghast at the sudden strife which arises, 95; his grief, 95, 97; marries Helche, 113; visited by Dietlieb, 146; gives Dietlieb Styria, 147; wars against Osantrix, 151; his death, 160

EUROPE. Story of "Reynard the Fox" circulated over, 35; destined to be infested with dragons, 120; Dietrich ruler of southern part, 160

EX-CAL'I-BUR. Arthur's sword, 289, 308

EY'STEIN. King of Sweden, 336; attacks Ragnar, 336; slain, 337

F

FA'ER-IE QUEENE. Spenser's poem, 380

FAF'NIR. Slain by Sigurd, 327

GLOSSARY AND INDEX

Faf'nis-bane. Surname of Sigurd, 327

Fairyland. Huon and Amanda in, 237

Falke. Horse obtained by Heime for Dietrich, 142 ; saves Dietrich, 144

Fa'solt. Brother of Ecke ; Dietrich defeats, 144 ; afterwards joins service of Dietrich, 145

Fa'ta Mor-ga'na. Same as Morgana the fay, 114

Fat'i-ma. Favourite attendant of Rezia, with whom she escapes, 229 ; is sold into slavery, 235 ; in Fairyland, 237 ; rescued by Huon and Sherasmin, 239

Fer'di-nand. The Cid at the court of, 345 ; shows favour to the Cid, 346–347 ; the duel, 349 ; complaints against, 351 ; defies the Pope, 352

Fer'ra-cute. A giant challenged by Charlemagne, 182 ; fights with Ogier, 183 ; defeats Ogier, 183 ; meets Roland, 183 ; who tries to convert him, 184 ; defeat and death of, 184

Fer'ra-gus. See Ferracute

Fierefiss (fyâr-e-fes'). Meets Parzival, 265–266 ; marries Repanse de Joie, 266

Fire-drake. A monster ; meets Beowulf, 14 ; is slain by him, 15

Flam'berge. Sword of Aymon, 201 ; owned by Renaud, 208 ; is broken, 213

Fountain of Youth, 375

France. Story of "Reynard the Fox" in, 35 ; Ogier marries widow of king of, 176 ; Vikings visit, 337

Franks and "Reynard the Fox," 35, 36 ; Franks and Hildegunde, 155

Fras-tra-da. Wife of Charlemagne ; her magic ring, 165 ; swallows this when dying, 166 ; the power of the ring, 166

Frie'sian Sea, 179

Frie'sians. Invasion of, 12

Fries'land. Invaded by Hygelac, 12

Fri-mou-tel'. Son of Titurel and Richoude ; named to succeed his father, 249 ; goes out into the world and dies, 250

Frute. Follower of Hettel ; accompanies him in his quest of Hilde, 23

G

Ga-la'fre. Huon and Sherasmin at court of, 238

Gal'a-had, Sir. Knighted by Lancelot, 298 ; occupies Siege Perilous, 299 ; sees Holy Grail, 300

Gal'y-en. Son of Oliver, 178

Galyen Rhetoré. A chanson de geste, 177

Ga'mu-ret. Father of Parzival, 250

Ga-ne-lon. Chosen as ambassador, 186 ; persuades Charlemagne that Roland is not calling for aid, 187 ; king regrets his advice, 189 ; his death, 191

Gan-har-din. Brother of Iseult ; accompanies Tristan to Cornwall, 325 ; helps to deliver Arthur from the Lady of the Lake, 325

Gar-a-die, Count. Captures Hagen, but is overawed by him, 21

Gar-ci'a, Don. King of Galicia, 352–354

Gar'den (same as Guarda). Wolfdietrich set down near, 131 ; Herbrand inherits, 134 ; invested by army, 155 ; taken by Dietrich, 158

Gar'eth, Sir. Knighted by Lancelot, 295 ; insulted by Lynette, 295 ; marries Lynette, 296

Gary. Follower of Gunther, 73, 87

Ga'wain. Adventures of, 261 ; slays giant, 264 ; his marriage, 264

Geates. Kingdom of, 4 ; Beowulf is escorted by, 10 ; death of their king, 12

GLOSSARY AND INDEX

GEL-FRAT. Ferryman killed by Hagen, 89

GENOA. Charlemagne and Duke of, 176

GEOFFREY DE BOUILLON. King of Jerusalem, 176; title given him by Renaud, 213

GEOFFREY OF MONMOUTH, 273, 379

GEP'I-DÆ. Settle in Pannonia, 102; quarrel with the Langobards, 103

GER'AINT. Brother of Gareth; joins Round Table, 296; marries Enid, 296; misunderstands her remark, 297; makes Enid accompany him on journey, 297; dies, 298

GERASMES (je-räme). See Sherasmin, 218

GER'HART. Claims hand of Liebgart, 132; denounced by Wolfdietrich, 133

GER'IMS-BURG. Stronghold of one of vassals of Ermenrich, 152

GER-LIN'DA. Receives Gudrun, 28; pretends kindness, 28–29; cruelty of, 30; in the siege, 32; her death, 33

GERMANY. Story of "Reynard the Fox" in, 35; greatest epic, the "Nibelungenlied," 59; poet von Ofterdingen, 59; Eckewart's faithfulness proverbial in, 81

GER'NOT. Son of Dankrat and Ute, 59; joins Gunther, 63; incited by Hagen to murder Siegfried, 75; supports Kriemhild, 80; angry with Hagen for removing the jewels, 82; slain by Rüdiger, 99

GIER'E-MUND. Wife of Isegrim the wolf; is insulted by Reynard, 37; wooed by Reynard, 38

GI-RARD'. 1. Brother of Huon, 215; killed by Charlot, 215. 2. Knight who steals Huon's estates, 239

GIS'EL-HER. Son of Dankrat and Ute, 59; joins Gunther, 63; reproves Hagen, 75; supports Kriemhild, 80; angry with

Hagen for removing the jewels, 82; falls in love with Dietelinde, 90

GODFREY OF BOUILLON. Crown of Jerusalem passed on to, 213

GOËMAGOT (gō-e-mä-got'). Corineus kills, 378

GOETHE. "Reineke Fuchs" of, 36

GO'MEZ, DON. Slain by the Cid, 345; Ximena, daughter of, 347

GO-TE-LINDE. Wife of Rüdiger; entertains Kriemhild, 85

GOTHS. See Geates. Name the symbol of courage, 17

GOTT'FRIED VON STRASS'BURG, 241, 273

GOZZOLI (got'so-lee). Painting of, 372

GRAIL. See Holy Grail

GRAM'O-FLAUS. Parzival champion of, 264

GRAN. Capital of Etzel, 85; Kriemhild there, 86, 87; Hungarian minstrels return to, 87

GREECE. Hertnit, earl of, 151; Vikings visit, 337; epics of, 371; Brutus goes to, 377

GREN'DEL. A monster, 3; perpetrates massacre, 4; Beowulf attacks, 5; they fight, 7; defeat of Grendel, 8; mother of, 9; killed by Beowulf, 11

GRIFFIN. Hagen carried off by, 19; slain, 20

GRIM. A giant; great depredations, 136; attacked by Dietrich, 136; killed, 137; brother to Sigenot, 137

GRIM'BART THE BADGER. Nephew to Reynard, 36; defends Reynard, 37; goes to call him to court, 44; absolves him, 45; hastens to his uncle's assistance, 51; instructs him how to return to court, 52

GRIM-HILD. See Kriemhild

GUARDA. See Garden

GU-DRUN. Same as Kriemhild. 1. Poem of, 18. 2. Daughter of Hettel and Hilde; her birth, 25; her beauty, 26; wooing of, 26–27; captured by Hart-

mut, 27 ; rejects his offers,
28 ; tortured by Gerlinda, 29 ;
Gudrun and Gerlinda, 31 ; rescued, 32 ; queen, 33 ; married,
34

GUER'IN DE MONT-GLAVE. A
chanson de geste, 176

GUI-ENNE'. Huon's patrimony,
237

GUIN'E-VERE. Marries Arthur,
290 ; is loved by Lancelot, 293 ;
her caprice, 294 ; accused of
death of a knight, 301 ; throws
away the necklace, 304 ; a
prisoner, 306 ; her death and
burial, 310

GUIS'CARD. Son of Aymon, 202

GUN'NAR. Same as Gunther

GUN'THER. Parentage, 59 ; the
tournament, 61 ; desires Brunhild, 65 ; goes to woo her, 66 ;
strives with her, 68 ; marries
her, 70 ; is humiliated by her,
71 ; is helped by Siegfried, 72 ;
receives visit from Kriemhild
and Siegfried, 73 ; incited by
Hagen to murder Siegfried, 75 ;
receives last message from Siegfried, 78 ; Kriemhild's rage
against, 79 ; plots with Hagen
for recovery of Nibelungen
hoard, 81 ; angry with Hagen
for removing the jewels, 82 ;
assists to destroy the Huns, 95 ;
is captured, 99 ; slain, 100 ;
King of Burgundy attacks
Walther, 156

GUR'NE-MANZ. Instructs Parzival in knighthood, 255

GU'TRUN. See Kriemhild

H

HA'CHE. Receives Rhine land, 134

HAD-BURG. Prophecy of, 88

HAD'U-BRAND. Son of Hildebrand, 159

HAGEN. 1. Son of Sigeband ;
birth and boyhood, 19 ; life in
cave, 20 ; slays the griffins,
20 ; is rescued and taken to
Issland, 21 ; is made king, 22 ;
marries, 22 ; pursues Hettel, 25.

2. Same as Högni, 59 ; uncle
of Siegfried ; joins Gunther,
63 ; accompanies Gunther to
Issland, 66–69 ; promises to
avenge Brunhild, 75 ; plots
against Siegfried, 75 ; reproved
by Giselher, 75 ; slays Siegfried,
78 ; plots with Gunther for
recovery of Nibelungen hoard,
81 ; steals keys of tower where
kept, 82 ; receives Rüdiger,
83 ; opposes Kriemhild's proposed marriage, 83 ; accompanies Gunther out of Worms,
87 ; steals swan maidens' robes,
88 ; acts as ferryman, 89 ;
makes compact with Volker,
92 ; cruelly slays Ortlieb, 95 ;
made a captive, 99 ; put to
death, 100

HAGEN OF TRONJE, 155–156

HAR'DRED. Son of Hygelac ;
his reign, 13

HAR'LUNGS. Sibich betrays, 153

HART'MUT. Prince of Nor-
mandy, 26 ; kidnaps Gudrun,
27 ; is pursued, 27 ; rescues
Gudrun, 28 ; his life abroad,
29 ; returns home, 29 ; prepares for wedding, 32 ; fights
against Ortwine, 32 ; made a
prisoner, 33 ; released and married, 34

HAS'SAN. See Sherasmin

HASTINGS. Battle of, 163

HA'WART. Death of, 96

HED'IN. Lover of Hilde, 18

HE'GE-LINGS. Legend of, 19 ;
news of Hilde's beauty reaches
land of, 22 ; Hilde flees with,
24, 33 ; in battle, 27, 32 ; turn
homewards, 33

HEI'ME. Challenges Dietrich, 142 ;
meets Wittich, 143 ; is banished
145 ; seizes sword Mimung,
151 ; restores to Wittich, 152

HEIN'RICH VON OF'TER-DING-EN.
His " Book of Heroes," 102

HELCHE. Wife of Etzel, 83 ;
daughter of Oda and Rotha,
113 ; Queen Helche, 157

HEL'DEN-BUCH. The "Book of
Heroes," 102, 161

GLOSSARY AND INDEX

HELIGOLAND. Rumours of Dietrich's courage reach, 143

HEL'-KAP-PE. See Tarnkappe

HELL. Bayard brought from, by Malagigi, 200 ; demons in, 275

HEL'MI-GIS. Rosamund incites to murder Alboin, 104 ; marries Rosamund, 105 ; his death, 105

HEN'NING. Complains against Reynard, 39

HENRY THE FOWLER. Hears accusation against Else, 270

HENRY III. Emperor of Germany ; complains to Pope, 351

HENRY VIII. Lord Berners translates " Huon of Bordeaux" for, 215

HEOR'OT. Hrothgar builds, 2 ; Beowulf's vigil in, 6 ; his second exploit there, 9 ; feast in, 12

HER'BART. Nephew of Dietrich ; elopes with Hilde, 154, 155

HER'BRAND. Son of Berchther ; inherits the city of Garden, 134 ; reputation as a traveller, 150

HER-GART. Sister to Herwig, 34

HERKA. Same as Helche

HEROES. German " Book of," 135 •

HER'RAT (or HERAND). Princess of Transylvania ; marries Dietrich, 159 ; death, 160

HERTNIT. Earl of Greece, 151

HER'WIG. King of Zealand ; wooes Gudrun the Beautiful, 26 ; rescues Gudrun from Gerlinda, 30 ; his happiness, 31 ; makes war upon Ludwig, 32 ; holds banquet, 33 ; returns home, 34

HER-ZE-LOI'DE. Daughter of Frimoutel, 249 ; her marriage, 250

HESSE. Gunther and his followers pass through, 63

HET'TEL. King of North Germany, 22 ; wooes Hilde, 23 ; marries Hilde, 25 ; has encounter with Herwig, 25–27 ; is killed, 27

HILD'BURG. 1. Hagen finds, 19. 2. Companion of Gudrun, 29 ; meets Ortwine, 30 ; is wooed by him, 31 ; rescued from Gerlinda, 32 ; marries Ortwine, 34. 3. Parentage of, 122 ; wooed by Hugdietrich, 123 ; marries him, 123 ; mother of Wolfdietrich, 123 ; entrusted to care of Sabene, 125

HIL'DE. 1. In the Edda, 18–19 ; daughter of Högni ; escapes with lover, Hedin, 18 ; Hagen marries, 22. 2. Daughter of Hagen and Hilde, 22 ; noted for her beauty, 22 ; wooed by Hettel, 23 ; kidnapped, 24 ; mother of Gudrun, 25 ; sees Gudrun carried off, 27 ; hears of death of Hettel, 28. 3. A giantess ; Dietrich's encounter with, 136. 4. Daughter of Arthur, 154 ; elopes with Herbart, 155

HIL'DE-BRAND. 1. Claims body of Rüdiger and fights Burgundians, 99 ; kills Kriemhild, 100. 2. Tutor to Dietrich, 135 ; kills Sigenot, 139 ; meets Wittich, 143 ; steals sword of Wittich, 143 ; in the Rose Garden, 147 ; the second Rose Garden adventure, 150 ; release of, 155 ; fights against his father, 159 ; then returns home, 160

HIL'DE-GARDE. Gets news of Roland's death, 193 ; becomes a nun, 194

HIL'DE-GRIM. Giant's helmet, 136

HIL'DE-GUNDE. Adventures of, 156

HINTZE. Complains of Reynard, 37 ; bears Reynard's message to Malepartus, 42 ; tricked by Reynard again, 43 ; again at court, 44 ; imprisoned, 50

HLE'DRA. Capital of Denmark 329

HOG'NI. Father of Hilde, 18 ; same as Hagen, 59

HOLGER. Same as Ogier, 172

HOLLAND. Hegelings sail to, with Hilde, 25

HOLY GRAIL, 241–272 ; origin of legend, 241 ; Titurel's mission regarding it, 244–245 ; temple of,

246 ; descent of, 248 ; Titurel's marriage and the guardianship of the cup, 249–250 ; Parzival's quest of, 251–256 ; the miracle of the Grail, 259 ; Gawain's quest for, 261 ; Trevrezent renounces, 265 ; Parzival finds, 266–267 ; Arthur searches for Grail, 268 ; Lohengrin summoned by, 268 ; legend of, 268 ; place at the Round Table, 279 ; appearance of, 299 ; Parzival, Lancelot, and Galahad saw, 300

HOLY LAND. Renaud sets out for, 213 ; story of Christ's passion in, 242

HO'RANT. Goes on quest for Hittel's sake, 23 ; his songs, 24 ; at the marriage of Gudrun, 34

HORN'BO-GI. Warrior of Dietrich ; meets Wittich, 143 ; father of Amalung, 150

HROTH'GAR. Descent of, 1 ; hall of, 2 ; troubled by Grendel, 3 ; welcomes Beowulf, 6 ; holds banquet, 7 ; congratulates Beowulf, 8 ; bewails Æschere, 9

HROUD'LANDUS. Same as Roland, 163

HUG, LORD, OF DORDOGNE. Slain by Charlemagne, 199 ; avenged by Aymon, 200

HUG-DIE'TRICH. 1. Son of Anzius, 122 ; marries Hildburg, 123 ; father of Wolfdietrich, 123 ; entrusts wife to care of Sabene, 125 ; suspicious of, 126 ; death, 126. 2. Son of Wolfdietrich, 135

HUGUES. King of Jerusalem, 177

HUNGARY. Etzel, King of, 83 ; Gunther sets out for, 87

HUNS. King and queen of, 83, 113 ; Kriemhild to marry king of, 84 ; king of, 146, 150 ; queen of, 157 ; court of, 159 ; Albanact wars against, 379

HU'ON OF BOR-DEAUX', 215–240 ; origin of, 215 ; his quest, 216 ; meets Oberon, 219 ; slays Angoulaffre, 224 ; wins Rezia, 226–230 ; at sea with Rezia, 230 ; shipwrecked, 231 ; bereft of wife and child, 233–234 ; pitied by Oberon, 235 ; reunited to Rezia, 236 ; in Fairyland, 237 ; other versions, 238–240

HU'O-NET. Son of Huon, 233

HYGD. Wife of Hygelac, 13

HY'GE-LAC. King of the Geates, 4 ; meets Beowulf, 6 ; his death, 12

HYR-CA'NI-A. Babican, king of, 226

I

ICE-LAND. The "Iliad" in, 373

IL'SAN. Brother of Hildebrand ; as a monk assists Dietrich, 145 ; acts foolishly with prize awarded him, 150

IM'E-LOT. King of Desert Babylonia, 109 ; ambushed by Rother, 110 ; captured, 110 ; escapes, 112 ; killed, 113

INCARNATION. Doctrine of ; Ferracute accepts, 184

IN-FAN-TES OF CARRION, 360–365

IN'GE-BORG. Wife of Sigurd Ring, 327

ING'EL-HEIM. Charlemagne's palace at, 165

IRE-LAND. 1. In Holland, 19. 2. Tristan goes to, 318 ; his exploits there, 319 ; Vikings visit, 337

I'RING. Killed by Hagen, 96

IR'-MIN-SUL. Charlemagne destroys the, 162

IRN'FRIED. The Thuringian killed by Hagen and Volker, 96 ;

IS'E-GRIM. Complains against Reynard, 37 ; Reynard enters into partnership with, 38 ; bound to rope of convent bell, 45 ; Reynard talks of early alliance with, 47 ; alleged by Reynard to be in conspiracy, 48 ; death of, 58

I'SEN-LAND. Princess of ; found by Hagen, 19

I-SEULT. 1. Sister of Morold, 317 ; healing aid sought by Tristan, 317. 2. Daughter of

Iseult with whom Tristan spends much time, 318 ; desired in marriage by Mark, king of Cornwall, 318 ; finds Tristan nearly killed by dragon, 319 ; marries Mark, 322 ; her death, 326. 3. Iseult of Brittany ; marries Tristan, thinking he loves her, 324 ; Tristan returns to her, 325 ; sees him die, 326

I-SOLDE. See Iseult

ISS-LAND. Brunhild, princess of, 59 ; visited by Gunther, who comes to woo her, 66 ; Siegfried brings a force to, 69

I'SUNG. Minstrel ; leads Wildeber, 151

I-TAL-IAN CYCLE OF ROMANCES, 370

ITALY (or AMALING LAND). Dietmar, king of, 151 ; Dietrich, king of, 151 ; vikings visit, 337

I-TO'NIE. Wife of Gramoflaus, 264

I'VAR. Eldest son of Ragnar, 333 ; and also a cripple, 336 ; kills Eystein's magic cow, 337 ; goes to live in Lunduna Burg, or London, 341 ; his power, 341–342

I'WO. Prince of Tarasconia, 205 ; gives Renaud his daughter Clarissa, 205 ; treachery of, 207 ; Renaud saves from death, 208

J

JACK THE GIANT-KILLER. Origin of story of, 378

JAM'BAS. Son of Ortgis, 140

JAMES, ST. Explains vision to Charlemagne, 179 ; and the Cid, 350

JARL HER'RAND. Father of Thora, 329

JER'AS-PUNT. Castle of Virginal, 141

JE-RU'SA-LEM. Besieged by Ogier, 175 ; Godfrey made king of, 176, 213 ; Charlemagne makes pilgrimage to, 177 ; and Vespasian, 242

JESUS CHRIST. James, the Apostre of, 179

JEWS, 242 ; lend money to the Cid, 358

JO'SEPH OF ARI-MA-THE'A. And the Holy Grail, 242 ; institutes the Round Table, 243 ; carries the Grail to Glastonbury, 244

JO'SI-ANE. Daughter of Frimoutel, 249

JOYEUSE (zhwȧ-yēz'). Sword of Charlemagne, 174

JOYEUSE GARDE. Guinevere takes refuge in, 294 ; Lancelot buried at, 310 ; Iseult, wife of Mark, carried to, 325

JUDGMENT DAY. Dietrich to lead Wild Hunt till, 161

JULIUS CÆSAR. Father of Oberon, 219, 281

JUTES. Same as Goths and Geates, 4

K

KAN'TART. Son of Henning, 39

KASPAR VON DER RHÖN. " Book of Heroes " edited by, 102

KAY, SIR. Foster-brother of Arthur, 280 ; in London, 286 ; receives sword from Arthur, 286

KLING'SOR. Castle of, 262 ; Gawain's adventures with, 263 ; death of, 264

KNIGHTS OF ST. JOHN, 369

KRA'KE. Her beauty, 332 ; marries Ragnar, 333 ; despised at court, 334 ; reveals own name of Aslaug, 334 ; her son Sigurd the Snake-eyed, 335 ; acclaimed as worthy to be queen, 335

KRIEM'HILD. 1. Childhood of, 59 ; her dream, 60 ; wooed by Siegfried, 61 ; at the tournament, 64 ; meets Siegfried, 64, 65 ; welcomes Brunhild, 70 ; marries Siegfried, 71 ; is given the Nibelungen hoard, 71 ; visits Brunhild with her husband, 73 ; quarrels with Brunhild, 74 ; confides in Hagen, 76 ; bewails fate of Siegfried 79 ; her brooding, 80 ; wooed

GLOSSARY AND INDEX

by Etzel, 83 ; consents to marry
Etzel, 84 ; marries Etzel, 85 ;
plans revenge on Hagen, 86;
receives guests, 91 ; sends Blödelin to murder Hagen, 94 ; is
slain, 100.   2. Of Burgundy,
150 ; widow of Siegfried,
marries Etzel, 159
KRY'ANT. Son of Henning, 39
KUNDRIE. Witch ; death of, 267
KUN'HILD. Sister of Dietlieb ;
kidnapped by Laurin, 147 ;
rescued by Dietrich, 148 ; delivers Dietrich and knights,
149 ; marriage and realm of, 150
KÜR'EN-BERG. Austrian minstrel, 59
KUR'VEN-AL. Foster-father to
Tristan, 313 ; seeks Tristan,
315 ; goes with him to Brittany
and thence to Cornwall, 325

L

LADY OF THE LAKE. Brings
sword to Arthur, 289 ; carries
off Lancelot du Lac, 292
LAM GOËMAGOT. Old name for
Plymouth, 378
LAMBERT LE CORT. Author of
" Alexandre le Grant," 374
" LAMENT." THE, 101
LAM'PE. Ill-treated by Reynard,
37 ; escorts Reynard home, 50 ;
murdered by Reynard, 51 ; the
murder discovered, 52 ; excuses
of Reynard, 53
LAN'CE-LOT DU LAC, SIR. Joined
by Ogier, 175 ; birth of, 292 ;
reputed parents of, 292 ; loves
Guinevere, 293 ; rescues her,
294 ; wanders away from court,
295 ; nursed by Elaine, 303 ;
offers Guinevere necklace, 304 ;
meets funeral barge of Elaine,
305 ; death of, 310 ; praises of,
311
LAN-GO-BAR'DI-AN CYCLE OF RO-
MANCES, 102–121
LAN-GO-BARDS. Settle in Pannonia (Hungary), 102 ; quarrel
with Gepidæ, 103
LATIN CHRONICLE. Recording

the adventures of Charlemagne,
163
LAU'RIN (see Alberich). His
kingdom, 147 ; attacked by
Dietrich, 148 ; conquered, 149 ;
marries Kunhild, 149
LA-VIN'IA. Mother of Brutus, a
niece of, 377
LAZARUS, SAINT. Seen by the Cid,
348
LEIR. Founder of Leicester, 379
LE-O'DE-GRAUNCE. King of Scot-
land ; Arthur and, 289
LEPANTO. Huon and Rezia reach,
230
LIEB'GART. Same as Sidrat.
Marries Ortnit, 118 ; called
Liebgart, 118 ; the evil present,
119 ; hears of death of Ortnit,
120 ; her grief, 120 ; Wolf-
dietrich has compassion for,
131 ; marries Wolfdietrich, 133 ;
crowned at Rome, 133 ; marries
Dietrich, 160
LOC-RINE'. Son of Brutus ; gave
name to province Locria, 379
LOD'BROK. See Ragnar
LOD-GER'DA. Marries Ragnar
Lodbrok, 329
LO'HEN-GRIN. Parentage of, 268 ;
champions Else, 271 ; end of his
story, 272
LOM'BARDS. Same as Langobards. Charlemagne wars
against, 162
LOMBARDY. Ruled over by Ortnit's ancestors, 122 ; Didier, king
of, 173
LON'DON. Founded, 341, 379
LONGFELLOW. " Tales of a Wayside Inn," 371
LON-GI'NUS. Rosamund takes
refuge with, 105 ; falls in love
with, 105
LORCH. Kriemhild takes up abode
at, 83
LOUIS. Youngest son of Charle-
magne, 195
LUCIFER. Cast out of Heaven, 241
LUD. Descendant of Brutus, 379
LU'DE-GAST. King of Denmark ;
threatens to invade Burgundy,
63

LU'DE-GER. King of Saxons; Gunther's wars with, 63, 76

LUD'WIG. King of Normandy; suitor of Gudrun, 26; kills Hettel, 27; throws Gudrun overboard, 28; is slain by Herwig, 32

LYN-ETTE'. Story of Gareth and, 295-296

M

MAC'E-DON, ALEXANDER, KING OF. Life related in "Alexandre le Grant," 374

MA-CHO-RELL'. Father of Sidrat, 114; Alberich carries challenge to, 117; sends dragons' eggs to Liebgart, 118

MA-BRI-AN'. A chanson de geste, 199

MAHOMET. See Mohammed

MALAGIGI (mal'à-jē-jē). The necromancer, same as Malagis; romances relating to, 199; presents Bayard, 200; rescues Bayard, 201; helps Aymon, 201; his stratagem, 206; to the rescue, 208; captures Charlemagne, 210

MAL'A-GIS. See Malagigi, 199

MAL'E-BRON. Servant to Oberon, 225; carries Huon to Yvoirin's court, 238

MA-LE-PAR'TUS. The home of Reynard, 40, 41, 42, 50, 51

MALORY. His version of " Morte d'Arthur," 292

MAN'TUA. Ermenrich takes, 155

MAP, WALTER. Works of, 241, 273, 292

MARK. King of Cornwall; receives Tristan, 315; makes Tristan his heir, 317; Tristan praises Iseult to, 318; goes to woo Iseult for Mark, 319; Iseult marries, 322; orders burial of Iseult and Tristan, 326

MARSIGLIO (mar-sēl'yō). Saracen king at Saragossa, 185; Charlemagne sends peace envoy to him, 186; an ambush, 187; is killed, 187

MAR-SIL'I-US. Same as Marsiglio, 185

MARTIN. 1. Parson's son, 43. 2. The ape, 53

MARTIN GONZALEZ. The Cid fights with, 349

MARY OF ENGLAND. The oath of Philip of Spain, 309

MAT'E-LAN. Hilde goes to, with Hettel, 25; Herwig comes to, 26; Hartmut comes to, 27; Hilde welcomes her daughter to, 33

MAU'GIS. A chanson de geste, 199

MAX-I-MIL'IAN I. Emperor of Germany, 18

MAY-ENCE'. Charlemagne's wife buried at, 166

ME-DE'A. Story of, 372

ME-LE'A-GANS. Guinevere a captive of, 294

ME-LI-A-DUS. Same as Rivalin, 312; visits King Mark, 312; marries Blanchefleur, 313; jealous of Iseult, 323

MER'AN. Hugdietrich confided to care of Berchther of, 122; Wolfdietrich educated at, 126; Hildburg seeks refuge at, 126; educated at, 126

MER'KI-NAU THE CROW. Accuses Reynard, 51

MER'LIN. Prophecy concerning Round Table, 244; origin of legend, 274; a prophet, 276; at Carduel, 278; as builder, 282; and Vivian, 283; connection with Round Table, 290; decrees that Arthur must fight before marriage, 290; explains " Siege Perilous," 291

MER-O-VIN'GI-AN rulers of the Franks, 36

MEUR'VIN. Another chanson de geste, 176

MIL'AN. Invested by army, 155

MIL'ON. Father of Roland, 169; wins the coveted jewel, 171; his death, 182

MIM'UNG. Sword of Wittich, 143; conquers Dietrich, 144; Heime steals, 151; Heime restores, 152

MO-HAM'MED. Salancadys, an idol made by, 180; Ferracute and, 184

MON-TAU-BAN. Renaud returns

to, 209 ; siege of, 209 ; Charlemagne carried prisoner to, 210 ; Aymon's sons escape from, 211

MONT-BRAND. See Yvoirin, 238

MONTFAUCON (môn-fō-kôn'). Adventure of Renaud and Bayard at, 209

MONT-SAL-VATCH, 245–256 ; chosen for reception of Holy Grail, 245 ; its situation, 245 ; Titurel guards, 246 ; Holy Grail appears on, 247 ; life of knights on, 249 ; Parzival arrives at, 256 ; Parzival again at, 266 ; his life there, 268 ; Else of Brabant upon, 272

MOOR'LAND. Kingdom of Siegfried, 26, 27

MOORS. And Christians, 202 ; king of, 205 ; and legend of Holy Grail, 241 ; plot of, to slay the Cid, 350

MOR'DRED. The traitor, 306 ; fights against Arthur, 307 ; is killed, 308

MORE, SAINT BENOÎT DE, 373

MOR'GANA. Shows vision to Ortnit, 114 ; predicts happiness of Ogier, 172 ; gives him a magic ring, 175 ; her son, 176 ; spirits Ogier away, 176 ; mother of Oberon, 219 ; and King Arthur, 309

MOR'OLD. Brother of the King of Ireland ; comes to claim tribute from Cornwall, 316 ; is challenged by Tristan, 316 ; slain, 317 ; his body carried back to Ireland, 317

MOSES. Sin against Holy Grail, 243

MUN-TA-BURE'. Castle, 114 ; besieged by Ortnit, 117 ; Alberich's devices concerning, 117

N

NA'GEL-RING. Sword given to Beowulf, 5 ; won by Dietrich from Grim, the giant, 137

NAISMES DE BAVIÈRE (näm de bäve-èr'). "Nestor of the Carolingian legends," 186

NA-VARRE'. Charlemagne's wars in, 182–185 ; king of, threatens Don Sancho, 353

NEN'NI-US. Writer of romances, 273, 376

NES'TOR. See Naismes de Bavière, 186

NETHERLANDS. Story of "Reynard the Fox" first written down in, 35 ; kingdom of, governed by Siegmund and Siegelind, 60

NI-BE-LUNG-EN HOARD, 71, 81, 82, 91, 160

NI'BE-LUNG-EN-LIED, 18, 59–101 ; records fall of the knights, 159

NI-BE-LUNGS. "Calamity of," 59 ; name given to Burgundians, 80, 88 ; go to court of Kriemhild, 91 ; their behaviour there, 93 ; the banquet, 94–95 ; the struggle in the hall, 96–97 ; more slaughter, 99 ; their extirpation, 100

NO'BEL. King of the animals, 36–48 ; is won over by Reynard's excuses, 48, 49 ; makes presents to Reynard, 50 ; angry against Reynard, 54 ; agrees to hear him, 55 ; appoints fight, 56 ; receives the fox into high favour, 57

NON'NEN-WORTH. Hildegarde retires to convent of, 194 ; Roland resides near, 195

NOR'MAN-DY. Ludwig, king of, 26 ; Gudrun taken to, 27

NOR'MANS. Pursued by Siegfried, 27 ; attacked by Hegelings, 27 ; victory of the Hegelings, 33 ; Ogier defends Paris against, 176 ; take Luna by stratagem, 337 ; found London, 341

NORSE. Origin of poem of Gudrun, 18

NORSEMEN. Kidnap Tristan, 314

NORWAY. See Wilkina Land

NU'DUNG. Only son of Rüdiger, 158 ; slain near Raben, 158

O

O'BE-RON. King of the fairies ; Ogier joins, 175 ; his castle seen by Huon, 219 ; his wrath, 220 ;

promises help to Huon, 221 ;
gift of the magic horn, 222 ; has
ring stolen from him, 223 ;
raises tent above Huon, 225 ;
again helps Huon, 229 ; his aid
on behalf of Rezia, 229 ; his
last command, 230 ; punishes
disobedience, 231 ; relents, 234 ;
is reconciled to Titania, 237 ;
other versions of story, 238

O'DA. Daughter of Constantine,
106 ; in danger, 112 ; rescued,
113, her daughter Helche, 113

O'DEN-WALD. Siegfried invited to
a hunt in, 77 ; death of Siegfried
in, 78

O-DI'LI-A. Wife of Dietmar, 135

O'DIN. Hrothgar's descent from,
1 ; Skeaf sent by, 2 ; worship
of, by Druids, 162

OF'TER-DING-EN. German poet, 59

O'GIER LE DANOIS. A *chanson
de geste*, 172, 176

O'GIER THE DANE. A paladin of
Charlemagne, 163, 172 ; in
France, 173 ; his vision, 175 ;
surprised by Turpin, 175 ; in
the East, 175 ; joins Arthur,
175–176 ; carried to Avalon,
176 ; other versions, 177 ; his
boasts, 178 ; defeated by Ferracute, 183

OLD TROY. Sigeminne, queen of,
128

OL'GER. See Ogier

OL'I-VANT. Horn of Roland ; its
last blast, 189

OL'I-VER. Paladin of Charlemagne, 163 ; fights with Roland, 177 ; his sword Altecler,
177 ; wins heart of princess,
178 ; in Charlemagne's camp,
210

OR-GUEIL-LEUSE'. Gawain declares his love to, 262

OR'I-LUS, LORD. Parzival's adventure with, 254 ; Parzival's
challenges to, 260

OR-LAN'DO FU-RI-O-SO, 282, 370

OR-LAN'DO IN-NA-MO-RA'TA, 370

ORT'GIS. The magician ; captures Virginal, 139 ; is challenged by Dietrich, 140

ORT-LIEB. Son of Etzel and
Kriemhild, 85 ; is murdered,
95

ORT'NIT. 1. The poem of, 102.
2. King of Lombardy, 113 ;
meets Alberich, 115, 116 ; accepts sword Rosen, 117 ; wooes
Sidrat, 118 ; slays giants, 119 ;
his death, 120 ; bewailed by
Liebgart, 120 ; Wolfdietrich
promises to avenge, 126 ; and
relates story to giantess who
helps him, 131 ; Liebgart follows out Ortnit's last wishes,
132–133

OR'TRUN. Sister of Hartmut, 28 ;
begs for mercy from Gudrun,
32 ; is taken prisoner by Hegelings, 33 ; her marriage, 34

ORT'WINE. 1. Son of Hettel and
Hilde, 25 ; brought up by
Wat, 26 ; comes to rescue
Gudrun, 30 ; wooes Hildburg,
31 ; his marriage, 34. 2. Vassal
of Gunther, 63, 87 ; incited by
Hagen to murder Siegfried,
75. 3. Son of Helche ; his help
promised by her to Dietrich,
158

O-SAN'TRIX. King of the Wilkina Land, 151 ; Etzel wars
against, 151

OSBORN. Same as Asprian, 107

OS'TRO-GOTHS. Defeated by Alboin, 104

O'THERE. Discoverer of the North
Cape ; sons of, 13

OT'NIT. See Ortnit, 113

OT'U-EL, SIR. Story of, 184

P

PAD'AUWE. Taken by Dietrich,
158

PAL'MER-INS. Cycle of, 370

PAM-PLO'NA. Siege of, 180, 182

PAN-DRA'SUS. King of Greece ;
defeated by Brutus, 377

PAN-NO'NI-A. Gepidæ and Langobards settle in, 102

PAPILLON (pä - pä - yon'). The
magic horse, 175–176

PAR'IS. 1. Judgment of, 55 ; picture of, in act of kidnapping Helen, 372. 2. Ogier defends against Normans, 176 ; city of, 206

PAR'ZI-VAL. Birth of, 250; childhood of, 251 ; in the world, 253 ; at court, 254 ; finds Sigune, 254 ; on Monsalvatch, 256 ; meets Sigune, 259 ; sits in Siege Perilous, 261 ; is again at Montsalvatch, 266 ; Amfortas healed through, 266 ; sees Holy Grail, 267

PAS'SAU. Kriemhild entertained at, 85 ; Hagen goes to, 90 ; funeral mass at, 101

PEDRO, SAN. Church of, 367

PEL'LI-NORE, SIR. Arthur and, 288 ; Arthur saved from, by Merlin, 288

PENDRAGON. Brother of Uther, 274

PEP'IN. Charlemagne son of, 162

PER-I-DE'US. Giant incited to murder Alboin, 104

PER'SI-A. Overthrown by Alexander, 375

PETER, ST. The Cid's vision of, 365

PIER-LE-PONT. Castle of Aymon, 202 ; Aya mistress of, 202 ; Aymon's sons leave, 205 ; they return to, 205

PILATE, 243

PIL'GRIM, BISHOP. Brother to Ute, 85 ; welcomes Hagen, 90 ; holds funeral mass, 101

PIN'A-BEL. Champion of Ganelon, 191

PLYMOUTH. See Lam Goëmagot

POLAND. See Reussen

POL-Y-OL'BI-ON. By Drayton, 380

POPE. Ban on Reynard, 49 ; and Charlemagne, 162 ; Huon visits, 217 ; blessing of, 230 ; and Arthur, 306 ; message to Ferdinand, 351

PORTUGAL. Hildburg, daughter of king of, 19

PO'RUS. Alexander's fight with, 375

PRI'AM. Descendants of, 376

PYR'E-NEES. Defeat in, 163, 186–187

R

RA'BEN. Same as Ravenna ; taken by Imperial army, 155 ; Ermenrich and Dietrich fight terrible battle near, 158

RAGNAR LOD'BROK. Romances regarding, 327 ; his parentage, 327 ; his bravery as a boy, 328 ; wooes Lodgerda, 329 ; rescues Thora, 330 ; origin of name Lodbrok, 331 ; is captivated by beauty of Krake, 332 ; marries her, 333 ; their sons, 334–335 ; sends his sons to battle, 336 ; his death, 339

RA-MI'RO, DON. Quarrel of Ferdinand with, 353

RAND'WER. Son of Ermenrich, 153

RAUCH-EL'SE. Her appearance, 127 ; helps Wolfdietrich, 128 ; reveals herself as Sigeminne, Queen of Old Troy, 128 ; marries Wolfdietrich, 128 ; their happiness and sorrow, 129 ; goes to Old Troy, 130 ; her death, 130

RAVENNA. See Raben

RED KNIGHT. Parzival and, 254 ; is slain, 255

RED SEA. Huon lost in, 217

REI-NE-KE FUCHS. Epic of, 35 ; Goethe's poem of, 36

REINOLD. See Renaud, 203

RE-NAUD DE MONTAUBAN. Paladin of Charlemagne, 163 ; meets Ferracute, 183 ; is defeated, 183 ; parents of, 202 ; wins Bayard, 203 ; and Flamberge, 203 ; avenges Alard, 204 ; marries Clarissa, 205 ; builds Montauban, 205 ; betrayed by Iwo, 207 ; his exploits, 208 ; is saved by Bayard, 209 ; agrees to sacrifice Bayard, 211 ; the tragedy, 212 ; death of Renaud 213

RE-PANSE' DE JOIE. Daughter of Frimoutel, 249 ; bears Holy Grail, 257 ; marries Fierefiss, 267

GLOSSARY AND INDEX

RESURRECTION. Doctrine of, rejected by Ferracute, 184

REUSSEN (rois'sen). Elias, prince of, 114 ; Waldemar, king of, 157

REYNARD THE FOX. Origin of story, 35 ; Reynard accused, 37 ; summoned to court, 40 ; his trick on Brown, 41 ; the second summons, 42 ; the trick on Hintze, 43 ; the third summons, 44 ; arrives at court, 46 ; the sentence, 47 ; his trick on Nobel, 48 ; is pardoned, 49 ; more accusations, 51 ; again at court, 53 ; his second defence, 54 ; his celebrated judgment, 55 ; his great fight, 57 ; received into high favour, 57

RE-ZI-A. Won by Huon, 228 ; at sea, 230 ; shipwrecked, 231 ; called Amanda, or Esclarmonde, 231

RHINE. Nibelungen hoard sunk in by Hagen, 82, 91 ; Charlemagne's palace near, 164 ; Renaud's body said to be flung into, 214 ; Lohengrin in swan boat on, 271

RHÖN, VON DER. Edited "Heldenbuch," 102

RICHARD. Son of Aymon, 202

RI-CHOU-DE. 1. Wife of Titurel ; her death, 249. 2. Her daughter, 249

RIMSTEIN. Vassal of Ermenrich, 152

RINALDO DE TREBIZONDE. A *chanson de geste*, 199

RI-VA-LIN. See Meliadus

ROBERT OF SICILY. In poem of Longfellow, 371

ROD-RI-GO DI'AZ. See the Cid, 344

ROG'ER. See Hrothgar

ROGERO. Rescues Angelica from sea-monster, 196

ROGERS. Translation of "Reineke Fuchs," 36

ROHAND. See Kurvenal, 313

RO'LAND. Paladin of Charlemagne, 163 ; parentage of, 168 ; his raid, 169 ; other legends regarding, 163, 170 ; is knighted, 171 ; fights with Oliver, 177 ; his sword Durandana, 177 ; his horn Olivant, 177 ; slays the giant Ferracute, 184 ; pursued by Sir Otuel, 185 ; the battle of Roncesvalles, 186 ; blows a last blast on his horn, 187 ; his death, 189 ; other versions, 189–195

RO'LAND RISE. See Meliadus

RO'LANDS-ECK. Retreat of Roland, 194

ROLLO. Famous Norman viking, 342

ROMABURG (ROME). Wolfdietrich crowned at, 134 ; Dietrich crowned here, 160

ROMAN DE TROIE (rō-môn' dĕ trwä). Translated into every European dialect, 373

ROMANCE LITERATURE. General survey, 369–380

ROMANS DE CHEVALERIE. Story of Roland, 163

ROME. See Romaburg. Martin, the ape, on the road to, 53 ; Dietrich and his men set out for, 145 ; Huon arrives at, 239

ROME LA GRANT, 376

RONCESVALLES (rŏn-ces-väl'yes). Battle of, 163, 178, 186–187, 193

ROSAMUND. Thurisind's granddaughter ; Alboin falls in love with, 103 ; marries Alboin, 103 ; plots Alboin's murder, 104 ; marries Helmigis, 105 ; death of, 105

ROSE GARDEN. Laurin's famous possession, 147 ; Kunhild goes to live there, 149 ; similar one at Worms, 150

RO'SEN. Sword of Ortnit, 116, 119, 132

RO'THER. King of Lombardy ; at Bari, 105 ; desires to marry Oda, 106 ; sends embassy, 106 ; goes himself to Constantinople, 107 ; wooes Oda, 109 ; carries off Imelot, 110 ; kidnaps Oda, 111 ; rescues her, 112–113

ROUMELIA. Wolfdietrich rides through deserts of, 127

ROUND TABLE. Prophecy con-

cerning. 244 ; established by
Merlin, 278 ; opening banquet,
279 ; general history of, 285–
311 ; Knights of the Round
Table, 290–291 ; Siege Perilous,
291 ; Gareth arrives at, 295 ;
the Holy Grail descends upon,
299

Ru'al. See Kurvenal

Rück-en-au, Frau, 54, 55, 56, 57

Rü'di-ger. 1. Vassal of Etzel ;
goes to woo Kriemhild for his
master, 83 ; at court of Gunther, 83–84 ; sends Eckewart
to warn Burgundians, 90 ; attacks Gunther, 98 ; is slain,
99. 2. Suggested helper of
Dietrich, 150 ; comes to rescue
of Dietrich, 157 ; Nudung,
only son of, 158

Ru'molt. Squire of Gunther, 87

Ru-ot'ze. Giantess who hatches
magic eggs, 119

Russia. See Reussen

Ruy Diaz. See the Cid, 344

Ry'ance of Ireland. His
cruelty, 289 ; Arthur fights
against, 289 ; is slain, 289

S

Sa-bene'. Accusations against
Hildburg, 125 ; is banished,
126 ; fights against Wolfdietrich, 127 ; is utterly routed, 133

Sa-bri-na. Daughter of Locrine ;
drowned in Severn, 379

Saforet. King of Moors, 205

Saints-bury, Professor, 273

Salancadys. Famous idol in
city of, 180

San Pe'dro de Car-den̄'a. The
Cid buried at, 367

San'cho, Don. King of Castile ;
the Cid serves, 353 ; leaves
Rome, 353 ; his wars, 354 ;
banishes the Cid, 355 ; is murdered, 356

San'gre-al. See Holy Grail, 267

Sar'a-cens. Charlemagne's exploits against, 162, 175 ; Charlemagne is commanded to again
encounter, 179–182 ; Saracen

knight challenged by Roland,
183 ; Ferracute dies a Moham-
medan, 184 ; devices of the,
185 ; ambush in valley of
Roncesvalles, 186 ; Sherasmin
taken by, 218 ; a drink from a
magic cup, 225

Sar-a-gos'sa, 185 ; siege of, 353

Satan. Malagigi offers services
to, 200 ; angry over number of
Christian converts, 275

Saxons. Ludeger, king of, 63 ;
and Arthur, 289

Saxony. Burgundians enter, 63

Scan-di-na'via. "Iliad"¡in, 373

Scot'land. Same as Albania, 379

Scratch-foot. One of the hens
killed by Reynard, 40

Senlis. Countess, discovers virtue
of magic ring, 176

Seine. Bayard drowned in, 212 ;
Flamberge cast into, 213

Shakes'peare, 373, 379

Shar-fe-neb'be. Wife of crow
Merkinau, 51

Sher-as-min'. Same as Gerasmes ; Huon finds, 217 ; accompanies Huon into forest, 218 ;
offends Oberon, 219 ; drinks
from Oberon's beaker, 221 ;
journeys to Bagdad, 223 ; is
faithful to Huon, 225 ; goes in
search of Rezia, 226 ; helps her
to escape, 229 ; embarks on
vessel for France, 231 ; a gardener, 235 ; in Fairyland, 237 ;
other versions, 238–239

Si'bich. His plots, 153 ; induces
Ermenrich to kill his sons,
153

Sid'rat, Princess, 114 ; vision
of, 114 ; is wooed by Ortnit, 118 ;
marries him, 118 ; called Liebgart, 118 ; bewails death of
Ortnit, 120

Siege Per'il-ous, 243 ; Parzival
occupies, 261 ; and Merlin,
284, 291 ; Galahad occupies,
299

Sie'ge-lind. 1. Queen of the
Netherlands, 60 ; the great
tournament, 61 ; death of, 73.
2. A swan maiden, 88

SIEG'FRIED. 1. King of Moorland ; suitor of Gunther, 26 ; invades Zealand, 27 ; his marriage, 34. 2. Same as Sigurd, 59 ; his parentage, 60 ; wooes Kriemhild, 61 ; at Gunther's court, 62 ; ruler of Nibelungen land, 62 ; fights for Gunther, 63 ; his return after victory, 64 ; sees Kriemhild, 64 ; meets Kriemhild, 64 ; goes with Gunther to Brunhild, 66 ; helps Gunther, 68 ; claims hand of Kriemhild, 71 ; subdues Brunhild for Gunther, 72 ; visits Gunther's court, 73 ; Hagen plots to murder, 75 ; is murdered, 78 ; mass said for, 82 ; his body removed to Lorch, 83 ; widow of, marries Etzel, 159

SIEG'MUND. King of the Netherlands, 60 ; holds a tournament, 61 ; receives Siegfried and Kriemhild, 72 ; invited to Worms, 73 ; hears news of Siegfried's death, 79 ; proposes a return home, 80

SI'GE-BAND. Father of Hagen, 19, 22

SI-GE-MIN'NE. Queen of Old Troy, 128. See Rauch-Else

SI-GE-NOT'. Brother to Grim, 137 ; Dietrich encounters, 138 ; his overthrow, 139

SIGUNE. Daughter of Josiane, 250 ; Parzival finds, 254

SI'GURD. Same as Siegfried, 59

SI'GURD RING. Father of Ragnar, 327 ; wooes Alfsol, 328

SI'GURD THE SNAKE-EYED. Son of Ragnar, 335 ; training entrusted to Norman pirate Hastings, 335

SI-MIL'DE. See Kunhild

SI-MILT. See Kunhild

SINDOLT. Joins Gunther, 63

SIN'TRAM. Dietrich delivers, 145

SKEAF. Son of Odin, 1

SKIOLD. Same as Skeaf

SKIOL'DUNGS. Dynasty of, 1

SONS OF AYMON, 199–215

SPAIN. Overrun by Saracens, 162 ; Saracens gain advantage in war, 185 ; Philip of, oath to relinquish crown to Arthur, 309

SPANISH CYCLE OF ROMANCE, 370

SPEN'SER. "Faerie Queene" of, 282, 380

ST. JAMES. Body of, 179

ST. OMER. Ogier in prison at, 172

STEIERMARK, DIETLIEB OF, 150

STONEHENGE. Built by Merlin, 282

STU'DAS. Father of Heime, 142

SUDERS (or TYRE). Ortnit sets sail for, 117

SUL-TAN. Sherasmin a gardener to, 235 ; Amanda to be sold to, 235 ; the daughter of, 236

SU'SAT. Dietrich goes to, 155 ; his second entry there, 158

SWANHILD. Daughter of Siegfried and Kriemhild, 153 ; brothers of, 159

SWAN MAIDENS. Prophesy to Hagen, 88 ; Wachilde a, 158

SWEDEN. Eadgils, king of, 13 ; same as Wilkina land, 151

SWEDES. Beowulf defeats, 5

SWEM'MEL. Hungarian minstrel, 86

SWORDS. See Nägeling, Nagelring, Mimung, Eckesax, Altecler, Excalibur, Tizona, Colada, Joyeuse, Durandana, Flamberge

SYRIA. Princess Sidrat, daughter of ruler of, 114

T

TAN'TRIS. Same as Tristan

TARN'KAP-PE. 1. Magic cloak owned by Siegfried, 62 ; its help to Gunther, 68 ; in chamber of Brunhild, 72. 2. Magic cap, worn by Laurin, 148

TCHIO-NA-TU-LAN'DER. Brought up with Parzival, 250 ; how killed, 254 ; embalmed remains, 259

TEM'PLARS. Guardians of the Holy Grail, 246 ; guided by the carbuncle, 247 ; renown of, 369

TEU-TON'IC CYCLE OF ROMANCE, 369

THAMES. Brutus visits, 379

THE-OD'O-RIC. Identified with Dietrich von Bern, 135; name given to Dietrich, 160; his tomb, 161

THE'OD-O-RI'CUS and Roland at Roncesvalles, 189

THES-SA-LO-NI'CA. Hugdietrich visits, 122; Berchther of Meran visits, 124

THIE'DRIC. Roland's squire, 191

THING, THE. Convoked by Hygd, 13; Ragnar recognised as ruler in place of Sigurd Ring, 327

THO'RA. Daughter of Jarl Herrand; her story, 329–331

THU'RI-SIND. Governor in Pannonia, 102

TIN-TA'GEL. 1. Gorlois, Lord of, 279. 2. A town in Cornwall, 313; Tristan arrives at, 315; Iseult sets out for, 320; Mark's marriage at, 322

TI-TA'NI-A. Queen of the fairies; Huon reaches land of, 232; reconciled to Oberon, 237

TIT'U-REL. Origin of, 241; his birth, 244; his descendants, 244; his vocation, 245; on Montsalvatch, 245–246; takes care of Holy Grail, 247; marries Richoude, 248; names his son king, 250; is troubled about sickness of Amfortas, 251; dies, 267

TITUS. Son of Vespasian, 243; cured of leprosy, 243

TI-ZO'NA. Sword of the Cid, 348; its value, 359; given to lords of Carrion, 362; to be put in embalmed hand of the Cid, 365; is drawn by dead hero, 367; its motto, 368

TO-LE'DO. 1. King of; dies, 359; Yahia succeeds, 359; Alfonso plots against, 359; Spanish assembly at, 363; the Cid leaves, 364. 2. School of, 200

TO'RO. City; given to Doña Elvira, 355

TOURMOUNT. Huon and Oberon journey to, 223

TRANSYLVANIA. Herrat, Princess of, 159

TREV'RE-ZENT. Son of Frimoutel, 249; Parzival visits, 265

TRIENT. Magic eggs sent to, 119

TRINITY. Doctrine of, Ferracute accepts, 183

TRISTAN. Joined by Ogier, 175; origin of the story, 312; versions of the story, 312; parents of, 313; birth of, 313; in Cornwall, 314; wounded, 317–319; wooes Iseult on behalf of Mark, 320; drinks the love potion, 321; in Brittany, 324; his death, 326

TRIS'TREM. See Tristan, 313

TRO'IL-US AND CRESSIDA. Story of, 373

TRONJE. Hagen of, at Etzel's court, 155

TROY. Sigeminne, Queen of Old Troy, 128; she dies there, 130; romances regarding, 371; New Troy, 379

TU'NIS. Amanda and the pirates wrecked near, 235; Galafre, king of, 238

TU-ROL'DUS. Author of "Chanson de Roland," 163

TU-RO'NUS. Nephew of Brutus, 378

TUR'PIN. Latin chronicle attributed to, 163; adviser to Charlemagne, 163, 166; Ogier surprised by, 175; in Spain, 180; administers baptism, 180; administers last aid to Roland, 189; his vision at Vienna, 196

TYRE (or SUDERS). Ortnit sets sail for, 117

TYROLIAN MOUNTAINS. Dietrich hunts in, 139; Kunhild prisoner in, 147

U

UL'FIN. Councillor of Uther, 279

U-LYS'SES. Story of, 372

UOTE (wō'te). See Ute (2), 137

UR-RA'CA, DOÑA. Daughter of the Cid, 352; deprived of her kingdom by Don Garcia, 353; pleads for Alfonso, 354; her bravery, 355; besieged, 355–356

GLOSSARY AND INDEX

U'ta. See Ute (2), 137

U'te. 1. Queen of Burgundy, 59; interprets Kriemhild's dream, 60; at the tournament, 64; sister to Bishop Pilgrim, 85; tries to keep Gunther from accepting Kriemhild's invitation, 87. 2. Marries Hildebrand, 137; is rejoined by him, 160

Uther. Son of Constans, 274; fights with Vortigern and Hengist, 278; Merlin builds palace for, 278; changed into the form of Gorlois, 280; marries Yguerne, 280; death of, 281; father of Arthur, 281; a descendant of Brutus, 380

V

Val-duer'na. Given to Rodrigo, 348

Vale of Thorns. See Roncesvalles

Va-len'ci-a. Taken by Moors, 360; the Cid master of, 361; besieged by Moors, 362; Felez Muñoz at, 363; again besieged by Moors, 365; its evacuation, 367–368

Val'kyrs. Ragnar warned by, 339

Va-ran'gian Guard, 342

Veillantif (vä-yan-tef'). Roland kills, 188

Vell'i-do. See Bellido. Murders Don Sancho, 356

Ver'gen. Kriemhild escorted to, by Gernot and Giselher, 85

Ve-ro'na (or Bern). Duke of, 135; tomb of Theodoric near, 161

Veronica. Her sacred cloth, 243

Ves-pa'si-an, 242–243

Vi-a'ne. Renaud meets Aude at siege of, 192

Vi-en'na. Library at, 18; marriage of Etzel and Kriemhild, 85; Bishop Turpin's vision at, 196

Vikings. Band of, visits various coasts, 337

Virgil. Enchanter in " Rome la Grant," 376

Virgin. Protects Angela, 224

Vir'gin-al. The ice-queen; appears to Dietrich, 138; marries Dietrich, 141; forsakes her husband, 154

Viv'i-an. Enchants Merlin, 283–284, kidnaps Arthur, 292

Vol'ker. Follower of Gunther, 63, 87; makes compact with Hagen, 92; slays a Hun, 94

Vol'sung. The race, 135

Vol'sunga Sa'ga, 59, 327

Vor'ti-gern. Made king and builds fortress, 274; Merlin prophesies regarding, 276

Vos'ges. See Walter von Wasgenstein

Vul-ca'nus, Mount. Malagigi's adventure at, 200

W

Wa'al, River, 25

Wace. Writer of metrical tale of Brutus, 376

Wa-chil'de and Wittich, 143, 158

Wack'er-los. Complaint of, 37

Wagner. Last opera of, based on Eschenbach's " Parzival," 241, 273

Wal'de-mar. King of Reussen; Dietrich wars against, 157; slain by Dietrich, 157; his palace, 157

Wa-leis'. Battle at, 25

Wal'gund of Thessalonica. Hugdietrich's visit to, 124; finds grandson with the wolf, 124

Wal'ther von Was'gen-stein. Champion warrior at Rome, 146; receives town of Gerimsburg, 152; a hostage, 155; in love with Hildegunde, 156; marries her, 157

Wat. Follower of Hettel; goes on quest, 23; his skill in athletic sports, 23; brings up Ortwine, 26; sets off as Gudrun's deliverer, 27; his coming foretold, 30 ; blows note of defiance on horn, 32 ; kills Gerlinda, 33

WAX'MUTH. Son of Hildburg, 126

WAY'LAND. See Wieland

WEAL'THEOW. Wife of Hrothgar, 8

WER'BEL. Hungarian minstrel sent from Kriemhild with message to Hagen, 86 ; hand cut off by Hagen, 95

WE'SER. See Wisara

WHIT'A-BY. Ragnar's sons fight here against English, 336

WHITSUNTIDE. Animals wont to assemble at, 36

WIE-LAND. The smith ; his weapons, 143, 201

WIG'LAF. Follower of Hardred, 13 ; accompanies Beowulf on last expedition, 14 ; is thanked by Beowulf, 15 ; his sorrow, 15

WIL-DE'BER (Wild Boar). Noted for strength, 145 ; rescues Wittich, 151 ; his clever scheme, 152

WILD HUNT. Dietrich leader of, 161

WIL-KI'NA LAND (NORWAY). Dietrich invades, 151

WILKINA SAGA, 135

WIN'CHESTER. See Camelot, 290

WISARA. Heime retires to wood on bank of, 145

WIT'IG. See Wittich

WIT'TICH. Son of Wieland ; seeks out Dietrich, 143 ; is defeated, 144 ; fights single-handed against twelve others, 145 ; accompanies Dietrich to Rose Garden, 147 ; the second Rose Garden adventure, 150 ; prisoner, 151 ; rescued, 152 ; Mimung restored to, 152 ; pursued by Dietrich, and saved by Wachilde, 158

WOLF-DIE'TRICH. Parentage of, 123 ; rescued from wolves, 124 ; entrusted to care of Sabene, 125 ; educated by Berchther, 126 ; helps Hildburg, 126 ; marries Rauch-Else, 128 ; goes

in search of Sigeminne, 129 ; Sigeminne restored to, 130 ; kills Sir Belligan, 131 ; takes compassion on Liebgart, 131 ; meets Alberich, 132 ; kills dragon, 132 ; marries Liebgart, 133 ; his descendants, 134

WOLF'HART. Nephew of Hildebrand ; goes on expedition with Dietrich, 138 ; in the Rose Garden, 147 ; the second Rose Garden adventure, 150

WOL'FRAM VON ESCH'EN-BACH. His " Book of Heroes," 102 ; his version of " Parzival," 241

WORMS. Favourite city of Dankrat, 59 ; Siegfried rides to, with eleven companions, 61 ; expedition on behalf of Gunther quits Worms, 63 ; Kriemhild arrives at, 73 ; Siegfried's body carried back to, 78 ; burial of Siegfried there, 79 ; the Nibelungen hoard brought to, 81 ; Rüdiger arrives at, 83 ; Werbel and Swemmel received at, 87

WÜL'PEN-SAND. Battle of, 27

X

XAN'TEN. Great tournament there, 60 ; Siegfried and Kriemhild journey to, 72

XI-ME'NA, DOÑA. Comes to court of Ferdinand to complain against the Cid, 346 ; her disdain, 347 ; is married by the Cid, 347 ; carries out last wishes of her husband, 367

Y

YA'HIA. Grandson of Alimaymon, 359

Y-GUERNE'. Wife of Gorlois, Lord of Tintagel, 279 ; her daughters, 279 ; marries Uther, 280 ; mother of Arthur, 281

GLOSSARY AND INDEX

Y-LYAS. Same as Elias. Prince of Reussen, Ortnit's uncle, 114

Y-SOLDE. See Iseult

Y'VOIR-IN OF MONT-BRAND. Uncle of Amanda, or Esclarmonde, 238

Y'WAIN. Grandson of Yguerne. 279

Z

ZAM'OR-A. Kingdom of Urraca, 353; siege of, 354; Urraca's defiance on behalf of, 355; Alfonso, king of, 357

ZEA'LAND. Herwig, king of, 26

ZEBEDEE. Son of, 179